The Practical Guide to Lotus 1-2-3

About the author

To stay at the forefront of PC technology and education, Patrick Bultema does selective consulting projects and teaches training courses in industry. He's also a popular and frequent speaker on PC topics. In addition to this book, Pat has written the companion book to this one:

The Least You Need to Know About Lotus for DOS

About the cover

Eleanor Rapp is the creator of *The Red Wall*, the monoprint featured on the cover.

In addition to our long standing support and concern for the environment, Mike Murach & Associates, Inc. has chosen to show our support for the fine arts by featuring works from California artists on the covers of our technical books.

The Practical Guide to Lotus 1-2-3

for DOS

Patrick Bultema

Mike Murach & Associates
4697 West Jacquelyn Avenue, Fresno, California
(209) 275-3335

Production Team

Editor
Cris Allen

Technical writer
Michael Farino

Graphics designer
Steve Ehlers

Other books for PC users

The Only DOS Book You'll Ever Need

The Least You Need to Know About DOS

The Least You Need to Know About Lotus 1-2-3 for DOS

The Least You Need to Know About WordPerfect for DOS

DOS, WordPerfect, and Lotus Essentials

Printed in the Unites States of America.

Cover art ©1992

10 9 8 7 6 5 4 3 2 1

ISBN: 0-911625-70-74

Library of Congress Cataloging-in-Publication Data

Bultema, Patrick, 1959-
The practical guide to Lotus 1-2-3 for DOS / Patrick Bultema.
p. cm.
Includes index.
ISBN 0-911625-70-4 (alk. paper) :
1. Lotus 1-2-3 (Computer file) 2. Business--Computer programs.
3. Electronic spreadsheets. I. Title.
HF5548.4.L67B853 1993
650'.0285'5369--dc20 93-497
CIP

Contents

Publisher's Preface

In 1989, *Lotus 1-2-3* release 3.0 became available. This release offered some important new features including three-dimensional spreadsheets. Although release 3.0 was intended to replace release 2.01, it soon became apparent that the demand for release 2 was going to continue. As a result, Lotus Development Corporation decided to provide an upgrade for release 2.01 called release 2.2. This release also offered some important new features including a cell linking feature, but it retained its one-dimensional nature.

Since then, Lotus Development Corporation has provided two upgrade paths. *Lotus* release 2.2 has been upgraded twice (releases 2.3 and 2.4), and release 3.0 has been upgraded twice (releases 3.1 and 3.4). Besides the enhancements that have been provided by each of these upgrades, add-in programs like *WYSIWYG*, *SmartIcons*, *Backsolver*, and the *Macro Library Manager* have been included with the recent releases, and each of these programs provides some new features.

The trouble with all of these enhancements is that they've made *Lotus 1-2-3* more difficult to master. They've added more options to the menus, which were already several layers deep and wide, so it's harder to find the options you're looking for. They've made it harder for you to identify the essential features that you need to master. And they've made it harder for you to figure out which advanced features you need and which ones you should avoid using.

In short, the *Lotus 1-2-3* enhancements of the last five years have been a mixed blessing. Yes, they've provided some new capabilities that most *Lotus* users can benefit from. But they've also created new instructional and reference problems that I don't think have been adequately addressed by the training and book publishing industries. As a result, most *Lotus* users today aren't taking full advantage of the enhancements of the last five years. And most *Lotus* users today aren't working more productively than they were five years ago.

That's why we've kept two goals in mind in writing this book. The first goal is to teach you how to use the *Lotus* features that you need for your projects as quickly and easily as possible. That includes the basic features of the early releases of *Lotus* as well as the advanced features of all the *Lotus* releases. The second goal is to provide a reference that's quick and easy to use...whether you're looking up an advanced feature that's completely new to you or a basic feature that you don't use often enough to have memorized.

How this book differs from all the other *Lotus* books on the shelf

During the last five years, so many *Lotus* books have been published that trying to select the right book for your requirements can be a difficult job. So let me quickly tell you some ways in which this book differs from the others on the shelf.

First, this book has a unique modular organization that lets you read the chapters in whatever sequence you prefer. That means you can learn whatever you need to learn when you need to learn it. If you study the table of contents, you can see that most of the chapters are based on the skills that a *Lotus* user needs to perform, not on the command structure of *Lotus*. That makes it easier for you to find the chapter that teaches the skills that you need for a specific requirement.

Second, we believe our book will help you learn more quickly than you can with any competing book. That's made possible by the modular organization of our book and our emphasis on summaries and illustrations. Although other books will help you learn *Lotus* too, most of them force you to learn at a frustratingly slow pace. Often, in fact, the pace is so slow that you decide that new functions and features aren't worth learning, so you stay with the ones you already know. With this book, though, you can learn a new *Lotus* skill any time you have ten minutes to spare.

Third, we believe our book is the most efficient *Lotus* reference book that's currently available. This again is made possible by the book's modular organization and our emphasis on summaries and illustrations. Because most of the chapters present the skills for a single purpose or a single feature, you can usually find everything you need to know in a single chapter. Then, you just have to look through the summaries and illustrations to find the information that you need.

Last, we believe this is the most practical *Lotus* book that you can find. That's why we call it *The Practical Guide to Lotus 1-2-3*. In each chapter, you not only learn specific *Lotus* skills, but you get practical advice on when and how best to use them. To keep the practical perspective, this book doesn't teach every option of each command because some just waste your time. But if you want to learn how to use all of the commands, functions, and features that let you get more done in less time, this book is for you.

What this book does

This book presents all of the functions and features that are available with any *Lotus 1-2-3* release from 2.0 through 2.4 and from 3.0 through 3.4. It also presents six of the seven add-in programs that come with releases 2.4 and 3.4. And it presents all of the functions, features, and add-in programs with a practical perspective so you can easily decide which ones you should be using for your projects.

If you look at the table of contents, you can see that this book is divided into five sections. Section 1 presents the skills that every *Lotus* user should master because these are the skills that help you work smarter and faster. Section 2 presents the skills that you need for special purposes such as working with large spreadsheets, sorting the data in a spreadsheet, and linking cells between spreadsheets. Most *Lotus* users need some but not all of these skills. Section 3 presents the skills that you need for making effective business presentations that include graphs. And section 4 presents three features that definitely aren't for everybody: including the macro feature, the database feature, and the *SmartIcons* feature. Then, the one chapter in section 5 presents practical advice for upgrading to a later *Lotus* release if you're not satisfied with the release you have and for upgrading your PC if you're not satisfied with the *Lotus* performance that you're getting from it.

To help you get the maximum benefit from this book, all of the chapters are written as independent modules. That means you can skip to any chapter in the book without reading the previous chapters. If, for example, you want to know how to import data from a database program into *Lotus*, you can skip to chapter 12. If you want to learn how to use add-in programs, you can skip to chapter 14. If you want to learn how to use a mouse and the *SmartIcons* with *Lotus*, you can skip to chapter 21. If you want to learn how to protect the cells in a spreadsheet so you can have someone else update it with no fear of lost formulas, you can skip back to chapter 9. And if you want to learn how to use *Lotus* to access data from an external database like a *dBase IV* or *Paradox* database, you can skip ahead to chapter 20.

How the summaries and illustrations help

To help you learn more easily, this book is packed with summaries and illustrations. In each chapter, you get summaries of the commands and keystrokes for the functions and features that are presented. You get examples of how the *Lotus* commands work, including before and after screen images. And you get step-by-step procedures so there's no mistaking what you have to do to perform a function. Summaries and illustrations like these make it easy for you to learn from this book, even when you're not at your PC.

But the summaries and illustrations are more than just learning aids. They're also the best reference materials we know of. If, for example, you want to use the /Data Fill command to enter a sequence of values into a range of cells, figure 1-6 shows you how to do that. If you want to sort the data in a range of cells, figures 10-1 through 10-5 show you what you need to know. And if you want to review all of the commands for setting defaults, figures 15-1 through 15-3 give you the summaries you need. Normally, when you use the figures for reference, you don't have to read the related text because the figures tell you everything you need to know.

Who this book is for

This book is designed for people who want to get more from *Lotus 1-2-3*. That includes the people who have recently taken a beginning course in *Lotus* and are now ready to learn more about *Lotus*. But it also includes the many thousands of people who have been using *Lotus* for years and still haven't mastered the *Lotus* skills that will help them get more done in less time.

What are the prerequisites for using this book? A minimum set of *Lotus 1-2-3* skills. In general, that means you should already know how to create, print, and save a simple spreadsheet. And it means that you should already know how to retrieve and modify an existing spreadsheet.

To find out whether you have the minimum set of skills, you can read the Introduction to this book. It reviews the skills that the book assumes that you have. If you can read and understand this introduction, you are ready for this book. And if you already know how to use another spreadsheet program, but not *Lotus 1-2-3*, you can probably learn the minimum set of *Lotus* skills from this introduction.

If you can't understand everything in the introduction, though, you need to learn more about *Lotus 1-2-3*. The best way to do that is to take the tutorial that's presented in the companion book to this one: *The Least You Need to Know About Lotus 1-2-3*. If you are already familiar with *Lotus 1-2-3* or some other spreadsheet program, you can complete this tutorial in three hours or less. And if you're a complete novice to PCs and to spreadsheet software, you can complete this tutorial in six hours or less. When you complete the tutorial, you're ready for this book.

In terms of hardware and software, this book is for anyone who uses *Lotus* for DOS, not *Windows*, on a PC with a hard disk. That includes users of all releases of *Lotus* from 2.0 through 2.4 and from 3.0 through 3.4. Because subsequent releases of *Lotus* probably won't have much effect on the skills presented in this book, you should be able to use this book with newer *Lotus* releases too.

Conclusion

We wrote this book because we don't think that any of the competing *Lotus* books have reached acceptable standards for training and reference in the 90's. In particular, other books don't do an adequate job of presenting the new features and add-in programs of the more recent *Lotus* releases. Within these pages, we've tried to raise the standards for *Lotus* books.

For those of you who may be interested, all of our books are developed by staff, not free-lance, writers so we have complete control over the quality of our books. In this case, the first draft of the manuscript was written by Pat Bultema, who left for another job before he completed the project. At that point, Michael Farino stepped in to write some additional topics and chapters and to provide the technical expertise for the completion of the project. Fortunately, some synergy resulted from the combination of perspectives and talents, so I think we ended up with a better book than we would have otherwise.

If you have any comments or criticisms, we would enjoy hearing from you. That's why there's a postage-paid comment form at the back of the book. I thank you for reading this book. And I sure hope it helps you work smarter, faster, and with more satisfaction. If it does, please drop me a note.

Mike Murach, Publisher
Fresno, California
January 15, 1993

What you should know how to do before you start using this book

This book is designed for someone who has a minimum set of *Lotus 1-2-3* skills. In general, that means you should already know how to create, print, and save a simple spreadsheet. And it means that you should already know how to retrieve and modify an existing spreadsheet.

To make sure that you have the minimum set of skills, this introductory chapter reviews the skills that the book assumes that you already have. If you already know how to use *Lotus 1-2-3*, you'll probably pick up a few ideas in this introduction that will help you improve your efficiency right away. If you already know how to use another spreadsheet program, but not *Lotus 1-2-3*, you can probably learn the minimum set of *Lotus* skills from this introduction. Either way, if you can read and understand this introduction, you are ready to benefit from this book. Then, you can read any chapter in this book to learn new skills or to refresh your memory about how to use a skill that you haven't quite mastered.

If you can't understand everything in this introduction, though, you need to learn more about *Lotus 1-2-3*. The best way to do that is to take the tutorial that's presented in the companion book to this one: *The Least You Need to Know About Lotus 1-2-3*. If you are already familiar with *Lotus 1-2-3* or some other spreadsheet program, you can complete this tutorial in three hours or less. And if you're a complete novice to PCs and to spreadsheet software, you can complete this tutorial in six hours or less.

Although *Lotus 1-2-3* is the official name of the spreadsheet program that this book covers, many people use just the name *Lotus* to refer to *Lotus 1-2-3*. As a result, I'll use just *Lotus* whenever that is appropriate from now on. As you can imagine, using this abbreviation will save hundreds of repetitions of the numbers *1-2-3* in the remainder of this book.

How to start *Lotus* and how to tell what release you're using

Of course, you should already know how you start *Lotus*. How you do that depends on how your PC is set up. If your PC displays a menu or a shell program when you start it up, you can probably start *Lotus* by selecting an option from a menu. If your PC displays the DOS command prompt, you may be able to start *Lotus* by entering a batch file command like *123* at the command prompt:

```
C:>123
```

But if that doesn't work, you can always start *Lotus* by entering a series of commands like this at the command prompt:

```
D:>c:
C:>cd \123
C:\123>123
```

When *Lotus* starts, it should display a *spreadsheet screen* like the second one in figure I-1. In some *Lotus* books or manuals, you'll see the spreadsheet referred to as a *worksheet*. You'll also see the spreadsheet screen referred to as the *worksheet screen*. In this book, though, I will use the terms *spreadsheet* and *spreadsheet screen* exclusively.

Some PCs, though, are set up so *Lotus* starts with the Access System menu shown in the first screen in figure I-1. Then, to get to the spreadsheet screen, all you have to do is press the Enter key. This selects the first option in the menu that leads to the spreadsheet screen. To start the Access System menu from the DOS command prompt, you usually enter *lotus* instead of *123* like this:

```
C:>cd \123
C:\123>lotus
```

When *Lotus* starts with the Access System menu screen, you can easily tell which release of *Lotus* is installed on your PC. In figure I-1 for example, the Access System menu screen shows that it is release 2.2. But even when *Lotus* starts with the spreadsheet screen, it first displays a temporary screen that indicates the release number. This screen is displayed for a few seconds, and then it's replaced by the spreadsheet screen.

The *Lotus* releases that are currently in use range from 2.0 through 2.4 and from releases 3.0 through 3.4. These releases are presented in more detail in chapter 22. For now, though, you should realize that this book works for all of these releases. That way, you can use this book no matter which release of *Lotus* you're using.

To make it easier to refer to the releases from 2.0 through 2.4, I will refer to them as the 2.*X* releases whenever that is appropriate. Similarly, I'll refer to the releases starting with 3.0 as the 3.*X* releases. Today, Lotus Development Corporation is continuing to develop both the 2.X and 3.X releases so both should be available for many years to come.

The Access System menu

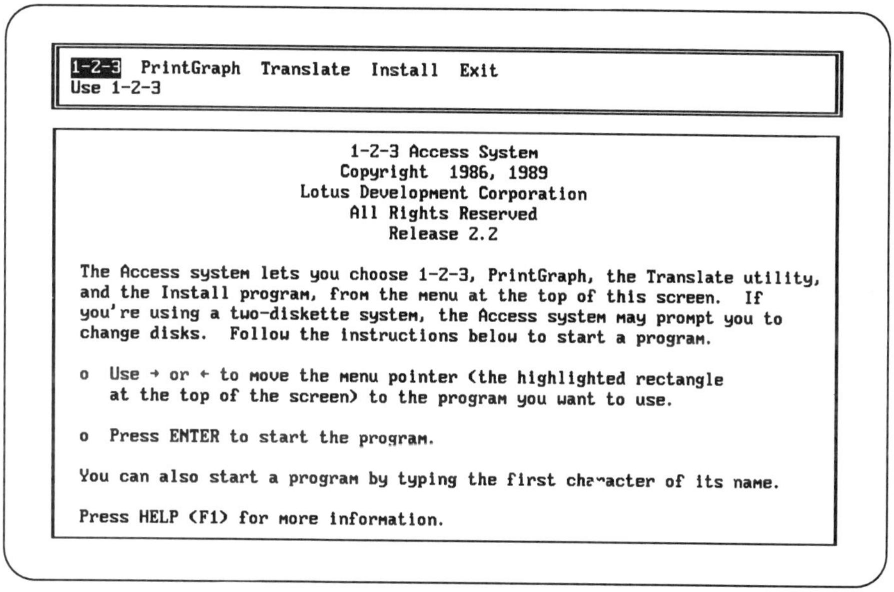

The spreadsheet (or worksheet) screen

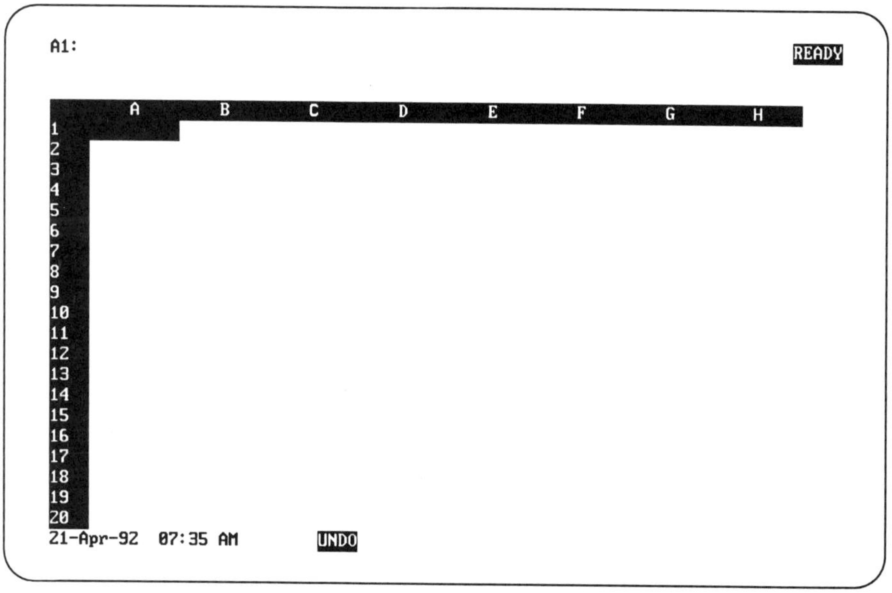

Figure I-1 The two starting screens for release 2.2 of *Lotus 1-2-3*

How to handle variations in the spreadsheet screen from one release of *Lotus* to another

In this book, all of the spreadsheet screens are for release 2.2 unless some other release is specifically identified. I'm using screens for that release because they are less cluttered than the screens for some of the later releases. So if you're using release 2.2 or an earlier release, your starting spreadsheet screen will look like the one in figure I-1. If you're using one of the later releases of *Lotus*, though, your starting screen will have some additional features. Although these additions shouldn't affect the way you use *Lotus*, you should at least know what they are.

Variations for releases 2.3 and 2.4 If you're using *Lotus* release 2.3 or 2.4, you'll see five small symbols on the right side of the spreadsheet screen. They are designed for use with the mouse. If you use *WYSIWYG* with release 2.4, you'll see an entire column of symbols on the right side of the screen. These symbols, called *icons*, are also designed for use with a mouse. In chapter 21, you can learn how to use the mouse and the icons with these releases of *Lotus*.

Variations for the 3.X releases If you're using one of the 3.X releases, the information in the upper left of the screen will look like this:

```
A:A1:
```

Here, the A: means that you're working on the first spreadsheet. These versions of *Lotus* allow you to work on more than one spreadsheet at a time. You'll also see an A over the column of numbers on the left side of the screen. In chapter 11, you can learn how to work on more than one spreadsheet at a time. There, you'll see that *Lotus* uses the letters B, C, and so on to identify the other spreadsheets.

If you use *WYSIWYG* with one of the 3.X releases, you can use a mouse for some operations. If you use *WYSIWYG* with release 3.4, you'll see a column of symbols on the right side of the screen. These symbols, called icons, are designed for use with a mouse. In chapter 21, you can learn how to use the mouse and the icons with *WYSIWYG*.

How to interpret the *Lotus* spreadsheet screen

To make sure that you know all of the terms that apply to the *Lotus* spreadsheet screen, figure I-2 presents them. Here, you can see that the main portion of the screen consists of vertical *columns* and horizontal *rows*. The columns are identified by letters, and the rows are identified by numbers. Although you can see only 20 rows in this screen, *Lotus* provides for rows numbered from 1 to 8192. Similarly, although you can see only five columns, *Lotus* provides for a total of 256. The first 26 are labeled A through Z, the next 26 from AA through AZ, the next 26 from BA through BZ, and so on to IV.

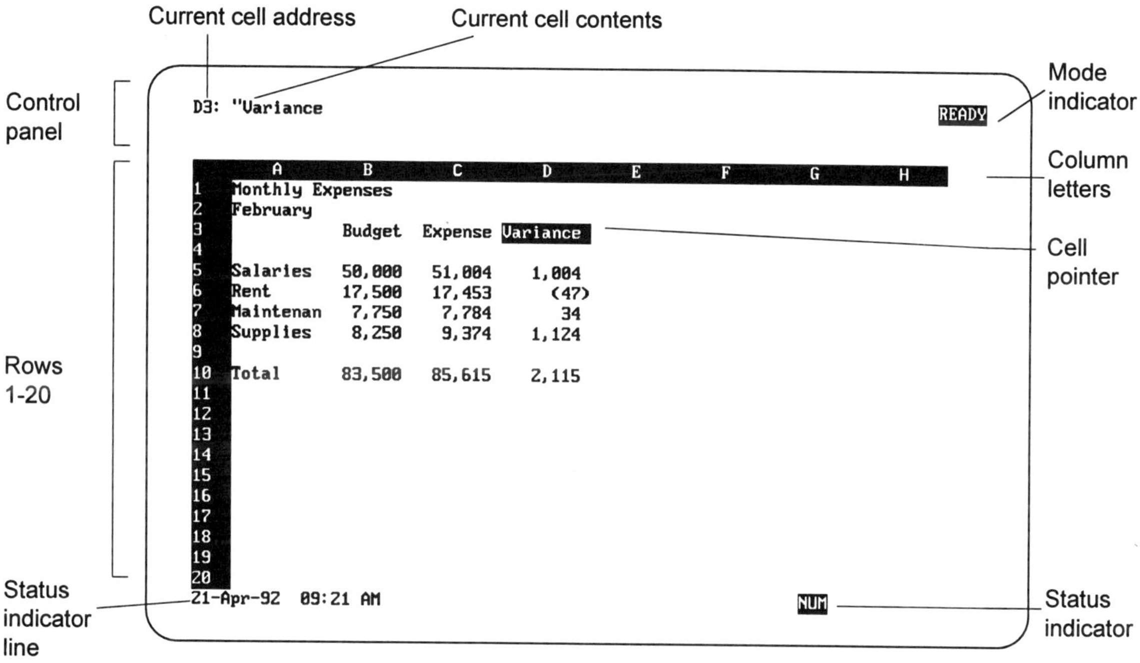

Figure I-2 The terms that apply to the *Lotus* spreadsheet screen

The intersection of a column and a row is called a *cell*. Each cell can be identified by a *cell address* that consists of its column letter and row number. Thus, A1 is the address of the cell in the first column and first row, and C4 is the address of the cell in the third column and fourth row.

The *cell pointer* is the highlight on the screen that points to just one cell. This cell is called the *current cell*. In figure I-2, the cell pointer is on D3 so the current cell is D3.

The top three lines of a spreadsheet screen are called the *control panel*. This panel consists of information that changes as you work with a spreadsheet. In figure I-2, the information on the left side of the panel gives the cell address of the current cell. On the right side of the panel, the *mode indicator* indicates that *Lotus* is ready for the next operation. This indicator changes as you perform specific operations.

The bottom line of a spreadsheet screen is called the *status indicator line*. On the left side of this line, you'll usually see the current date and time as in figure I-2. On some systems, though, you may see the file name for the spreadsheet that's in use instead of the date and time.

To the right of the file name or the date and time, you may find one or more *status indicators*. In figure I-2, the NUM status indicator is shown; in figure I-1, the UNDO indicator is shown. When the UNDO indicator is on, you can "undo" the last change that you made to the spreadsheet you're working on by pressing the F4 key while you hold down the Alt key. In chapter 3, you'll learn how to turn off this feature if it is on, and you'll learn why we recommend that you keep it off.

How to use the keyboard with *Lotus*

Two kinds of keyboards are in use today: the 84-key keyboard and the 101-key keyboard. On the right side of both keyboards is a ten-key numeric pad. To use these numeric pads correctly, you have to know how the Num-lock key works.

If you study the numeric pads, you can see that each numbered key within the numeric pad also has a control function, with the exception of the 5-key. For instance, the 7-key is also the Home key; the 8-key is also the Up arrow key; and the 9-key is also the Page-up (PgUp) key. Then, if the Num-lock light is on, each of the keys represents its decimal value or the decimal point. If the Num-lock light is off, each of the keys represents its control function. To turn the Num-lock light on or off, you press the Num-lock key.

Because this doubling up of keyboard meanings can cause some entry errors, most people prefer the 101-key keyboard. Here, the control functions of the numeric pad are duplicated on control keys that are located between the typewriter keys and the numeric pad. Then, if you keep the Num-lock light on, you can use the control pad for control functions and the numeric pad for numeric entries. Because *Lotus* normally requires that you use control functions along with numeric data entry, the 101-key keyboard is especially useful for *Lotus* applications.

Figure I-3 summaries the control keys that you'll use most frequently with *Lotus*. The Arrow keys move the cell pointer around the spreadsheet. The pointer moves one cell in the direction of the arrow for each keystroke. In contrast, the Page-up and Page-down keys move the cell pointer up or down a full screen with each keystroke. Similarly, the Tab key and the Shift+Tab keystroke combination (that means you press the Tab key while you hold down the Shift key) moves the cell pointer a full screen to the right or left with each keystroke. And the Ctrl+Right arrow and the Ctrl+Left arrow combinations also move the cell pointer a full screen to the right or left.

To return the cell pointer to cell A1 with a single keystroke, you press the Home key. The counterpart to this is the combination of the End and Home keys. In this case, you press the End key; then, you press the Home key (you don't hold one down while you press the other). This moves the cursor to the lower right corner of the spreadsheet. That's the cell that's at the intersection of the right-most column and the lowest row that are used by the spreadsheet.

When you use the Num-lock key to turn the Num-lock light on, the NUM indicator appears in the status indicator line at the bottom of the *Lotus* screen.

Keys	Function
Arrow key	Move the cell pointer one cell in the direction of the arrow.
Page-up	Move the cell pointer up one screen.
Page-down	Move the cell pointer down one screen.
Tab	Move the cell pointer one screen to the right.
Shift+Tab	Move the cell pointer one screen to the left.
Ctrl+Right arrow	Move the cell pointer one screen to the right.
Ctrl+Left arrow	Move the cell pointer one screen to the left.
Home	Move the cell pointer to the home position (A1).
End Home	Move the cell pointer to the cell that is at the intersection of the bottom row and the right-most column that are used in the spreadsheet.
Num-lock	Turn the Numeric lock function on if it's off; turn it off if it's on.
Scroll-lock	Turn the Scroll lock function on if it's off; turn it off if it's on. When Scroll-lock is off, the cell pointer moves when you press the Arrow keys. When Scroll-lock is on, the cell pointer stays where it is and the entire window moves. Usually, you'll want to leave this off.
F1	Access the *Lotus* Help feature.
F2	Edit a label, value, or formula.
/	Access the *Lotus* menu system.
Esc	Cancel an operation or go back one step within a command or menu.

Figure I-3 Some of the control keys that affect *Lotus* operations

Similarly, the Caps-lock key turns the Caps-lock light on or off. When it's on, the typewriter keyboard is set so all letter keystrokes enter capital letters instead of lowercase letters. Then, the CAPS status indicator appears in the status indicator line.

The Scroll-lock key works like the other lock keys in that it turns the Scroll-lock light on or off. If it's on, the SCROLL indicator appears in the status indicator line. To appreciate what this key does, you need to experiment with it on your PC because it's hard to describe. Normally, though, you won't want to use this feature so you'll probably keep the

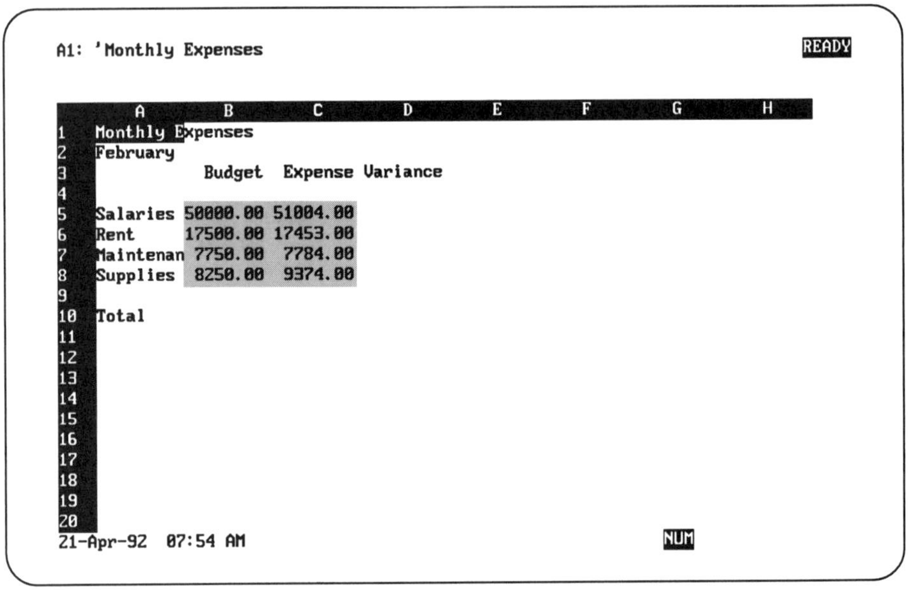

Figure I-4 The labels (unshaded) and values (shaded) of the expense spreadsheet

Scroll-lock light off. As a result, I won't say any more about this feature in this book.

The keys numbered from F1 through F10 on the 84-key keyboard and from F1 through F12 on the 101-key keyboard are called *function keys*. Two of the most useful of these are the F1 and F2 keys. You use the F1 key to access the *Lotus* Help feature and the F2 key to edit the entry in a cell.

The last two keys in this summary are the Slash (/) key and the Esc (Escape) key. The Slash key is used to access the *Lotus* menu system. The Esc key can be used to cancel an operation or a command.

How to enter labels into a spreadsheet

If you've used *Lotus* before, you should already know how to enter labels into a spreadsheet. In the spreadsheet in figure I-4, for example, the labels are the cell entries that aren't shaded.

A *label* is used for descriptive purposes. It can't be operated upon numerically. To enter a label into a cell, you type the letters or numbers that the label contains. As you type the entry, *Lotus* displays it in the second line of the control panel at the top of the screen. Then, you press the Enter key to put the label into the current cell.

If you make any mistakes as you type the label, you can use the Backspace key to erase characters so you can type the correct ones. Similarly, you can press the Esc key to clear the entry from the control panel so you can start over.

If you discover an error after you've pressed the Enter key, you can correct the error by re-entering the label. Then, the new label replaces the old label. Another way to correct a label after you've pressed the Enter key is to edit the old label. To start the editing operation, you press the F2 key. When editing, you can use the Arrow keys to go to the characters you want to edit; you can use the Delete key to delete characters; and so on. This is explained in detail in chapter 1.

When you start an entry with a letter, *Lotus* automatically assumes that you're entering a label. As a result, it turns the LABEL mode indicator on. On almost all systems, *Lotus* also precedes the characters that you enter with an apostrophe ('). This apostrophe means that the label should be aligned on the left side of the cell that it's entered into. This is called *left alignment*. In figure I-4, you can see that the label in the control panel is preceded by an apostrophe, even though the apostrophe doesn't show in cell A1. You can also see that the label is left aligned in cell Al.

If you want to enter a label so it is aligned on the right side of a cell, you start the entry with a quotation mark ("). In the spreadsheet in figure I-4, for example, the labels in cells B3, B4, and B5 have *right alignment*. If you want to center a label in the cell, you start the entry with a caret (^).

If you want to enter a label that starts with a number, you have to precede it by either an apostrophe, a quotation mark, or a caret . If you don't start the entry with one of these prefixes, *Lotus* won't recognize it as a label. If, for example, you enter

21DELTA

into a cell without a prefix, *Lotus* assumes that you're entering a value as soon as you type the digit 2. As a result, it displays the VALUE mode indicator. Then, when you press the Enter key after you've typed the entire label, *Lotus* thinks you made an entry error because a value can't include letters. That's why it beeps, displays the EDIT indicator, and won't accept the entry until you correct it.

When you enter a label that's wider than the cell, the label overlaps into the cell or cells on the right if those cells are empty. For instance, the label in cell A1 in figure I-4 extends into column B. That's okay until you enter data into the cells that the label has overflowed into. Then, the label overflow disappears. This is illustrated by cell A7 in figure I-4. Here, the last two characters in the label aren't displayed. To display them, you have to use a *Lotus* command to increase the width of the column.

To speed up the entry process, you can use one of the Arrow keys instead of the Enter key to complete each label entry. Using an Arrow key to complete an entry is equivalent to pressing the Enter key and then pressing the Arrow key. As a result, using an Arrow key saves you one keystroke for each label that you enter.

How to enter values into a spreadsheet

A *value* contains numeric data that will usually be operated upon numerically. In the spreadsheet in figure I-4, for example, the values are shaded. To enter a value into a cell, you use the same basic procedure that you use for entering labels. First, you type the value for the cell. Here again, *Lotus* displays the number that you're entering on the control panel as you type it. It also displays the VALUE mode indicator as soon as you enter the first digit of the number. If you discover an error as you're typing, you can backspace and correct it. Then, when you press the Enter key, the value is entered into the current cell.

As you enter values, you should realize that there's often a difference between what you enter for a cell and what is displayed for it. For instance, the value 50000 may be displayed as 50000.00. That's because the way that the value is displayed depends on the format that's been applied to its cell. To change the format for one or more cells in a spreadsheet, you use the one of the *Lotus* commands.

If you want to enter values that contain decimal places, you use the decimal point on the numeric pad or the period on the typewriter keyboard. If you want to enter a negative value, you start the entry with a minus sign. If you enter a value that's too wide for the current cell, the cell is filled with asterisks like this:

```
*********
```

or a special notation like this:

```
1.2E+08
```

Then, you can either enter a value with fewer digits, or you can use one of the *Lotus* commands to increase the width on the column.

To speed up the entry process, you can use an Arrow key instead of the Enter key to complete each value entry. Using an Arrow key to complete an entry is equivalent to pressing the Enter key and then pressing the Arrow key. As a result, using an Arrow key saves you one keystroke for each value that you enter into a spreadsheet.

How to enter a formula into a spreadsheet using the anchor-and-point method

When you enter a *formula* into a cell, you often use *operators* like the plus sign (+) for addition, the minus sign (-) for subtraction, the asterisk (*) for multiplication, and the slash (/) for division. In figure I-5, for example, you can see how you use operators as you enter the formula for cell D5 using the *anchor-and-point method*. The formula in this cell is supposed to subtract the value in cell B5 from the value in cell C5.

Step 1:

Move to the appropriate cell and press the Plus key.

```
D5:                                                              VALUE
+

      A         B         C         D         E         F         G         H
1  Monthly Expenses
2  February
3              Budget   Expense Variance
4
5  Salaries 50000.00 51004.00
6  Rent     17500.00 17453.00
```

Step 2:

Move to the first cell you want to refer to in the formula.

```
C5: 51004                                                        POINT
+C5

      A         B         C         D         E         F         G         H
1  Monthly Expenses
2  February
3              Budget   Expense Variance
4
5  Salaries 50000.00 51004.00
6  Rent     17500.00 17453.00
```

Step 3:

Press the next operator you need for the formula.

```
D5:                                                              VALUE
+C5-

      A         B         C         D         E         F         G         H
1  Monthly Expenses
2  February
3              Budget   Expense Variance
4
5  Salaries 50000.00 51004.00
6  Rent     17500.00 17453.00
```

Step 4:

Move to the next cell you want to refer to in the formula.

```
B5: 50000                                                        POINT
+C5-B5

      A         B         C         D         E         F         G         H
1  Monthly Expenses
2  February
3              Budget   Expense Variance
4
5  Salaries 50000.00 51004.00
6  Rent     17500.00 17453.00
```

Step 5:

Press the Enter key to complete the formula.

```
D5: +C5-B5                                                       READY

      A         B         C         D         E         F         G         H
1  Monthly Expenses
2  February
3              Budget   Expense Variance
4
5  Salaries 50000.00 51004.00  1004.00
6  Rent     17500.00 17453.00
```

Figure I-5 How to enter a formula into a spreadsheet using the anchor-and-point method

In step 1, you use the Arrow keys to move to cell D5. Then, you enter the plus operator (+) using either the typewriter keyboard or the numeric pad. The plus sign tells *Lotus* that you're entering a formula for the current cell. As soon as *Lotus* receives the plus sign, it displays the VALUE mode indicator to show that it expects either a value or a formula.

In step 2 in figure I-5, you move the cell pointer to the first cell you want to refer to in the formula (cell C5). *Lotus* then displays the POINT mode indicator. In step 3, you enter the next operator you need for the formula. To enter a minus sign, you can use either the hyphen on the typewriter keyboard or the minus sign on the numeric keypad. *Lotus* then returns the cell pointer to the original cell as shown in step 3.

In step 4, you move the cell pointer to the next cell you want to refer to in the formula (cell B5). In step 5, you press the Enter key to complete the formula. *Lotus* then enters the formula into the original cell, performs the calculation, and displays the result as shown in step 5.

Here again, you can see that there's a difference between what a cell contains and what is displayed for the cell. In steps 1 through 4 in figure I-5, you can see that *Lotus* displays the formula on the second line of the control panel as you create it. Then, in step 5, you can see that *Lotus* displays the completed formula in the first line of the control panel right after the cell address for the current cell. You can also see that the cell itself contains the value that has been calculated by the formula. How this value is displayed depends on the format that has been applied to its cell.

How to enter an @function into a spreadsheet using the anchor-and-point method

To add the values in the Budget column of figure I-4, you can enter a formula using the anchor-and-point method. In this case, though, you would have to point to four different cells so the formula would end up like this:

```
+B5+B6+B7+B8
```

This isn't too bad for a short column of numbers, but you can see that it's inefficient for a long column.

To simplify the entry of a formula like this, *Lotus* provides *@functions* (pronounced *at function* because the @ symbol is the *at sign*). One of these @functions is the @SUM function (pronounced *at sum*). It can be used to add the values in a column or row. A formula can contain one or more @functions combined with other operators. Often, though, a formula consists of just one @function.

Figure I-6 shows you how to enter the @SUM function into cell B10 of the expense spreadsheet. In step 1, you move the cell pointer to this cell. Then, you type the function name, @SUM, followed by a left parenthesis. As you

Step 1:

Move to the appropriate cell and type: @sum(

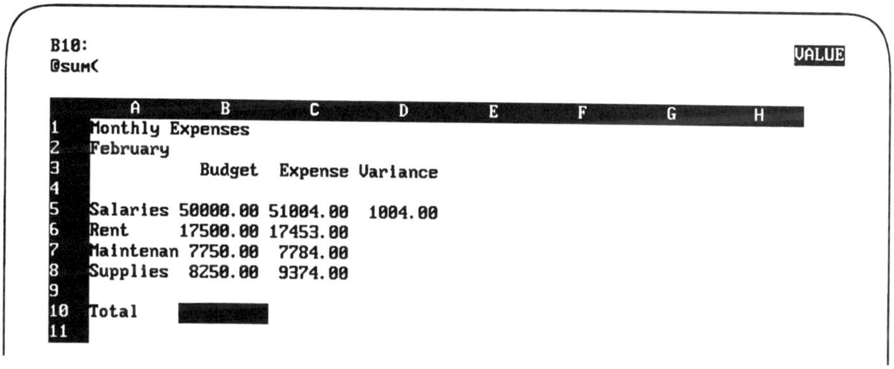

Step 2:

Move to the first cell in the range that you want to sum.

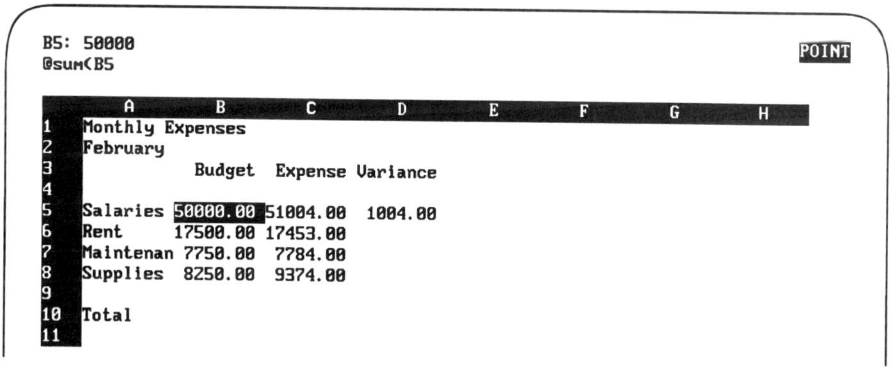

Step 3:

Press the Period key and use the Arrow keys to highlight the range.

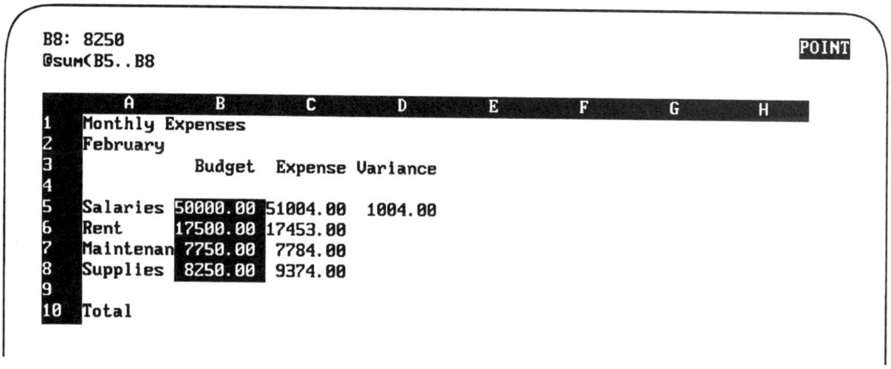

Figure I-6 How to enter the @SUM function into a spreadsheet using the anchor-and-point method (part 1 of 2)

Step 4:

Type a right parenthesis.

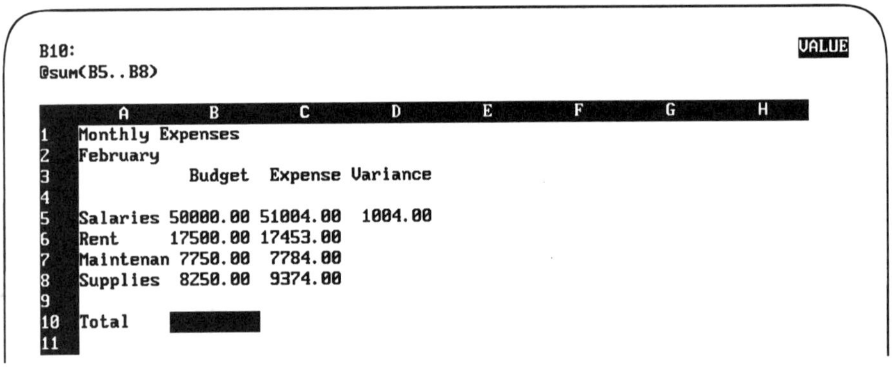

Step 5:

Press the Enter key.

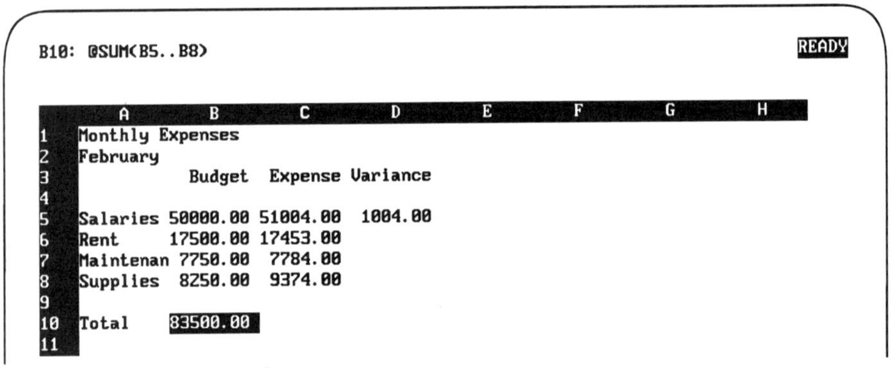

Figure I-6 How to enter the @SUM function into a spreadsheet using the anchor-and-point method (part 2 of 2)

type, *Lotus* displays the formula on the second line of the control panel. It also displays the VALUE mode indicator.

In steps 2 and 3, you highlight the cells that contain the values you want totaled. In *Lotus* terminology, this group of cells is called a *range*. To identify this range, you move the cell pointer to the cell at one corner of the range as shown in step 2. Then, you press the period key (.) and highlight the rest of the range as shown in step 3. As you do this, *Lotus* creates an address that identifies the range as shown in the second line of the control panel in step 3. Here, *B5..B8* is called a *range address*. It consists of the cell address of the first cell in the range, two periods (even though you only entered one), and the cell address of the last cell in the range. As you identify the range, *Lotus* displays the POINT mode indicator.

To complete the @SUM function, you type a right parenthesis as shown in step 4. That returns the cell pointer to the original cell. Then, to complete the formula, you press the Enter key. That tells *Lotus* to enter the formula into the original cell, perform the calculation, and display the result as shown in step 5.

Although the @SUM function is usually used to add a range that is contained within a single column or row, you should know that a range can consist of any adjacent cells that form a rectangle. For instance, all of the range addresses that follow are acceptable:

```
A1..D16
E5..G12
B21..F5
```

To enter a range using the anchor-and-point method, you move the cell pointer to the cell at one corner of the range, enter a period, and move the cell pointer to the cell at the far corner of the range.

How to use the *Lotus* menu system to access commands

To perform functions like increasing the width of a column, printing a spreadsheet, and saving a spreadsheet on your PC's hard disk, you use *commands*. To access a *Lotus* command, you use the *Lotus* menu system. To activate this system, you press the Slash key. When you do, *Lotus* displays the *menu* in the control panel at the top of the screen as shown in figure I-7. The first menu that is displayed is the Main menu.

To select an option from this or any other *Lotus* menu, you can press the Right and Left arrow keys to move the highlight to the option you want and then press the Enter key. At the Main menu in figure I-7, for example, you can press the Right arrow key twice to move the highlight from the Worksheet option to the Copy option. Then, when you press the Enter key, *Lotus* starts the Copy command.

To select an option more quickly, you press the first letter of the option. This is equivalent to moving the highlight to the option and pressing the Enter key. If, for example, you press the key for the letter *m* when you're at the Main menu in figure I-7, the Move command is started.

When you select an option from a menu, it can start a command or take you to another menu. Although the Copy and Move options in the Main menu start commands, most of the other options lead to menus. If, for example, you select the Worksheet option, it takes you to the Worksheet menu shown in figure I-7. The Global option from this menu takes you to a third-level menu. And the Format option from this menu takes you to a fourth-level menu.

When you move the highlight to an option that takes you to another menu, *Lotus* displays the options available on the next menu on the third line of the control panel. In the first level of figure I-7, for example, the third line of the control panel displays the options of the Worksheet menu. In the second

Level 1:

The Main menu

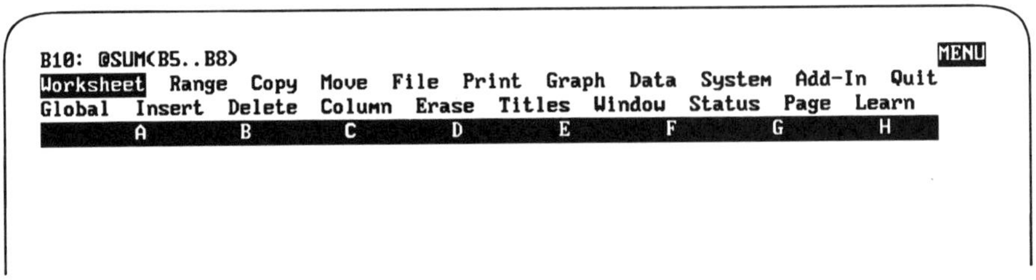

Level 2:

The /Worksheet menu

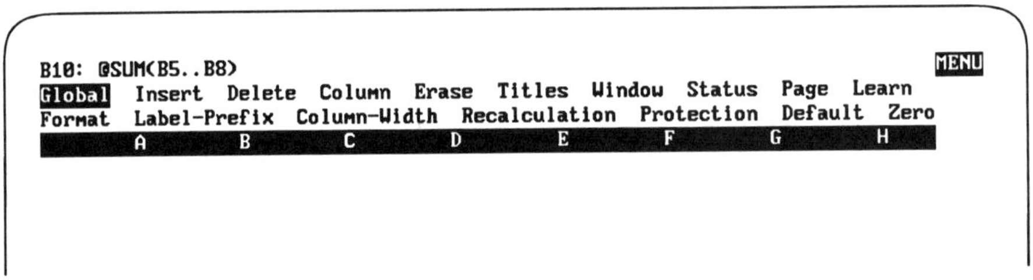

Level 3:

The /Worksheet Global menu

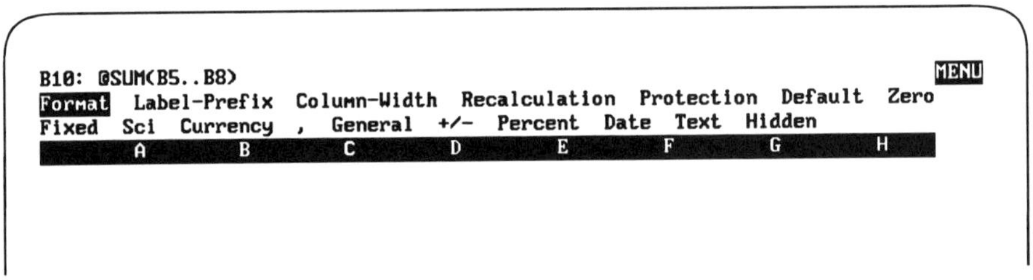

Level 4:

The /Worksheet Global Format menu

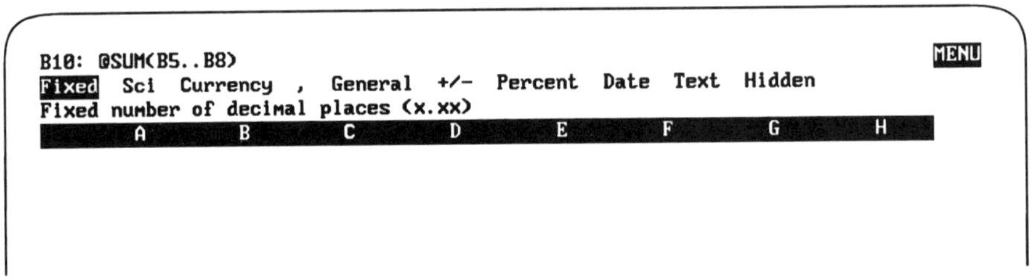

Figure I-7 Four levels of the *Lotus* menu system

level, the third line of the control panel displays the options of the Global menu. By looking at this third line in the control panel as you highlight the options in a menu, you can make sure that an option is going to take you where you want to go before you select it. When the highlight is on an option that starts a command, the third line in the control panel gives a brief description of the command's function.

If at any point you select the wrong option from a menu, you can back up to the previous menu by pressing the Esc key. If, for example, you select the Range option on the Main menu instead of the Copy option, you can return to the Main menu by pressing the Esc key once. If you reach the third level of the menu system, you can return to the Main menu by pressing the Esc key twice.

To identify a command, you can use the names of the menu options that lead to the command starting with a slash. For instance, the Copy command can be referred to as the /Copy command. And the highlighted command at the third level in figure I-7 can be referred to as the /Worksheet Global Format command.

How to use the essential *Lotus* commands

Figure I-8 summarizes the commands that you should know when you start this book. To access one of these commands, you type the Slash key followed by the first letters of the word in the command name. For instance, to access the /Worksheet Column Set-width command, you type:

```
/wcs
```

And to back out of the command, you press the Esc key three times.

With just the commands in figure I-8, you can create and edit simple spreadsheets. Then, as you read and use this book, you'll learn how to use commands that help you work more efficiently. You'll also learn how to use commands that let you perform new functions like protecting the data in a spreadsheet or creating a graph from a spreadsheet. To make sure that you know how to use the commands in figure I-8, I'll review some of the most important ones now.

How to use the /File Directory and /File Retrieve commands You can use the /File Directory command to set the drive and directory for your spreadsheet files. If you do this as you start a *Lotus* session, the setting will stay in effect until you exit from *Lotus*. As a result, you will only have to specify the file name when you want to retrieve or save a spreadsheet. You won't have to specify the drive and directory for it.

The use of the /File Directory command is illustrated in figure I-9. After you start the command by typing /fd, the prompt asks you for the directory name. Then, you type in a directory specification that includes the drive and directory that you want to use for your spreadsheet files, and you press the

Command name	Next level	Function	Operation
/Worksheet Insert	Column	Insert one or more columns into a spreadsheet.	Highlight the location and number of columns to be inserted; then, press the Enter key.
	Row	Insert one or more rows into a spreadsheet.	Highlight the location and number of rows to be inserted; then, press the Enter key.
/Worksheet Delete	Column	Delete one or more columns from a spreadsheet.	Highlight the columns to be deleted; then, press the Enter key.
	Row	Delete one or more rows from a spreadsheet.	Highlight the rows to be deleted; then, press the Enter key.
/Worksheet Column	Set-Width	Increase or decrease the width of a column.	Presented in chapter 3.
/Worksheet	Erase	Erase a spreadsheet from internal storage.	Type Y when *Lotus* asks whether you're sure.
/Copy		Copy the labels, values, or formulas from one range of cells to another.	See figure I-10
/Range	Format	Format the data in a range of cells.	Select the formatting option. If necessary, type the number of decimal places that should be used and press the Enter key. Then, highlight the range of cells that the format should apply to and press the Enter key.
	Erase	Erase the data from a range of cells.	Highlight the range of cells to be erased; then, press the Enter key.
/Print Printer	Range	Set the range of cells that are to be printed.	See figure I-12.
	Go	Print all of the cells in the print range.	See figure I-12.
	Page	Skip the paper in the printer to the top of the next page.	See figure I-12.

Figure I-8 A summary of the commands you should know before you start to use this book (part 1 of 2)

Command name	Next level	Function	Operation
/File	Directory	Identify the directory that you want to use for your spreadsheet files.	See figure I-9.
	Retrieve	Retrieve a spreadsheet from a file on a hard disk or diskette.	See figure I-9.
	Save	Save a spreadsheet to a file on a hard disk or diskette.	See figure I-13.
/Quit		Exit from Lotus.	See figure I-14.

Figure I-8 A summary of the commands you should know before you start to use this book (part 2 of 2)

Enter key. After that, *Lotus* displays the directory you specified whenever you retrieve or save a file. However, this default setting will be lost when you exit from *Lotus*. In chapter 3, you can learn how to use the /Worksheet Global Default Directory command to change the directory so it stays in effect from one *Lotus* session to another.

Once you set the directory to the one you want, it's easier to use the /File Save and /File Retrieve commands. In figure I-9, for example, you can see how the /File Retrieve command works once you've set the directory. After you start the command by typing /fr, *Lotus* displays the directory you want in the second line of the control panel followed by one of these extensions:

```
*.wk1  *.wk?  *.wk*
```

The extension that's displayed depends on the release of *Lotus* that you're using. This just means that the command is waiting to be told which file you want to retrieve. On the third line of the control panel, *Lotus* displays the names of the first five spreadsheet files in the directory. In this case, the directory contains only two files, so only two are shown.

To identify the file that you want to retrieve, you can type the name of the file (without the extension) and press the Enter key. Or, you can use the Left and Right arrow keys to move the highlight on the third line of the control panel to the name of the file that you want and then press the Enter key. If there are more than five spreadsheet files in the directory, the hidden names will scroll into view as you use the Arrow keys.

If you don't set the default directory to the one you want before you use the /File Retrieve command, you can give a complete file specification to override the default directory. To do this, press the Esc key twice to clear the

How to use the /File Directory command

1. Start the command by typing /fd. *Lotus* then displays a prompt like this:

```
Enter current directory: C:\123
```

2. At the prompt, enter the specification for the directory that you want to use as in this example:

```
Enter current directory: C:\123\DATA
```

3. Press the Enter key. This directory specification stays in effect until you change it or you exit from *Lotus*.

How to use the /File Retrieve command after you've set the directory to the one you want

1. Start the command by typing /fr. *Lotus* then displays a control panel like this:

```
A1:
Name of file to retrieve: C:\123\DATA\*.wk?
FEBEXP.WK1       MAREXP.WK1
```

   In the third line, you can see the names of the files that are stored in the default directory.

2. To specify the file you want, use the Right and Left arrow keys to highlight the file name on the third line of the control panel or type the name of the file you want at the prompt, as in this example:

```
Name of file to retrieve: C:\123\DATA\MAREXP
```

   When you type in the file name, you don't have to include an extension because *Lotus* assumes an acceptable extension of either WK1 or WK3.

3. Press the Enter key. When *Lotus* retrieves the file, it replaces any spreadsheet that you've been working on.

Figure I-9 How to use the /File Directory and /File Retrieve commands

default directory from the prompt in the control panel. Then, enter a specification that includes the drive, the directory, and the file name. If your specification is correct, *Lotus* will retrieve the file you want, no matter what the default directory is.

If you're working on one spreadsheet and you use the /File Retrieve command to retrieve another spreadsheet, the spreadsheet that you're working on is lost. That's why you must be sure to save one spreadsheet before you retrieve another. When you use release 2.3 or 2.4, *Lotus* displays a warning message if the file that you retrieve is going to replace a spreadsheet that you've been working on. But when you use one of the other releases, *Lotus* doesn't give you any warning that you're going to lose the spreadsheet that you're working on.

How to use a command that requires a range specification

Commands like the /Copy and /Range commands require a range specification. In figure I-10, for example, you can see how the /Copy command is used to copy the formula in cell D5 to cells D6..D8. To start this operation, you move the cell pointer to the cell that you want to copy (or the first cell in the range of cells you want to copy). Then, you access the command by typing */c*. That takes you to the screen shown in step 1 of figure I-10.

In this step, you identify what *Lotus* calls the *copy FROM range*. That's the cell or cells that you want to copy. (If you're using release 2.3 or 2.4, *Lotus* calls this the *Copy what? range*.) In this example, you want to copy the contents of one cell, and that cell is already identified in the control panel: D5..D5. As a result, all you have to do to is press the Enter key.

In step 2, *Lotus* asks you for the *copy TO range*. That's the cell or cells that you want to copy the formula to. (If you're using release 2.3 or 2.4, *Lotus* calls this the *Copy where? range*.) To identify this range, you can use the anchor-and-point method. First, use the Down arrow key to move the cell pointer down one cell. Next, type one period. Last, press the Down arrow key two times to highlight the range shown.

When you press the Enter key in step 3, *Lotus* copies the formula from cell D5 to each cell in the copy TO range. As it does this, it adjusts the cell addresses in the formulas so they work in the new locations. For instance, the formula in cell D5 is changed from

```
+C5-B5
```

to

```
+C6-B6
```

as it's moved from cell D5 to D6. After the formulas are copied, *Lotus* calculates the new values and displays them in the cells. If a copied formula can't be calculated properly in its new cell, *Lotus* displays ERR in the cell.

As you use many of the *Lotus* commands, you are asked to specify a range of cells, columns, or rows. For instance, the /Copy command asks you to specify both a Copy-from range and a Copy-to range. The /Print Printer command asks you to specify the range of cells that should be printed. And the /Worksheet Delete Column and the /Worksheet Delete Row commands ask you to specify the range of columns or rows that should be deleted. Now, I want to make sure that you know how to specify a range within a command.

Figure I-11 summarizes the two methods for specifying the first range of cells, columns, or rows that are required by a command. Both methods use the anchor-and-point method. In method 1, you move the cell pointer to the first cell in the range before you start the command. In method 2, you start the command first. Then, when the command asks for the range, you move the cell pointer to the first cell in the range. In this case, though, you have to press

Step 1:

Highlight the cell that contains the formula you want to copy, select the /Copy command, and press the Enter key.

```
D5: +C5-B5                                                         POINT
Enter range to copy FROM: D5..D5

        A             B         C         D         E       F       G
1  Monthly Expenses
2  February
3                   Budget   Expense  Variance
4
5  Salaries         50,000    51,004     1,004
6  Rent             17,500    17,453
7  Maintenance       7,750     7,784
8  Supplies          8,250     9,374
9
10 Total            83,500
11
```

Step 2:

Use the anchor-and-point method to highlight the range of cells you want to copy the formula to. That is, move the cell pointer to D6: type one period; and move the cell pointer to cell D8.

```
D8:                                                                POINT
Enter range to copy TO: D6..D8

        A             B         C         D         E       F       G
1  Monthly Expenses
2  February
3                   Budget   Expense  Variance
4
5  Salaries         50,000    51,004     1,004
6  Rent             17,500    17,453
7  Maintenance       7,750     7,784
8  Supplies          8,250     9,374
9
10 Total            83,500
11
```

Step 3:

Press the Enter key to complete the command.

```
D5: +C5-B5                                                         READY

        A             B         C         D         E       F       G
1  Monthly Expenses
2  February
3                   Budget   Expense  Variance
4
5  Salaries         50,000    51,004     1,004
6  Rent             17,500    17,453      (47)
7  Maintenance       7,750     7,784        34
8  Supplies          8,250     9,374     1,124
9
10 Total            83,500
11
```

Figure I-10 How to use the /Copy command to copy a formula

Method 1

1. Move the cell pointer to the first cell in the range that's going to be used by the command.
2. Start the command.
3. When the command asks for the range, move the cell pointer to the last cell in the range and press the Enter key.

Method 2

1. Start the command.
2. When the command asks for the range, press the Esc key if the current cell isn't the first one that should be in the range.
3. Move the cell pointer to the first cell in the range.
4. Type a period (dot) to continue the range address.
5. Move the cell pointer to the last cell in the range and press the Enter key.

Figure I-11 Two ways to use the anchor-and-point method to specify the first range of cells, columns, or rows within a command

the Esc key before moving the cell pointer to the first cell because the *Lotus* commands assume that the current cell is going to be the first one in the range.

After you've specified the first cell with either method, you complete the range specification. If you're using method 1, you just move the cell pointer to the last cell in the range. If you're using the method 2, though, you have to type a dot before you move the cell pointer to the last cell in the range. Then, you press the Enter key so the command can continue.

Remember that *Lotus* specifies a range address with two dots like this

```
C2..C9
```

even though you enter only one dot to continue a range address. If a range consists of only a single cell, of course, you just press the Enter key after you've identified the cell. You don't have to type a dot and then press the Enter key.

A few of the *Lotus* commands like the /Copy and /Move commands require two range addresses. To specify the second range, you just move the cell pointer to the first cell in the range, type a dot, move the cell pointer to the last cell, and press Enter. In this case, you don't have to press the Esc key before you move the cell pointer to the first cell in the range because the command makes no assumption about what the first cell is going to be.

If you make a mistake as you specify a range, you can go back one step at a time by pressing the Esc key. If, for example, you realize that the first cell is wrong after you press the dot, you can press the Esc key twice to reset the first cell. Or, you can press the Esc key as many times as are needed to back completely out of the command and start over.

You should also know that you don't have to use the anchor-and-point method for identifying a range. If you prefer, you can type the range and press the Enter key. In this case, you type the address of the first cell in the range, one dot, and the address of the last cell in the range. In general, though, I recommend that you use the anchor-and-point method for identifying a range because you're less likely to make an error.

How to use the /Print Printer command to print a spreadsheet
To print a spreadsheet, you use the /Print Printer command as summarized in figure I-12. The first time you print a spreadsheet you have to use the Range option to specify the range of cells that you want to print. This range can include the entire spreadsheet or just a portion of it.

After you select the Range option, you can use the anchor-and-point method to identify the range. If, for example, you want to identify the range from cell A1 through D10, you start by using the Home key to move the cell pointer to the cell A1. Then, you type one dot. Last, you move the cell pointer to cell D10 and press the Enter key. The easiest way to move the pointer to cell D10 is to press the End key followed by the Home key.

The first time you print a spreadsheet you may also want to set the margins or page length for the printed page. You can use the /Print Printer Options menu to set these values. In chapters 3 and 4, you can learn how to set these options in detail.

After you specify the range and set the margins the way you want them, you're ready to print the spreadsheet. After you make sure that the printer is ready and the paper is aligned properly, select the Go option to print the spreadsheet. Then, to skip to the next page, press the Page option.

When *Lotus* completes the print job, you can return to the spreadsheet in one of two ways. First, you can press the Esc key three times. Second, you can select the Quit command to exit from the Print menu.

How to use the /File Save command to save a spreadsheet If you shut off your PC or exit from *Lotus* without saving your spreadsheet, your work is lost. That's why it's so important that you understand what the /File Save command does and how it works. As you will see, this command works differently for a new spreadsheet than it does for an old one.

The first example in figure I-13 shows you how to use the /File Save command to save a spreadsheet for the first time. In step 1, the prompt in the control panel asks you to supply the file name that should be used for the new file. It also shows the directory that the new file will be stored in unless you specify otherwise:

```
Enter name of file to save: C:\123\DATA\*.wk1
```

This tells you that the *default directory* is \123\DATA on the C drive. The *.wk1 means that *Lotus* is waiting for you to enter a file name and that the

The /Print Printer menu

```
B10: @SUM(B5..B8)                                                MENU
Range  Line  Page  Options  Clear  Align  Go  Quit
Specify a range to print
        A          B        C        D        E        F        G
```

The range for the expense spreadsheet

```
D10: @SUM(D5..D8)                                                POINT
Enter print range: A1..D10

        A          B        C        D        E        F        G
1   Monthly Expenses
2   February
3                   Budget  Expense Variance
4
5   Salaries        50,000   51,004    1,004
6   Rent            17,500   17,453     (47)
7   Maintenance      7,750    7,784       34
8   Supplies         8,250    9,374    1,124
9
10  Total           83,500   85,615    2,115
11
```

A typical sequence of commands for printing a small spreadsheet for the first time

1. Use the /Print Printer Range command to specify the range of cells to be printed. Normally, the range is from A1 to the cell that's at the intersection of the bottom row and right-most column of the spreadsheet. You can use the anchor-and-point method to identify this range. To move to the lower right corner of the spreadsheet, you can use the End Home key sequence.
2. Use the /Print Printer Go command to print the spreadsheet.
3. Use the /Print Printer Page command to advance the paper to the top of the next form.
4. Use the /Printer Printer Quit command to exit from the command.

Figure I-12 How to print a spreadsheet and skip to the top of the next page

extension is going to be WK1. If you're using release 3.X, you'll see a slightly different prompt:

```
Enter name of file to save: C:\123\DATA\FILE0001.WK3
```

Here, FILE0001.WK3 means that *Lotus* is waiting for you to enter a file name and that the extension is going to be WK3.

If the default directory is the one you want to save the spreadsheet in, you enter just a file name as shown in step 2 of figure I-13. Here, FEBEXP has been entered without an extension because *Lotus* will add an extension of WK1 or WK3 automatically. Then, when you press the Enter key, the spreadsheet is saved in the default directory in a file named either FEBEXP.WK1 or FEBEXP.WK3, depending on the release of *Lotus* you're using. Because release 2.2 has been used for the example in figure I-24, the extension is WK1.

If the default directory shown in step 1 isn't the one you want to use, you can override it by giving a file specification that includes the directory. To do that, press the Esc key twice to clear the assumed directory so the second line in the control panel looks like this:

```
Enter name of file to save:
```

Then, you enter a complete specification for the file you want to save. If, for example, you want to store the spreadsheet in a file named FEBEXP in the LTSDATA directory on the D drive, you can enter a specification like this:

```
Enter name of file to save: D:\LTSDATA\FEBEXP
```

When you create a file name for a spreadsheet, you must of course follow the DOS rules for file names. You should also try to create file names that you'll remember later on. In this example, FEBEXP is used to indicate that the file contains an expense (EXP) summary for the month of February (FEB).

The second example in figure I-13 shows you how to use the /File Save command to save a spreadsheet for the second time. After you select the /File Save command, *Lotus* displays the prompt shown in step 1. This prompt shows you the file name that you used to save the file the first time so you don't have to enter it again. Instead, you just press the Enter key.

However, because there's already a file on the hard disk with the file name you've just used, *Lotus* doesn't store the spreadsheet on the disk right away. Instead, it displays the prompt shown in step 2 to warn you that another file with the same name exists. Then, to save the new version of the spreadsheet in place of the old one, you select the Replace option. That's what you usually want to do. But to cancel the command and return to the spreadsheet without replacing the old file, you can select the Cancel option.

The third example in figure I-13 shows you how to use the /File Save command to save an old spreadsheet with a new name. After you select the /File Save command, *Lotus* displays the prompt shown in step 1. This prompt shows you the file name that you used to save the file the last time: FEBEXP. But suppose that's not the name you want for the new spreadsheet file. To enter the name for the new file, you press the Esc key once to clear the old file name, type the new file name (MAREXP), and press the Enter key. This time *Lotus* stores the file on disk without presenting any message because there isn't a file on the disk named MAREXP.

How to use the /Quit command to exit from *Lotus* When you're ready to end your *Lotus* session and return to DOS, you use the /Quit command.

How to save a spreadsheet for the first time

1. Start the /File Save command by typing /fs. *Lotus* then displays a prompt like this:

   ```
   Enter name of file to save: C:\123\DATA\*.wk1
   ```

2. Type a file name:

   ```
   Enter name of file to save: C:\123\DATA\febexp
   ```

   Then, when you press the Enter key, the file is saved on the hard disk.

How to save a spreadsheet for the second time

1. Start the /File Save command by typing /fs. *Lotus* then displays a prompt like this:

   ```
   Enter name of file to save: C:\123\DATA\FEBEXP
   ```

2. Press the Enter key to save the file. *Lotus* then displays a prompt like this:

   ```
   Cancel  Replace  Backup
   ```

   Select the Replace option to save the spreadsheet using the same file name as before.

How to save an old spreadsheet with a new file name

1. Start the /File Save command by typing /fs. *Lotus* then displays a prompt like this:

   ```
   Enter name of file to save: C:\123\DATA\FEBEXP
   ```

2. Type a new file name:

   ```
   Enter name of file to save: C:\123\DATA\marexp
   ```

   Then, when you press the Enter key, the file is saved on the hard disk.

Figure I-13 How to use the /File Save command

When you start this command, *Lotus* displays a message like the first one in figure I-14. This gives you a chance to change your mind. If you select the No option, *Lotus* returns to the spreadsheet screen. If you select the Yes option, you exit from *Lotus* and return to DOS.

If you're using release 2.2 or any one of the later releases, *Lotus* displays a message like the second one in figure I-14 if you select the /Quit command before you saved the last changes to the spreadsheet you were working on. If you want to lose the changes you've made, you select the Yes option. But if you don't want to lose the changes you've made, you select the No option to return to the spreadsheet. Then, you can save the spreadsheet to disk and issue the /Quit command again.

The message that's displayed when you select the /Quit command

```
E1: "MAREXP                                                    MENU
No  Yes
Do not end 1-2-3 session; return to READY mode
        A         B         C         D         E         F         G
1   Monthly Expenses                          MAREXP
2   March
3                 Budget   Expense Variance
4
```

The message that's displayed if you try to exit from *Lotus* before you saved the last changes you've made to a spreadsheet (releases 2.2 and later)

```
E1: "MAREXP                                                    MENU
No  Yes
WORKSHEET CHANGES NOT SAVED!  End 1-2-3 anyway?
        A         B         C         D         E         F         G
1   Monthly Expenses                          MAREXP
2   March
3                 Budget   Expense Variance
4
```

Figure I-14 The exit messages that are displayed by the /Quit command

If you're using one of the earlier releases of *Lotus*, you must be sure to save the last changes to a spreadsheet before you exit from *Lotus*. That's because these releases of *Lotus* don't provide the warning message shown in figure I-14.

How to enter the current date into a spreadsheet

Most PCs today automatically keep track of the current date and time. On the older PCs, you are asked to enter the correct date and time as part of the DOS start-up procedure. Either way, the current date is available to *Lotus* so you can use it in your spreadsheets. To access the date from DOS and put it in a cell, you use an @function. To format the date entry, you use the /Range Format command. This is illustrated in figure I-15.

When you enter @NOW into a cell, *Lotus* puts a number in the cell that represents the current date. This is illustrated in the first step in figure I-15. Here, the number 33,683 represents March 19, 1992. Then, to format this number so it makes sense, you use the /Range Format Date command.

When you start the /Range Format Date command, you are given five different options. After you select one of these options, the command asks you for the range of cells to be formatted. In this case, only one cell needs to be formatted so you press the Enter key when the correct cell is highlighted.

1. Move the cell pointer to the cell that you want to put the current date in. Type @NOW and press the Enter key. At this point, Lotus will display the number of the day in the cell like this:

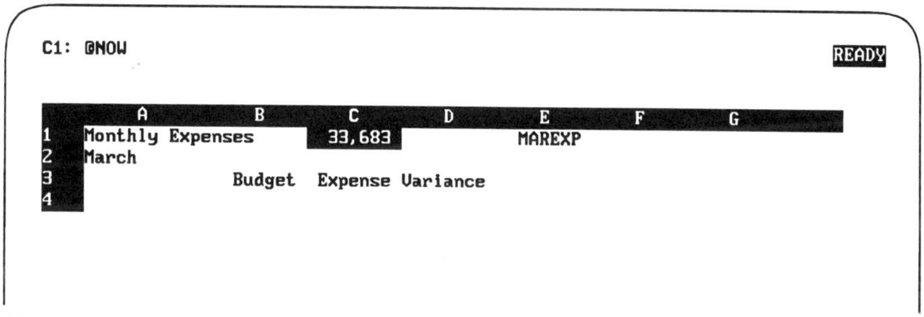

2. Use the /Range Format Date command to format the date cell. After you select one of the five options of the Date format, you highlight the cell to be formatted and press the Enter key. If, for example, you select the Long International format, *Lotus* will display the date like this if the column is wide enough for it:

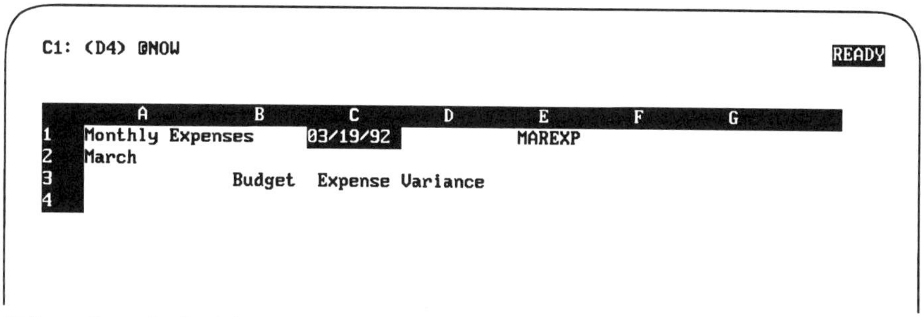

3. If the column isn't wide enough, use the /Worksheet Column Set-Width command to increase the width of the column so the date is displayed properly.

Figure I-15 How to enter the current date into a spreadsheet

When you use the @NOW function, the date is automatically updated each time you modify a spreadsheet. As a result, this function is frequently used in one of the top lines of a spreadsheet to indicate the date that the spreadsheet was printed. That way, you can easily identify the versions of a spreadsheet that were prepared on different dates.

How to use the *Lotus* Help feature

As you work with *Lotus*, you should realize that the Help feature is only a keystroke away. To access it, just press the F1 function key. If you're not using a command, a general Help-index screen like the one in figure I-16 is displayed. Then, you can highlight the topic that you're interested in and press the Enter key to get the information. To get back to the spreadsheet, you press the Esc key one or more times.

If you press the F1 key when you're using a command, the Help feature gives specific information about the command you're using. This saves time because you don't have to use the Help index. In figure I-16, for example, you can see the help information that's displayed for the /Worksheet Global Format command.

Because the *Lotus* Help feature is a good one, you should try it whenever you're not sure how a command or feature works. The limitation of the Help feature is that it doesn't always give you the information you need, and it doesn't show you the relationships between features. In practice, then, the best reference materials are a book like this one in combination with the Help feature.

How to use *Lotus* for business applications

Once you master the skills that I just presented, you should be able to apply those skills to your own business spreadsheets. For instance, you should be able to create, print, and save a spreadsheet like the one in figure I-17. This is a simple spreadsheet that compares actual expenses to budgeted expenses and calculates the variance between the two.

Using the same set of *Lotus* skills, you should be able to retrieve a spreadsheet like the one in figure I-17 and modify it so it looks like the one in figure I-18. For this modification, you need to increase the width of the first column, edit the labels in that column, insert a new row into the spreadsheet, make sure that the @SUM function in the total line still works, and so on. If necessary, you should be able to save the modified spreadsheet with a new name so both the old and the new spreadsheets are stored on the hard disk.

How to use *Lotus* for "what if" analysis

Although many people use *Lotus* just to organize and summarize data in spreadsheets like the one in figure I-18, one of the most exciting uses of *Lotus* is for *what-if analysis*. Because *Lotus* recalculates all of the cells in a spreadsheet so quickly, you can try many different assumptions in just a few minutes to see "what will happen if." If you're a manager, what-if analysis is likely to be the major benefit that you'll get from *Lotus*. If you learn to do this type of analysis well, it will help you make better business decisions.

The Help Index screen

```
A1:                                                              HELP

1-2-3 Help Index

About 1-2-3 Help          Linking Files            1-2-3 Main Menu
Cell Formats              Macro Basics             /Add-In
Cell/Range References     Macro Command Index      /Copy
Column Widths             Macro Key Names          /Data
Control Panel             Mode Indicators          /File
Entering Data             Operators                /Graph
Error Message Index       Range Basics             /Move
Formulas                  Recalculation            /Print
@Function Index           Specifying Ranges        /Quit
Function Keys             Status Indicators        /Range
Keyboard Index            Task Index               /System
Learn Feature             Undo Feature             /Worksheet

To select a topic, press a pointer-movement key to highlight the topic and then
press ENTER.  To return to a previous Help screen, press BACKSPACE.  To leave
Help and return to the worksheet, press ESC.

21-Apr-92  07:39 AM                                    NUM
```

The Help screen that's displayed when you press the F1 key while using the /Worksheet Global Format command

```
B10: @SUM(B5..B8)                                                HELP
Fixed  Sci  Currency  ,  General  +/-  Percent  Date  Text  Hidden
Fixed number of decimal places (x.xx)

/Worksheet Global Format -- Sets the default cell format, the way 1-2-3
 displays data, in the worksheet.  Note that changing the cell format only
 affects the display of data, not the data itself.

 1. Select /Worksheet Global Format.
 2. Select a format and complete any further prompts or menu selections
    for that format.
 3. If a column is not wide enough to display a value in the format
    you selected, 1-2-3 fills the cell with * (asterisks).  Use
    /Worksheet Column Set-Width to widen the column and redisplay
    the value.

 To change the format of data in a range, and not the entire worksheet,
 use /Range Format.  To return the worksheet to the default format
 setting, use /Worksheet Global Format General.

Numeric Formats     /Worksheet Global     Worksheet Commands     Help Index
21-Apr-92  08:42 AM                                    NUM
```

Figure I-16 Two Help screens

In this introduction, I'm going to illustrate what-if analysis with only one example. Figure I-19 shows a spreadsheet that can be used to make profit-and-loss projections for the next year. Because some of the expenses are related to sales, this spreadsheet shows sales at five different levels. The variable expenses are then calculated as a percent of sales using the percents from the previous year. Thus, the cost of goods sold is 41 percent of sales; the order handling expense is 4.6 percent of sales; and the bad debt expense is 2.8 percent of sales. The other expenses are treated as fixed costs so they stay the same at all five sales levels.

Once you've set up a spreadsheet like the one in figure I-19, you're ready to do some what-if analysis. And one of the first questions is: What if the cost of goods sold could be reduced? To see how this would affect profits, you just change the formulas in the cost-of-goods-sold row and all the other values are automatically recalculated. In figure I-20, for example, you can see the projections when the cost of goods sold is assumed to be 38% instead of 41% of sales. As you can see, this variable can have a dramatic effect on profits.

Another good question is: What if the marketing budget were increased or decreased? To see how this could affect profits, you change just the values in the marketing row and all of the other values are recalculated. In figure I-21, for example, you can see the possible results when marketing costs are increased to $400,000 per year and the cost of goods sold is kept at 41% of sales. If you compare this spreadsheet with the one in figure I-19, you can see that the $100,000 increase in marketing costs would have to increase sales by about $200,000 in order to justify the cost increase. So perhaps an increase in marketing costs isn't the best way to increase profits.

By now, I hope you get the idea. If you set up a spreadsheet right, you can quickly consider many strategic alternatives. The more closely your spreadsheet models the real world, the better your projections will be. But even simple spreadsheets and simple what-if manipulations can help you see relationships that you are likely to miss otherwise.

When you set up a spreadsheet for what-if analysis, you want to set it up so you can change the assumptions as efficiently as possible. In the spreadsheet in figure I-21, for example, you have to change only the marketing expense in cell D2 when you want to try another value. The marketing expense values for levels 1 through 5 are automatically changed to the value in cell D2. Similarly, if you want to change one of the fixed expenses, you have to change only the level-1 value in the row; the values for levels 2 through 5 are automatically changed to the level-1 value.

Figure I-22 shows the labels, values, and formulas that I used in the cells of the spreadsheet in figure I-21. To make this easier to follow, the row numbers are printed to the right of the spreadsheet and the column letters are printed beneath it. Here, you can see that cost of goods sold is the sales value times .41 (41 percent). You can see that the formula for marketing in level 2

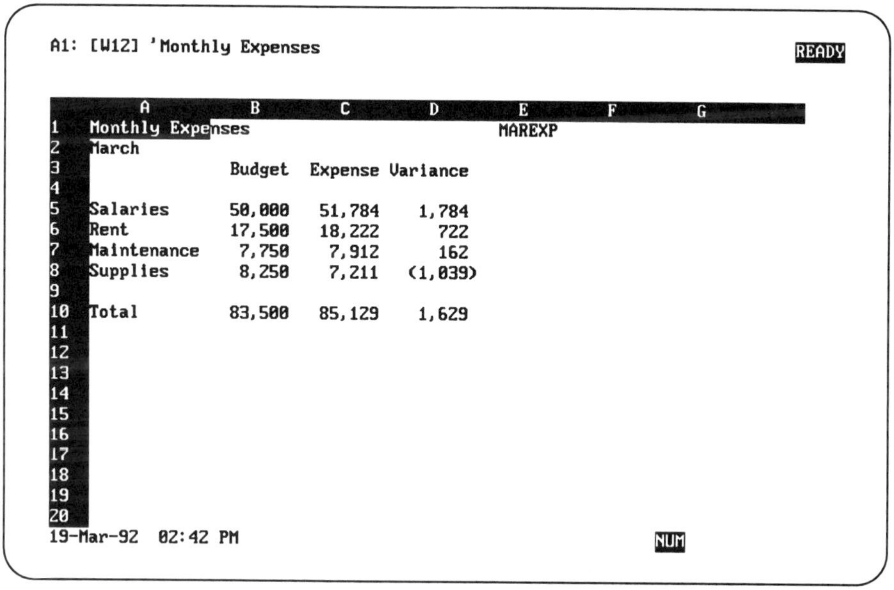

A1: [W12] 'Monthly Expenses READY

	A	B	C	D	E	F	G
1	Monthly Expenses				MAREXP		
2	March						
3		Budget	Expense	Variance			
4							
5	Salaries	50,000	51,784	1,784			
6	Rent	17,500	18,222	722			
7	Maintenance	7,750	7,912	162			
8	Supplies	8,250	7,211	(1,039)			
9							
10	Total	83,500	85,129	1,629			
11							
12							
13							
14							
15							
16							
17							
18							
19							
20							

19-Mar-92 02:42 PM NUM

Figure I-17 A simple spreadsheet that you should be able to create using the skills presented in this introduction

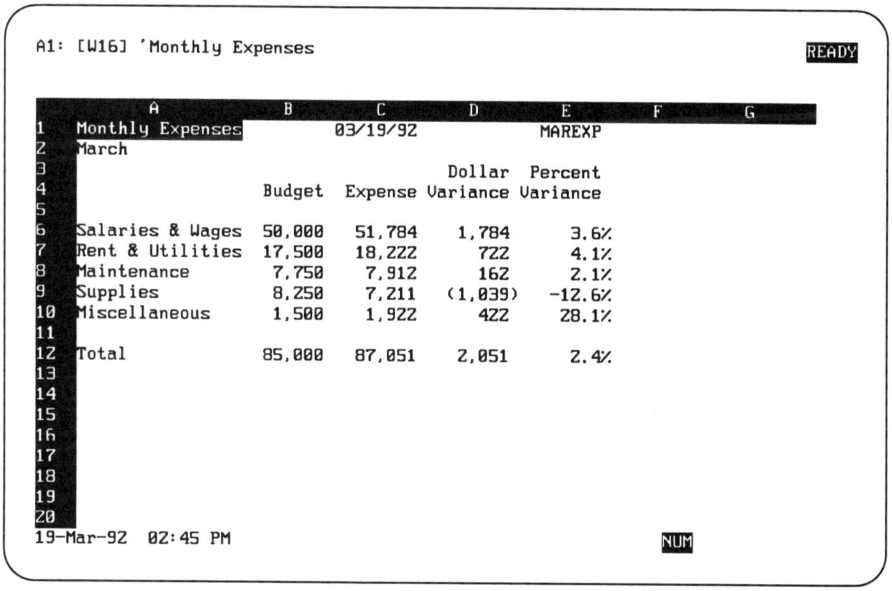

A1: [W16] 'Monthly Expenses READY

	A	B	C	D	E	F	G
1	Monthly Expenses		03/19/92		MAREXP		
2	March						
3				Dollar	Percent		
4		Budget	Expense	Variance	Variance		
5							
6	Salaries & Wages	50,000	51,784	1,784	3.6%		
7	Rent & Utilities	17,500	18,222	722	4.1%		
8	Maintenance	7,750	7,912	162	2.1%		
9	Supplies	8,250	7,211	(1,039)	-12.6%		
10	Miscellaneous	1,500	1,922	422	28.1%		
11							
12	Total	85,000	87,051	2,051	2.4%		
13							
14							
15							
16							
17							
18							
19							
20							

19-Mar-92 02:45 PM NUM

Figure I-18 A spreadsheet that you should be able to develop by modifying the spreadsheet in figure I-17

Proforma P&L Projection		COGS=	41.0%		PFORMA
Profit center 21		Marketing=	$300,000		
Level	1	2	3	4	5
Sales	2,600,000	2,700,000	2,800,000	2,900,000	3,000,000
Cost of goods sold	1,066,000	1,107,000	1,148,000	1,189,000	1,230,000
Gross profit	1,534,000	1,593,000	1,652,000	1,711,000	1,770,000
Salaries & wages	650,000	650,000	650,000	650,000	650,000
Rent & utilities	215,000	215,000	215,000	215,000	215,000
Equip. & maintenance	95,000	95,000	95,000	95,000	95,000
Order handling	117,000	121,500	126,000	130,500	135,000
Marketing	300,000	300,000	300,000	300,000	300,000
Miscellaneous	17,500	17,500	17,500	17,500	17,500
Total	1,394,500	1,399,000	1,403,500	1,408,000	1,412,500
Operating profit	139,500	194,000	248,500	303,000	357,500
Bad debt	75,400	78,300	81,200	84,100	87,000
Interest	35,000	35,000	35,000	35,000	35,000
Total	110,400	113,300	116,200	119,100	122,000
Before tax profit	29,100	80,700	132,300	183,900	235,500

Figure I-19 A spreadsheet that can be used to project profit and loss

sets the value equal to the same one as in level 1; the formula in level 3 sets the value equal to level 2; and so on. That's why you have to change only the level-1 value when you want to change all of the values in the row.

To create a spreadsheet like this, you concentrate on the data in column B. Once you set that column up so it accurately represents fixed and variable expenses, you can quickly set up the other columns by copying formulas from one range of cells to another. In fact, if you look at the contents of the cells in columns C through F, you can see that none of them contain values; they all contain formulas.

The point of showing you the formulas in this spreadsheet is to show you that you already know everything you need to know to create a spreadsheet that you can use for what-if analysis. As you go through this book, you'll learn other skills that will help you create spreadsheets like this in ways that are more sophisticated. For instance, chapter 2 shows you how to use an absolute address in a formula so you have to change just the percentage in cell D1 when you want to change all of the cost-of-goods-sold values in row 8.

Proforma P&L Projection		COGS=	38.0%		PFORMA
Profit center 21		Marketing=	$300,000		
Level	1	2	3	4	5
Sales	2,600,000	2,700,000	2,800,000	2,900,000	3,000,000
Cost of goods sold	988,000	1,026,000	1,064,000	1,102,000	1,140,000
Gross profit	1,612,000	1,674,000	1,736,000	1,798,000	1,860,000
Salaries & wages	650,000	650,000	650,000	650,000	650,000
Rent & utilities	215,000	215,000	215,000	215,000	215,000
Equip. & maintenance	95,000	95,000	95,000	95,000	95,000
Order handling	117,000	121,500	126,000	130,500	135,000
Marketing	300,000	300,000	300,000	300,000	300,000
Miscellaneous	17,500	17,500	17,500	17,500	17,500
Total	1,394,500	1,399,000	1,403,500	1,408,000	1,412,500
Operating profit	217,500	275,000	332,500	390,000	447,500
Bad debt	75,400	78,300	81,200	84,100	87,000
Interest	35,000	35,000	35,000	35,000	35,000
Total	110,400	113,300	116,200	119,100	122,000
Before tax profit	107,100	161,700	216,300	270,900	325,500

Figure I-20 The spreadsheet in figure I-19 after one assumption has been changed

But you don't have to learn more skills before you start using what-if analysis. Start using it right away. It can help you become a better manager.

How to get the most from *Lotus*

If you already have the skills reviewed in this chapter and you can apply them to business spreadsheets like those shown in figures I-18 through I-22, you're ready to benefit from this book. Now, to conclude this introduction, please take the time to read the three recommendations that follow. If you accept these recommendations, they will help you get the maximum benefit from *Lotus* and from this book.

Master the essential *Lotus* skills So often, I see people struggling with *Lotus* because they've never mastered the essential *Lotus* skills. My first recommendation, then, is to take the time to master those skills. If you do, you will get more done in less time. You'll also be able to apply *Lotus* to a wider range of business requirements.

```
Proforma P&L Projection          COGS=      41.0%          PFORMA
Profit center 21            Marketing=   $400,000
```

Level	1	2	3	4	5
Sales	2,600,000	2,700,000	2,800,000	2,900,000	3,000,000
Cost of goods sold	1,066,000	1,107,000	1,148,000	1,189,000	1,230,000
Gross profit	1,534,000	1,593,000	1,652,000	1,711,000	1,770,000
Salaries & wages	650,000	650,000	650,000	650,000	650,000
Rent & utilities	215,000	215,000	215,000	215,000	215,000
Equip. & maintenance	95,000	95,000	95,000	95,000	95,000
Order handling	117,000	121,500	126,000	130,500	135,000
Marketing	400,000	400,000	400,000	400,000	400,000
Miscellaneous	17,500	17,500	17,500	17,500	17,500
Total	1,494,500	1,499,000	1,503,500	1,508,000	1,512,500
Operating profit	39,500	94,000	148,500	203,000	257,500
Bad debt	75,400	78,300	81,200	84,100	87,000
Interest	35,000	35,000	35,000	35,000	35,000
Total	110,400	113,300	116,200	119,100	122,000
Before tax profit	(70,900)	(19,300)	32,300	83,900	135,500

Figure I-21 The spreadsheet in figure I-19 after another assumption has been changed

To make it easier for you to master the essential skills, the chapters in the first section of this book present the skills in a form that is designed for efficient learning and reference. These chapters present plenty of new information that will help you use *Lotus* more productively. But they also summarize all of the skills presented in this introduction.

So take the time to read all five chapters in the next section. Refer to those chapters whenever you need to refresh your memory. And use all of the skills so often that you master them. In the long run, the time that you spend mastering those skills will be paid back many times over in the form of increased productivity.

Become familiar with the other *Lotus* functions and features

Sections 2 through 4 of this book present *Lotus* functions and features for special purposes. As a result, it's possible that you won't ever need any of them. More likely, though, some will come in handy as you use *Lotus* for new

Proforma P&L Projection		COGS=	41.0%		PFORMA	1
Profit center 21		Marketing=	$400,000			2
========	========	========	========	========	========	3
Level	1	2	3	4	5	4
========	========	========	========	========	========	5
Sales	2,600,000	+B6+100000	+C6+100000	+D6+100000	+E6+100000	6
						7
Cost of goods sold	+B6*0.41	+C6*0.41	+D6*0.41	+E6*0.41	+F6*0.41	8
						9
Gross profit	+B6-B8	+C6-C8	+D6-D8	+E6-E8	+F6-F8	10
						11
Salaries & wages	650,000	+B12	+C12	+D12	+E12	12
Rent & utilities	215,000	+B13	+C13	+D13	+E13	13
Equip. & maintenance	95,000	+B14	+C14	+D14	+E14	14
Order handling	+B6*0.045	+C6*0.045	+D6*0.045	+E6*0.045	+F6*0.045	15
Marketing	+D2	+B16	+C16	+D16	+E16	16
Miscellaneous	17,500	+B17	+C17	+D17	+E17	17
Total	@SUM(B12..B17)	@SUM(C12..C17)	@SUM(D12..D17)	@SUM(E12..E17)	@SUM(F12..F17)	18
						19
Operating profit	+B10-B18	+C10-C18	+D10-D18	+E10-E18	+F10-F18	20
						21
Bad debt	+B6*0.029	+C6*0.029	+D6*0.029	+E6*0.029	+F6*0.029	22
Interest	35,000	+B23	+C23	+D23	+E23	23
Total	+B22+B23	+C22+C23	+D22+D23	+E22+E23	+F22+F23	24
						25
Before tax profit	+B20-B24	+C20-C24	+D20-D24	+E20-E24	+F20-F24	26
========	========	========	========	========	========	27
A	B	C	D	E	F	

Figure I-22 The spreadsheet in figure I-21 with its formulas shown

applications. For instance, you'll need the skills in chapter 7 if you start working with large spreadsheets. You'll need the skills in chapter 10 if you want to sort the data in a spreadsheet. You'll need the skills in chapter 11 if you want to link the data between two spreadsheets. You'll need the skills in chapter 16 if you want to graph the data in a spreadsheet. And so on.

With that in mind, I recommend that you at least browse through the chapters in sections 2 through 4. That way, you'll become familiar with the other functions and features that *Lotus* offers. Then, if you need one of those functions or features later on, you'll know where you can find it. Since the chapters in these sections are designed for quick instruction and efficient reference, you don't have to remember the skills that these chapters present. You just need to be able to refer to them when you need them.

To make the chapters in sections 2 through 4 as useful as possible, they are written as independent modules. As a result, you don't have to read them in sequence. Whenever you have ten or twenty minutes to learn a new skill, you can select a chapter, read it, and take another step toward mastering *Lotus*.

Do your own development work If you're a busy manager, it's tempting to delegate *Lotus* work to a subordinate. But I don't recommend that. At the least, I recommend that you develop your own spreadsheets for the analytical applications. As you develop them, you'll get ideas for making them more useful that you'll never get if you delegate the development work.

Once you've established the spreadsheets, you can delegate the work of keeping them up-to-date to someone else. You can even set up the spreadsheets so the formulas and labels can't be changed by entry error as explained in chapter 9.

Whenever a spreadsheet has to be modified due to changes in your operations, though, you should consider doing the work yourself. Please don't think of this as clerical work; think of it as analytical work. There's no question in my mind that *Lotus* can make good managers even better, but only if they do the development work themselves.

Terms

spreadsheet screen
worksheet
worksheet screen
spreadsheet
2.X
3.X
icon
mode indicator
status indicator line
status indicator
function key
label
left alignment
right alignment
value
formula
operator
anchor-and-point method
@function
column
row
cell
cell address
cell pointer
current cell
control panel
range
range address
command
menu
copy FROM range
copy what? range
copy TO range
copy where? range
dot
default directory
what-if analysis

Objectives

***Lotus* skills**

1. Enter any label into any cell of a spreadsheet with either left or right alignment. The label may start with a letter, digit, or special character.
2. Enter a positive or negative value with or without decimal positions into any cell of a spreadsheet.
3. Enter a formula into any cell of a spreadsheet using the anchor-and-point method.
4. Enter a formula that consists of a single @SUM function into any cell of a spreadsheet using the anchor-and-point method.

5. Use the commands presented in this chapter to perform any of the following functions:
   a) Set the default directory for a *Lotus* session.
   b) Retrieve a spreadsheet from the default directory or from another directory.
   c) Erase the current spreadsheet from internal storage and retrieve another one.
   d) Set the width for any column in a spreadsheet.
   e) Insert one or more rows or columns into a spreadsheet.
   f) Delete one or more rows or columns from a spreadsheet.
   g) Copy the labels, values, or formulas from one range of cells to another range of cells.
   h) Format the values in a range of cells.
   i) Erase the contents in a range of cells.
   j) Print a spreadsheet.
   k) Save a spreadsheet for the first time.
   l) Save a spreadsheet for the second time.
   m) Save an old spreadsheet in a new file.
   n) Exit from *Lotus*.

6. Use the @NOW function to enter the current date into any cell of a spreadsheet. Then, use the /Range Format command to apply a proper format to the date.
7. Use the *Lotus* Help feature to get information about any of the functions you're trying to perform or the commands you're trying to use.

Application skills

8. Use *Lotus* to create, print, and save a simple spreadsheet like the one in figure I-17.
9. Use *Lotus* to retrieve a spreadsheet like the one in figure I-17 and modify it so it looks like the one in figure I-18.
10. Use *Lotus* for what-if analysis.

Pretest

1. Create, print, and save the spreadsheet in figure I-17.
2. Retrieve the spreadsheet that you created in the first test item. Next, modify it so it looks like the spreadsheet in figure I-18. Then, print it and save it in its original location on the hard disk.

Section 1

The essential Lotus 1-2-3 skills

This section presents the essential skills that all *Lotus* users should have. For ease of use, each chapter in this section is treated as an independent module so you don't have to read the chapters in sequence. However, you should take the time to read all of the chapters in this section because the skills that they present can help you work more productively.

The chapters in this section, like all the chapters in this book, are designed so they can be used efficiently for both training and reference. When you use them for training, you read them from start to finish. But when you use them for reference, you usually don't have to read the text. In most cases, you can refresh your memory about how to use a function or feature just by studying the figures in the chapter.

Chapter 1

How to enter and edit the labels and values of a spreadsheet

In this chapter, I'll summarize all of the rules and commands that you need to enter and edit labels and values. Since this book assumes that you already use *Lotus*, this chapter will reinforce many of the skills you already have, and it may present some skills that you don't have. As a result, you should scan this chapter even if you think that you know most of what it presents.

To start, you'll learn all the rules for entering labels and values. Next, you'll learn how to edit labels and values so you don't have to re-enter them from scratch when you want to change them. Last, you'll learn how to use two commands that affect the entry process.

Two ways to complete an entry

Before I give you all the rules for entering labels and values, I want to remind you that there are two ways to complete an entry. The first way is to press the Enter key. In this case, the cell pointer remains in the cell that you were working on.

The second way to complete an entry is to press an Arrow key. In this case, the label or value is accepted and the cell pointer is moved one cell in the direction indicated by the Arrow key. Often, using an Arrow key is more efficient than using the Enter key. That's why you'll probably use Arrow keys to complete your entries most of the time.

How to enter labels into a spreadsheet

Whenever you begin an entry with a letter, *Lotus* assumes that it's a label so it automatically places an apostrophe (') in front of the entry in the control panel. In *Lotus* terminology, this apostrophe is called a *label prefix*. *Lotus* uses this prefix to identify the entry as a label, but the prefix isn't displayed in the cell or printed in the spreadsheet.

Prefix	Meaning	Cell entry	Cell display [W10]
'	Align left	'JAN '1Q1993	JAN 1Q1993
"	Align right	"JAN "1Q1993	JAN 1Q1993
^	Center	^JAN ^1Q1993	JAN 1Q1993
\	Repeat the next characters until the current cell is filled	\= \H \123	========== HHHHHHHHHH 1231231231

Note: [W10] indicates that the cells are ten characters wide.

Figure 1-1 The four label prefixes you can use to align labels and repeat characters

If a label doesn't start with a letter, you have to enter the label prefix yourself to tell *Lotus* that your entry should be a label, not a value or a formula. If, for example, you want to enter the year 1992 as a label, you must start the entry with a label prefix. Otherwise, *Lotus* will think that 1992 is a value. Similarly, if you want to enter a label that starts with a plus sign, a minus sign, or a left parenthesis, you must start the entry with a label prefix. Otherwise, *Lotus* will think that you're starting a value or a formula.

Figure 1-1 summaries the four label prefixes that you can use when you enter a label. Each one causes a different type of label alignment. The apostrophe (') aligns a label on the left of its cell. The quotation mark (") aligns a label on the right of its cell. And the caret (^) centers a label within its cell.

When you enter a label that is larger than a cell, the label continues into the cells to the right if they aren't already filled. In this case, *Lotus* aligns the label on the left of the first cell no matter what prefix you use. Then, when you change the width of the column to display the entire label, *Lotus* aligns the label according to its prefix.

The fourth prefix in figure 1-1 is the backslash (\). You use this prefix when you want to repeat one or more characters across a cell. This prefix is useful when you want to put separating lines in a spreadsheet. If you look ahead to figure 1-7, you can see this done in row 5 of the heading. To enter lines like these, you just enter \= in the first cell of one row. Then, you can copy the contents of this cell to the other cells in the row. Because the repeat prefix is used, the cells will be filled no matter how wide they are. Usually, the equal sign (=) or the minus sign (-) is the character that's repeated to form the separating line.

Cell entry	[W10] (,2) Cell display	[W10] (F2) Cell display	[W10] (C2) Cell display	[W10] (F1) Cell display
123	123.00	123.00	$123.00	123.0
1234	1,234.00	1234.00	$1,234.00	1234.0
123.45	123.45	123.45	$123.45	123.4
12345.67	12,345.67	12345.67	*********	12345.7
-123	(123.00)	-123.00	($123.00)	-123.0
-1234	(1,234.00)	-1234.00	*********	-1234.0
-123.45	(123.45)	-123.45	($123.45)	-123.4
-12345.67	*********	-12345.67	*********	-12345.7
+123	123.00	123.00	$123.00	123.0
+1234	1,234.00	1234.00	$1,234.00	1234.0
+123.45	123.45	123.45	$123.45	123.5

Notes:

[W10]	indicates that the columns are ten characters wide.
(,2)	indicates Comma format with two decimal positions.
(F2)	indicates Fixed format with two decimal position.
(C2)	indicates Currency format with two decimal positions.
(F1)	indicates Fixed format with one decimal position.
**********	indicates the formatted value is too wide for the column.

Figure 1-2 How four different formats affect the way values are displayed in a spreadsheet

How to enter values into a spreadsheet

When you start an entry with a digit or a plus or minus sign, *Lotus* assumes that you are entering a value. Within a value, you can only use one plus or minus sign, one decimal point, and the digits zero through nine.

To enter a positive value, you usually just start with the first digit of the value, but you can also start with a plus sign. In contrast, when you enter a negative value, you must start the entry with a minus sign. To enter a value with decimal places, you enter the decimal point in the appropriate place within the value.

Figure 1-2 illustrates valid values as they are entered into cells and as they are displayed by *Lotus*. As you can see, a value in a cell can be displayed in more than one format. As you'll learn in chapter 3, the format can be set for the whole spreadsheet, or it can be set for a range of cells. If a value has more digits than can be displayed properly within a cell, either the cell is filled with asterisks, or the value is displayed in exponential notation. How the over-long value is displayed depends on the default format that's set for the spreadsheet.

1. Move the cursor to the cell you want to edit and press the F2 (Edit) key.
2. Modify the entry using the keys shown in figure 1-4.
3. Press the Enter key.

Figure 1-3 How to edit the contents of a cell

The four formats that are illustrated in figure 1-2 are the Comma format with two decimal places (,2); the Fixed format with two decimal places (F2); the Currency format with two decimal places (C2); and the Fixed format with one decimal place (F1). Here, you can see that the Comma and Currency formats put parentheses around negative values, while the Fixed format puts a minus sign before a negative value. You can also see that the Currency format puts a dollar sign ($) before each value.

If a value has more decimal places than can be displayed by the format for the cell, the value is rounded to the correct number of decimal places for the display. Then, the unnecessary decimal places are truncated. Thus, the value 123.45 is displayed as 123.5 in the F1 format, and the value 12345.67 is displayed as 12345.7. You should remember, though, that this rounding and truncation is only for display. The cells still contain the original values that were entered into them. And *Lotus* will use the original values when it performs operations on them.

How to edit the contents of a cell

When you want to change a label or value for a cell after you've entered it, you can re-enter it. Then, the new entry replaces the old one. Often, though, it's more efficient to *edit* the contents of the cell.

To edit a cell, you do the three steps that are summarized in figure 1-3. To activate the edit feature in step 1, you press the F2 key. *Lotus* then transfers the entry that's in the current cell to the second line of the control panel so you can edit it in step 2. During this step, you can use any of the editing keys that are summarized in figure 1-4. After you've made the required changes, you press the Enter key in step 3 to return the edited entry to the current cell.

When you use the keyboard to type new characters while you're editing, *Lotus* is either in *Insert mode* or *Typeover mode*. In Insert mode, the characters that you type are inserted into the entry. In Typeover mode, the characters that you type replace the original characters in the entry. When Typeover mode is active, the OVR indicator appears at the bottom of the screen. To toggle between these two modes, you use the Insert key.

The most useful editing keys are probably the Home key to move the cursor to the start of the entry, the Left and Right arrow keys to move the

Key	Function
F2	Start the editing operation.
Left arrow	Move the cursor left one character.
Right arrow	Move the cursor right one character.
Backspace	Erase the character to the left of the cursor.
Delete	Erase the character at the cursor position.
Insert	Toggle between the *Insert* and *Typeover* modes. When the Insert mode is activated, the characters you enter are inserted at the cursor position. When the Typeover mode is activated, *Lotus* displays a OVR indicator at the bottom of the screen and the characters you enter overwrite the existing characters.
Home	Move the cursor to the first character.
End	Move the cursor to the last character.
Ctrl+Left arrow	Move the cursor to the left by five characters.
Ctrl+Right arrow	Move the cursor to the right by five characters.
Enter	End the editing operation.

Figure 1-4 The keys you can use to edit the contents of a cell

cursor from one character to the next, and the Backspace and Delete keys to delete characters. After you edit a few cells, you'll see how easy it is to use the Edit feature.

How to use the /Range Label command to change the label alignment for a range of cells

The /Range Label command lets you change the alignment for a range of cells. To use it, you use the procedure in figure 1-5. After you start the command, you select an alignment option. Then, you highlight the range of cells that the option should be applied to and press the Enter key.

When *Lotus* performs this command, it doesn't apply the alignment option to the cells. Instead, it changes the label prefixes for the labels in the cells. So this is a way to change the label prefixes for a range of cells after you've entered the labels. Remember, though, it doesn't do any good to use the /Range Label command on a range of cells before you enter labels into them because this command works on the labels themselves, not on the cells.

1. Select the appropriate alignment option from the /Range Label menu:

   `Left   Right   Center`

2. Highlight the range of labels that you want to align as prompted by the control panel:

   `Enter range of labels:   B3..D4`

   Then, press the Enter key.

Figure 1-5 How to use the /Range Label command to change the alignment of labels in a range of cells

How to use the /Data Fill command to enter a sequence of values into a range of cells

Occasionally, you'll want to enter a sequence of numbers into a spreadsheet. For instance, you may want to enter the numbers 1 through 36 to identify the 36 monthly payments required for repayment of a loan. Although you could enter these numbers manually, *Lotus* provides the /Data Fill command to help you speed up the process.

Figure 1-6 summarizes the procedure for using the /Data Fill command. In step 1, you highlight the range of cells that you want to fill. This is called the *fill range*. In step 2, you specify the *start value* for the sequence of numbers, and you specify the *step value* you want to use in step 3. If, for example, you want to enter the numbers 1 through 25, the start value is 1 and the step value is 1. If you want to enter the values 10 through 100 counting by fives, the start value is 10 and the step value is 5.

In step 4, you can enter the *stop value* for the sequence of numbers and press the Enter key. However, if you want to fill the entire fill range, you can just press the Enter key to accept the maximum stop value of 8191. Then, *Lotus* enters the sequence of values that you specified into the fill range, stopping when the last cell in the Fill range is filled.

Figure 1-7 shows a loan amortization spreadsheet that contains a sequence of numbers. To create this spreadsheet, I used the /Data Fill command to enter the payment numbers. In this case, I highlighted about 75 rows in column 1 of the spreadsheet because I didn't want to take the time to figure out what the last cell in the fill range was going to be. Then, since the period of the loan is for 60 months, I specified 60 as the stop value so the filling operation would stop at that number.

1. Highlight the range you want to use for the sequence as prompted by the control panel:

   ```
   Enter fill range:  A1..A36
   ```

   Then, press the Enter key.

2. Enter the value that you want for the first number in the sequence as prompted by the control panel:

   ```
   Enter fill range:  A1..A36
   Start: 1
   ```

   Then, press the Enter key.

3. Enter the step value you want to use for the sequence as prompted by the control panel:

   ```
   Enter fill range:  A1..A36
   Start: 1                 Step: 1
   ```

   Then, press the Enter key.

4. Enter the stop value you want for the sequence as prompted by the control panel:

   ```
   Enter fill range:  A1..A36
   Start: 1                 Step: 1                     Stop : 8191
   ```

   Then, press the Enter key. Usually, you can accept the default value of 8191 because the entries will stop when the last cell in the Fill range is filled.

Figure 1-6 How to use the /Data Fill command to enter a sequence of numbers into a range of cells

How to use the /Range Value command to convert formulas to values

Occasionally, you'll want to convert the formulas in a range of cells to their values. To illustrate, suppose you've created the spreadsheet in figure 1-8. Here, the sales totals in column D are the result of formulas that add the values in columns B and C. But now you decide that you would like to delete columns B and C to show just the total sales and commission for each salesperson. To do that without losing the values in column D, you must first convert the formulas in that column to values.

Of course, you could re-enter the values into the cells and thus replace the formulas. But re-entering the values is not efficient, and it's easy to make an error when you type so many cell entries. That's why *Lotus* provides the /Range Value command. Figure 1-9 shows you how to use this command. In step 1, you identify the copy FROM range that contains the formulas that you want to convert. In step 2, you identify the copy TO range that should receive the values. Normally, you want to put the values in the cells that originally contained the formulas so the TO range is the same as the FROM range. As a result, all you have to do is press the Enter key in step 2. When you do, the

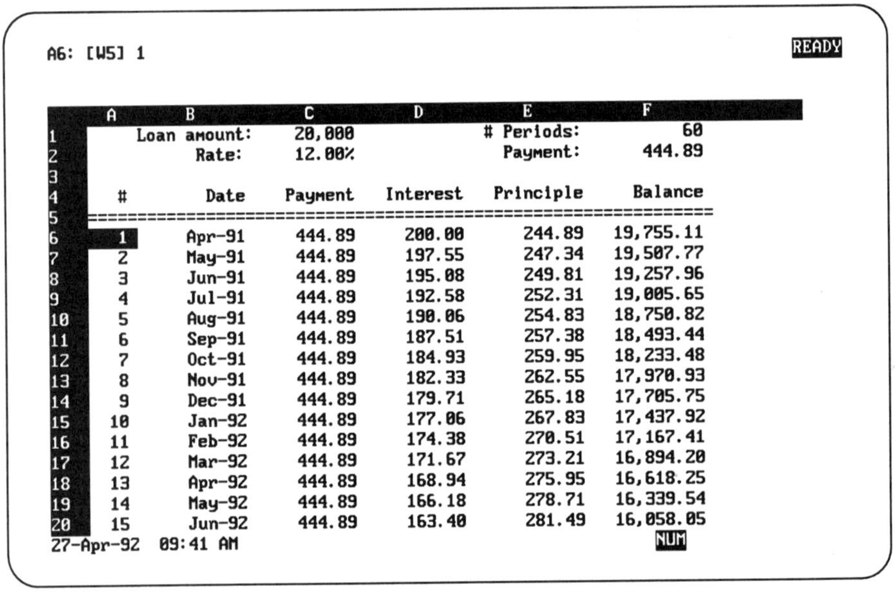

A6: [W5] 1 READY

	A	B	C	D	E	F
1		Loan amount:	20,000		# Periods:	60
2		Rate:	12.00%		Payment:	444.89
3						
4	#	Date	Payment	Interest	Principle	Balance
5	======	======	======	======	======	======
6	1	Apr-91	444.89	200.00	244.89	19,755.11
7	2	May-91	444.89	197.55	247.34	19,507.77
8	3	Jun-91	444.89	195.08	249.81	19,257.96
9	4	Jul-91	444.89	192.58	252.31	19,005.65
10	5	Aug-91	444.89	190.06	254.83	18,750.82
11	6	Sep-91	444.89	187.51	257.38	18,493.44
12	7	Oct-91	444.89	184.93	259.95	18,233.48
13	8	Nov-91	444.89	182.33	262.55	17,970.93
14	9	Dec-91	444.89	179.71	265.18	17,705.75
15	10	Jan-92	444.89	177.06	267.83	17,437.92
16	11	Feb-92	444.89	174.38	270.51	17,167.41
17	12	Mar-92	444.89	171.67	273.21	16,894.20
18	13	Apr-92	444.89	168.94	275.95	16,618.25
19	14	May-92	444.89	166.18	278.71	16,339.54
20	15	Jun-92	444.89	163.40	281.49	16,058.05

27-Apr-92 09:41 AM NUM

Figure 1-7 A sequence of numbers created by the /Data Fill command used for the number of loan payments in an amortization spreadsheet

formulas in the FROM range are converted to values. In this figure, for example, you can see that the formula in cell D4 (+B4+C4) is converted to its value of 201,668.

Now that the formulas in column D have been converted to values, you can delete columns B and C that were pointed to by the formulas in column D. After you delete these columns, you get the revised spreadsheet shown in figure 1-10 that shows the total sales and commission for each salesperson.

I want to warn you about using the /Range Value command if you happen to be using manual recalculation mode. (If you are using this mode, the CALC indicator appears in the status line at the bottom of your screen.) When you use this mode, formulas aren't recalculated each time you change the value in a cell. They are only recalculated when you press the F9 (Calc) key. That's why you should make sure that you've pressed the F9 key to recalculate all of the formulas in a spreadsheet before you use the /Range Value command. That way, you can be sure that the /Range Value command converts the formulas to the correct values. Manual calculation mode is discussed in chapter 7. But I wanted to mention it here because this mode can affect the results you get from the /Range Value command.

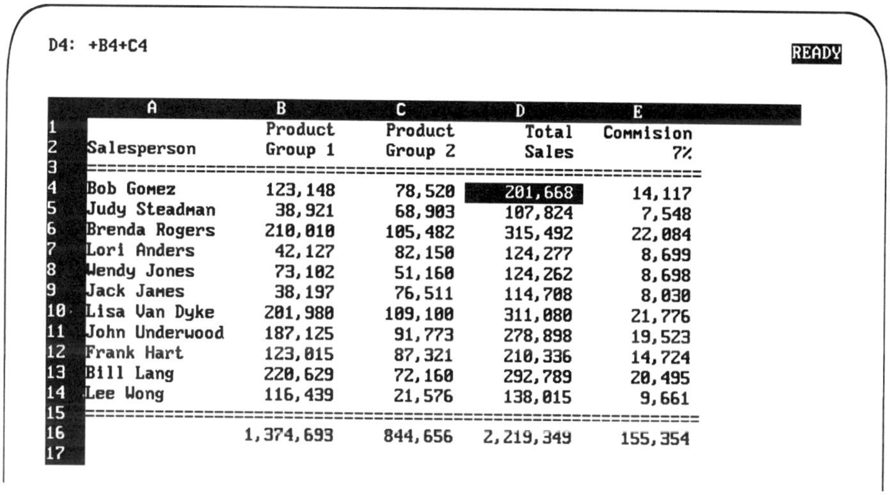

	A	B	C	D	E
1		Product	Product	Total	Commision
2	Salesperson	Group 1	Group 2	Sales	7%
3	==========	==========	==========	==========	==========
4	Bob Gomez	123,148	78,520	201,668	14,117
5	Judy Steadman	38,921	68,903	107,824	7,548
6	Brenda Rogers	210,010	105,482	315,492	22,084
7	Lori Anders	42,127	82,150	124,277	8,699
8	Wendy Jones	73,102	51,160	124,262	8,698
9	Jack James	38,197	76,511	114,708	8,030
10	Lisa Van Dyke	201,980	109,100	311,080	21,776
11	John Underwood	187,125	91,773	278,898	19,523
12	Frank Hart	123,015	87,321	210,336	14,724
13	Bill Lang	220,629	72,160	292,789	20,495
14	Lee Wong	116,439	21,576	138,015	9,661
15	==========	==========	==========	==========	==========
16		1,374,693	844,656	2,219,349	155,354
17					

Figure 1-8 A spreadsheet with formulas in column D that are based on values in columns B and C

Discussion

The basic skills that you need for entering and editing labels and values are easy to learn. The key to doing these tasks, then, is doing them as efficiently as possible. That means using the commands and keystrokes presented in this chapter. So if you haven't done so already, take a few minutes to try these commands and keystrokes so you'll remember them. Then, you'll save time the next time you need to edit an entry, enter a sequence of numbers, align labels, or convert formulas to values.

Terms

label prefix
edit a cell
Insert mode
Typeover mode
fill range
start value
step value
stop value

Objectives

1. Enter any label into any cell of a spreadsheet. The label may start with a letter, digit, or special character, and it may require left, right, or center alignment.
2. Enter a positive or negative value with or without decimal places into any cell of a spreadsheet.
3. Use the *Lotus* editing feature to edit any label or value.
4. Use the /Range Label command to change the label prefix of the labels in a range of cells.

Step 1:

After you select the /Range Value command, highlight the range of cells that contains the formulas you want to convert. Then, press the Enter key.

```
D4: +B4+C4                                                            POINT
Enter range to copy FROM: D4..D14
```

	A	B	C	D	E
1		Product	Product	Total	Commision
2	Salesperson	Group 1	Group 2	Sales	7%
3	==========	==========	==========	==========	==========
4	Bob Gomez	123,148	78,520	201,668	14,117
5	Judy Steadman	38,921	68,903	107,824	7,548
6	Brenda Rogers	210,010	105,482	315,492	22,084

Step 2:

Highlight the range of cells to receive the values. Often, this is the same as the first range so the first cell in the range is already highlighted. When the correct range has been highlighted, press the Enter key.

```
D4: +B4+C4                                                            POINT
Enter range to copy TO: D4
```

	A	B	C	D	E
1		Product	Product	Total	Commision
2	Salesperson	Group 1	Group 2	Sales	7%
3	==========	==========	==========	==========	==========
4	Bob Gomez	123,148	78,520	201,668	14,117
5	Judy Steadman	38,921	68,903	107,824	7,548
6	Brenda Rogers	210,010	105,482	315,492	22,084

The spreadsheet after the formulas have been converted to values

```
D4: 201668                                                            READY
```

	A	B	C	D	E
1		Product	Product	Total	Commision
2	Salesperson	Group 1	Group 2	Sales	7%
3	==========	==========	==========	==========	==========
4	Bob Gomez	123,148	78,520	201,668	14,117
5	Judy Steadman	38,921	68,903	107,824	7,548
6	Brenda Rogers	210,010	105,482	315,492	22,084
7	Lori Anders	42,127	82,150	124,277	8,699
8	Wendy Jones	73,102	51,160	124,262	8,698
9	Jack James	38,197	76,511	114,708	8,030
10	Lisa Van Dyke	201,980	109,100	311,080	21,776
11	John Underwood	187,125	91,773	278,898	19,523
12	Frank Hart	123,015	87,321	210,336	14,724
13	Bill Lang	220,629	72,160	292,789	20,495
14	Lee Wong	116,439	21,576	138,015	9,661
15	==========	==========	==========	==========	==========
16		1,374,693	844,656	2,219,349	155,354
17					

Figure 1-9 How to use the /Range Value command to convert formulas to values

B4: 201668 READY

	A	B	C	D	E
1		Total	Commision		
2	Salesperson	Sales	7%		
3	============	============	============		
4	Bob Gomez	201,668	14,117		
5	Judy Steadman	107,824	7,548		
6	Brenda Rogers	315,492	22,084		
7	Lori Anders	124,277	8,699		
8	Wendy Jones	124,262	8,698		
9	Jack James	114,708	8,030		
10	Lisa Van Dyke	311,080	21,776		
11	John Underwood	278,898	19,523		
12	Frank Hart	210,336	14,724		
13	Bill Lang	292,789	20,495		
14	Lee Wong	138,015	9,661		
15	============	============	============		
16		2,219,349	155,354		
17					

Figure 1-10 The spreadsheet in figure 1-8 after the formulas in column D have been converted to values and columns B and C have been deleted

5. Use the /Data Fill command to enter a sequence of numbers into a range of cells.
6. Use the /Range Value command to convert the formulas in a range of cells to their current values.

Chapter 2

How to enter and edit the formulas and @functions of a spreadsheet

Formulas define the calculations in a spreadsheet. In this chapter, I'll summarize all the rules that apply to the use of formulas. I'll present five @functions. And I'll present some advanced uses of formulas and @functions.

If you have a reasonably strong mathematical background, none of the material in this chapter should be difficult for you. If you don't, some of the mathematical notation may be confusing. For most business spreadsheets, though, the formulas are relatively simple so the mathematical notation usually isn't a problem.

How to enter formulas and @functions into a spreadsheet

Lotus provides two methods for entering formulas and @functions into a spreadsheet. They are the anchor-and-point method and the direct entry method.

The anchor-and-point method In figure 2-1, you can see how to use the *anchor-and-point method* to enter a typical formula. In step 1, you move the cell pointer to the cell that you want to put the formula in. In step 2, you enter a mathematical operator like a plus sign to tell *Lotus* that you're starting a value or a formula. Then, you move the cell pointer to the first cell that you want in the formula.

In step 3, you continue by typing another operator. Then, you point to the next cell to be used in the formula. In step 4, you continue with the next operators, cells, and values until the formula is complete. In step 5, you press the Enter key to tell *Lotus* that the formula is complete.

When you enter an @function like the @SUM function into a cell, you have to start with the name of the function. Next, if the function contains parentheses, you have to type the left parenthesis. At this point, you can use

1. Move the cell pointer to the cell that you want to use for the formula.
2. Type the operator that you want to start the formula with so *Lotus* will identify your entry as a value or a formula. Often, this is a plus sign. Then, move the cell pointer to the first cell used by the formula.
3. Type the next operator that's required. Then, move the cell pointer to the next cell that's required.
4. Continue in this way until the formula is complete.
5. Press the Enter key.

Figure 2-1 How to use the anchor-and-point method to enter a formula

the anchor-and-point method to highlight the cell or range required by the function. To finish the function, you type the right parenthesis and press the Enter key.

The direct entry method When you use the *direct entry method*, you just type in the formula or @function. This method is summarized in figure 2-2. In step 1, you move the cell pointer to the one you want to enter the formula into. In step 2, you type the formula. If, for example, you're in cell D5 and you want to enter a formula that adds the values in cells B5 and C5, you type the following:

```
+B5+C5
```

As you type the formula, *Lotus* displays it on the second line of the control panel. Then, in step 3, you press the Enter key to tell *Lotus* that the formula is complete.

When you enter a range using the direct entry method, you type the address of the first cell in the range. Next, you enter one period (or dot). Then, you type the address of the last cell in the range. A typical range entry, for example, will look like this:

```
B5.B14
```

Then, when the formula is entered into the cell, *Lotus* displays the range with two dots like this:

```
B5..B14
```

If you want to, you can type two dots as you enter the range, but only one is necessary.

You'll probably use the anchor-and-point method more than the direct entry method for two reasons. First, the anchor-and-point method is easier to use because you don't have to know the addresses of the cells that you want to refer to in the formula; you just point to the cells you want. Second, you're

1. Move the cell pointer to the cell that you want to use for the formula.
2. Type the formula that you want to enter for the cell. Be sure that you start with an operator so *Lotus* will identify your entry as a value or a formula.
3. Press the Enter key.

Figure 2-2 How to use the direct entry method to enter a formula

less likely to make a mistake when you use the anchor-and-point method because you don't have to type cell addresses. Sometimes, though, it's more efficient to use the direct entry method. And for some of the more complicated formulas, you have to use the direct entry method.

How *Lotus* evaluates a formula that doesn't contain parentheses

When *Lotus* calculates the value of a formula, it does the operations within the formula in a prescribed sequence. This sequence depends on the operators used within the formula. As you can see in figure 2-3, each operator has an *order of precedence*. For instance, multiplication and division operations are done before addition and subtraction operations. And exponentiation ("raising to the power of") is done before multiplication and division.

If two or more operators within a formula have the same order of precedence, the operations are done from left to right, one order of precedence at a time. In this formula, for example,

```
+9*9+3/3
```

the first operation is nine times nine (+9*9=81); the second operation is three divided by three (3/3=1); and the last operation adds the two results together (81+1=82).

The second order of precedence in figure 2-3 simply means that signed numbers are evaluated before the next two orders of precedence. In this formula, for example,

```
-9+3/3
```

the first operation is to treat the nine as a minus nine; the second operation is three divided by three (3/3=1); and the last operation adds the two results together (-9+1= -8) so the resulting value is minus eight. If the addition had been done before the nine was treated as a negative number, the resulting value would be minus ten.

For many formulas, you don't have to worry about the order of precedence because it's obvious how they're going to be interpreted. As your

Operator	Operation	Order of precedence
^	Exponentiation	1
+	Positive number	2
-	Negative number	
*	Multiplication	3
/	Division	
+	Addition	4
-	Subtraction	

Examples of *Lotus* formulas	Calculated values
`+10+3*5`	`25`
`+9+9/3`	`12`
`-9+3/3`	`-8`
`+9*9+3/3`	`82`
`+5^2`	`25`
`+3*5^2`	`75`
`+2+3*5^2`	`77`

Figure 2-3 The order of precedence that *Lotus* uses when it interprets a formula that doesn't contain parentheses

formulas get more complicated, though, you have to be sure that they get interpreted the way you want them to be. The best way to do that is to use parentheses in your formulas.

When and how to use parentheses within a formula

When the operations within a formula aren't going to be interpreted the way you want them to be, you can use parentheses to override the order of precedence. You can also use parentheses when a formula gets so complicated that it's hard for you to figure out what the sequence of operations is going to be. By using parentheses, you can be sure a formula is going to work the way you want it to.

When a formula contains parentheses, *Lotus* calculates the expressions in the parentheses before it uses its order of precedence and its left-to-right rules. This is illustrated by the examples in figure 2-4. If one set of parentheses is contained within another set, *Lotus* calculates the value of the expression in the innermost set of parentheses first. Within a set of parentheses, the order of

Formula	Calculated value
(10+3)*5	65
(9+9)/3	6
(-9+9)/3	0
(2+3)*5^2	125
((2+3)*5)^2	625

Figure 2-4 How parentheses affect the way that *Lotus* interprets a formula

precedence still applies. And after all the expressions contained in parentheses are calculated, the order of precedence still applies.

When you use parentheses in a formula, you must make sure that you enter an equal number of left and right parentheses. If you don't enter parentheses in balanced sets, *Lotus* won't accept the formula when you press the Enter key. Instead, it activates the Edit mode so you can correct the formula.

The five @functions that you're most likely to use

Figure 2-5 presents the five @functions you're most likely to use. If you find that you need other functions, *Lotus* probably provides the one you want. Chapter 6 of this book covers some additional @functions and so does your *Lotus* manual.

When you use an @function, you must make sure that you use the exact entry form that it requires. This form can be referred to as the *syntax* of the function. As you can see in figure 2-5, the syntax for each function starts with a *function name* like @NOW or @SUM. For most functions, this is followed by a set of parentheses that contains one or more *arguments*. Although the @NOW function doesn't require an argument, the next three functions in figure 2-5 require an argument consisting of the range of cells to be operated upon. The last function in figure 2-5, the @ROUND function, requires two arguments that I'll explain in a moment.

The @NOW function This function returns the date number for the current date. It gets this information from your computer's internal clock. As a result, the date generated by an @NOW formula is constantly updated. Before the date number makes sense, however, you have to use the /Range Format Date command to give it an appropriate format.

Function name	Syntax (arguments)	Function
`@NOW`	`@NOW`	Provide the current date
`@SUM`	`@SUM(range)`	Add the values in the range specified in the argument
`@AVG`	`@AVG(range)`	Derive the average of the values in the range specified in the argument
`@COUNT`	`@COUNT(range)`	Count the number of cells that aren't empty in the range specified in the argument
`@ROUND`	`@ROUND(value,decimal-places)`	Round the value specified in the argument to the number of decimal places specified in the argument

Figure 2-5 Five useful @functions

The @SUM, @AVG, and @COUNT functions The @SUM function adds the values in the range of cells given as its argument. To start the entry of this function, you type the function name and the left parenthesis. Then, you can enter the range using the anchor-and-point method or the direct entry method. To finish the function, you type the right parenthesis and press the Enter key.

You enter the @AVG and @COUNT functions in the same way that you enter the @SUM function. Only the function names are different. The @COUNT function counts the number of entries in the range of cells that's given as its argument. The @AVG function both adds and counts the entries in the range that's given; then, it divides the total by the count to get the average.

Figure 2-6 illustrates the use of the @SUM, @AVG, and @COUNT functions. Here, the @SUM functions add the numbers in each column. And the @COUNT functions count the number of entries in each column. In figure 2-6, you can see that the count for each column is ten even though there are 13 rows in the range. In other words, *Lotus* doesn't count the three cells that are empty in each range. Similarly, to derive the @AVG function, *Lotus* divides by 10, not by 13.

If you want the @AVG and @COUNT functions to work right, you must make sure that the cells that appear to be empty actually are empty. That's why you shouldn't get in the habit of entering one space into a cell to make it appear to be empty when it isn't. If a cell contains an apostrophe (label prefix) followed by one or more spaces, *Lotus* doesn't treat it as empty. As a result, the @AVG and @COUNT functions won't return the results that you want.

If you're using release 2.4 or 3.4, you should know that you can use one of the *SmartIcons* to create an @SUM function with a single click of a mouse.

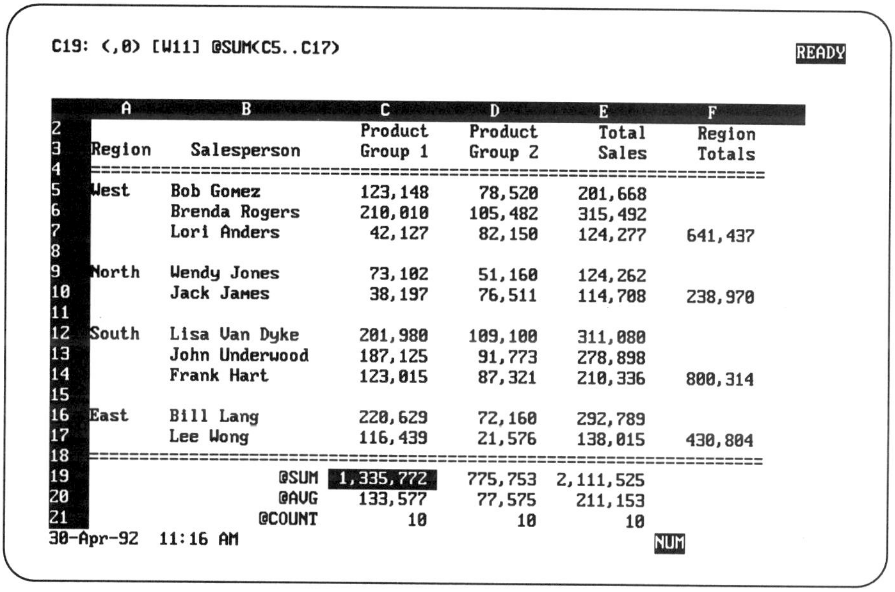

C19: (,0) [W11] @SUM(C5..C17) READY

	A	B	C	D	E	F
2			Product	Product	Total	Region
3	Region	Salesperson	Group 1	Group 2	Sales	Totals
4	========	============	==========	==========	==========	==========
5	West	Bob Gomez	123,148	78,520	201,668	
6		Brenda Rogers	210,010	105,482	315,492	
7		Lori Anders	42,127	82,150	124,277	641,437
8						
9	North	Wendy Jones	73,102	51,160	124,262	
10		Jack James	38,197	76,511	114,708	238,970
11						
12	South	Lisa Van Dyke	201,980	109,100	311,080	
13		John Underwood	187,125	91,773	278,898	
14		Frank Hart	123,015	87,321	210,336	800,314
15						
16	East	Bill Lang	220,629	72,160	292,789	
17		Lee Wong	116,439	21,576	138,015	430,804
18	========	============	==========	==========	==========	==========
19		@SUM	1,335,772	775,753	2,111,525	
20		@AVG	133,577	77,575	211,153	
21		@COUNT	10	10	10	

30-Apr-92 11:16 AM NUM

Figure 2-6 Values derived by the @SUM, @AVG, and @COUNT functions

Often, this is more efficient than entering the function through the keyboard. To learn more about the use the mouse and *SmartIcons*, please read chapter 21.

The @ROUND function Unlike the other mathematical @functions, the @ROUND function requires two arguments as you can see in figure 2-5. The first argument is the value to be rounded. This can be the value itself, the cell address of the value, or the formula that creates the value. The second argument is the number of decimal places that you want to round the value to.

Figure 2-7 illustrates the operation of the @ROUND function. It also shows how a formula or function can be used as the first argument of this function. As you can see, the second argument can be negative if you want the value rounded to the left of the decimal point. When you use the @ROUND function, the resulting value in the cell is actually rounded.

When should you use the @ROUND function? When you want to drop some of the decimal places that *Lotus* is carrying for one or more cells. For instance, if you multiply a value with two decimal places by another value with two decimal places, the result has four decimal places; and *Lotus* carries them in the cell. Similarly, if you divide one value by another, *Lotus* carries the result to as many as 15 decimal places. It's easy to forget this, though, because *Lotus* displays only the number of decimal places that the cell formats call for. And *Lotus* rounds the value that is displayed.

In most spreadsheets, carrying the extra decimal places creates no inaccuracies so you don't need to use the @ROUND function to drop the extra

@ROUND function	Resulting value
@ROUND(2437.289,2)	2437.29
@ROUND(2437.289,0)	2437
@ROUND(2437.289,4)	2437.289
@ROUND(2437.289,-1)	2440

Examples of @ROUND functions within formulas

```
@ROUND(C5/D5,1)
@ROUND(@SUM(B4..B14),2)
```

Figure 2-7 How the @ROUND function works

places. Occasionally, though, the extra decimal places lead to minor inaccuracies because *Lotus* uses all the places when it does calculations, not just those that are displayed. Then, to correct those inaccuracies, you can use the @ROUND function within those formulas that create the extra decimal places.

How to edit a formula or @function

In chapter 1, I showed you how to edit a label or value entry. Now, I want you to know that you can use the same methods to edit a formula or an @function. This is particularly useful when you need to modify a lengthy formula, and you don't want to take the time to enter it again using the anchor-and-point method.

The keys that you need for using the edit feature are summarized in figure 1-4 of the last chapter. To activate the edit feature, you press the F2 (Edit) key. Next, you can use several of the control keys to get to the portion of the formula that you want to modify. Then, you can insert characters, modify them, or delete them. After you've made the changes, you press the Enter key to replace the old formula or @function with the new one.

When and how to use relative, absolute, or mixed addresses in formulas

Lotus provides for three different types of cell addresses that you can use in formulas. These are summarized in figure 2-8. The type of address doesn't affect the results of a formula when it is in its original cell. However, the address type does determine how a formula is copied from one cell to another.

The first type of cell address is the *relative address*. When a relative address is copied, the row and column in the address are adjusted relative to the cell

Types of addresses	Examples	Meaning when copied	How each type appears in a formula
Relative	A3 C17	Adjust both the column and the row	+A3+B3 +C17*.07
Absolute	$A$3 $C$17	Adjust neither the column nor the row	+$A$3+B3 +$C$17*.07
Mixed	$A3	Adjust the row but not the column	+$A3*B3
	C$17	Adjust the column but not the row	+C$17*.07

Figure 2-8 The three types of addresses you can use in a formula

that it is copied to. If, for example, a formula is copied two cells to the right and three cells down, a relative address in the formula is changed so it points to a cell two cells to the right and three cells below the original address. This is the kind of address you use most of the time because it usually works the way you want it to.

The second type of cell address is the *absolute address*. When it is copied, the address isn't adjusted at all. It has a dollar sign ($) to the left of the column identifier and another dollar sign to the left of the row identifier as in this example:

```
$B$5
```

You probably won't need to use this type of address often, but it is useful in some situations.

The third type of cell address is the *mixed address*. It has a dollar sign to the left of either the column or row identifier indicating that the identifier associated with the dollar sign shouldn't be adjusted when the formula is copied. It has no dollar sign to the left of the other part of the address indicating that it should be adjusted. Thus,

```
$C7
```

is a mixed address with an absolute column identifier and a relative row identifier. Similarly,

```
D$10
```

has an absolute row identifier and a relative column identifier so it is a mixed address. Like absolute addresses, you probably won't use mixed addresses often, but they can save you time in some situations.

Two ways to create an absolute or mixed address

1. Use the direct entry method to enter the formula. As you type the addresses in the formula, put in whatever dollar signs are needed.
2. First, use the anchor-and-point method to enter a formula with relative addresses. Then, put in whatever dollar signs are needed by editing the formula.

The use of the F4 (Absolute) key with either method

Each time you press the F4 key, the address in the formula that the cursor is on gets changed to another format. If, for example, the cursor is on address B4, it gets changed as follows with four repetitions of the F4 key:

```
B4
$B$4
B$4
$B4
B4
```

Figure 2-9 How to create an absolute or mixed address

How to create a relative, absolute, or mixed address To create a relative address within a formula, you can use the anchor-and-point or the direct entry method. To create an absolute or a mixed address, though, you can't just use the anchor-and-point method because that doesn't put a dollar sign in an address. Instead, you can use one of two general methods to create the address. These methods are summarized in figure 2-9.

First, you can use the direct entry method to create an absolute or mixed address. That's the most straightforward way to enter an address the way you want it. Second, you can use the anchor-and-point method to enter the relative address. Then, when the formula is complete, you can edit the relative address, thus inserting the required dollar sign or signs.

To help you get an address the way you want it, you can use the F4 (Absolute) key to convert the address from one form to another. You can use this key when you're using the direct entry method or the anchor-and-point method to enter a formula. You can also use it when you're editing a formula. The first time you press the F4 key, *Lotus* switches the current address in a formula to an absolute address. The next time you press the F4 key, it switches the address to a mixed address (relative on the column, and absolute on the row). When you press the F4 key again, it switches the address to another mixed address (absolute on the column, and relative on the row). And if you press the F4 key again, *Lotus* converts the address back to a relative address.

Part 1:

The original formula in cell D5 that uses the relative addresses B5 and C5.

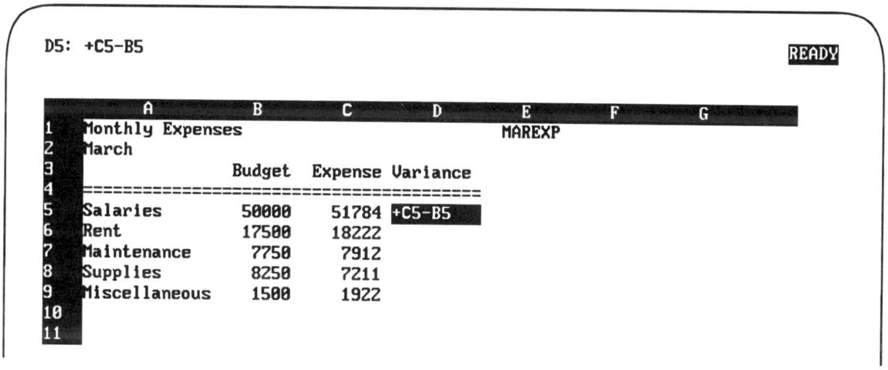

Part 2:

When the formula is copied to cells D6 through D9, *Lotus* adjusts the relative addresses in the formulas as shown here.

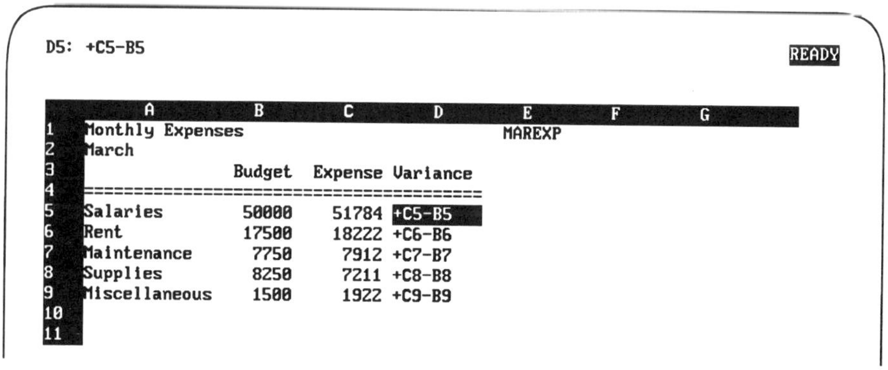

Figure 2-10 How *Lotus* adjusts a relative address when you copy a formula

When and how to use a relative address in a formula Generally, you use relative addresses in formulas. Then, when the formulas are copied, the addresses are adjusted so they work correctly in their new locations. Although that's usually what happens, you need to understand how this works so you'll know when to use absolute or mixed addresses.

Figure 2-10 shows what happens when you copy a formula with relative addresses down a column. Here, to help you understand what happens, the formulas are displayed in column D instead of the values that are derived from them. In cell D5, the formula is this:

```
+C5-B5
```

Since the addresses in the formula are relative, *Lotus* interprets the formula as this: "Get the number that's one column to the left in the same row as this cell; then, from it, subtract the number that's two columns to the left in this row."

Part 1:

A formula in cell D6 that uses a relative and an absolute address.

```
D6: (,2) +C6*(1+$D$1)                                                    READY

       A          B              C              D             E
1  Monthly expense           %Increase           15%
2  Budget planning
3                            Current yr.     Next yr.
4                             Mon/budget    Mon/budget
5                            --------------------------
6              Auto mileage      150.00        172.50
7              Airfare           500.00
```

Part 2:

When the formula is copied to cells D7 through D12, the absolute address isn't adjusted so the formula still works correctly.

```
D7: (,2) +C7*(1+$D$1)                                                    READY

       A          B              C              D             E
1  Monthly expense           %Increase           15%
2  Budget planning
3                            Current yr.     Next yr.
4                             Mon/budget    Mon/budget
5                            --------------------------
6              Auto mileage      150.00        172.50
7              Airfare           500.00        575.00
8              Auto rental       250.00        287.50
9              Lodging           400.00        460.00
10             Meals             400.00        460.00
11             Supplies          150.00        172.50
12             Misc.              50.00         57.50
13                           --------------------------
14                            $1,900.00     $2,185.00
15
```

Figure 2-11 How to use an absolute address in a formula so the cell address isn't adjusted when the formula is copied

Then, when the formula is copied, *Lotus* modifies the cell addresses to establish the same relationship in the new location. As a result, the row identifiers are increased as the formula is copied down the column, but the column identifiers stay the same.

When and how to use an absolute address in a formula Figure 2-11 presents a spreadsheet that uses a formula with an absolute address. This formula is entered in cell D6:

```
+C6*(1+$D$1)
```

It multiplies the value in the column to its left by a value of one plus the value in cell D1. However, cell D1 is entered as an absolute address. Then, when this formula is copied down the D column, the relative address (C6) is changed to C7, C8, and so on, but the absolute address stays at D1. As a result, all of the values in column C are multiplied by a value of one plus the value in cell D1. As a result, all of the values in column D are increased by 15 percent.

I hope it's obvious why you need to use an absolute address for cell D1 in the example in figure 2-11. If you used a relative address instead, the cell address would be adjusted to cell D2 when the formula was copied to cell D7; it would be adjusted to cell D3 when the formula was copied to cell D8; and so on. Since D2 and D3 don't contain acceptable values, this wouldn't work at all.

You can see, then, how you can use an absolute address when you want to use a value in one fixed cell in the formulas for other cells. Then, when you change the value in the one fixed cell, all of the other cells are adjusted accordingly. This is useful when you create many types of spreadsheets for what-if analysis.

When and how to use a mixed address in a formula Occasionally, you need *Lotus* to adjust one portion of an address when you copy it, but not the other. Sometimes, you need it to adjust the column portion of the address, but not the row portion. And sometimes, you need it to adjust the row portion of the address, but not the column portion. In short, you need a mixed address.

Figure 2-12 presents a spreadsheet with a formula that requires two mixed addresses. It is the formula for cell D6:

```
+$C6*(1+D$4)
```

This formula multiplies the value in the column to its left by a value of one plus the value in cell D4. However, both cells C6 and D4 are entered as mixed addresses. Then, when this formula is copied down the D column, the first mixed address ($C6) is changed to $C7, $C8, and so on, but the other mixed address stays at D4. That's what you want. And when the formula in cell D6 is copied to cells E6 through E12, the first mixed address is changed to $C6, $C7, $C8, and so on, and the second mixed address is changed to E$5, which is also what you want. Finally, when the formula in cell D6 is copied to cells F6 through F12, the mixed addresses are again changed the way you want them to be changed.

This example illustrates how useful mixed addresses can be when you're doing what-if analysis. However, you can also see that using them can be tricky. As a result, you may decide you don't want to use mixed addresses. If so, you can get the same results by entering more formulas with relative addresses. When used correctly, though, mixed addresses can help make you more productive.

Part 1:

The formula in cell D6 uses two mixed addresses.

```
D6: (,2) +$C6*(1+D$4)                                                  READY

   A       B               C            D            E            F
1  Monthly expense
2  Budget planning
3                     Current Yr   % Increase   % Increase   % Increase
4                     Mon/Budget        10.0%        15.0%        20.0%
5                    --------------------------------------------------
6   Auto mileage          150.00       165.00
7   Airfare               500.00
8   Auto rental           250.00
```

Part 2:

When the formula is copied to cells D7 through D12 and to cells E6 through F12, the mixed addresses are adjusted so the formula still works correctly.

```
F12: (,2) +$C12*(1+F$4)                                                READY

   A       B               C            D            E            F
1  Monthly expense
2  Budget planning
3                     Current Yr   % Increase   % Increase   % Increase
4                     Mon/Budget        10.0%        15.0%        20.0%
5                    --------------------------------------------------
6   Auto mileage          150.00       165.00       172.50       180.00
7   Airfare               500.00       550.00       575.00       600.00
8   Auto rental           250.00       275.00       287.50       300.00
9   Lodging               400.00       440.00       460.00       480.00
10  Meals                 400.00       440.00       460.00       480.00
11  Supplies              150.00       165.00       172.50       180.00
12  Misc.                  50.00        55.00        57.50        60.00
13                   --------------------------------------------------
14                     $1,900.00    $2,090.00    $2,185.00    $2,280.00
15
```

Figure 2-12 How to use mixed addresses in a formula so it works correctly when it is copied

How to detect and correct circular references

A *circular reference* occurs when a formula contains an address that refers to the cell that the formula is in. This is illustrated by the spreadsheet in figure 2-13. Here, the @SUM function in cell D14 includes cell D14 in its own range. As a result, the formula tries to include the result of its calculation in the calculation.

When a circular reference occurs, the displayed value is usually inaccurate, and it changes each time *Lotus* recalculates the spreadsheet. That's why *Lotus* always alerts you to this condition by displaying a CIRC indicator at the bottom of the display.

To correct the problem in figure 2-13, you move the cell pointer to cell D14 and press the F2 key to edit the formula. Next, you change the range address to D4..D12 to exclude cell D14 from the range. Then, when you press

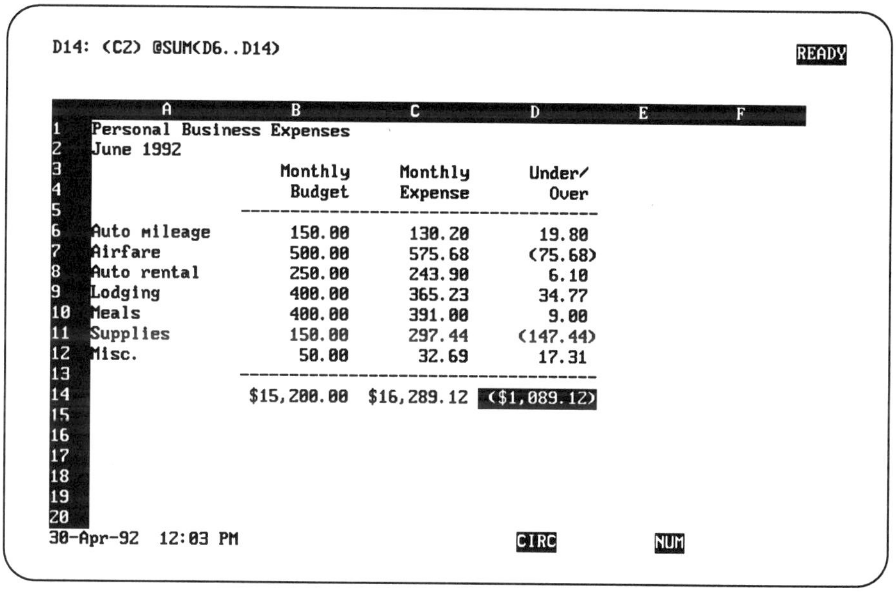

Figure 2-13 A spreadsheet that contains a circular reference in an @SUM function

the Enter key to return the formula to the cell. The CIRC indicator will disappear unless there's another circular reference in the spreadsheet.

How to use the /Worksheet Status command to find a circular reference In order to correct a circular reference, you must be able to find it. In a large spreadsheet, that can be a challenging task. That's why *Lotus* provides the /Worksheet Status command to help you find circular references.

Figure 2-14 shows the screen *Lotus* displays when you select the /Worksheet Status command. In the middle of this screen, you can see the information about circular references. Here, *Lotus* shows that a circular reference exists in the current spreadsheet at cell D14.

Unfortunately, this command displays only one circular reference address at a time. So if several circular references exist, you must issue the /Worksheet Status command to find the first circular reference. Then, after you correct the first reference, you must repeat the process until you've found and corrected all of the circular references.

How to use the *Auditor* add-in program to find circular references
As you've just seen, the /Worksheet Status command can find only one error at a time. That's why the later releases of *Lotus* (starting with 2.3 and 3.1+) come with a *spreadsheet auditor program* called the *Auditor*. This program makes it much easier to track down circular references and other types of

```
D14: (C2) @SUM(D6..D14)                                             STAT
Press any key to continue...

                     Global Settings
  Conventional memory:   102214 of 103040 Bytes (99%)
  Expanded memory:       (None)

  Math coprocessor:      (None)

  Recalculation:
    Method               Automatic
    Order                Natural
    Iterations           1

  Circular reference:    D14

  Cell display:
    Format               (G)
    Label prefix         ' (left align)
    Column width         9
    Zero suppression     No

  Global protection:     Disabled

30-Apr-92  01:06 PM                          CIRC        NUM
```

Figure 2-14 How to use the /Worksheet Status command to find a circular reference

errors. However, it requires the use of the *add-in facility* of *Lotus*. If you don't already know how to use the add-in facility, you can learn how to use it in chapter 14 of this book.

Figure 2-15 shows how you can use the *Auditor* to find the circular references in the spreadsheet in figure 2-13. Part 1 shows the menu the *Auditor* displays when you invoke it. Part 2 shows the listing the *Auditor* displays when you select the Circs command from the menu. Here, you can see that there are actually three cells that contain circular references in the spreadsheet. And the *Auditor* shows the addresses of all three.

If you have a release of *Lotus* that doesn't come with *Auditor*, you should know that several companies sell spreadsheet auditor programs. The most popular one is called *The Cambridge Spreadsheet Analyst*. So if you create large, complex spreadsheets or if you're responsible for reviewing other people's spreadsheets for accuracy, you have two auditing options. First, you can upgrade to a later release of *Lotus* to get the *Auditor*. Second, you can buy a spreadsheet auditor program like *The Cambridge Spreadsheet Analyst*.

Discussion

As I said at the start of this chapter, some of the material in this chapter is likely to be difficult for you if your mathematical background is limited. So keep in mind that most business spreadsheets don't require complex formulas or mixed addresses. And if you enter your formulas carefully, you probably won't ever encounter a circular reference.

Part 1:

The menu of the *Auditor* program

```
D14: (C2) @SUM(D6..D14)                                                  MENU
Precedents  Dependents  Formulas  Recalc-List  Circs  Options  Quit
Identify all cells involved in circular references
         A          ─────── Auditor Settings ──────── E          F
1   Personal Business  Range              ┌Report Method┐
2   June 1992          [A1..IV8192·····]  │( ) Highlight│
3                                         │(*) List     │
4                                         │( ) Trace    │
5                --                       └─────────────┘
6   Auto mileage
7   Airfare            Press F2 (EDIT) to edit settings
8   Auto rental
9   Lodging              400.00      365.½½      34.77
10  Meals                400.00      391.00       9.00
11  Supplies             150.00      297.44    (147.44)
12  Misc.                 50.00       32.69      17.31
13              ------------------------------------
14                   $19,000.00  $18,325.26  ($1,225.26)
15
16
17
18
19
20
22-Jan-92  02:09 PM                           CIRC        NUM
```

Part 2:

A listing of all the circular references that the *Auditor* found in the spreadsheet

```
List  ◄  ►  ▲  ▼  ?                                               CIRCS

B14              C14              D14
```

Figure 2-15 How to use the *Auditor* program of *Lotus* to find a circular reference

For maximum productivity, however, you do need to know how to use both the anchor-and-point and the direct entry methods for entering formulas and @functions. You do need to know how to use parentheses within a formula to make sure that *Lotus* interprets your formulas the way you want them interpreted. You should know how to edit a formula so you don't have to re-enter it from scratch. And once in a while you're likely to have a need for absolute addresses.

Terms

anchor-and-point method	relative address
direct entry method	absolute address
order of precedence	mixed address
@function	circular reference
syntax	spreadsheet auditor program
function name	add-in facility
argument	

Objectives

1. Enter a formula into any cell of a spreadsheet using either the anchor-and-point method or the direct entry method. The formula may or may not include one or more @functions.
2. Given a formula that may or may not include one or more sets of parentheses, describe the sequence of operations that *Lotus* will perform when it evaluates the formula.
3. Use any of the five @functions presented in this chapter in a *Lotus* spreadsheet:

@NOW	@AVG	@ROUND
@SUM	@COUNT	

4. Use the *Lotus* editing feature to edit any formula.
5. Use relative, absolute, or mixed addresses in the formulas of a spreadsheet so the formulas can be copied properly to other cells in the spreadsheet.
6. Identify and correct a circular reference in a spreadsheet using the /Worksheet Status command.
7. Explain how a spreadsheet auditor program can be used to find circular references.

Chapter 3

The commands that every *Lotus* user should know how to use

Because *Lotus* provides so many commands, it's easy to forget the names of the commands you already know how to use. And it's hard to figure out which of the dozens of *Lotus* commands you actually need to know. The menu system doesn't make this any easier because it isn't always logical.

With that in mind, this chapter presents a complete summary of the commands that we believe every *Lotus* user ought to know. Because this chapter assumes that you already know how to access and use *Lotus* commands, the emphasis is on the functions of the commands, not on their operational details. At this stage of your development, that's all you should need.

When you complete this chapter, you'll know how to use all of the commands that you need for working with most business spreadsheets. If you use these commands as you work with *Lotus*, you'll soon have most of the commands in this chapter memorized. But whenever you need to refresh your memory, you'll be able to use the summaries in this chapter for quick and efficient reference.

Another look at the *Lotus* menu system

Figure 3-1 presents the Main *Lotus* menu for release 2.2 along with its subordinate menus. Although the options and names of options in a menu vary from one release to another, the basic options are the same in all releases of *Lotus*. The shaded options are the ones that are summarized in this chapter.

If you study the selections in the Main menu in figure 3-1, you can see that seven of them lead to subordinate menus, but four of them start commands or actions. Similarly, some of the selections in the seven subordinate menus lead to lower level menus, and some start commands. This continues as you go deeper into the menu structure, and sometimes you have to go six levels deep before a command is started. In all, the *Lotus* menu system presents several dozen menus with a total of more than 200 selections. Is it any wonder, then, that many *Lotus* users have a hard time figuring out which commands they should be using?

A summary of the essential commands in menu sequence

Figure 3-2 presents a summary of the commands presented in this chapter. In general, the /Worksheet commands apply to the entire spreadsheet. The /Range, /Copy, and /Move commands apply to a range of one or more cells. The /File commands are used to set directories, save files, and retrieve files. The /Printer commands are used to set print options and print spreadsheets. The /Data Fill command is used to enter a sequence of values into a range of cells. And the /Quit command is used to exit from *Lotus*.

When you see the term *global* in a command name, it means that the command applies to the entire spreadsheet. For instance, the /Worksheet Global Column-Width command lets you set the column width for all of the columns in the spreadsheet. However, you can override the default by using the /Worksheet Column Set-Width command. Similarly, the /Worksheet Global Format command lets you set the format for all of the cells in the spreadsheet. But you can override it by using the /Range Format command.

As you study the summary in figure 3-2, you can see that two function keys can be used with a few of the commands. You can use the F6 (Window) key to display settings screens for the /Worksheet Global, /Worksheet Global Default, and /Print Printer commands. And you can use the F3 (Name) key to display a list of all the files in a directory when either the /File Retrieve or the /File Save command has been accessed. Both the F3 and the F6 keys are *toggle keys;* they turn the related screen on of it's off, and they turn it off if it's on. Unfortunately, the F6 key doesn't work for any of the commands in figure 3-2 with *Lotus* releases 3.0 and 3.1, and it only works for the /Print Printer command with *Lotus* release 3.4.

If you already feel comfortable using *Lotus* commands, this summary may be all that you need for now. If you try the commands shown as you experiment with spreadsheets of your own, you'll quickly see how they work. And if you need additional information, you can refer to the figures given in figure 3-2. However, if you don't feel comfortable learning the commands by experimenting with them on your own, please read on.

A summary of the essential commands in functional groupings

When you create and use *Lotus* spreadsheets, you perform functions like formatting cells, copying cells, inserting and deleting columns, and retrieving and saving files. Unfortunately, though, the *Lotus* menu system isn't arranged

The Main menu

`Worksheet  Range  Copy  Move  File  Print  Graph  Data  System  Add-in  Quit`

The Worksheet menu

`Global  Insert  Delete  Column  Erase  Titles  Window  Status  Page  Learn`

The Range menu

`Format  Label  Erase  Name  Justify  Prot  Unprot  Input  Value  Trans  Search`

The File menu

`Retrieve  Save  Combine  Xtract  Erase  List  Import  Directory  Admin`

The Print menu

`Printer  File`

The Data menu

`Fill  Table  Sort  Query  Distribution  Matrix  Regression  Parse`

The Graph menu

`Type  X  A  B  C  D  E  F  Reset  View  Save  Options  Name  Group  Quit`

The Add-In menu

`Attach  Detach  Invoke  Clear  Quit`

Main menu options that start commands

`Copy  Move  System  Quit`

Figure 3-1 The *Lotus* menu system

Command name	Next level	Function	Refer to
/Worksheet Global F6 (Window)	Format	Set the formats for all of the cells in the spreadsheet	Figure 3-6, 3-7
	Label-Prefix	Set the default label prefix for all the labels that are entered into the spreadsheet	Figure 3-5
	Column-Width	Set the widths for all of the columns in the spreadsheet	Figure 3-8
	Default F6 (Window)	Set the permanent default values for the print margins, the file directory, and so on	Figure 3-3, 3-4, 3-15, 3-16
/Worksheet Insert	Column	Insert one or more columns into a spreadsheet	Figure 3-9
	Row	Insert one or more rows into a spreadsheet	Figure 3-9
/Worksheet Delete	Column	Delete one or more columns from a spreadsheet	Figure 3-9
	Row	Delete one or more rows from a spreadsheet	Figure 3-9
/Worksheet Column	Set-Width	Increase or decrease the width of a column	Figure 3-8
	Reset-Width	Reset the column widths to the global default	Figure 3-8
	Hide	Hide one or more columns	Figure 3-10, 3-11
	Display	Display one or more hidden columns	Figure 3-10
	Column-Range	Set the width of a range of columns	Figure 3-8
/Worksheet	Erase	Erase a spreadsheet from internal memory	Figure 3-18
	Titles	Freeze the titles at the top or side of a spreadsheet	Figure 3-12, 3-13
	Status	Display the Global setting screen, which identifies the location of a circular reference and summarizes memory usage	Figure 2-14, 7-3

Figure 3-2 A summary of the most useful *Lotus* commands (part 1 of 2)

Command name	**Next level**	**Function**	**Refer to**
/Range	Format	Set the format for a range of cells	Figure 3-6, 3-7
	Label	Change the label prefixes of the labels in a range of cells	Figure 3-5
	Erase (Delete key)	Erase the data from a range of cells	Figure 3-14
	Value	Convert the formulas in a range of cells to values	Figures 1-8, 1-9, 1-10
/Copy		Copy the labels, values, or formulas from one range of cells to another	Figure 3-14
/Move		Move the labels, values, or formulas from one range of cells to another	Figure 3-14
/File	Retrieve F3 (Name)	Retrieve a spreadsheet file	Figure 3-16, 3-17
	Save F3 (Name)	Save a spreadsheet to a file on a hard disk or diskette	Figure 3-16
	Directory	Identify the directory that you want to use for your spreadsheet files	Figure 3-16
/Print Printer F6 (Window)	Range	Set the range of cells that are to be printed	Figure 3-15
	Page	Skip the paper in the printer to the top of the next page	Figure 3-15
	Options	Set print options like the margin sizes and page length	Figure 3-15
	Align	Tell *Lotus* that the paper is aligned properly in the printer	Figure 3-15
	Go	Print all of the cells in the print range	Figure 3-15
	Quit	Exit from the Print menu	Figure 3-15
/Data	Fill	Enter a sequence of values into a range of cells	Figure 1-6, 1-7
/Quit		Exit from *Lotus*	I-14

Figure 3-2 A summary of the most useful *Lotus* commands (part 2 of 2)

by function. That's why it's often difficult to remember the name of the command you need for a specific function. That's also why it's often difficult to find the command you need by searching through the *Lotus* menus. As you work with the summaries presented in this section, I think you'll get a better perspective on which commands you need for what purposes and on how the commands work together.

How to set defaults Figure 3-3 summarizes the primary commands that you need for setting defaults. Note that all of these commands start with /Worksheet Global. This means that they apply to the entire spreadsheet. I'm presenting these commands first because they can help you get a spreadsheet or a *Lotus* session set up right. If, for example, you set the default format the way you want it, you'll often save time later on because you won't have to set the formats for as many cells on a range-by-range basis.

The first three commands in figure 3-3 set defaults for the spreadsheet you're working on. But these defaults are not carried over from one spreadsheet to the next. Thus, the /Worksheet Global Format command sets the default format for just the spreadsheet you're working on. The /Worksheet Global Label-Prefix command sets the default label prefix for just the spreadsheet you're working on. And the /Worksheet Global Column-Width command sets the default column width for just the spreadsheet you're working on.

In contrast, the /Worksheet Global Default commands set defaults that are carried over from one spreadsheet to the next. Also, if you perform the /Worksheet Global Default Update command after you set the defaults, the defaults are carried over from one *Lotus* session to the next. In other words, they become *permanent defaults* that last until you change the settings and perform the /Worksheet Global Default Update command again. However, if you don't update the defaults that you set, they are cancelled when you exit from *Lotus* and the previous defaults are reset.

If you look at levels 4 and 5 of the /Worksheet Global Default command in figure 3-3, you can see that you can use this command to set print defaults like margins and page length. I'll tell you more about these defaults when I present the /Print Printer command. You can also use the /Worksheet Global Default command to set the default directory that will be used for your spreadsheet files. And you can use it to set other defaults like whether the status indicator line shows the date and time or whether the beeper beeps when *Lotus* detects an error condition. If you want any of these to become permanent defaults, remember to use the /Worksheet Global Default Update command after you've set them.

One of the Other defaults that you can set on some releases of *Lotus* is the Undo setting. When this setting is "enabled," the word UNDO appears in the status indicator line. Then, you can "undo" the last command that you performed by pressing the F4 key while you hold down the Alt key. We

Levels 1 & 2	**Level 3**	**Level 4**	**Level 5**	**Function**
/Worksheet Global F6 (Window)	Format			Set the format for all of the cells in the spreadsheet
	Label-Prefix			Set the default label prefix for all the labels that are entered into the spreadsheet
	Column-Width			Set the widths for all of the columns in the spreadsheet
	Default F6 (Window)	Printer	Left	Set the default value for the left print margin
			Right	Set the default value for the right print margin
			Top	Set the default value for the top print margin
			Bottom	Set the default value for the bottom print margin
			Pg-Length	Set the default page length for the printer
			Quit	Exit from the Printer menu
		Directory		Set the default directory for retrieving and saving files
		Status		Display the default settings screen
		Update		Update the default settings so they become the permanent defaults
		Other	Clock	Set the status indicator line so it shows either the current filename or the date and time
			Undo	Turn the *Lotus* Undo feature on or off (it's usually best to keep it off)
			Beep	Turn the beeper on or off for error conditions
		Quit		Exit from the Default menu

Figure 3-3 The commands for setting defaults

recommend that you "disable" this option, however, because it requires extra internal memory so it reduces the size of the spreadsheet that you can create. In addition, this feature slows *Lotus* down, and you should rarely need to use it.

If you look again at figure 3-3, you can see that the F6 (Window) key is shown for the /Worksheet Global commands and again for the /Worksheet Global Default commands. When you press this key after you access a /Worksheet Global command, a Global Settings screen like the one in figure 3-4 is either turned off or on. This is the same screen that you get when you perform the /Worksheet Status command. When you press the F6 key after you access a /Worksheet Global Default command, a Default Settings screen like the one in figure 3-4 is either turned off or on. This is the same screen that you get when you perform the /Worksheet Global Default Status command. So if your release of *Lotus* supports the F6 key, be sure to experiment with it.

If you're using release 2.3 or 2.4, you can edit a settings screen instead of using *Lotus* commands to update the screen. To do this, you press the F2 (Edit) key when a screen is displayed. Then, you can use the Tab key to move from one entry in the settings screen to another, and you can make changes to the settings right in the settings screen. If you have one of the *Lotus* releases that supports this, you shouldn't have any trouble editing the settings screens so I won't say any more about them in this book.

Although figure 3-3 summarizes the global settings and defaults you're most likely to want to change, there are some others. In particular, all releases of *Lotus* provide commands for changing the default printer from one printer to another. This is useful if you're working on a PC that has access to more than one printer. If you're interested in the other commands for setting defaults, please refer to chapter 15.

How to align labels Figure 3-5 summarizes the commands you need for aligning labels in their cells. When you start a new spreadsheet, the label prefix default is the apostrophe. This means that *Lotus* starts each label that you enter with an apostrophe when you don't enter a label prefix yourself. The apostrophe means the label will be left aligned in the cell.

To change the default, you can use the /Worksheet Global Label-Prefix command. This default applies only to the spreadsheet you're working on and only to labels that are entered after you set the default. Also, you can override the default for any label just by starting the entry with the label prefix of your choice. For most spreadsheets, you'll want the apostrophe as the default prefix, so you'll rarely use this command.

If you want to change the label prefixes and thus the alignment for a range of cells, you can use the /Range Label command. This actually changes the label prefixes for all of the labels in the range of cells that you specify. However, this doesn't affect labels that you enter after the command has been performed. When you enter a new label, *Lotus* assumes the default label prefix unless you override it with a prefix of your own.

The Global Settings screen

```
A1: [W16] 'Monthly Expenses                                          MENU
Format  Label-Prefix  Column-Width  Recalculation  Protection  Default  Zero
Fixed  Sci  Currency  ,  General  +/-  Percent  Date  Text  Hidden
 ------------------------------- Global Settings -------------------------
|  Conventional memory:   96256 of 97168 Bytes (99%)                      |
|  Expanded memory:       (None)                                          |
|                                                                         |
|  Math coprocessor:      (None)                                          |
|                                                                         |
|  Recalculation:                                                         |
|    Method               Automatic                                       |
|    Order                Natural                                         |
|    Iterations           1                                               |
|                                                                         |
|  Circular reference:    (None)                                          |
|                                                                         |
|  Cell display:                                                          |
|    Format               (,0)                                            |
|    Label prefix         ' (left align)                                  |
|    Column width         9                                               |
|    Zero suppression     No                                              |
|                                                                         |
|  Global protection:     Disabled                                        |
 -------------------------------------------------------------------------
04-May-92  04:09 PM                                               NUM
```

The Default Settings screen

```
A1: [W16] 'Monthly Expenses                                               MENU
Printer  Directory  Status  Update  Other  Autoexec  Quit
Save new default settings in configuration file
 ------------------------------- Default Settings --------------------------
| Printer:                                   Directory: C:\123\DATA          |
|   Interface      Parallel 1                                                |
|   Auto linefeed  No                        Autoexecute macros: Yes         |
|   Margins                                                                  |
|     Left 4   Right 76  Top 2  Bottom 2     International:                  |
|   Page length    66                          Punctuation       A           |
|   Wait           No                            Decimal         Period      |
|   Setup string                                 Argument        Comma       |
|   Name           Epson FX, RX & JX/L...         Thousands       Comma       |
|                                              Currency          Prefix: $   |
| Add-In:                                      Date format (D4)  A (MM/DD/YY)|
|   1                                          Time format (D8)  A (HH:MM:SS)|
|   2                                          Negative          Parentheses |
|   3                                                                        |
|   4                                        Help access method: Removable   |
|   5                                        Clock display:      Standard    |
|   6                                        Undo:               Disabled    |
|   7                                        Beep:               Yes         |
|   8                                                                        |
 ----------------------------------------------------------------------------
04-May-92  04:12 PM                                                NUM
```

Figure 3-4 The Global Settings screen and the Default Settings screen that can be displayed using the F6 (Window) key

Command name	Next level	Function
/Worksheet Global Label-Prefix	Left	Set the default label prefix to the apostrophe (') for left alignment
	Right	Set the default label prefix to the quotation mark (") for right alignment
	Center	Set the default label prefix to the caret (^) for centered alignment
/Range Label	Left	Change the label prefix in a range of cells to the apostrophe (') for left alignment
	Right	Change the label prefix in a range of cells to the quotation mark (") for right alignment
	Center	Change the label prefix in a range of cells to the caret (^) for centered alignment

Figure 3-5 The commands for aligning labels

How to format the values in cells Figure 3-6 summarizes the commands that you can use for setting the formats of cells. The first command, the /Worksheet Global Format command, sets the default format for all of the cells in a spreadsheet. As a result, you should use this command to set the default to the one that will be used most often in the spreadsheet you're working on. In contrast, the /Range Format command is used to apply a format to a range of cells.

Figure 3-7 summarizes the ten formatting options that can be applied to a cell. Of these, the first four are the most useful for business spreadsheets. The Comma (,), Currency, and Percent formats are commonly used for cells that contain values. And one of the Date formats should be used with the value that is returned by the @NOW function. Note that the Percent format takes a decimal value, moves the decimal point two places to the right, rounds the new value to the number of decimal positions specified for the format, and displays it with a percent sign after it.

Command name	Next level	Function
/Worksheet Global Format	See figure 3-7	Set the format for all the cells in a spreadsheet
/Range Format	See figure 3-7	Set the format for a range of cells
/Range Format Reset		Remove the formats that have been applied to a range of cells and reset the formats to the default format

Figure 3-6 The commands for setting cell formats

If you're using *Lotus* for business spreadsheets, you probably won't have any need for the other formats shown in figure 3-7. But there is one that you should at least know about; it's called the Text format. When it is applied to the cell, the contents of the cell are displayed, even if the cell contains a formula. If, for example, a cell contains this formula

```
+C9-D14
```

that's what is displayed for the cell. Then, if you print the spreadsheet, the formulas are printed. This format can be useful when you want to check a spreadsheet to make sure that all of the formulas have been entered correctly.

In the third column of figure 3-7, you can see the format code that's shown in the control panel when the highlighted cell has been formatted by the /Range Format command. Thus, (,2) means Comma format with two decimal positions, and (P0) means Percent format with zero decimal positions. If the highlighted cell has the default format, however, the format code isn't displayed in the control panel.

The last command in figure 3-6 is the /Range Format Reset command. This command removes the formats that have been applied to a range of cells and returns their formats to the default format. This command can be useful when you've applied the wrong formats to a range of cells.

How to set the width of columns Figure 3-8 summarizes the commands you need for setting the widths of columns. The /Worksheet Global Column-Width command can be used to set the default width for all the columns in the spreadsheet. If you don't use this command, the default width is nine characters.

The /Worksheet Column Set-Width and the Reset-Width commands can be used to set or reset the width for a single column. When you set the width for a column, you can enter the number of characters that you want as the

Option	Decimal positions or date option	Format code shown in control panel	Cell value or contents	Cell display [W10]
, (Comma)	2	,2	5780.001	5,780.00
	0	,0	-234	(234)
Currency	2	C2	5780.001	$5,780.00
	0	C0	-234	($234)
Percent	2	P2	0.15782	15.78%
	0	P0	0.95	95%
Date	DD-MMM-YY	D1	33689.65459	26-Mar-92
	DD-MMM	D2	33689.65459	26-Mar
	MMM-YY	D3	33689.65459	Mar-92
	Long Intn'l	D4	33689.65459	03/26/92
	Short Intn'l	D5	33689.65459	30/26
Fixed	2	F2	5780.001	5780.00
	0	F0	-234	-234
Sci	2	S2	5780.001	5.78E+03
	0	S0	-234	-2E+02
General	N/A	G	5780.001	5780.001
	N/A	G	-234	-234
+/-	N/A	+	7	+++++++
	N/A	+	-2	- -
Text	N/A	T	-234	-234
	N/A	T	+C9-D14	+C9-D14
Hidden	N/A	H	5780.001	
	N/A	H	-234	

Figure 3-7 The ten *Lotus* format options for cells

Command name	Function
/Worksheet Global Column-Width	Set the column width of all the columns in a spreadsheet that you haven't set using one of the /Worksheet Column commands
/Worksheet Column Set-Width	Set the width of one column in a spreadsheet
/Worksheet Column Reset-Width	Reset the width of a column to the default column width
/Worksheet Column Column-Range Set-Width	Set the width of one or more columns in a spreadsheet
/Worksheet Column Column-Range Reset-Width	Reset the width of one or more columns to the default column width

Figure 3-8 The commands for setting column widths

column width, or you can use the Left and Right arrow keys to increase or decrease the width of the column.

The /Worksheet Column Column-Range Set-Width and Reset-Width commands can be used to set or reset the widths of more than one column. These commands were introduced with release 2.2 of *Lotus*. After you select one of these commands, you highlight the range of columns that you want to set or reset the width for. Then, you continue with the command.

How to insert and delete columns and rows Figure 3-9 summarizes the commands for inserting and deleting columns and rows. After you select one of these commands, you highlight the range of columns or rows that you want to insert or delete. Then, you press the Enter key.

How to hide and expose columns When you work on some spreadsheets, it makes sense to hide one or more columns instead of deleting them. Then, you can print the spreadsheet with the columns hidden. Afterwards, you can expose the hidden columns and continue working.

Figure 3-10 summarizes the two commands you need for hiding and exposing columns. When you use the /Worksheet Column Hide command, you highlight the columns you want to hide and press the Enter key. In figure 3-11, for example, you can see a spreadsheet with nine columns hidden, columns E through M, as indicated by the column letters at the top of the spreadsheet.

Command name	Function
/Worksheet Insert Row	Insert one or more rows into a spreadsheet
/Worksheet Insert Column	Insert one or more columns into a spreadsheet
/Worksheet Delete Row	Delete one or more rows from a spreadsheet
/Worksheet Delete Column	Delete one or more columns from a spreadsheet

Figure 3-9 The commands for inserting and deleting rows and columns

To expose hidden columns, you start the /Worksheet Column Display command. When you do this, the hidden columns are displayed with an asterisk next to the column letter to indicate that they're hidden. Then, you move the cursor to a cell in the first column that you want to expose. If you want to expose more than one column, you type one dot and highlight the range of columns that you want to expose. When you press the Enter key, the columns that were hidden are displayed as usual.

Hiding columns is particularly useful when you're working with wide spreadsheets. Then, you can hide the columns you don't need so a spreadsheet will fit on a single page. That's possible because *Lotus* only prints the columns that are displayed. Hiding columns is also useful when you want to compare columns that aren't adjacent. In figure 3-11, for instance, I wanted to compare the data for the first quarter of the year with the annual averages. Hiding columns E through M made this comparison easy.

How to freeze titles on the screen When you scroll down a spreadsheet past the twentieth row, the top rows of the spreadsheet disappear. As a result, you can't see the titles that identify the columns of the spreadsheet. Similarly, when you scroll to the right past the last column that is displayed, the left columns of the spreadsheet disappear. As a result, you can't see the labels that identify the rows of the spreadsheet. In either case, the spreadsheet becomes more difficult to work with.

To overcome this problem, *Lotus* provides the /Worksheet Titles command as summarized in figure 3-12. This command lets you *freeze the titles* so they always appear on the screen. As you can see, you can freeze the titles that identify the rows, the columns, or both.

Command name	Function
/Worksheet Column Hide	Hide one or more columns in a spreadsheet
/Worksheet Column Display	Display one or more columns in a spreadsheet

Figure 3-10 The commands for hiding and exposing columns

```
A1: [W21] 'Balance sheet changes by month                                READY

              A              B        C        D          N        O
1   Balance sheet changes by month          05/18/92   BALMONTH
2   ============================================================
3                           JAN      FEB      MAR      AVERAGE
4   ============================================================
5   Current assets
6     Cash in bank         15,869    9,110   13,033     12,671
7     Accounts receivable 279,754  248,034  265,086    264,291
8     Inventory           234,621  217,302  234,580    228,834
9     Prepaid expenses     14,801    9,779    4,624      9,735
10                        ----------------------------------------
11        TOTAL          $545,045 $484,225 $517,323   $515,531
12  ============================================================
13  Current liabilities
14    Accounts payable    129,736   79,562   56,125     88,474
15    Line of credit      119,000  145,200  102,550    122,250
16                        ----------------------------------------
17        TOTAL          $248,736 $224,762 $158,675   $210,724
18  ============================================================
19  Quick ratio              2.19     2.15     3.26       2.45
20  ============================================================
18-May-92  09:49 AM                                        NUM
```

Figure 3-11 A spreadsheet with nine hidden columns

To create a title across the top of a spreadsheet, you move the cell pointer to the first row below the rows that you want to freeze. If, for example, you want to freeze the first four rows of the spreadsheet in figure 3-13, you move the cell pointer to row 5. Then, you select the /Worksheet Titles Horizontal command to freeze the rows. If you look at the second part of this figure closely, you can see that *Lotus* displays rows 21 through 32 right after the title rows.

Command name	Option	Function	Operation
/Worksheet Titles	Horizontal	Freeze the rows above the cell pointer as titles for each screen	Move the cell pointer to the first row below the rows that you want to use as title rows. Then, select this command and option.
	Vertical	Freeze the columns to the left of the cell pointer as titles for each screen	Move the cell pointer to the first column to the right of the ones that you want to use as title columns. Then, select this command and option.
	Both	Freeze the rows above the cell pointer and the columns to the left of the cell pointer as titles for each screen	Move the cell pointer to the first cell that's below the rows that you want to use as title rows and to the right of the columns that you want to use as title columns. Then, select this command and option.
	Clear	Unfreeze all the title rows and columns	Select the command from anywhere in the current spreadsheet.

Figure 3-12 The command for freezing titles on a spreadsheet screen

The Vertical and Both options work in much the same way that the Horizontal option works. If, for example, you want to freeze just column A, you move the cell pointer to column B and select the /Worksheet Titles Vertical command. And if you want to freeze both column A and rows 1 through 4, you move the cell pointer to cell B5 and select the /Worksheet Titles Both command.

The fourth option in figure 3-12 is the Clear option. You use this when you want to unfreeze all of the columns or rows that have been frozen as titles. When you perform this command, it doesn't matter where the cell pointer is in the spreadsheet.

A spreadsheet that doesn't have frozen titles

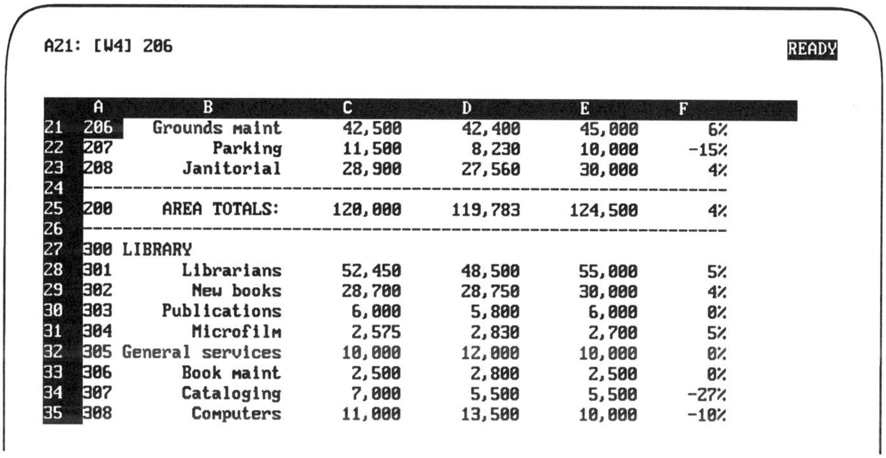

A21: [W4] 206 READY

	A	B	C	D	E	F
21	206	Grounds maint	42,500	42,400	45,000	6%
22	207	Parking	11,500	8,230	10,000	-15%
23	208	Janitorial	28,900	27,560	30,000	4%
24	-----	-----	-----	-----	-----	-----
25	200	AREA TOTALS:	120,000	119,783	124,500	4%
26	-----	-----	-----	-----	-----	-----
27	300	LIBRARY				
28	301	Librarians	52,450	48,500	55,000	5%
29	302	New books	28,700	28,750	30,000	4%
30	303	Publications	6,000	5,800	6,000	0%
31	304	Microfilm	2,575	2,830	2,700	5%
32	305	General services	10,000	12,000	10,000	0%
33	306	Book maint	2,500	2,800	2,500	0%
34	307	Cataloging	7,000	5,500	5,500	-27%
35	308	Computers	11,000	13,500	10,000	-10%

The same spreadsheet with the first four rows frozen as titles

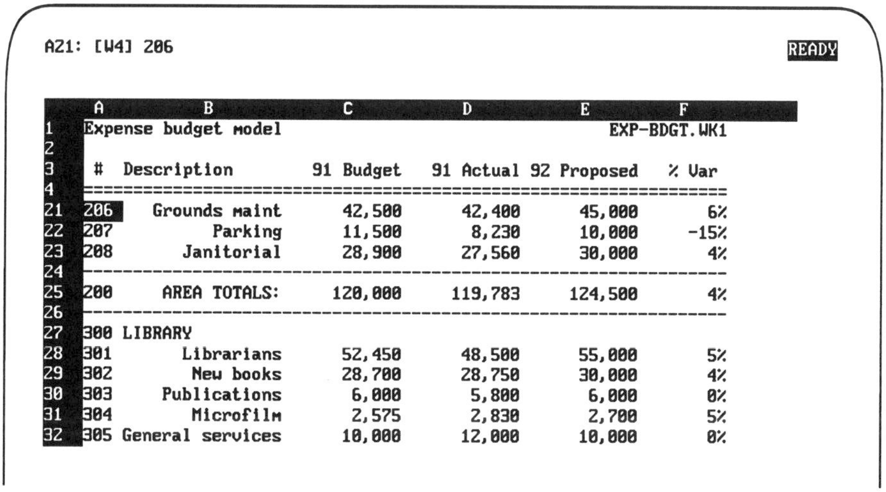

A21: [W4] 206 READY

	A	B	C	D	E	F
1	Expense budget model				EXP-BDGT.WK1	
2						
3	#	Description	91 Budget	91 Actual	92 Proposed	% Var
4	=====	=====	=====	=====	=====	=====
21	206	Grounds maint	42,500	42,400	45,000	6%
22	207	Parking	11,500	8,230	10,000	-15%
23	208	Janitorial	28,900	27,560	30,000	4%
24	-----	-----	-----	-----	-----	-----
25	200	AREA TOTALS:	120,000	119,783	124,500	4%
26	-----	-----	-----	-----	-----	-----
27	300	LIBRARY				
28	301	Librarians	52,450	48,500	55,000	5%
29	302	New books	28,700	28,750	30,000	4%
30	303	Publications	6,000	5,800	6,000	0%
31	304	Microfilm	2,575	2,830	2,700	5%
32	305	General services	10,000	12,000	10,000	0%

Figure 3-13 A spreadsheet with and without frozen titles

How to copy, move, and erase cell entries Figure 3-14 summarizes the commands for copying, moving, and erasing cell entries. When you use these commands, you highlight the range of cells that you want to operate on. Then, if you're copying or moving cells, you highlight the receiving range of cells. Often, the command will work the way you want it to if you only highlight the first cell in the receiving range. When the ranges have been properly identified, you press the Enter key to complete the command.

Command name	Function
/Copy	Copy the contents and formats from one range of cells to another
/Move	Move the contents and formats from one range of cells to another
/Range Erase (Delete key)	Erase the contents but not the formats of a range of cells

Figure 3-14 The commands for copying, moving, and erasing the contents of cells

Note in figure 3-14 that both the cell contents and the cell formats are copied by the /Copy command and moved by the /Move command. However, the /Range Erase command erases the cell contents, but leaves the cell formats intact. Although this may appear to be inconsistent, that's usually the way you want these commands to work.

If you're using release 2.3, 2.4, or 3.4, you should know that you can use the Delete key instead of the /Range Erase command to erase the contents of the cell at the cell pointer. If you're using release 3.4 with a mouse, you can also highlight a range of cells before you press the Delete key to erase the contents in the entire range.

How to print spreadsheets Figure 3-15 summaries the commands for setting print options and printing spreadsheets. If you're using a 2.X release of *Lotus*, the related commands display Default Settings and Print Settings screens that you can hide by pressing the F6 (Window) key. If you're using release 3.4, only the Print Settings screen is supported.

If you use the /Worksheet Global Default Printer command to set the permanent print defaults the way you want them for most spreadsheets, you won't have to use the /Print Printer Option command for most spreadsheets. Generally, the print defaults should be set for a wide spreadsheet that can accommodate seven or eight *Lotus* columns. Then, you only have to override the defaults when they aren't appropriate for the spreadsheet you're working on.

If you're using a printer that prints at 10 characters per inch on standard 8-1/2 by 11 inch paper, a Left margin of 5 and a Right margin of 80 provide for half-inch margins with 75 characters between the margins. If your printer prints at 12 characters per inch, a Left margin of 6 and a Right margin of 96 provide for half-inch margins with 90 characters between the margins. If you set the Top and Bottom margins at 4, *Lotus* will skip 6 lines at the top and bottom of each page because it skips 2 lines in addition to the margins you

Command name	Next level	Next level	Function
/Worksheet Global Default F6 (Window)	Printer	Left	Set the default for the left print margin
		Right	Set the default for the right print margin
		Top	Set the default for the top print margin
		Bottom	Set the default for the bottom print margin
		Pg-Length	Set the default for the number of lines on each page
		Quit	Exit from the Printer command
/Print Printer Options F6 (Window)	Margins	Top	Set the top print margin for a spreadsheet
		Bottom	Set the bottom print margin for a spreadsheet
		Left	Set the left print margin for a spreadsheet
		Right	Set the right print margin for a spreadsheet
	Pg-Length		Set the number of lines to be printed on each page of a spreadsheet
/Print Printer F6 (Window)	Range		Set the range of cells that are to be printed
	Page		Skip the paper in the printer to the top of the next page
	Align		Tell *Lotus* that the paper is aligned properly in the printer
	Go		Print all the cells in the print range
	Quit		Exit from the Print menu

Figure 3-15 The commands for setting print options and printing spreadsheets

set. Finally, the Page length is usually set to 66 for a dot-matrix printer because this is standard for an 11 inch page with 6 lines printed per inch. If you're using a laser printer, though, you usually set the Page length to 60.

When you set the margins for any printer, you may have to experiment with them a bit before you get them to work exactly the way you want them to. On my printer, for example, a Top margin setting of 2, which should skip four lines before printing, actually skips six lines. And a Bottom margin setting of 2, which should leave a bottom margin of four lines, actually leaves a margin of only two lines.

Similarly, the Left and Right margin settings might not work exactly the way you want them to. For instance, many printers can't print the full width of the paper. Instead, they require a small margin like a quarter inch on each side of the form. As a result, a printer that's set for printing 10 characters per inch can't print the full line when the Left margin is set to 1 and the Right margin is set to 84 because those margins are too narrow. In that case, the printer will either ignore the extra characters for each line or roll them over to the next print line. In either case, you know that you've exceeded the printer's maximum printing width. Then, you must reset the margins with fewer characters per line.

On many printers, you can change the printing of your printer from 10 characters per inch to one or more of these settings: 12, 15, 17, or 20 characters per inch. You can usually do that just by pressing a button or two on the printer itself. However, you can also control that from within the *Lotus* program. I'll show you how in the next chapter. When you switch from one setting to another, whether you do it manually or from within the *Lotus* program, you must adjust the *Lotus* margins to accommodate the line widths.

Once you've got the print settings the way you want them, you use the Range, Go, and Page options to set the range of cells, to print them, and to skip the printed form to the next page. When *Lotus* completes the print job, you can return to the spreadsheet in one of two ways. First, you can press the Esc key three times. Second, you can select the Quit command to exit from the Print menu.

Occasionally, *Lotus* gets confused as it is printing so it skips to the middle of a page instead of the top of the page. Then, the next page that's printed gets started in the middle of the page. To correct this problem, first realign the form in the printer. Then, use the Align option of the /Print Printer command to tell *Lotus* that the form is aligned properly. After that, the Go and Page options should work the way you want them to.

When you print long or wide spreadsheets, printing often becomes a problem. For instance, you may have trouble getting the margins to work the way you want them to; you may want to print headings on each page of a long spreadsheet; or you may want to print a wide spreadsheet sideways so all of the columns can be printed on one page. To learn more about printing and to learn the skills you need for printing long or wide spreadsheets, please read the next chapter.

Command name	Option	Function
/Worksheet Global Default Directory		Set the default drive and directory that *Lotus* will use for spreadsheet files
/File Directory		Set the drive and directory that *Lotus* will use for the spreadsheet files in the current work session
/File Retrieve F3 (Name)		Retrieve a spreadsheet from the hard disk or a diskette
/File Save F3 (Name)	Cancel	Cancel the command and return to Ready mode
	Replace	Replace the file on disk with the current spreadsheet
	Backup	Replace the file on disk with the current spreadsheet, but also save a backup copy of the current spreadsheet using the same file name and the extension BAK

Figure 3-16 The commands for setting directories, saving files, and retrieving files

How to set directories, save spreadsheets, and retrieve spreadsheets

Figure 3-16 summarizes the commands for setting directories, retrieving spreadsheet files, and saving them. If you're the only *Lotus* user on your PC and you only use one directory, you should use the /Worksheet Global Default Directory command to set the default directory to the one you use. After you set the directory, you use the /Worksheet Global Default Update command to make the default directory permanent so it carries over from one *Lotus* session to another. If you share a PC with several *Lotus* users or you use several different directories for *Lotus* files, you can use the /File Directory command to set the directory each time you start a *Lotus* session.

Once you've set the directory to the one you want to use, you can use the /File Save and /File Retrieve commands to save files into that directory and retrieve files from that directory. When you create a name for a new file, you don't have to specify the drive or directory information because that's assumed.

```
A1:                                                                              FILES
Name of file to retrieve: C:\123\DATA\*.wk?
          SLSDATA.WK1     02/28/92        10:39           3257
1QSLS.WK1         2QSLS.WK1       3QSLS.WK1       4QSLS.WK1       EXPENSES.WK1
MODIFED.WK1       NRTH-SLS.WK1    QTR-SLS.WK1     SLS&COM.WK1     SLS-SUM.WK1
SLSDATA.WK1       STH-SLS.WK1     WEST-SLS.WK1    EXPENSES\       SALES\
```

Figure 3-17 The file listing that is displayed when you press the F3 (Name) key

If you want to display all of the files in the default directory as you use the Save or Retrieve commands, you can press the F3 (Name) key to display a listing like the one in figure 3-17. Then, to retrieve a file, you just highlight the one you want and press the Enter key.

When you use the F3 key to view all the spreadsheet files in a directory, the second line of the control panel displays information for the highlighted file. In figure 3-17, you can see the date and time that the SLSDATA file was last saved and the size of the file expressed in bytes.

If the default directory contains any subdirectories, they are also displayed when you use the F3 key to view the files in the directory. In figure 3-17, for example, these two subdirectories are displayed at the end of the listing: EXPENSES\ and SALES\. To view the spreadsheets in one of these subdirectories, you move the highlight to the one you want and press the Enter key. When you exit from the command, the default directory is reinstated.

When you use the /File Save command to save a spreadsheet with the name of a file that's already on the disk, you get the three options shown in figure 3-16: Cancel, Replace, and Backup. The Cancel option means to cancel the command so the spreadsheet isn't saved, and Replace means to replace the old file with the current spreadsheet. Normally, those are the only options you need to use.

When you use the Backup option, *Lotus* saves the spreadsheet as usual with a WK1 or WK3 extension, but it also creates a copy of the original spreadsheet with a BAK extension. If, for example, you're saving a file named YTDSLS using *Lotus* release 2.2, *Lotus* saves one copy of the current spreadsheet in a file named YTDSLS.WK1, and it creates a copy of the original spreadsheet named YTDSLS.BAK. Both of these files are saved in the same directory.

Although they are saved in the same directory, they have different extensions so the files with the BAK extension aren't listed with the files that have the WK1 or WK3 extension when you use the /File Retrieve command.

```
A1: [W16] 'Monthly Expenses                                                    MENU
No  Yes
Do not erase the worksheet; return to READY mode
          A              B         C         D         E         F         G
1   Monthly Expenses            05/04/92            MAREXP
2   March
3                                          Dollar   Percent
4                        Budget   Expense Variance Variance
5
6   Salaries & Wages    50,000    51,784     1,784      3.6%
7   Rent & Utilities    17,500    18,222       722      4.1%
8   Maintenance          7,750     7,912       162      2.1%
9   Supplies             8,250     7,211   (1,039)    -12.6%
10  Miscellaneous        1,500     1,922       422     28.1%
11
12  Total               85,000    87,051     2,051      2.4%
13
14
```

Figure 3-18 The message displayed by the /Worksheet Erase command

To retrieve a BAK file, you must type in the BAK extension as part of the file specification. Although some people use BAK files to give themselves an extra measure of security, these files can quickly get out of control. As a result, most *Lotus* users don't ever need the BAK option.

How to erase a spreadsheet from internal memory Occasionally, you'll want to clear a spreadsheet from the screen so you can create a new one from scratch. To do that, you use the /Worksheet Erase command. This command erases the current spreadsheet from the internal memory of your PC.

Before the command erases the current spreadsheet, though, it displays the prompt shown in figure 3-18. This gives you a chance to make sure that you've saved your work. If you respond with the letter *y*, you lose your work if you haven't already saved it. If you respond with the letter *n*, you return to the spreadsheet you've been working on.

Discussion

If you master all the commands that are summarized in this chapter, you will become a proficient *Lotus* user. Using just the commands presented here, you will be able to create and use spreadsheets for most business purposes. Then, when you need to perform functions that can't be done using just these commands, you can refer to the other chapters in this book.

Terms

global
default
toggle key
permanent default
freeze
title

Objective

Use any one of the commands presented in this chapter to perform its intended function.

Chapter 4

How to print spreadsheets that are long or wide

When you create a spreadsheet that's too long or wide to print on a single page, it becomes more difficult to read the printed copy. That's because the pages aren't numbered, the column and row identifiers aren't repeated on all of the pages, the printer may skip to the next page at an inappropriate row in the spreadsheet, and so on. Fortunately, though, *Lotus* provides several commands and capabilities that let you print long and wide spreadsheets so they're easy to read.

In this chapter, you'll start by learning how to use some commands that can be applied to all spreadsheets. Next, you'll learn how to use two commands that apply to long spreadsheets. Then, you'll learn how to use two commands that apply to wide spreadsheets. Last, you'll learn how to clear print settings and how to save more than one group of print settings for a single spreadsheet.

The printing commands that you can use for all spreadsheets

Figure 4-1 summarizes the printing commands for setting, saving, and clearing print options. The options in this summary apply to all spreadsheets including those that are long, wide, or both long and wide. You've already been introduced to the commands for setting the margins and page length in chapter 3, but the other commands are new ones.

If you're using *Lotus* releases 2.2, 2.3, 2.4, or 3.4, a Print Settings screen like the one in figure 4-2 is displayed when you start the /Print Printer command. To turn this screen off so you can see the spreadsheet, you can press the F6 (Window) key. Then, to turn the screen back on, just press the key again. As you can see in this figure, the Print Settings screen shows the settings for the print margins as well as several other settings that you'll learn to use in this chapter.

Command name	Next level	Next level	Next level	Function
/Worksheet Global Default F6 (Window)	Printer	Left		Set the default for the left print margin
		Right		Set the default for the right print margin
		Top		Set the default for the top print margin
		Bottom		Set the default for the bottom print margin
		Pg-Length		Set the default for the number of lines on each page
		Setup		Set the default pitch for printing
		Quit		Exit from the Default command
/Print Printer Options F6 (Window)	Margins	Top		Set the top print margin for a spreadsheet
		Bottom		Set the bottom print margin for a spreadsheet
		Left		Set the left print margin for a spreadsheet
		Right		Set the right print margin for a spreadsheet
	Pg-Length			Set the number of lines to be printed on each page of a spreadsheet
	Header			Create a header that will be printed on each page
	Footer			Create a footer that will be printed on each page
	Setup			Set the pitch to be used when the spreadsheet is printed
/Print Printer Clear F6 (Window)				Clear some or all of the current print settings (see figure 4-24)
/Print Printer Options (release 3.X)	Advanced	Layout	Pitch	Set the pitch to be used when the spreadsheet is printed
	Name			Create, delete, or select a named group of print settings for the current spreadsheet (see figure 4-25)

Figure 4-1 The commands for setting, clearing, and saving print options that can used with all spreadsheets

```
D3: "Variance                                                    MENU
Range  Line  Page  Options  Clear  Align  Go  Quit
Print the specified range
---------------------------- Print Settings ----------------------------
  Destination:  Printer

  Range:        A1..H10

  Header:       @|March Expenses|Page #
  Footer:

  Margins:
    Left 6    Right 96    Top 4    Bottom 4

  Borders:
    Columns
    Rows

  Setup string: \027\077

  Page length:  66

  Output:       As-Displayed (Formatted)

27-May-92  01:29 PM                                      NUM
```

Figure 4-2 The Print Settings screen that can be displayed by using the F6 (Window) key

Similarly, when you use the /Worksheet Global Default command with *Lotus* release 2.2, 2.3, or 2.4, a Default Settings screen is displayed. This screen includes the defaults that apply to print settings. To turn the Default Settings screen on or off, you also use the F6 key.

How to set the print margins for a spreadsheet Figure 4-3 shows how the margin settings in figure 4-2 are applied to a standard 8-1/2 by 11 inch page. These settings are designed for printing with 12 characters per inch, or a maximum of 102 characters across an 8-1/2 inch page. Here, the Left margin is 6 and the Right margin is 96. Those settings provide for half-inch margins, and 90 characters can be printed between the margins. If your printer prints at 10 characters per inch, a Left margin of 5 and a Right margin of 80 provide for half-inch margins, and 75 characters can be printed between the margins.

The Top margin in figure 4-2 and 4-3 is 4. Thus, six lines are skipped at the top of each printed page because *Lotus* automatically skips two lines on its own. Similarly, the Bottom margin in figure 4-2 and 4-3 is 4. Thus, six lines are skipped at the bottom of each printed page.

The Page length in figure 4-2 and 4-3 is set at 66. This is the standard setting for an 11 inch page with 6 lines per vertical inch when you're using a dot-matrix printer. Because six lines are skipped at the top and bottom of each page, 54 lines can be printed on each page. When you're using a laser printer, though, the Page length is usually set to 60.

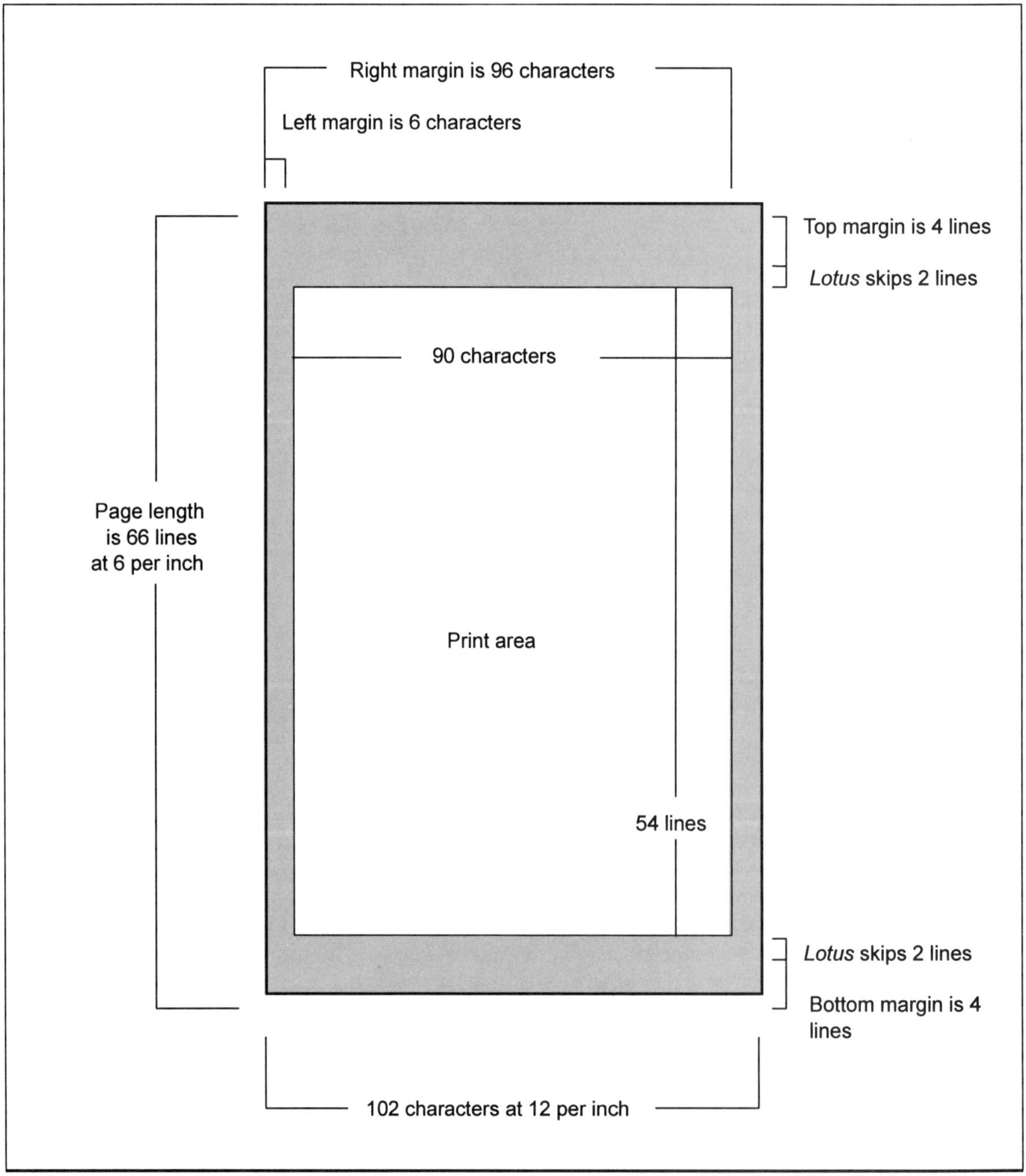

Figure 4-3 The print options in figure 4-2 as they are applied to a standard 8-1/2 by 11 inch page when printed by a dot-matrix printer

Command name	Next level	Function	Operation
/Print Printer Options	Header	Create a header that will be printed on each page	Type a one-line header; then, press the Enter key.
	Footer	Create a footer that will be printed on each page	Type a one-line footer; then, press the Enter key.

Figure 4-4 The commands for creating headers and footers

When you set the margins for any printer, you may have to experiment with them a bit before you get them to work exactly the way you want them to. On my printer, for example, a Top margin setting of 2 should skip four lines before printing. However, six lines are actually skipped. And a Bottom margin setting of 2 should leave four blank lines at the bottom of the page, but this setting actually leaves only two blank lines.

Similarly, the Left and Right margin settings might not work exactly the way you want them to. For instance, many printers can't print the full width of the paper. Instead, they require a small margin like a quarter inch on each side of the form. As a result, a printer that's set for printing 10 characters per inch can't print the full line when the Left margin is set to 1 and the Right margin is set to 84 because these settings don't leave that small margin required by the printer. Then, the printer will either ignore the extra characters for each line or roll them over to the next print line. In either case, you know that you've exceeded the maximum printing width. As a result, you must reset the margins with fewer characters per line.

If you use the /Worksheet Global Default command to set the permanent print defaults the way you want them for most spreadsheets, you won't have to use the /Print Printer Options command for most spreadsheets. Then, when a spreadsheet passes the limits of the default margin settings, you can adjust the margins for just that spreadsheet. If a spreadsheet still won't fit on a page after you've adjusted the margins, you can use some of the other skills presented in this chapter to print the spreadsheet in a form that's easy to read.

How to add a header or footer to a spreadsheet Figure 4-4 summarizes the two commands you can use for creating *headers* and *footers*. Then, figure 4-5 shows you how to use the special symbols that are designed for a header or a footer. As you'll see, these two commands and special symbols make it easy to create headers and footers.

To create a header, you select the /Print Printer Options Header command. Then, at this prompt:

```
Enter header:
```

Character	Function
¦	Control the alignment of the header or footer. The first of these characters causes the entry that follows to be centered. The second one causes the entry that follows to be aligned on the right print margin.
#	Automatically insert the appropriate page number in the header or footer.
@	Automatically insert the current date in a header or footer.

Examples

Header	Result
`Budget`	`Budget`
`¦¦Budget`	`                                        Budget`
`Budget¦¦#`	`Budget                                      1`
`@¦Budget¦Page #`	`07-Jan-92            Budget            Page 1`

Figure 4-5 How to use the special characters for headers and footers

you type the header and press the Enter key. Although the header doesn't appear on the screen, it will be printed on each page of the spreadsheet. You create a footer in the same way, but you start the process with the /Print Printer Options Footer command. Like a header, the footer doesn't appear on the screen, but it will be printed on each page of the spreadsheet.

If you look back to the Print Settings screen in figure 4-2, you can see that the spreadsheet will be printed with a header. This header will be printed after the number of lines given in the Top margin setting. Then, *Lotus* will skip two lines before it starts printing the rows of the spreadsheet. If you add a footer to a spreadsheet, *Lotus* skips two lines after the last row that's printed; then, it prints the footer. After it prints the footer, it skips the number of lines in the Bottom margin. If you look ahead to figures 4-11 and 4-19, you can see headers and a footer that have been used for printing a long and a wide spreadsheet.

The special characters in figure 4-5 are easy to use. The vertical bar controls the alignment of entries; the # character inserts the page number; and the @ character inserts the current date. The first vertical bar in a header causes the next entry to be centered; the second vertical bar causes the next entry to be aligned on the right print margin.

Because using a header makes it easy for you to print the date at the top of a spreadsheet, you may want to use headers for all of your spreadsheets, even the ones that are only one page long. That way, you don't have to use the @NOW function to put the date in the spreadsheet. Then, if you also put the file name and page number in the header, all your spreadsheets will have a standard heading. Usually, you can put all the information you need to identify the spreadsheet and its pages in the header, so there's no need for a footer.

How to use the /Print Printer Options Setup command to set the pitch for a spreadsheet The number of characters that are printed in an inch can be referred to as the *pitch*. Today, most dot-matrix printers have a 10 pitch setting (10 characters per inch, or 10 cpi) and a 12 pitch setting. Most printers today also offer a *condensed mode* of 17 pitch, though the exact number of characters per inch may vary slightly. For instance, my printer prints at 16.7 cpi in condensed mode. If you're using a laser printer, the type sizes may not be referred to in terms of *pitch*, but similar size alternatives are offered. To find out the capabilities of your printer, you should refer to your printer manual.

One way to set the pitch for a spreadsheet is to set it on your printer manually. With many printers, you can set the pitch by pressing a button on the top or front of the printer. With other printers, you can set the pitch by using a built-in LCD display and menu system. Either way, your printer manual should tell you how to set the pitch on your printer manually.

Often, though, it's better to use *Lotus* to set the pitch for a spreadsheet. That way, you don't have to remember to adjust your printer manually before you print a spreadsheet. As a result, your spreadsheet will always print the way you want it to.

Figure 4-6 shows you how to use the /Print Printer Options Setup command for setting the pitch. When you use this command, you enter a special code called a *setup string*. If, for example, you're using an Epson

Command name

/Print Printer Options Setup

How to use this command

1. Start the /Print Printer Options Setup command.
2. Type the setup string for the pitch that you want to use. Figure 4-7 lists the setup strings for some of the most commonly used printers.
3. Press the Enter key.

Related command

/Print Printer Options Margins

Use this command to change the left and right margins so they are appropriate for the pitch that will be used to print the spreadsheet. Figure 4-8 shows the margin settings for half-inch margins when you use one of the five most common pitch settings.

Figure 4-6 The command for setting the pitch that will be used to print the spreadsheet

printer and you want the spreadsheet to be printed in condensed pitch, you enter this setup string: \015. Later, when you tell *Lotus* to print the spreadsheet, this setup string gets sent to the printer to tell it what pitch to use.

If you look back to the print settings screen in figure 4-2, you can see that the setup string is \027\077. This sets the pitch to 12 on my Epson LQ printer. Some of the setup strings for the most commonly used pitches and printers are given in figure 4-7. Remember, though, that many printers offer more than just two or three pitches. To find all of the setup strings that you can use for your printer, you should use your printer manual.

When you send a setup string to a printer, the printer continues to use that pitch setting until it receives a new setup string. So if you use a setup string to switch your printer to condensed pitch for one spreadsheet, you must switch it back when you want to print a spreadsheet in normal pitch. You can do that by sending it another setup string or by using the switches on the printer to change the pitch manually.

When you use the /Print Printer Options Setup command to change the pitch for a spreadsheet, you should also change the left and right margins to provide for the pitch. To do that, you use the /Print Printer Options Margins command. Then, to set one-half inch margins for pitches of 10, 12, 15, 17, and 20 characters per inch, you can use the settings shown in figure 4-8.

Printer	10 pitch	12 pitch	Condensed pitch
Epson X series	\018	\027\077	\015
IBM Proprinter	\018	\027\058	\015
Okidata Microline	\030	\028	\029
Toshiba P321	\027\093	(none)	\027\091
HP LaserJet	\027E	\027(s0p12H	\027s(s16.66H

Figure 4-7 The setup strings for setting the pitch on some of the most commonly used printers

Pitch (cpi)	Left margin	Right margin	Total characters between margins	Maximum characters in each line
10	5	80	75	85
12	6	96	90	102
15	8	120	112	127.5
17	9	136	127	144.5
20	10	160	150	170

Figure 4-8 Half-inch margin settings for the most common pitches using standard 8-1/2 by 11 inch paper

If, for example, you're using 17 pitch, you set the left margin at 9 and the right margin at 136. Then, 127 characters can be printed between the margins. If you need to print more characters than that on each line, you can reset the margins until you reach the maximum number of characters that your printer can print on each line.

If you look back to figure 4-1, you can see that you can use the /Worksheet Global Default Printer Setup command to establish a default setup string for new spreadsheets. For instance, you can use this command to set this default for 12 pitch printing. Then, you don't have to remember to set the type size manually on the printer before you start each print job.

How to use the /Print Printer Options Advanced Layout Pitch command to set the pitch for a spreadsheet (release 3.X) Figure 4-9 shows you how to use the /Print Printer Options Advanced Layout Pitch command for setting the pitch. By using this command, you can set the pitch to standard, condensed, or expanded mode without having to remember and enter setup strings. The other benefit of this command is that you don't have to adjust the left and right margins when you use it. Instead, *Lotus*

Command name (release 3.X)

/Print Printer Options Advanced Layout Pitch

The three options at the next level

Standard	The default pitch for your printer (often, 10 characters per inch)
Compressed	A pitch with smaller characters and more characters per inch than the default pitch (often, 17 characters per inch)
Expanded	A pitch with larger characters and fewer per inch than the default pitch (often, 5 characters per inch)

How to use this command

1. Start the /Print Printer Options Advanced Layout Pitch command.
2. Select one of the three options shown above.
3. Press the Enter key.

Related command

None. You don't have to use any other commands because *Lotus* automatically adjusts the margins to correspond to the pitch selection.

Figure 4-9 The command for setting the pitch when you use *Lotus* release 3.X

automatically adjusts the margins to correspond to your pitch selection. Unfortunately, this command doesn't work with all printers. As a result, you'll have to experiment with your printer to see if it works.

How to print a long spreadsheet

When you create a spreadsheet that's too long to print on a single page, the spreadsheet becomes difficult to read. This is illustrated by the spreadsheet in figure 4-10. As you can see, this spreadsheet doesn't have headers that print the date and page number on each page. If you look at the second page in this example, you can see that the column identifiers aren't repeated. And the budget data for the Administration category is split over two pages.

Expense budget model EXP-BDGT.WK1

#	Description	91 Budget	91 Actual	92 Proposed	% Var
100	INSTRUCTION				
101	Faculty	1,500,000	1,543,800	1,600,000	6%
102	Depart. support	250,000	258,210	250,000	0%
103	Instruct. aids	148,000	142,900	150,000	1%
104	Lab expense	52,000	43,800	48,000	-8%
105	Printing	28,000	28,590	29,000	3%
106	Teacher's aids	55,000	58,100	60,000	8%
100	AREA TOTALS:	2,033,000	2,075,400	2,137,000	5%
200	FACILITIES				
201	Building maint	85,000	82,000	85,000	0%
202	Debt service	150,700	148,230	145,000	-4%
203	New building	35,700			
204	Utilities	28,900			
205	Waste disposal	8,200			
206	Grounds maint	42,500			
207	Parking	11,500			
208	Janitorial	28,900			
200	AREA TOTALS:	120,000			
300	LIBRARY				
301	Librarians	52,450			
302	New books	28,700			
303	Publications	6,000			
304	Microfilm	2,575			
305	General services	10,000			
306	Book maint	2,500			
307	Cataloging	7,000			
308	Computers	11,000			
300	AREA TOTALS:	120,225			
400	PROMOTION				
401	Staff	48,000			
402	Office expense	10,500			
403	Alumni relations	14,500			
404	Public relations	12,000			
405	Mailings	15,000			
406	Literature	7,400			
407	Guest day	3,000			
400	AREA TOTALS:	110,400			
500	ADMINISTRATION				
501	President's off.	150,000			
502	Provost's off.	120,000			
503	Admissions	78,000			
504	Registrar	82,000			
505	Testing	12,000			

Page 1

506	Business off.	172,000	159,000	160,000	-8%
507	Foundation	57,000	55,000	58,000	2%
508	Computers	21,000	24,000	18,000	-17%
509	Security	28,000	29,300	32,000	13%
510	Audit services	2,800	3,000	3,000	7%
511	Legal services	10,700	9,650	10,500	-2%
512	Insurance	73,000	78,900	82,000	11%
513	Conting fund	25,000	21,000	25,000	0%
500	AREA TOTALS:	831,500	814,950	844,500	2%
600	STUDENT SERVICES				
601	Student employ.	15,000	13,500	14,000	-7%
602	Placement	27,000	29,500	30,000	10%
603	Counseling	34,000	32,000	34,000	0%
604	Health	75,000	75,120	75,000	0%
605	Housing	58,900	59,200	60,000	2%
606	Financial aid	95,000	94,700	94,000	-1%
607	FA services	35,000	28,900	30,000	-17%
608	Student assoc	24,000	23,100	25,000	4%
600	AREA TOTALS:	363,900	356,020	362,000	-1%
700	RESEARCH				
701	Grant props	12,000	13,975	12,000	0%
702	Research support	50,000	52,000	55,000	9%
703	Office suport	28,900	24,780	28,000	-3%
704	Other	15,000	13,460	14,000	-7%
700	AREA TOTALS:	105,900	104,215	109,000	3%

Page 2

Figure 4-10 How *Lotus* prints a long spreadsheet by default

The spreadsheet in figure 4-11 is the same one as in figure 4-10. However, headers and footers are printed on each page. Column identifiers are printed on each page. And the whole Administration category is printed on the same page. These improvements make the spreadsheet easier to read.

Figure 4-12 summarizes the commands that you need for making printing improvements to a long spreadsheet. Since I've already explained how to add headers and footers to a spreadsheet, I won't mention these commands again. Instead, I'll show you how to tell *Lotus* when you want it to skip to a new page and how to add repeating column headings to a spreadsheet. Once you learn how to use these commands, you can make the improvements shown in figure 4-11 in just a few minutes.

How to insert a page break in a spreadsheet By default, *Lotus* inserts a *page break* based on the settings for the top and bottom margins. After the last line that will fit on the first page is printed, *Lotus* inserts a page break and starts printing on the second page. Often, this page break occurs where you don't want it to. Of course, you can experiment with the top and bottom margin settings to get the page to break where you want it, but there's an easier way to get the page to break where you want it to.

To insert a page break where you want one to occur, you use the /Worksheet Page command as summarized in figure 4-13. When you perform this command, a *new page symbol* is inserted into the spreadsheet. The symbol consists of four dots as shown in this figure (cell A48 of the spreadsheet). Then, when you print the spreadsheet, a page break occurs at the symbol and the row below the symbol becomes the first line on the next page.

When you perform the /Worksheet Page command, you must insert the new page symbol in the first column of the row. Otherwise, *Lotus* doesn't recognize the symbol so it doesn't skip to the next page. Instead, *Lotus* reads the symbol as a character and it just prints the four dots.

As you can see in figure 4-13, *Lotus* inserts a new row in a spreadsheet when you use the /Worksheet Page command. As a result, the best way to remove the page break is to delete the entire row. If you erase the new page symbol but don't delete the row, your spreadsheet will contain an extra blank row.

How to print repeating borders in a spreadsheet When you print a spreadsheet of two or more pages, the spreadsheet is easier to read if the rows that contain the column identifiers are printed at the top of each page. The repeated rows are referred to as a *border*. To create a border, you use the /Print Printer Options Borders Rows command as summarized in figure 4-14.

When you perform this command, it prompts you for the range of cells to use for the border. You can enter the range of cells using either the anchor-and-point or the direct entry method. When you press the Enter key, the

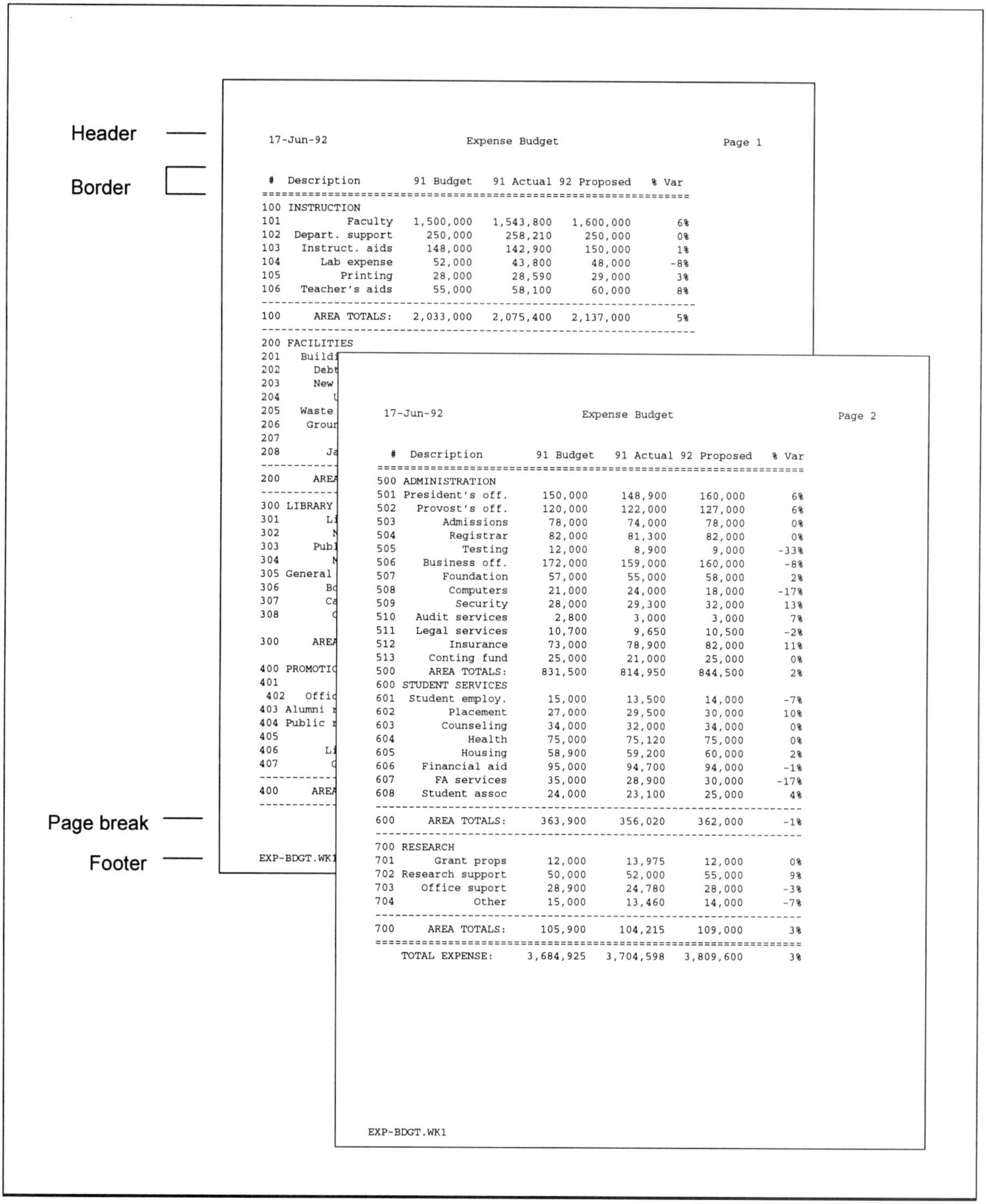

17-Jun-92 Expense Budget Page 1

#	Description	91 Budget	91 Actual	92 Proposed	% Var
100	INSTRUCTION				
101	Faculty	1,500,000	1,543,800	1,600,000	6%
102	Depart. support	250,000	258,210	250,000	0%
103	Instruct. aids	148,000	142,900	150,000	1%
104	Lab expense	52,000	43,800	48,000	-8%
105	Printing	28,000	28,590	29,000	3%
106	Teacher's aids	55,000	58,100	60,000	8%
100	AREA TOTALS:	2,033,000	2,075,400	2,137,000	5%
200	FACILITIES				
201	Buildi				
202	Debt				
203	New				
204	U				
205	Waste				
206	Grour				
207					
208	Ja				
200	AREA				
300	LIBRARY				
301	Li				
302	M				
303	Publ				
304	M				
305	General				
306	Bo				
307	Ca				
308	C				
300	AREA				
400	PROMOTIC				
401					
402	Offic				
403	Alumni r				
404	Public r				
405					
406	Li				
407	C				
400	AREA				

EXP-BDGT.WK1

17-Jun-92 Expense Budget Page 2

#	Description	91 Budget	91 Actual	92 Proposed	% Var
500	ADMINISTRATION				
501	President's off.	150,000	148,900	160,000	6%
502	Provost's off.	120,000	122,000	127,000	6%
503	Admissions	78,000	74,000	78,000	0%
504	Registrar	82,000	81,300	82,000	0%
505	Testing	12,000	8,900	9,000	-33%
506	Business off.	172,000	159,000	160,000	-8%
507	Foundation	57,000	55,000	58,000	2%
508	Computers	21,000	24,000	18,000	-17%
509	Security	28,000	29,300	32,000	13%
510	Audit services	2,800	3,000	3,000	7%
511	Legal services	10,700	9,650	10,500	-2%
512	Insurance	73,000	78,900	82,000	11%
513	Conting fund	25,000	21,000	25,000	0%
500	AREA TOTALS:	831,500	814,950	844,500	2%
600	STUDENT SERVICES				
601	Student employ.	15,000	13,500	14,000	-7%
602	Placement	27,000	29,500	30,000	10%
603	Counseling	34,000	32,000	34,000	0%
604	Health	75,000	75,120	75,000	0%
605	Housing	58,900	59,200	60,000	2%
606	Financial aid	95,000	94,700	94,000	-1%
607	FA services	35,000	28,900	30,000	-17%
608	Student assoc	24,000	23,100	25,000	4%
600	AREA TOTALS:	363,900	356,020	362,000	-1%
700	RESEARCH				
701	Grant props	12,000	13,975	12,000	0%
702	Research support	50,000	52,000	55,000	9%
703	Office suport	28,900	24,780	28,000	-3%
704	Other	15,000	13,460	14,000	-7%
700	AREA TOTALS:	105,900	104,215	109,000	3%
	TOTAL EXPENSE:	3,684,925	3,704,598	3,809,600	3%

EXP-BDGT.WK1

Figure 4-11 The spreadsheet in figure 4-10 with a header, a footer, a border, and a page break

Command name	Next level	Next level	Function
/Worksheet Page			Insert a page break into a spreadsheet
/Print Printer Options	Header		Create a header that will be printed on each page
	Footer		Create a footer that will be printed on each page
	Borders	Rows	Identify the rows that should be printed after the header on each page
/Print Printer Options Advanced Layout (release 3.X)	Line-Spacing	Compressed	Set the vertical spacing of the printed lines to compressed printing

Figure 4-12 The commands for printing long spreadsheets so they're easier to read

range of cells is added to the list of print settings for the spreadsheet as shown in figure 4-15. Here, the border range is A1..F2.

When you use a border, you should also change the print range for the spreadsheet. Otherwise, the border will print twice on the first page. First, it prints as a border. Then, it prints as part of the print range. In figure 4-15, the print range has been changed so it excludes rows 1 and 2. As a result, the first page of the spreadsheet will print correctly.

How to print more lines to the vertical inch Most printers print at six lines per vertical inch, but some printers can print at either six or eight lines per inch. If your printer has that capability, you can use the last command in figure 4-12 to specify that you want to print more lines per inch. Often, though, the compressed printing is difficult to read so you should use one of the other options for printing long spreadsheets.

How to print a wide spreadsheet

When you create a spreadsheet that is so wide that it can't be printed on a single page, *Lotus* prints it as shown in figure 4-16. Here, you can see that *Lotus* printed as many columns as it could print within the left and right margins of the first page. And it printed the remaining columns on the second page. If a spreadsheet has so many columns that it can't be printed on two pages, *Lotus* continues with as many pages as are necessary until all of the columns in the print range are printed.

Command

/Worksheet Page

Function

Insert a page break in a spreadsheet to tell *Lotus* where one printed page ends and the next one begins.

How to use this command

1. Move the cell pointer to the row that you want to print at the top of the next page. The cell pointer must be on the first column in this row. Otherwise, the command won't work properly.
2. Execute the /Worksheet Page command.
3. The new page symbol (: :) is then displayed to indicate where the page will break when you print the spreadsheet. Here, you can see that the page break occurs at row 48 of the spreadsheet.

```
A49: [W4] 500                                                         READY

     A          B              C           D           E          F
41  404 Public relations    12,000      13,100       8,000       -50%
42  405         Mailings    15,000      14,900      18,000        17%
43  406       Literature     7,400       7,180       7,400         0%
44  407        Guest day     3,000       2,850       3,000         0%
45  ----------------------------------------------------------------
46  400     AREA TOTALS:   110,400     114,550     110,900         0%
47  ----------------------------------------------------------------
48  ::
49  500 ADMINISTRATION
50  501 President's off.   150,000     148,900     160,000         6%
51  502   Provost's off.   120,000     122,000     127,000         6%
52  503       Admissions    78,000      74,000      78,000         0%
53  504        Registrar    82,000      81,300      82,000         0%
54  505          Testing    12,000       8,900       9,000       -33%
```

How to remove the new page symbol

/Worksheet Delete Row

Figure 4-13 The command for inserting a page break into a spreadsheet

Command name

/Print Printer Options Borders Rows

How to use this command

1. Start the /Print Printer Options Borders Rows command.
2. Use the anchor-and-point or the direct entry method to enter the range of cells that should be used for the border.
3. Press the Enter key.

Related command

/Print Printer Range

Use this command to change the print range for the spreadsheet. The print range shouldn't include the rows in the border range. If it does, the border rows will print twice on the first page.

Figure 4-14 The command for creating a border that is repeated at the top of each printed page

```
A1: [W4] ^#                                                          MENU
Range  Line  Page  Options  Clear  Align  Go  Quit
Print the specified range
                                   Print Settings
  Destination:  Printer

  Range:        A3..F86

  Header:       @|Expense Budget|Page #
  Footer:       EXP-BDGT.WK1

  Margins:
    Left 5     Right 80    Top 2    Bottom 4

  Borders:
    Columns
    Rows        A1..F2

  Setup string:

  Page length:  66

  Output:       As-Displayed (Formatted)

25-Jun-92  12:15 PM                                          NUM
```

Figure 4-15 The Print Settings screen with the borders option and print range set for the spreadsheet printed in figure 4-11

1991 Sales Summary Analysis 06/18/92 SALESSUM91

PRODUCT	JAN	FEB	MAR	APR	MAY	JUN
Product 1	92,520	74,016	90,670	120,276	118,426	93,445
Product 2	130,050	104,040	127,449	169,065	166,464	131,351
Product 3	170,582	136,465	167,170	221,756	218,344	172,287
Product 4	54,441	43,553	53,352	70,773	69,684	54,985
GROUP 1:	447,593	358,074	438,641	581,870	572,918	452,068
Product 5	66,614	53,292	65,282	86,599	85,266	67,281
Product 6	93,636	74,909	91,763	121,727	119,854	94,572
Product 7	122,819	98,255	120,362	159,664	157,208	124,047
Product 8	39,198	31,358	38,414	50,957	50,173	39,589
GROUP 2:	322,267	257,814	315			
TOTALS:	769,860	615,888	751			

Page 1

JUL	AUG	SEP	OCT	NOV	DEC
72,166	82,343	99,922	122,126	78,642	64,764
101,439	115,745	140,454	171,666	110,543	91,035
133,054	151,818	184,228	225,168	144,994	119,407
42,464	48,452	58,796	71,862	46,275	38,109
349,123	398,358	483,400	590,822	380,454	313,315
51,959	59,287	71,944	87,931	56,622	46,630
73,036	83,336	101,127	123,600	79,591	65,545
95,799	109,309	132,644	162,121	104,396	85,973
30,574	34,886	42,333	51,741	33,318	27,438
251,368	286,818	348,048	425,393	273,927	225,586
600,491	685,176	831,448	1,016,215	654,381	538,901

Page 2

Figure 4-16 How *Lotus* prints a wide spreadsheet by default

Command name	Next level	Next level	Next level	Function
/Print Printer Options	Borders	Columns		Identify the columns that will print on the left side of each page
	Setup			Set the pitch that will be used to print the spreadsheet
/Print Printer Options (release 3.X)	Advanced	Layout	Pitch	Set the pitch that will be used to print the spreadsheet
			Orientation	Set the printing orientation to portrait or landscape

Figure 4-17 The commands for printing wide spreadsheets so they're easier to read

Sometimes, this method of printing wide spreadsheets is acceptable. If you place the printed pages side by side, they accurately present the data in the spreadsheet. You can even tape the pages together and copy them when you want to distribute the data. But often, it's better if you can print the spreadsheet in a way that is easier to handle and read.

One way to print more columns on a page is to buy a printer with a wide carriage. Then, you can print 130 or more characters in a single line with standard sized type. However, a printer with a wide carriage costs more than one with a standard 8-1/2 inch carriage. And even a wide carriage may not be enough to accommodate all of the columns in a spreadsheet. In that case, you need to use one or more of the printing techniques presented in this chapter.

Figure 4-17 summarizes the commands you can use for printing wide spreadsheets. If you use a smaller type size, you can often print a wide spreadsheet on a single page as shown in figure 4-18. To print a spreadsheet this way, you use the commands for setting the margins and pitch as I explained earlier in this chapter. Here, the spreadsheet is printed at 17 pitch instead of the 12 pitch used in figure 4-16.

If you don't like to use condensed type because it's too small or if your printer doesn't provide for it, you can use the other commands in figure 4-17 to print a wide spreadsheet in a readable form. One way to do that is to print the spreadsheet with side borders. Another way is to print the spreadsheet sideways on the page.

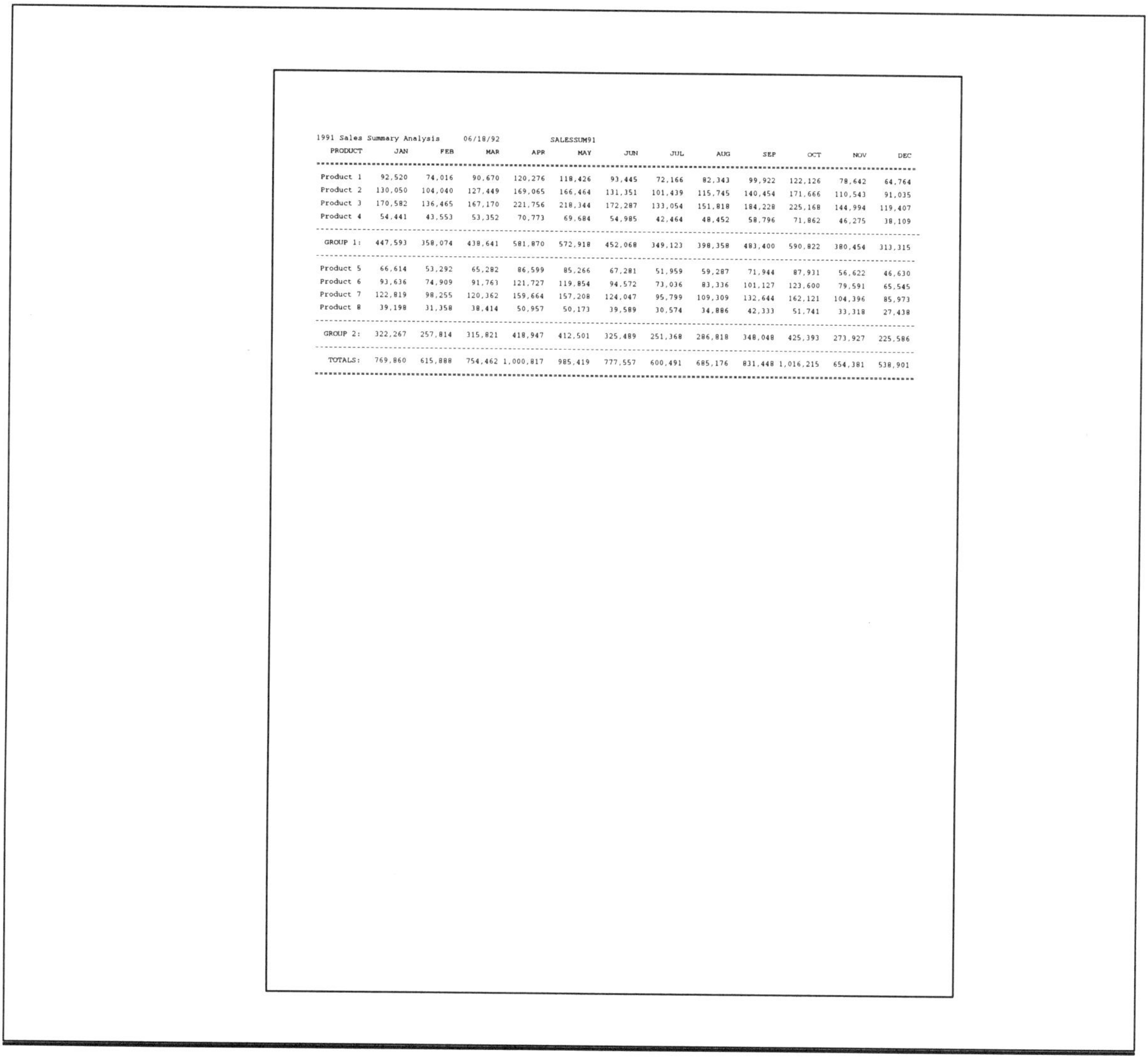

1991 Sales Summary Analysis 06/18/92 SALESSUM91

PRODUCT	JAN	FEB	MAR	APR	MAY	JUN	JUL	AUG	SEP	OCT	NOV	DEC
Product 1	92,520	74,016	90,670	120,276	118,426	93,445	72,166	82,343	99,922	122,126	78,642	64,764
Product 2	130,050	104,040	127,449	169,065	166,464	131,351	101,439	115,745	140,454	171,666	110,543	91,035
Product 3	170,582	136,465	167,170	221,756	218,344	172,287	133,054	151,818	184,228	225,168	144,994	119,407
Product 4	54,441	43,553	53,352	70,773	69,684	54,985	42,464	48,452	58,796	71,862	46,275	38,109
GROUP 1:	447,593	358,074	438,641	581,870	572,918	452,068	349,123	398,358	483,400	590,822	380,454	313,315
Product 5	66,614	53,292	65,282	86,599	85,266	67,281	51,959	59,287	71,944	87,931	56,622	46,630
Product 6	93,636	74,909	91,763	121,727	119,854	94,572	73,036	83,336	101,127	123,600	79,591	65,545
Product 7	122,819	98,255	120,362	159,664	157,208	124,047	95,799	109,309	132,644	162,121	104,396	85,973
Product 8	39,198	31,358	38,414	50,957	50,173	39,589	30,574	34,886	42,333	51,741	33,318	27,438
GROUP 2:	322,267	257,814	315,821	418,947	412,501	325,489	251,368	286,818	348,048	425,393	273,927	225,586
TOTALS:	769,860	615,888	754,462	1,000,817	985,419	777,557	600,491	685,176	831,448	1,016,215	654,381	538,901

Figure 4-18 The spreadsheet in figure 4-16 after it has been printed on a single page with condensed print

How to print a wide spreadsheet with repeating borders When you print a wide spreadsheet on two or more pages, the spreadsheet is easier to read if you repeat the row identifiers in the first column of the spreadsheet as shown in figure 4-19. Then, the second page of the spreadsheet makes sense without referring to the first page to see what each row represents. In this example, the spreadsheet is also printed with headers that put the date and page number on each page.

27-May-92 Sales Analysis Summary 1991 Page 1

SALESSUM91

PRODUCT	JAN	FEB	MAR	APR	MAY	JUN
Product 1	92,520	74,016	90,670	120,276	118,426	93,445
Product 2	130,050	104,040	127,449	169,065	166,464	131,351
Product 3	170,582	136,465	167,170	221,756	218,344	172,287
Product 4	54,441	43,553	53,352	70,773	69,684	54,985
GROUP 1:	447,593	358,074	438,641	581,870	572,918	452,068
Product 5	66,614	53,292	65,282	86,599	85,266	67,281
Product 6	93,636	74,909	91,763	121,727	119,854	94,572
Product 7	122,819	98,255	120,362	159,664	157,208	124,047
Product 8	39,198	31,358	38,414	50,957	50,173	39,589
GROUP 2:	322,267	257,814	315			
TOTALS:	769,860	615,888	754			

27-May-92 Sales Analysis Summary 1991 Page 2

SALESSUM91

PRODUCT	JUL	AUG	SEP	OCT	NOV	DEC
Product 1	72,166	82,343	99,922	122,126	78,642	64,764
Product 2	101,439	115,745	140,454	171,666	110,543	91,035
Product 3	133,054	151,818	184,228	225,168	144,994	119,407
Product 4	42,464	48,452	58,796	71,862	46,275	38,109
GROUP 1:	349,123	398,358	483,400	590,822	380,454	313,315
Product 5	51,959	59,287	71,944	87,931	56,622	46,630
Product 6	73,036	83,336	101,127	123,600	79,591	65,545
Product 7	95,799	109,309	132,644	162,121	104,396	85,973
Product 8	30,574	34,886	42,333	51,741	33,318	27,438
GROUP 2:	251,368	286,818	348,048	425,393	273,927	225,586
TOTALS:	600,491	685,176	831,448	1,016,215	654,381	538,901

Figure 4-19 The spreadsheet in figure 4-16 after it has been printed with headers and column borders

Command name

/Print Printer Options Borders Columns

How to use this command

1. Start the /Print Printer Options Borders Columns command.
2. Use the anchor-and-point or the direct entry method to enter the range of cells that should be used for the border.
3. Press the Enter key.

Related command

/Print Printer Range

Use this command to change the print range for the spreadsheet. The print range shouldn't include the columns in the border range. If it does, the border columns will print twice on the first page.

Figure 4-20 The command for creating a border that is repeated on the left side of each page

To repeat the row identifiers, you use the /Print Printer Options Borders Columns command as summarized in figure 4-20. This command lets you identify the column or columns that you want repeated on each page of the spreadsheet. Usually, you just want to repeat column A on each page so column A is the border.

When you start this command, it asks you for range of cells that you want to use for the border. Then, you enter the range of cells using either the anchor-and-point or the direct entry method. When you press the Enter key, the range of cells is added to the list of print settings for the spreadsheet as shown in figure 4-21. Here, the border range is A3..A20.

When you use a border, you should also change the print range for the spreadsheet. Otherwise, the border will be printed twice on the first page. First, it prints as a border. Then, it prints as part of the print range. In figure 4-21, the print range has been changed so it excludes column A. As a result, the first page of the spreadsheet will print correctly.

How to print a spreadsheet in landscape mode (release 3.X)

Figure 4-22 shows a spreadsheet that has been printed in two different modes. *Portrait mode* is the normal orientation for a report, and *landscape mode* is a

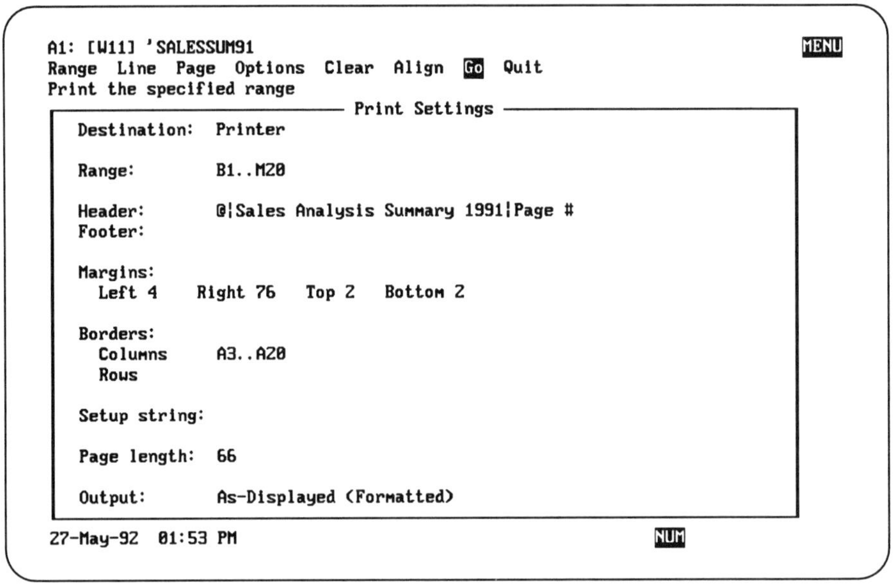

Figure 4-21 The Print Settings screen with the borders option and print range set for the spreadsheet printed in figure 4-19

sideways orientation. When you print a wide spreadsheet in landscape mode, you can often print it on a single page without condensed type.

However, landscape mode only works with the 3.X releases of *Lotus*, and it doesn't work with all printers. In particular, releases 3.0 and 3.1 require a laser printer, and release 3.4 doesn't work with all dot-matrix printers. The best way to find out whether this feature works with your printer is to try it.

Figure 4-23 shows you how to use the /Print Printer Options Advanced Layout Orientation command to print a spreadsheet in landscape mode. But the process isn't as easy as you might expect because *Lotus* doesn't automatically adjust to the new print orientation. As a result, you must issue commands that adjust the page length and set a new right margin before you print a spreadsheet in landscape mode. You may also have to experiment with these settings before you can get them to work correctly with your printer.

How to use a sideways print utility to print in landscape mode

If you aren't using *Lotus* release 3.X, you can use a *sideways print utility* to print a spreadsheet in landscape mode. A program like this will do the job for you even if you're using *Lotus* release 2.0 and a simple dot-matrix printer. Before you can use a sideways print utility, though, you must install and run it under *Lotus 1-2-3* as an *add-in program.*

Portrait

1991 Sales Summary Analysis 06/18/92 SALESSUM91

PRODUCT	JAN	FEB	MAR	APR	MAY	JUN	JUL	AUG	SEP	OCT	NOV	DEC
Product 1	92,520	74,016	90,670	120,276	118,426	93,445	72,166	82,343	99,922	122,126	78,642	64,764
Product 2	130,050	104,040	127,449	169,065	166,464	131,351	101,439	115,745	140,454	171,666	110,543	91,035
Product 3	170,582	136,465	167,170	221,756	218,344	172,287	133,054	151,818	184,228	225,168	144,994	119,407
Product 4	54,441	43,553	53,352	70,773	69,684	54,985	42,464	48,452	58,796	71,862	46,275	38,109
GROUP 1:	447,593	358,074	438,641	581,870	572,918	452,068	349,123	398,358	483,400	590,822	380,454	313,315
Product 5	66,614	53,292	65,282	86,599	85,266	67,281	51,959	59,287	71,944	87,931	56,622	46,630
Product 6	93,636	74,909	91,763	121,727	119,854	94,572	73,036	83,336	101,127	123,600	79,591	65,545
Product 7	122,819	98,255	120,362	159,664	157,208	124,047	95,799	109,309	132,644	162,121	104,396	85,973
Product 8	39,198	31,358	38,414	50,957	50,173	39,589	30,574	34,886	42,333	51,741	33,318	27,438
GROUP 2:	322,267	257,814	315,821	418,947	412,501	325,489	251,368	286,818	348,048	425,393	273,927	225,586
TOTALS:	769,860	615,888	754,462	1,000,817	985,419	777,557	600,491	685,176	831,448	1,016,215	654,381	538,901

Landscape

1991 Sales Summary Analysis 06/18/92 SALESSUM91

PRODUCT	JAN	FEB	MAR	APR	MAY	JUN	JUL	AUG	SEP	OCT	NOV	DEC
Product 1	92,520	74,016	90,670	120,276	118,426	93,445	72,166	82,343	99,922	122,126	78,642	64,764
Product 2	130,050	104,040	127,449	169,065	166,464	131,351	101,439	115,745	140,454	171,666	110,543	91,035
Product 3	170,582	136,465	167,170	221,756	218,344	172,287	133,054	151,818	184,228	225,168	144,994	119,407
Product 4	54,441	43,553	53,352	70,773	69,684	54,985	42,464	48,452	58,796	71,862	46,275	38,109
GROUP 1:	447,593	358,074	438,641	581,870	572,918	452,068	349,123	398,358	483,400	590,822	380,454	313,315
Product 5	66,614	53,292	65,282	86,599	85,266	67,281	51,959	59,287	71,944	87,931	56,622	46,630
Product 6	93,636	74,909	91,763	121,727	119,854	94,572	73,036	83,336	101,127	123,600	79,591	65,545
Product 7	122,819	98,255	120,362	159,664	157,208	124,047	95,799	109,309	132,644	162,121	104,396	85,973
Product 8	39,198	31,358	38,414	50,957	50,173	39,589	30,574	34,886	42,333	51,741	33,318	27,438
GROUP 2:	322,267	257,814	315,821	418,947	412,501	325,489	251,368	286,818	348,048	425,393	273,927	225,586
TOTALS:	769,860	615,888	754,462	1,000,817	985,419	777,557	600,491	685,176	831,448	1,016,215	654,381	538,901

Figure 4-22 The spreadsheet in figure 4-18 printed in both portrait and landscape orientations

Command name (release 3.X)

/Print Printer Options Advanced Layout Orientation

The two options at the next level

Portrait	Vertical orientation as shown in figure 4-22
Landscape	Horizontal orientation as shown in figure 4-22

How to use this command

1. Start the /Print Printer Options Advanced Layout Orientation command.
2. Select the Landscape option.
3. Press the Enter key.

Related commands

1. Use the /Print Printer Options Pg-Length command to reduce the page length to accommodate landscape orientation.
2. Use the /Print Printer Options Margins Right command to set the right margin so it will accommodate the increased line length of landscape orientation.

Notes

The Landscape option of the /Print Options Advance Layout Orientation command will only work with printers that can print in landscape mode. If your printer can't, this command will have no effect on the printing.

Figure 4-23 The command for printing a spreadsheet in landscape mode when you use *Lotus* release 3.X

The most popular sideways print utility is called *Sideways*, and it sells for about $70. Before you buy it, though, you should know that it can take a long time to print a spreadsheet when you use a utility. For instance, it took over three minutes to print the one page spreadsheet in figure 4-22 on a dot-matrix printer. In addition, the characters that *Sideways* prints on a dot-matrix printer aren't always as easy to read as the normal print. As a result, it may be more practical for you to use one of the other techniques presented in this chapter for printing wide spreadsheets.

Command name	Next level	Function
/Print Printer Clear	All	Clear all the current print settings and return to the default settings
	Range	Clear the current print range
	Borders	Clear the current border settings
	Format	Clear the current format settings like the margin and page-length settings

Figure 4-24 The command for clearing print settings

How to clear print options

When you set print options like the margins and page length, they are saved with the spreadsheet when you use the /File Save command. *Lotus* also saves the settings for the header, footer, border, print range, and so on. Then, if you want to change one or more of these settings, you can reset them using the appropriate commands.

Sometimes, though, you may want to change some of the settings back to the defaults without taking the time to use the individual commands. In that case, you can use the /Print Printer Clear command as summarized in figure 4-24. To return all of the print settings to the defaults, you select the All option. To clear just the print range, you select the Range option. To clear just the border, you select the Borders option. And to clear just the formatting options such as the margins and page length, you select the Format option.

How to save more than one group of print settings for a single spreadsheet (release 3.X)

If you're using *Lotus* release 3.X, you can save more than one group of print settings for the same spreadsheet. For instance, you can save one group of settings for printing the entire spreadsheet and another group of settings for printing just the rows that relate to the Administration category of the spreadsheet. Or, you can save one group of settings for printing a spreadsheet in portrait orientation and another group for printing it in landscape orientation.

To save and use the settings, you use the /Print Printer Options Name command as summarized in figure 4-25. After you set the print settings the way you want them, you use the Create option of the /Print Printer Options Name command to save the print settings. When you start this command, it

Command name

/Print Printer Options Name

Next Level	**Function**
Create	Assign a name to the current print settings so you can use them again without having to specify each setting again
Use	Select a named group of print settings that you have saved for use with the current spreadsheet
Delete	Delete a named group of print settings

How to save a print setting

1. Start the /Print Printer Options Name Create command.
2. Type the name to be used for the current print settings at this prompt:

   ```
   Enter print settings name:
   ```

   The name can be up to 15 characters long, and it can consist of any combination of letters, digits, or symbols except <<.
3. Press the Enter key to save the named print settings.

How to retrieve a print setting

1. Start the /Print Printer Options Name Use command.
2. From the list of print settings that appears after the prompt, select the name of the setting you want by highlighting it or by typing it:

   ```
   Enter print settings name to use:
   PORTRAIT    LANDSCAPE
   ```
3. Press the Enter key.

Figure 4-25 The *Lotus* release 3.X commands for saving and retrieving the print settings that apply to a spreadsheet

asks you for the name that you want to use for the print settings. This name is called the *print settings name*. It can be up to 15 characters long, and it can include letters, digits, or symbols. After you type the name and press the Enter key, the print settings are saved using the name that you specified.

To change from one group of print settings to another, you select the Use option of the /Print Printer Options Name command. Then, the available print setting names are displayed on the third line of the control panel. To select the one you want to use, highlight it and press the Enter key. Then, you can print the spreadsheet using the standard /Print commands.

If you want to modify a group of print settings after you've named them, you use /Print Printer Options Name Use command to access the named print settings. Next, you modify the settings. Then, you use the Create option of the /Print Printer Options Name command to save the current print settings with the original print settings name.

If you decide that you want to delete a print settings name, you do so by selecting the Delete option. Then, you select the name that you want deleted. When you press the Enter key, the print settings name is deleted along with its print settings.

How to use background printing for lengthy print jobs

If you're using *Lotus* release 2.X or release 3.4, you have to wait for a spreadsheet to print before you can continue your work on a spreadsheet. With releases 3.0 and 3.1, however, you don't have to wait. Once you send a job to the printer, you can continue your work. This is possible because releases 3.0 and 3.1 automatically provide for *background printing*. This just means that the printing is done independently.

If waiting for a printer when you're using release 2.X or 3.4 is slowing you down, you can use a utility program to provide for background printing. The use of this utility is explained in detail in chapter 15. This chapter also shows you how to control the background printing that is done by releases 3.0 and 3.1.

Discussion

If your PC has more than one printer available to it and you don't know how to switch from one printer to the other, chapter 15 shows you how to make the switch. Then, you can switch to a wide-carriage printer or a laser printer before printing a wide or a long spreadsheet. If you're using release 2.X, you use the Interface and Name options of the /Worksheet Global Default Printer command. But if you're using release 3.X, you can use that command or one of the /Print Printer commands to make the switch.

As you use the /Print Printer command for release 3.X as described in this chapter, you'll see some options for enhanced printing. One of these options, for example, lets you use one typeface for the header and the footer of a spreadsheet and another typeface for the spreadsheet itself. Although some of these enhancement options are presented in chapter 17, most are so limited that they aren't useful.

On the other hand, if you're using one of the *Lotus* releases that includes the *WYSIWYG* add-in program, I recommend that you read chapter 18 to learn more about it. Here, you'll learn how you can use *WYSIWYG* to adjust the fonts that are used in a spreadsheet so more characters can be printed both horizontally and vertically on the page. You'll also learn how to use *WYSIWYG* for landscape printing. For some printers, this works when the *Lotus* capability for landscape printing doesn't.

Terms

header
footer
pitch
condensed mode
setup string
new page symbol
border
portrait mode
landscape mode
sideways print utility
add-in program
print settings name
background printing

Objectives

1. Print a long spreadsheet in a form that's easy to read by using the *Lotus* commands for inserting page breaks, printing headers and footers, and printing borders.
2. Print a wide spreadsheet in a form that's easy to read by using the *Lotus* commands for printing borders, printing with more characters per inch, and printing in landscape mode.
3. If you're using *Lotus* release 3.X, save two or more groups of print settings for one spreadsheet. Then, retrieve any one of the named print settings for use in a printing operation.

Chapter 5

Five guidelines that will help you work more efficiently

This chapter presents five quick guidelines that will help you work more efficiently. The first two are relatively trivial, but they will save you a little time if you follow them. The next two are more significant so they can save you a considerable amount of time if you follow them. The last one is one that some of you won't want to follow, but it's probably the most important one.

Identify each spreadsheet with title, date, and filename

It's easy to create spreadsheet files, and it's easy to create variations of the same spreadsheet file. That's why this first guideline encourages you to identify each spreadsheet with title, date, and filename as shown in figure 5-1.

If you put the filename in one of the first rows, you'll always remember the name you used for the file. In figure 5-1, the filename is PFORMA93. And if you use the @NOW function to put the date in one of the first rows, you'll always be able to tell which version of a printed spreadsheet was done on the most recent date.

It doesn't matter much where you put these items of information as long as they're easy to identify. For instance, many of the other examples in this book show the filename over the right-most column of the spreadsheet, not in cell A2. Either form is okay, but once you find a form that you like, you may as well use it as the standard for all your spreadsheets.

If you prefer to use headers to identify your spreadsheets as described in chapter 4, that's okay too. When you put the current date in the header, you don't have to use the @NOW function in the spreadsheet itself, and the header is printed on every page. The disadvantage is that you can't see what the header contains unless you use the /Print Printer Options Header command or you print the spreadsheet.

Proforma Projection for 1993	12-Jun-92		COGS =		41.0%
PFORMA93			Marketing =		$300,000
Level	1	2	3	4	5
Sales	2,600,000	2,700,000	2,800,000	2,900,000	3,000,000
Cost of goods sold	1,066,000	1,107,000	1,148,000	1,189,000	1,230,000
Gross profit	1,534,000	1,593,000	1,652,000	1,711,000	1,770,000
Salaries & wages	650,000	650,000	650,000	650,000	650,000
Rent & utilities	215,000	215,000	215,000	215,000	215,000
Equip. & maintenance	95,000	95,000	95,000	95,000	95,000
Order handling	117,000	121,500	126,000	130,500	135,000
Marketing	300,000	300,000	300,000	300,000	300,000
Miscellaneous	17,500	17,500	17,500	17,500	17,500
Total	1,394,500	1,399,000	1,403,500	1,408,000	1,412,500
Operating profit	139,500	194,000	248,500	303,000	357,500
Bad debt	75,400	78,300	81,200	84,100	87,000
Interest	35,000	35,000	35,000	35,000	35,000
Total	110,400	113,300	116,200	119,100	122,000
Before tax profit	29,100	80,700	132,300	183,900	235,500

Figure 5-1 A spreadsheet with a heading that identifies the spreadsheet and documents its assumptions

Document any assumptions in the spreadsheet heading

If you make certain assumptions in a spreadsheet that aren't obvious, it makes sense to document them in one of the first rows of the spreadsheet. The spreadsheet in figure 5-1, for example, documents the facts that 41 percent is used for calculating the cost of goods sold and $300,000 is used as the marketing expense. Then, if you change the assumptions and reprint the spreadsheet, you can tell at a glance which spreadsheet has made which assumptions.

When you document the assumptions as shown in figure 5-1, you should use the values in the document portion of the spreadsheet in the formulas in the body of the spreadsheet. Then, if the cost of goods sold assumption is changed to 39 percent, all the related values in the spreadsheet will reflect this change. To do this for a spreadsheet like the one in figure 5-1, though, requires the use of absolute addresses as explained in chapter 2.

```
Monthly Expenses          06/12/92              MAREXP
March
                                        Dollar  Percent
                   Budget   Expense  Variance  Variance

Salaries & Wages   50,000    51,784     1,784      3.6%
Rent & Utilities   17,500    18,222       722      4.1%
Maintenance         7,750     7,912       162      2.1%
Supplies            8,250     7,211   (1,039)    -12.6%
Miscellaneous       1,500     1,922       422     28.1%

Total              85,000    87,051     2,051      2.4%
```

Figure 5-2 A monthly expense spreadsheet that can be used as the basis for starting new expense spreadsheets

Use old spreadsheets or template spreadsheets as the basis for new ones

After you work with *Lotus* for a while, you'll probably realize that many of your spreadsheets are similar. If that's true, this guideline encourages you to use old spreadsheets as the basis for new ones. To say this another way, try to avoid starting a new spreadsheet from scratch.

In figure 5-2, for example, you can see the spreadsheet for a March expense summary. Obviously, you can use this spreadsheet as the basis for any monthly expense summary. When you want to create the spreadsheet for April, you can retrieve the spreadsheet for March, change the March data to April data, print the spreadsheet, and save the new spreadsheet with a new filename.

Often, though, it makes sense to use an old spreadsheet as the basis for a new one, even when the two spreadsheets aren't that similar. Most spreadsheets, for instance, require heading information and row identifiers like those in figure 5-2. And many business spreadsheets require the Comma format with zero decimal places as the global default. So if you just start with an old spreadsheet that has some column width and formatting similarities, it's better than starting from scratch.

If you regularly use the same type of spreadsheet for data summaries, you should consider creating a *template spreadsheet* (or just *template*) that you can use for starting the spreadsheets. In figure 5-3, for example, you can see a template spreadsheet that has been created from the spreadsheet in figure 5-2. Here, I've put question marks in all the cells that require new data. Then, to create an expense summary for a new month, all you have to do is enter data in those cells that contain question marks. That will put proper values in the

Monthly Expenses		06/12/92		???EXP
??				
			Dollar	Percent
	Budget	Expense	Variance	Variance
Salaries & Wages	50,000	??	(50,000)	ERR
Rent & Utilities	17,500	??	(17,500)	ERR
Maintenance	7,750	??	(7,750)	ERR
Supplies	8,250	??	(8,250)	ERR
Miscellaneous	1,500	??	(1,500)	ERR
Total	85,000	0	(85,000)	ERR

Figure 5-3 A template spreadsheet that can be used as the basis for starting new expense spreadsheets

cells that show ERR. When you're done, you can save the file with a new name like JUNEXP as indicated by the filename in the cell in the upper right-hand corner of the spreadsheet. When I use a template like this, I give it a filename like TEMPEXP to indicate that it is a template.

Plan a complicated spreadsheet before you start creating it

When you create a simple spreadsheet, you can usually design it as you create it on your PC. For more complicated spreadsheets, though, it makes sense to take a few minutes to plan what you're going to do before you start doing it. In figure 5-4, for example, you can see a written plan for a spreadsheet that is going to summarize data at three levels: monthly, quarterly, and yearly. These summaries are going to be based on the detailed sales data for each of the twelve months in a year.

For a spreadsheet this complicated, it often helps to do a sketch of the spreadsheet layout as shown in figure 5-5. Here, the four areas of the spreadsheet are laid out on a diagonal. Then, if you want to delete or insert one or more columns or rows in any one of the four areas, it won't affect the data in the other areas. If you don't design your spreadsheet on a diagonal, deleting a row in one data area can affect the data in another area.

In general, I recommend that you keep your spreadsheets simple so I hope you won't create and use many spreadsheets that are as complicated as the one in figure 5-5. One way to simplify is to use a separate spreadsheet for each of the data areas of a large spreadsheet. For instance, you can use one spreadsheet for each of the twelve months in figure 5-5, one for each of the

Year-to-date summary	Get total sales information from Quarterly summaries Show sales by salesperson and region Calculate year-to-date sales
Quarterly summaries	Get product group sales information from Monthly sales summaries Calculate quarterly product group sales Show sales by product groups, salesperson, and region Calculate total sales
Monthly sales summaries	Get product group sales information from Monthly sales data Show sales by product groups, salespeople, and region Calculate total sales Calculate commissions
Monthly sales data	Enter monthly sales data for each product Calculate sales by product group for each salesperson

Figure 5-4 A detailed listing of the functions for a sales summary spreadsheet

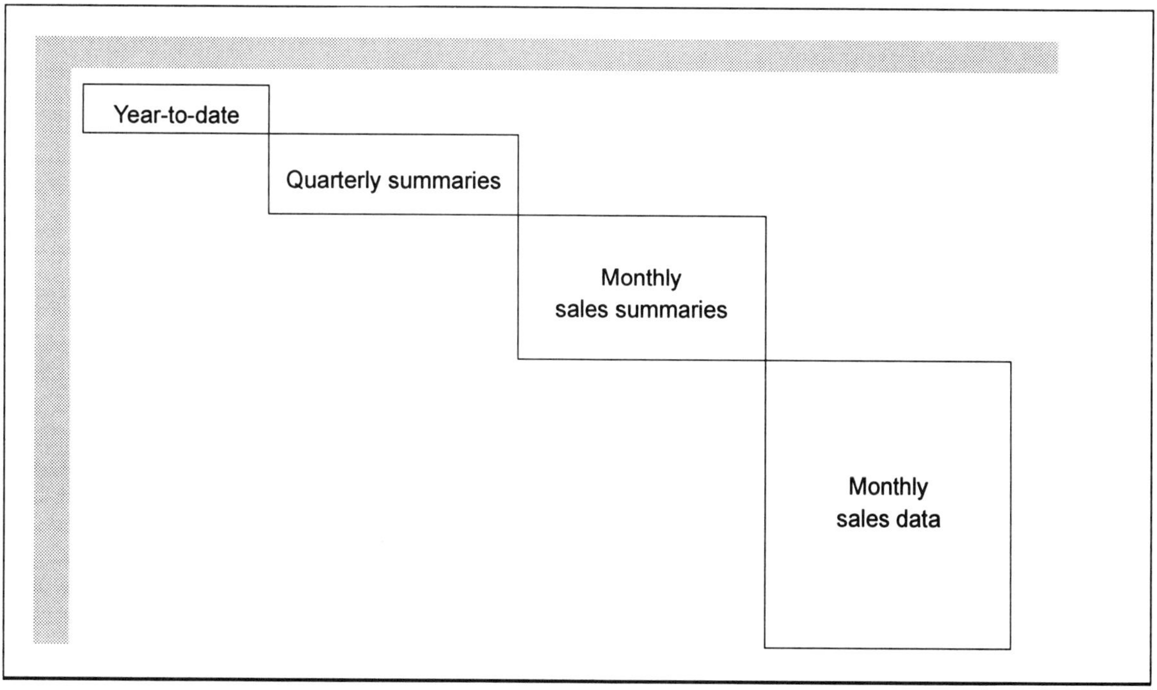

Figure 5-5 A map of the sales summary spreadsheet

four quarters, and so on. In this case, you may have to take data from one spreadsheet and re-enter it into another, but each spreadsheet will be so easy to use that you're likely to save time overall.

If you're using *Lotus* release 2.2 or later, though, you can link the cells in one spreadsheet with those in another. Then, you don't have to re-enter data from one spreadsheet to another. This makes it more practical to simplify a large spreadsheet by dividing it into several smaller spreadsheets. So if you frequently use large spreadsheets, I recommend that you read chapter 11 to learn how to link cells between spreadsheets.

Do your own development work

Although it's tempting to delegate *Lotus* work to a subordinate, I just can't recommend that. At the least, I recommend that you develop your own spreadsheets for the analytical applications. As you develop them, you'll get ideas for making them more useful that you'll never get if you delegate the development work.

Once you've established the spreadsheets, you can delegate the work of keeping them up-to-date to someone else. Whenever a spreadsheet has to be modified due to changes in your operations, though, you should consider doing the work yourself. But don't think of this as clerical work; think of it as analytical work. There's no question in my mind that *Lotus* can make good managers even better, but only if they do the development work themselves.

Discussion

All five of the guidelines in this chapter can help you get more done. If I were to add a sixth, it would be to keep your spreadsheets simple. Although you would think that would be easy advice to follow, many *Lotus* users seem to enjoy complexity. Sometimes, it takes extra effort to keep a spreadsheet simple, but that usually pays off in the long run.

Terms

template spreadsheet
template

Objectives

1. Describe the use of a template spreadsheet.
2. Follow the five guidelines presented in this chapter as you create and use spreadsheets of your own.

Section 2

Lotus 1-2-3 skills for special purposes

This section consists of ten chapters. Each one presents the *Lotus* skills that you need for a specific purpose such as working with large spreadsheets, sorting the data in a spreadsheet, linking cells between spreadsheets, and transferring data into *Lotus* from another program. For ease of use, each chapter in this section is treated as an independent module so you can read the chapters in whatever sequence you prefer.

Chapter 6

How to use the most practical @functions

In chapter 2, you learned how to use these five @functions: @NOW, @SUM, @AVG, @COUNT, and @ROUND. If you use *Lotus* just for simple spreadsheets, these may be the only @functions you'll ever need. However, you should at least be aware of the other types of @functions that are available to you.

In this chapter, I'll introduce you to the eight types of @functions that *Lotus* provides. Then, I'll show you how to use 17 of the most useful @functions for business applications. When you finish this chapter, you'll know what kind of @functions are available to you and how you might want to use them. Then, if you need one of them later on, you can refer back to this chapter for the operational details.

An introduction to the eight types of @functions that *Lotus* provides

Lotus release 2.4 provides 93 different @functions. Some of the earlier releases provide a few less, and the later releases will probably provide a few more. Regardless of the total number of @functions provided, however, they can be divided into the eight types that are summarized in figure 6-1.

As you can see in this figure, the first type of @function performs operations that are related to the date and the time. In chapter 2, you learned how to use the @NOW function. In this chapter, you'll learn how to use the others listed here.

The second type of @function in figure 6-1 performs statistical operations. In chapter 2, you learned how to use these three simple ones: @SUM, @AVG, and @COUNT. However, *Lotus* also provides statistical functions that perform operations like calculating the standard deviation of a list of values. I'll show you how to use @MIN, @MAX, @STD, and @VAR in this chapter.

The third type of @function in figure 6-1 performs financial operations. If your specialty is finance, you shouldn't have any trouble using these @functions because they use terminology and perform operations that you are already familiar with. Even if your specialty isn't finance, though, some of these @functions may be useful to you. So in this chapter, I'll show you how to use @FV, @PMT, and @DDB.

The fourth type of @function in figure 6-1 performs mathematical operations like getting the absolute value of a number or getting the sine or cosine of an angle. If your specialty is mathematics, you shouldn't have any trouble using these @functions because they use terminology and perform operations that you are already familiar with. In chapter 2, I showed you how to use the @ROUND function because it's occasionally useful for business applications. The only other mathematical @function that you're likely to use for business applications is @SQRT, so I'll describe it in this chapter.

The fifth type of @function figure 6-1 performs logical operations. These operations can be used in conjunction with any of the other types of @functions. In this chapter, I'll show you how to use the primary logical @function, the @IF function, because it's useful for some business applications.

The last three types of @functions in figure 6-1 perform special, string, and database operations. The special @functions perform operations like getting information about a cell or its contents. The string @functions perform operations like counting the number of characters in a label. And the database @functions perform operations like getting the average of the values in a database given certain selection criteria. In general, though, you shouldn't need any of these for business applications. That's why they're not covered in this book.

If you want information about some of the @functions that aren't covered in this chapter, you can learn about them by reading your *Lotus* manual. In fact, one of the sections in your manual presents all of the @functions for your release, and the @functions are arranged in alphabetical order within this section so they're easy to find.

How to use 17 @functions for business applications

Now, I'll show you how to use 17 of the @functions in figure 6-1. I've picked the ones that you're most likely to use for business applications. Before I start, though, I want to make sure that you remember what the syntax of a *Lotus* @function is.

The syntax of an @function Figure 6-2 summarizes the *syntax* of an @function. As you may remember from chapter 2, the *syntax* of an @function always starts with the *function name*. With few exceptions, the function name is followed by one or more *arguments* in parentheses. If there is more than one argument, the arguments are separated by commas as shown in this figure.

When you enter an @function into a formula, the arguments can be values, cell addresses, or formulas. The first argument in figure 6-2, for example, represents the principal amount of a loan. When you use this argument in an @function, though, the principal can be expressed as a value

@Function type	Typical functions	Examples
Date and time	Get the current date and time	`@NOW`
	Get the current date only	`@TODAY`
	Convert a label that looks like a date to its date value	`@DATEVALUE`
Statistical	Get the total of the values in a range	`@SUM`
	Get the average of the values in a range	`@AVG`
	Count the non-empty cells in a range	`@COUNT`
	Get the standard deviation of the values in a range	`@STD`
Financial	Calculate the periodic payment required to pay off a loan	`@PMT`
	Calculate the future value of a series of equal payments	`@FV`
Mathematical	Round a value	`@ROUND`
	Take the square root of a value	`@SQRT`
	Return the integer portion of a value	`@INT`
	Generate a random number between 0 and 1	`@RAND`
	Get the sine, cosine, or tangent of an angle	`@SIN` `@COS` `@TAN`
Logical	Take one action if a condition is true; take another if it's false	`@IF`
Special	Return information about a cell or its contents	`@CELL`
	Count the number of columns in a range	`@COLS`
	Count the number of rows in a range	`@ROWS`
String	Count the number of characters in a string	`@LENGTH`
	Convert the characters in a string to lowercase	`@LOWER`
Database	Get the average of the fields in a database table based on certain criteria	`@DAVG`
	Count the non-empty fields in a database table based on certain criteria	`@DCOUNT`

Figure 6-1 The eight types of @functions that *Lotus* provides

Function name **Arguments**

```
@PMT(principal,interest,term)
```

Figure 6-2 The syntax of a typical @function

@Function name	Syntax(arguments)	Function
`@NOW`	`@NOW`	Return the date value for the current date and time.
`@TODAY`	`@TODAY`	Return the date value for the current date only.
`@DATEVALUE`	`@DATEVALUE(date)`	Convert a label that looks like a date to its date value.
`@TIMEVALUE`	`@TIMEVALUE(time)`	Convert a label that looks like a time to its time value.
`@DATE`	`@DATE(year,month,day)`	Return the date number based on the argument values. For instance, @DATE(92,04,14) returns the date value for April 14, 1992.

Figure 6-3 Five date and time @functions

(10000), a cell address for a cell that contains a value (D4), or a formula that calculates a value (C4+D4). You'll see examples of these different types of arguments as you continue with this chapter.

How to use five date and time @functions Figure 6-3 summarizes five date and time @functions. As I explained in chapter 2, you use the @NOW function to get the current date. However, *Lotus* returns the date as a number like 33938 to represent November 30, 1992. Then, to display this number as a date, you use the /Range Format Date command to give the cell one of five date formats.

What I didn't explain in chapter 2 is that the number that *Lotus* gets for the @NOW function includes the current time as well as the current date. At 12 noon on November 30, 1992, for example, *Lotus* gets this number:

```
33938.5
```

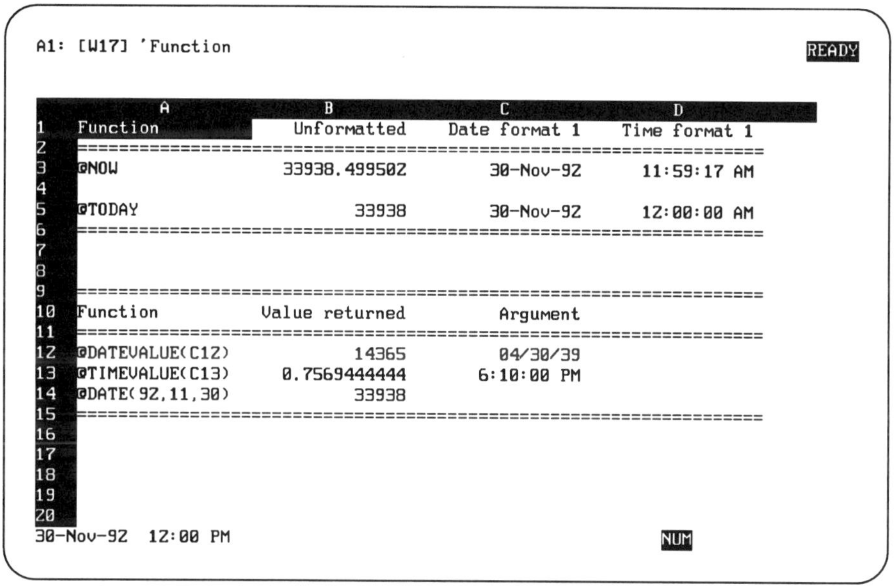

```
A1: [W17] 'Function                                                    READY

              A                  B               C                D
1   Function                Unformatted     Date format 1    Time format 1
2   =================================================================
3   @NOW                 33938.499502       30-Nov-92        11:59:17 AM
4
5   @TODAY                      33938       30-Nov-92        12:00:00 AM
6   =================================================================
7
8
9   =================================================================
10  Function              Value returned        Argument
11  =================================================================
12  @DATEVALUE(C12)             14365            04/30/39
13  @TIMEVALUE(C13)      0.7569444444          6:10:00 PM
14  @DATE(92,11,30)             33938
15  =================================================================
16
17
18
19
20
30-Nov-92  12:00 PM                                          NUM
```

Figure 6-4 The five date and time @functions used in a spreadsheet

Here, the number to the left of the decimal represents the date. This is the day number counting from January 1, 1900, as day 1. Then, the number to the right of the decimal point represents the time as the portion of the day that has gone by. Since 12 noon represents half a day, the decimal fraction above is .5.

Figure 6-4 shows the five @functions in figure 6-3 as they are used in a spreadsheet. Here, you can see that the @TODAY function is like the @NOW function, but it returns the current day number only, not the decimal fraction for the time. In the example for the @NOW function, you can see that the decimal fraction is .499502. It represents 11:59:17 AM. To convert the time portion of a date number to a readable format, you use one of the options of the /Range Format Date Time command. In figure 6-4, I used the first option to format the time.

The @DATEVALUE and @TIMEVALUE functions take a valid date like 04/03/39 or a valid time like 6:10 PM and convert it to the *Lotus* date or time value. In figure 6-4, for example, you can see how these functions can be used with arguments that are the addresses for cells that contain labels. Then, if the label is in an acceptable format for a date or time, the @DATEVALUE and @TIMEVALUE functions perform the conversions.

The last @function in figure 6-4, @DATE, converts an argument like

```
(92,11,30)
```

@Function name	Syntax(arguments)	Function
`@SUM`	`@SUM(range)`	Calculate the sum of the values in a range
`@AVG`	`@AVG(range)`	Calculate the average value in a range
`@COUNT`	`@COUNT(range)`	Return the number of non-empty cells in a range
`@MIN`	`@MIN(range)`	Return the lowest value in a range
`@MAX`	`@MAX(range)`	Return the highest value in a range
`@STD`	`@STD(range)`	Calculate the standard deviation of a range of values
`@VAR`	`@VAR(range)`	Calculate the variance of a range of values

Figure 6-5 Seven statistical @functions

to the *Lotus* day number. When you use this @function, you can enter the actual year, month, and day values as arguments. Or, you can enter cell addresses that point to cells that contain year, month, and day values.

The benefit of the *Lotus* date system is that it lets you perform calculations on dates and times. If, for example, you want to know how many days have passed between two dates, you can subtract one date number from the other. Or if you want to enter the date number for every Wednesday in a year into a range of cells, you can add multiples of seven to the date number for the first Wednesday in the year.

How to use seven statistical @functions Figure 6-5 summarizes the seven statistical @functions that come with *Lotus* release 2.4. In chapter 2, you were introduced to the first three of these, and the last four work the same way as the first three. The argument for all seven @functions is just the range of cells that you want to operate upon.

Figure 6-6 illustrates the use of the seven statistical @functions. Here, you can see that the @MIN and @MAX functions extract the minimum and maximum values from a range of values, but these values are easy to identify when the range of values is small. Similarly, from a statistical point of view, the @STD and @VAR functions aren't of much use when the range of values is small, or when the values are widely divergent as shown here. That's why few *Lotus* users ever need these @functions for business spreadsheets.

```
A1: [W14] 'Product group                                          READY

        A                  B           C       D       E       F
1  Product group         $ Sales
2
3  Group A               164,191
4  Group B               171,297
5  Group C               115,335
6  Group D             1,220,039
7  Group E               274,149
8  Group F               592,989
9  Group G                44,972
10 Group H               463,862
11 Group I             1,876,107
12
13          @SUM       4,922,941
14          @AVG         546,993
15        @COUNT               9
16          @MIN          44,972
17          @MAX       1,876,107
18          @STD         580,138
19          @VAR 336,560,417,294
20
01-Dec-92  05:13 PM                                       NUM
```

Figure 6-6 The seven statistical @functions used in spreadsheet

How to use three financial @functions Figure 6-7 presents the eleven financial @functions that *Lotus* release 2.4 provides. As I said earlier, you shouldn't have any trouble using these @functions if your specialty is finance. And if your specialty isn't finance, you probably won't need these @functions. Just in case you do need them, though, here are some ideas that will help you use them.

If you review the arguments and functions in figure 6-7, you can see that all of the financial @functions perform calculations that deal with time periods. So when you specify the arguments in one of these @functions, you must make sure that the arguments measure time consistently. If, for example, you specify the term of a loan in months, then you must also specify the interest rate in months.

If the time units in your spreadsheet aren't consistent, you can adjust them when you specify the arguments as shown in figure 6-8. In the first example, the annual interest rate in the second argument is divided by 12 so it is consistent with the monthly payment periods. In the second example, the annual rate is divided by 12 and the payment period is multiplied by 12 so the arguments are consistent to produce a monthly payment.

When you use one of the financial @functions, you should realize that the *ordinary annuity method* is used for performing the calculations. This method assumes that the payments or investments are made at the end of each period. This is the method that's usually used for financial calculations. Occasionally, though, you may need to perform a calculation using the *annuity due method*.

@Function name	Syntax(arguments)	Function
Ordinary annuities		
`@PMT`	`@PMT(principal,interest,term)`	Calculate the amount of the periodic payments for a loan
`@FV`	`@FV(payment,interest,term)`	Calculate the future value of a series of equal payments
`@PV`	`@PV(payment,interest,term)`	Calculate the present value of a series of equal payments
`@TERM`	`@TERM(payment,interest,future-value)`	Calculate the number of equal payments needed to reach a future value
Capital budgeting		
`@NPV`	`@NPV(disount-rate,cash-flow-range)`	Calculate the net present value of a series of cash flows
`@IRR`	`@IRR(estimate,cash-flow-range)`	Calculate the internal rate of return for a series of cash flows
Single-sum compounding		
`@RATE`	`@RATE(future-value,investment,term)`	Calculate the interest rate required for a lump-sum investment to grow to a future value
`@CTERM`	`@CTERM(rate,future-value,investment)`	Calculate the number of periods required for a lump-sum investment to grow to a future value
Depreciation		
`@DDB`	`@DDB(cost,salvage,life,period)`	Calculate the double-declining depreciation of an asset for one period
`@SLN`	`@SLN(cost,salvage,life)`	Calculate the straight-line depreciation of an asset for one period
`@SYD`	`@SYD(cost,salvage,life,period)`	Calculate the sum-of-years-digit depreciation of an asset for one period

Figure 6-7 Eleven financial @functions

```
B6: (F2) @PMT(B3,B4/12,B5)                                            READY

      A                B          C          D                  E
1   Example 1                            Example 2
2
3   Loan amount:       20,000            Loan amount:       20,000
4          Rate:       12.00%                   Rate:       12.00%
5      # Months:           60                  Years:            5
6       Payment:       444.89                Payment:       444.89
7
8   The formula: @PMT(B3,B4/12,B5)       The formula: @PMT(E3,E4/12,E5*12)
9
10
```

Figure 6-8 Two @PMT functions that use consistent units of time

This method assumes that the payments or investments are made at the start of each period. To use this method, you must adjust the @function.

To illustrate, figure 6-9 shows how you can use the @FV function to perform a future value calculation using the ordinary annuity and annuity due methods. Here, the formulas appear to the right of the cells that contain them. As you can see, you don't have to adjust this @function to get the future value using the ordinary annuity method. But you need to multiply the @function by one plus the interest rate to get the future value using the annuity due method. To find out what you need to do to adjust each of the financial @functions to use the annuity due method, you can look up the @function in your *Lotus* manual.

The spreadsheet in figure 6-10 shows how you can use the value that you get from one of the financial @functions to provide a complete summary of financial transactions. Here, the @PMT function is used in cell F2 to get the monthly payment required to pay off a $20,000 loan in five years at 12 percent interest. The result, $444.89, is used in the rows that follow to set up a complete payment table. In column D, the formulas multiply the previous balance by the interest rate to get the interest amount for the month. In column E, the formulas subtract the monthly interest amount from the monthly payment to get the monthly principal amount. In column F, the formulas subtract the monthly principal amount from the previous balance to get the new balance.

The spreadsheet in figure 6-11 is another example of how you can use the values from financial @functions to provide a complete table of financial information. Here, the @DDB function is used in each of the five rows of a depreciation table. If you refer back to figure 6-7, you can see that the @DDB function calculates the double-declining depreciation amount for one period of an asset's life. To use this function, you must provide four arguments that represent the cost of the asset, the salvage value of the asset, the depreciation

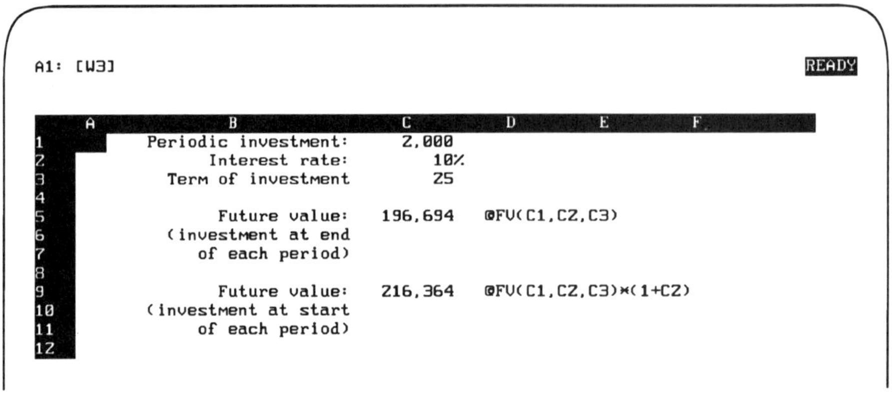

Figure 6-9 The @FV function used to perform an ordinary annuity calculation and an annuity due calculation

life of the asset, and the period for the calculation. In this example, absolute cell addresses are used for the first three arguments, and a mixed address is used for the fourth argument. As a result, the formula in cell F3 can be copied to cells F4 through F7 to complete the depreciation table.

How to use the @SQRT mathematical function Although *Lotus* release 2.4 provides 17 mathematical @functions, you may never need any of them in your business spreadsheets. In chapter 2, I showed you how to use the @ROUND function, but you should only need that one if you're working with values that can lead to rounding errors.

The only other mathematical @function that you're likely to use in business spreadsheets is the @SQRT function:

```
@SQRT(value)
```

It performs the square root operation on its single argument, which must be a positive value or zero. Not too many business calculations require the use of this operation, but a few do. For example, our company uses @SQRT in a formula that calculates the economical order quantity for printing orders.

How to use the @IF logical function Lotus release 2.4 provides nine logical @functions, but the @IF function is the most useful one for business spreadsheets. As a result, it's the only one that I'll present in this chapter.

Figure 6-12 presents the syntax of the @IF function along with the operators that you can use within its first argument. If you review the syntax, you can see that the first argument represents a test. Then, if the test is true, the second argument is performed. If the test is false, the third argument is performed.

F2: (,2) @PMT(C1,C2/12,F1) READY

	A	B	C	D	E	F
1		Loan amount:	20,000		# periods:	60
2		Rate:	12.00%		Payment:	444.89
3						
4	#	Date	Payment	Interest	Principle	Balance
5	======	======	======	======	======	======
6	1	Apr-92	444.89	200.00	244.89	19,755.11
7	2	May-92	444.89	197.55	247.34	19,507.77
8	3	Jun-92	444.89	195.08	249.81	19,257.96
9	4	Jul-92	444.89	192.58	252.31	19,005.65
10	5	Aug-92	444.89	190.06	254.83	18,750.82
11	6	Sep-92	444.89	187.51	257.38	18,493.44
12	7	Oct-92	444.89	184.93	259.95	18,233.48
13	8	Nov-92	444.89	182.33	262.55	17,970.93
14	9	Dec-92	444.89	179.71	265.18	17,705.75
15	10	Jan-93	444.89	177.06	267.83	17,437.92
16	11	Feb-93	444.89	174.38	270.51	17,167.41
17	12	Mar-93	444.89	171.67	273.21	16,894.20
18	13	Apr-93	444.89	168.94	275.95	16,618.25
19	14	May-93	444.89	166.18	278.71	16,339.54
20	15	Jun-93	444.89	163.40	281.49	16,058.05

01-Dec-92 05:21 PM NUM

Figure 6-10 The @PMT function used as the basis for a table that shows the portion of each payment that goes to principal and interest

F3: @DDB($B$3,$B$4,$B$5,$E3) READY

	A	B	C	D	E	F	G	H
1	Double-declining depreciation							
2								
3	Cost:	85,000		Year	1	34,000		
4	Salvage:	20,000		Year	2	20,400		
5	Life:	5		Year	3	10,600		
6				Year	4	0		
7				Year	5	0		
8						=========		
9						65,000		
10								
11								

Figure 6-11 The @DDB function used to develop a depreciation table

By using the conditional operators in figure 6-12, you can set up a test that compares two values. This is illustrated by the spreadsheet in figure 6-13. Here, the @IF function in cell E4 is:

```
@IF(D4>200000,0.08,0.07)
```

The syntax of the @IF function

```
@IF(test,true-action,false-action)
```

The conditional operators that can be used in an @IF function

Operator	Meaning	Condition test example
=	Equals	`B4=C4`
<>	Does not equal	`D12<>3.14`
>	Greater than	`B4>C4`
<	Less than	`1000<D12`
>=	Greater than or equal to	`F21>=1000`
<=	Less than or equal to	`F21<=20000`

The logical operators that can be used in an @IF function

Operator	Meaning	Condition test example
#AND#	Join two or more conditional tests using AND logic	`B1<5#AND#B1>1`
#OR#	Join two or more conditional tests using OR logic	`B1=5#OR#B1=1`
#NOT#	Perform a negative test	`#NOT#B1<5#AND#B1>1`

Figure 6-12 The @IF function and its operators

As a result, the test in the first argument is:

```
D4>200000
```

This test is true when the value in cell D4 is greater than 200,000. Then, if the test is true, the value in the second argument (0.08) is put in cell E4. But if the test is false, the value in the third argument (0.07) is put in cell E4. In other words, this formula is used to establish the commission rate at either 7 or 8 percent for each sales representative.

```
E4: (P0) [W6] @IF(D4>200000,0.08,0.07)                                    READY

         A              B           C            D        E          F
1                    Product     Product       Total
2     Salesperson    Group 1     Group 2       Sales    Rate    Commission
3   ==================================================================
4   Bob Gomez        123,148      78,520     201,668      8%     16,133.44
5   Judy Steadman     38,921      68,903     107,824      7%      7,547.68
6   Brenda Rogers    210,010     105,482     315,492      8%     25,239.36
7   Lori Anders       42,127      82,150     124,277      7%      8,699.39
8   Wendy Jones       73,102      51,160     124,262      7%      8,698.34
9   Jack James        38,197      76,511     114,708      7%      8,029.56
10  Lisa Van Dyke    201,980     109,100     311,080      8%     24,886.40
11  John Underwood   187,125      91,773     278,898      8%     22,311.84
12  Frank Hart       123,015      87,321     210,336      8%     16,826.88
13  Bill Lang        220,629      72,160     292,789      8%     23,423.12
14  Lee Wong         116,439      21,576     138,015      7%      9,661.05
15  ==================================================================
16                 1,374,693     844,656 2,219,349              171,457.06
17
18  Assumptions:     7% commission rate if Total sales are under 200,000
19                   8% commission rate if Total sales are over 200,000
20
01-Dec-92  05:06 PM                                              NUM
```

Figure 6-13 An @IF function that sets the commission rate based on the total sales

By using the logical operators in figure 6-12, you can set up a test that combines conditional tests. This is illustrated by the spreadsheet in figure 6-14. Here, the test in the first argument in the @IF function in cell F4 is:

D4>200000#AND#E4=1

This test is true when the value in cell D4 is greater than 200,000 and the value in cell E4 is equal to 1. In other words, this test combines two conditional tests with AND logic. That means that both conditions must be true for the test to be true. In contrast, when you use OR logic, the test is true if either condition is true; both conditions don't have to be true.

If you look again at the @IF function in cell F4 of figure 6-14, you can see that the second and third arguments are formulas. Here again, if the test is true, the formula in the second argument is performed. If the test is false, the formula in the third argument is performed. If you study the formulas, you can see that sales representatives with status 1 get 7 percent commission on the first $200,000 in sales and 10 percent thereafter. In contrast, sales representatives with status 2 don't qualify for the 10 percent commission.

If necessary, you can use @IF functions as the arguments in other @IF functions. That means you can perform tests within tests. For business spreadsheets, though, you should rarely need to go beyond one level of testing.

```
F4: (,2) [W13] @IF(D4>200000#AND#E4=1,200000*0.07+(D4-200000)*0.1,D4*0.07) READY

       A                B            C            D        E        F
1                    Product      Product       Total
2     Salesperson    Group 1      Group 2       Sales  Status  Commission
3  ==============================================================
4  Bob Gomez          123,148      78,520     201,668      2     14,116.76
5  Judy Steadman       38,921      68,903     107,824      2      7,547.68
6  Brenda Rogers      210,010     105,482     315,492      1     25,549.20
7  Lori Anders         42,127      82,150     124,277      1      8,699.39
8  Wendy Jones         73,102      51,160     124,262      2      8,698.34
9  Jack James          38,197      76,511     114,708      2      8,029.56
10 Lisa Van Dyke      201,980     109,100     311,080      1     25,108.00
11 John Underwood     187,125      91,773     278,898      2     19,522.86
12 Frank Hart         123,015      87,321     210,336      1     15,033.60
13 Bill Lang          220,629      72,160     292,789      1     23,278.90
14 Lee Wong           116,439      21,576     138,015      2      9,661.05
15 ==============================================================
16               1,374,693     844,656   2,219,349          165,245.34
17
18 Assumptions:    7% commission rate on sales under 200,000
19                 10% commission rate on sales in excess of 200,000
20                 Status 2 employees not eligible for higher tier
01-Dec-92  05:04 PM                                          NUM
```

Figure 6-14 An @IF function that calculates the commission based on the total sales and the status code

Discussion

As I mentioned at the beginning of this chapter, *Lotus* provides dozens of @functions that I didn't present in this chapter. In addition, you can buy sets of special-purpose @functions for use with *Lotus*. These @functions are called *add-in @functions* because they require the use of the add-in program facility that's provided by *Lotus*. If you do use add-in @functions, you may want to read chapter 14 because it covers the add-in program facility that *Lotus* provides.

Terms

syntax
function name
argument
ordinary annuity method
annuity due method
add-in @function

Objectives

1. Identify those @functions (if any) that you are likely to need in future spreadsheets.
2. Use this chapter or the *Lotus* manual for looking up the operational details for any of the @functions that you want to use in your spreadsheets.
3. Use whichever @functions you need in your spreadsheets.

Chapter 7

Four skills for working with a large spreadsheet

In this chapter, you'll learn four skills for working with a large spreadsheet. First, you'll learn how to move the cell pointer as efficiently as possible. Second, you'll learn how to minimize the delays that are caused when you enter data into a large spreadsheet. Third, you'll learn how to keep track of the amount of internal memory that your spreadsheet is using. And fourth, you'll learn how to use the Windows feature that *Lotus* provides to view two separate areas of a spreadsheet at the same time.

As you will see, efficiently moving the cell pointer is useful for any spreadsheet that takes more than one screen to view. The next three skills, though, apply primarily to much larger spreadsheets. Minimizing calculation delays is useful only if you are bothered by the delays that occur while *Lotus* recalculates a spreadsheet. Tracking memory use is useful only if the internal memory of your PC is so limited or your spreadsheets are so large that there isn't always enough memory for the spreadsheets you create. And viewing two areas of a spreadsheet at the same time is useful primarily when you need to compare the results in different areas of the spreadsheet. With that perspective, you can decide for yourself which of the last three skills presented in this chapter you need to learn.

How to move the cell pointer in a large spreadsheet

Figure 7-1 presents the keystroke combinations that you can use to move the cell pointer within a spreadsheet. Undoubtedly, you already know that the Arrow keys move the cell pointer one cell at a time in the direction of the arrow. In contrast, the Page-up and Page-down keys move the cell pointer up or down a full screen with each keystroke. Similarly, the Tab key and the Shift+Tab keystroke combination move the cell pointer a full screen to the right or left with each keystroke. The Ctrl+Right arrow and the Ctrl+Left arrow combinations also move the cell pointer a full screen to the right or left. In *Lotus* terminology, the keystrokes for the full screen movements to the right and left are referred to as the *big right* and *big left* combinations.

To return the cell pointer to cell A1 with a single keystroke, you press the Home key. The counterpart to this is the combination of the End and Home keys. In this case, you press the End key; then, you press the Home key (you don't hold one down while you press the other). This moves the cell pointer to the lower right corner of the spreadsheet. That's the cell that's at the intersection of the right-most column and the lowest row that are used by the spreadsheet.

When you use the End key followed by one of the Arrow keys, the movement of the cell pointer depends on the contents of the current cell. If the current cell is empty when you press the End key followed by the Right arrow key, the cell pointer moves to the right until it reaches the first cell that contains data. If the current cell contains data, the cell pointer moves to the right until it reaches the last cell in succession that contains data. As a result, the cell pointer always stops on a cell that contains data.

Using the End key with the Arrow keys lets you quickly move the cell pointer to the last cell in a row or column that contains data. If, for example, the cell pointer is in the middle of a long column of data, you can move the cell pointer to the bottom of the column by pressing the End key followed by the Down arrow key. Then, if you want to return the cell pointer to the top of the column, you can press the End key followed by the Up arrow key. Although it may be difficult for you to appreciate this cell pointer movement when you read about it, you'll find that it's easy to use if you just experiment with it for a minute or two.

The End Arrow key combinations are also useful when you're specifying ranges within formulas or commands. For instance, you can use the End key followed by an Arrow key to move the cell pointer when you're entering the range of an @SUM function using the anchor-and-point method. And you can use a key combination like that when you're highlighting the range to be operated upon by a command.

The last two key combinations in figure 7-1 use the F5 (Goto) key. You can use these key combinations to move to any cell or named range in the spreadsheet. First you press the F5 key followed by the cell address or range name. Then, you press the Enter key.

However, you can't always tell which cell address you want the cell pointer moved to. That's particularly true when you're working with a large spreadsheet. That's why you often use the F5 key in combination with range names. If you don't know how to create and use range names, you can learn how in the next chapter.

How to minimize the delays for recalculation

By default, *Lotus* automatically recalculates the formulas in a spreadsheet every time you enter a label, value, or formula. *Lotus* calls this *automatic recalculation*. If the spreadsheet you're using is small or your PC is fast, you

Keystrokes	Function
Arrow keys	Move the cell pointer one cell in the direction of the arrow.
Page-up	Move the cell pointer up one screen.
Page-down	Move the cell pointer down one screen.
Tab	Move the cell pointer one screen to the right (big right).
Shift+Tab	Move the cell pointer one screen to the left (big left).
Ctrl+Right arrow	Move the cell pointer one screen to the right (big right).
Ctrl+Left arrow	Move the cell pointer one screen to the left (big left).
Home	Move the cell pointer to the home position (A1).
End Home	Move the cell pointer to the cell that is at the intersection of the bottom row and the right-most column that are used in the spreadsheet.
End Right arrow End Left arrow End Up arrow End Down arrow	Move the cell pointer in the direction of the arrow. If the cell pointer starts on an empty cell, move it to the first non-empty cell. If the cell pointer starts on a cell that contains data, move it to the last cell in succession that contains data (stop before the first empty cell).
F5 (Goto)	Start the Goto operation. Then, enter the address of the cell that you want the cell pointer moved to. When you press the Enter key, the cell pointer jumps to that cell address.
F5 (Goto)	Start the Goto operation. Then, type the range name for the range that you want the cell pointer moved to. If you can't remember the range name, press the F3 (Name) key to display all the range names for the spreadsheet. Then, type the range name or use the Arrow keys to highlight the range name. When you press the Enter key, the cell pointer jumps to the first cell in the named range.

Figure 7-1 The keystrokes for efficiently moving the cell pointer in a spreadsheet

may not notice the delay that occurs as your PC performs this recalculation. But if the spreadsheet is large or your PC is slow, you may have to wait for several seconds while the spreadsheet is recalculated. And if you're using *Lotus* release 2.X, you can't work on the spreadsheet until it has been recalculated.

If you find that you're waiting for your PC every time that you make an entry in a spreadsheet, you may want to change the calculation mode from automatic to *manual recalculation*. When you do that, *Lotus* recalculates the

Command name	Option	Function
/Worksheet Global Recalc	Automatic	Recalculate the spreadsheet each time you enter a label, value, or formula. This is the default setting.
	Manual	Recalculate the spreadsheet only when you press the F9 (Calc) key. To remind you that you're using manual mode, the CALC indicator appears at the bottom of your screen.

Figure 7-2 The command for setting the recalculation mode

spreadsheet only when you press the F9 (Calc) key. As a result, you can enter data into the cells of the spreadsheet without waiting for your PC to recalculate the entire spreadsheet after each entry. Then, after you enter all the data, you can press the F9 key to recalculate the spreadsheet.

To change the recalculation mode between manual and automatic, you use the /Worksheet Global Recalc command as summarized in figure 7-2. Then, when you save the spreadsheet, *Lotus* also saves the recalculation setting.

To remind you that you're in manual recalculation mode, *Lotus* displays a CALC indicator at the bottom of the screen. If you use the spreadsheet results that are displayed or printed when this indicator is on, the data is likely to be inaccurate because you don't know when the calculations were last made. To clear this indicator and recalculate the entire spreadsheet, you press the F9 key.

If you're using *Lotus* release 3.X, you may not need to use the manual mode because these releases use a *background operation* to perform the recalculation. That means that you can use the spreadsheet at the same time that *Lotus* is recalculating it. The recalculation process still slows the operation of the spreadsheet down, though. So if the operation is slow enough to bother you, you may still want to change from automatic to manual recalculation mode.

Another way to deal with recalculation delays, no matter what *Lotus* release you're using, is to install a *math co-processor* in the systems unit of your PC. Often, when you install a co-processor, the recalculation time is cut by 50 percent or more. This is particularly true for PCs with 8088 or 80286 processors. At a cost of $100 to $300, this can be a relatively inexpensive way to improve the speed of *Lotus* calculations. For more information on this and other hardware upgrades, you should read chapter 22.

You can tell if your PC has a math co-processor or not by using the /Worksheet Status command to display the Global Settings screen. If you look at the screen in figure 7-3, for example, you can see that the PC doesn't have a co-processor.

```
B3: [W11] "1992                                                        STAT
Press any key to continue...

                         Global Settings
  Conventional memory:    323104 of 326128 Bytes (99%)
  Expanded memory:        2286176 of 3029560 Bytes (75%)

  Math coprocessor:       (None)

  Recalculation:
    Method                Automatic
    Order                 Natural
    Iterations            1

  Circular reference:     (None)

  Cell display:
    Format                (G)
    Label prefix          ' (left align)
    Column width          9
    Zero suppression      No

  Global protection:      Disabled

30-Nov-92  02:31 PM                                          NUM
```

Figure 7-3 The Global Settings screen that is displayed by the /Worksheet Status command

How to keep track of the amount of internal memory used by a spreadsheet

When you create a spreadsheet that requires more internal memory than your computer has, *Lotus* displays the MEM indicator at the bottom of the screen. Then, you must either redesign the spreadsheet so it uses less memory or break it up into smaller spreadsheets. Usually, though, it's better to check the amount of internal memory that's available for your spreadsheet as you go along. That way, you can adjust the design of your spreadsheet to deal with the memory limitation before you run out of memory.

As you work on a large spreadsheet, you can use the /Worksheet Status command to find out how much internal memory is still available for your spreadsheet. When you start this command, it displays a Global Settings screen like the one shown in figure 7-3. At the top of this screen, *Lotus* displays information about the internal memory in your PC. With release 2.X, the first line shows the amount of *conventional memory* that's available for the spreadsheet and the second line shows information about the *expanded memory* that's available for the spreadsheet. If your PC doesn't have expanded memory, *Lotus* displays the word *none* in this second line. With release 3.X, all of the available memory is treated as one large block; there isn't a separate line for conventional and expanded memory.

In figure 7-3, the first line of the display indicates that 323,104 bytes of conventional memory are still available for the spreadsheet. That's equivalent to 99 percent of the 326,128 bytes that were originally available for the spreadsheet. Similarly, 2,286,176 bytes of expanded memory are still available for the spreadsheet. That's 75 percent of the 3,029,560 bytes that were originally available for the spreadsheet. In other words, the PC started with more than 3MB of memory available for the spreadsheet and most of that hasn't yet been used.

But what if the display indicates that your spreadsheet has already used more than 90 percent of the available memory, and you know that you've got a lot more work to do on the spreadsheet? Rather than keep on going, you should redesign the spreadsheet, or you should buy more internal memory for your PC. Don't keep on going until the MEM indicator comes on. If you do, the redesign process becomes much more difficult. If you decide that more memory will solve your problem, please read chapter 22. It provides more information on upgrading internal memory.

How to use the Window feature to view two areas of a spreadsheet at the same time

Occasionally, when you create a large spreadsheet, you need to view two areas of it so you can compare results. If, for example, you're trying to balance a budget, you want to be able to make changes to the budget model and see how these changes affect the "bottom line." Of course, you can always make a change and then move the cursor. But that isn't efficient. That's why *Lotus* provides a feature that lets you view two areas of a spreadsheet at the same time.

Figure 7-4 summarizes the commands and keystrokes for using the *Windows* feature. The /Worksheet Window Horizontal and Vertical commands activate the Windows feature; the Horizontal command creates a horizontal window, and the Vertical command creates a vertical window. The Sync and Unsync commands control whether or not the cell pointer movements in the windows are linked to each other. The best way to understand how these commands affect the Windows feature is to experiment with them. The Clear command clears any windows you have set. And the F6 (Window) key moves the cell pointer from one window to the other.

To illustrate, figure 7-5 shows a budget model spreadsheet with the horizontal Windows feature in use. Here, the top window shows the top portion of the spreadsheet. The bottom window shows the bottom portion of the spreadsheet that has the expense totals. By using the Windows feature like this, you can make changes to individual line items and see how the changes affect the total expense figures at the same time.

Discussion

Even with the skills presented in this chapter, a large spreadsheet is harder to create and use than a small spreadsheet. So before you start developing a large spreadsheet, you should consider the use of two or more smaller spreadsheets instead. To make this practical, *Lotus* releases 2.X and 3.X

Command name	Option	Function
/Worksheet Window	Horizontal	Create a horizontal window at the row that the cell pointer is on
	Vertical	Create a vertical window at the column that the cell pointer is on
	Sync	Synchronize the windows so that the movement of the cell pointer shifts both windows
	Unsync	Unsynchronize the windows so that the movement of the cell pointer shifts only the current window
	Clear	Clear all windows from the screen
Keystroke		**Function**
F6 (Window)		Move the cell pointer from one window to the next

Figure 7-4 The commands and keystrokes for using the Window feature

provide ways to share data between spreadsheets and to link the data in the cells of one spreadsheet to the cells in another spreadsheet. In chapter 11, you can learn how how to use the commands and features for sharing and linking data.

When you do need to use a large spreadsheet, though, you should consider using range names. Range names can help you organize a large spreadsheet. You can use them with the F5 (Goto) key to move easily around a large spreadsheet. And they make it easier for you to create formulas and to use other *Lotus* commands within the spreadsheet. If you read the next chapter, you'll see what I mean.

Terms

big right
big left
automatic recalculation
manual recalculation
math co-processor
background operation
conventional memory
expanded memory

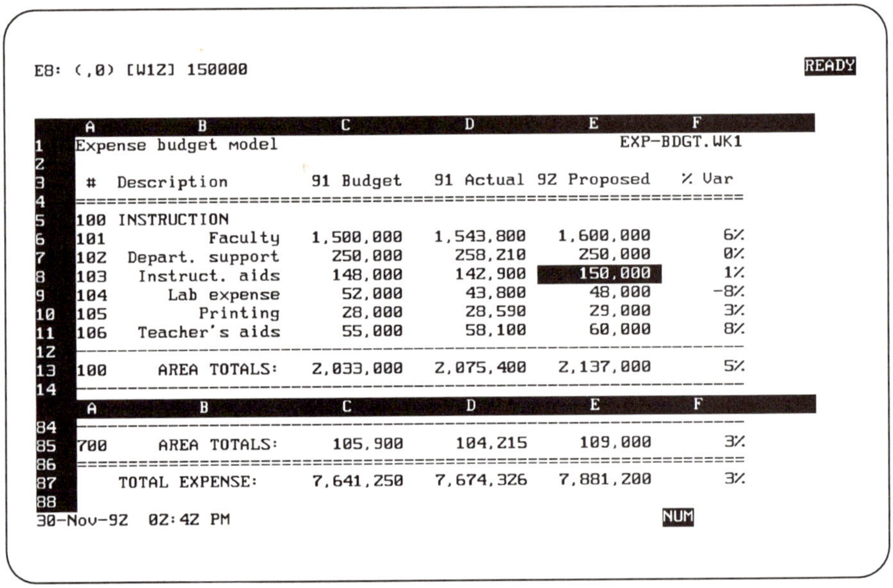

Figure 7-5 Two areas of a large spreadsheet displayed at the same time using the Window feature

Objectives

1. Use the keystrokes *Lotus* provides for moving the cell pointer around a large spreadsheet.
2. Use manual recalculation to minimize recalculation delays when you're working on a large spreadsheet.
3. Display the amount of internal memory that is still available for the spreadsheet you're working on.
4. Use the Window feature to view two areas of a spreadsheet simultaneously.

Chapter 8

How to use range names to organize a spreadsheet

As a spreadsheet grows and as the layout of the spreadsheet gets more complex, it gets more difficult to move the cell pointer to different portions of the spreadsheet. If, for example, you're working on a spreadsheet like the one in figure 8-1, it is difficult to move the pointer to the start of the monthly sales summaries. If you've read chapter 7, you know that you can use the F5 (Goto) key to move to the first cell in this area of the spreadsheet, but to do that you have to know that the address of this cell is Z41.

To help organize a spreadsheet, *Lotus* lets you assign *range names* to ranges within a spreadsheet. Because it's easier to remember the range names than the actual cell addresses, you can use the F5 (Goto) key to easily move the cell pointer to the start of the named range. Also, range names can make it easier to execute *Lotus* commands and to create formulas.

How to create and manage range names

Figure 8-2 summarizes the commands that you can use for working with range names. The first of these commands is the /Range Name Create command that's illustrated in figure 8-3. When you start this command, *Lotus* asks you for the range name that you want to use. After you type the name and press the Enter key, *Lotus* asks you for the range of cells that you want the range name applied to. In this example, the range of cells is A1 through E20 and is named YTD-SUM.

Figure 8-4 summarizes the rules for creating range names. As you can see, a range name can be up to 15 characters in length, and it can include letters, digits, symbols, or spaces. However, the name shouldn't be a valid cell address. Also, the name shouldn't start with a digit or a mathematical operator if you want to use the name in a formula later on. When you type the name, it doesn't matter whether you use lowercase or uppercase letters because *Lotus* will treat them all as uppercase letters.

If you want to change the range for a range name, you can use the /Range Name Create command again. This time, you use the same name that you used the first time. Then, you enter the corrected range address.

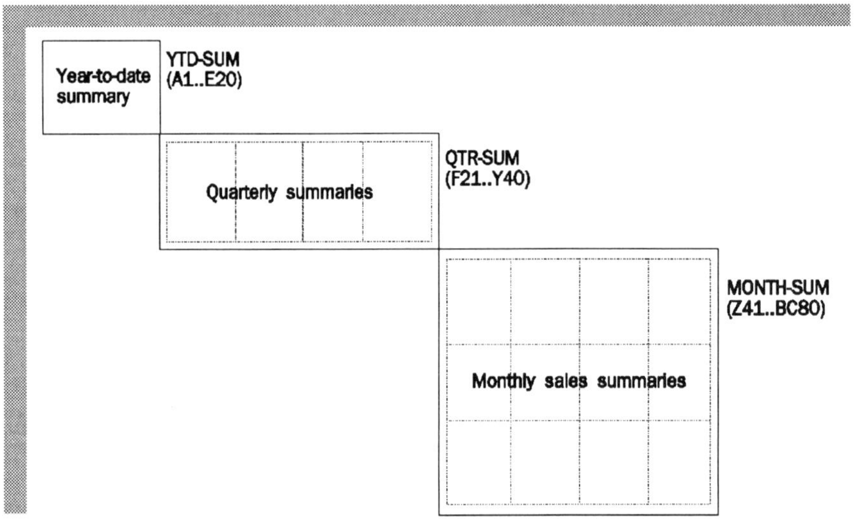

Figure 8-1 How range names can be used to identify the portions of a large spreadsheet

You should realize, though, that the range addresses for named ranges are automatically updated when you insert or delete columns or rows within the ranges. As a result, you don't have to update the ranges when you make these modifications to a spreadsheet.

If you want to delete a range name, you use the /Range Name Delete command as illustrated in figure 8-5. Here, you can see how *Lotus* displays range names on the third line of the control panel when you start the command. If all of the range names don't fit on this line, you can use the Left or Right arrow keys to scroll to the names that aren't shown. Or, you can press the F3 (Name) key to display all of the names at once. When you see the name you want to delete, you can type it at the prompt, or you can highlight the name on the screen. Then, when you press the Enter key, the range name is deleted.

If you're having trouble keeping track of all the range names that you've created for a spreadsheet, you can create a table of range names and their ranges in another area of the spreadsheet. To do that, you use the /Range Name Table command as illustrated in figure 8-6. To start, *Lotus* asks you for the range of cells that should be used for the table. Often, the best place for that range is outside the lower right corner of the spreadsheet. In figure 8-1, for example, cell BD81 is ideal for the first cell of the range name table. After you identify the first cell in this range and press the Enter key, *Lotus* creates a table like the one shown in step 2 of figure 8-6. Since the first column in the

Command name	Option	Function
/Range Name	Create	Create a range name and apply it to a range of cells
	Delete	Delete one range name at a time without affecting the data in the range
	Reset	Delete all of the range names for a spreadsheet without affecting the data in each range
	Table	Create a two-column table in the spreadsheet that lists all of the range names and their ranges

Figure 8-2 The commands for creating and managing range names

1. Type the range name as prompted by the control panel:

   `Enter name: ytd-sum`

   Then, press the Enter key.

2. Enter the range of cells that the name should be applied to as prompted by the control panel:

   `Enter name: ytd-sum                Enter range: A1..E20`

   You can enter the range by the direct entry or the anchor-and-point method. Then, press the Enter key.

Figure 8-3 How to use the /Range Name Create command to create a range name

table contains the range names, you may have to increase the width of this column to 15 so the full names are displayed. This is illustrated in step 3 of figure 8-6.

Unfortunately, *Lotus* doesn't automatically update the range name table every time you make a change to the spreadsheet that affects the table. So when you add or delete a range name, or when you add or delete rows or columns within the ranges, the table is no longer accurate. Then, to update the table, you have to perform the /Range Name Table command again.

The last command in figure 8-2 that you need to manage range names is the /Range Name Reset command. You use this command when you want to delete all of the range names from a spreadsheet. Normally, you shouldn't have to do that, though, so you may never need this command.

The rules

1. A range name can't consist of more than 15 characters.
2. A range name can be any combination of letters, digits, and symbols, including spaces.
3. A range name shouldn't be a valid cell address.
4. If you want to use a range name in a formula, the name shouldn't start with a digit or a mathematical operator.
5. All letters in a range name are treated as uppercase, so it doesn't matter whether you use lower- or uppercase to enter them.

Valid range names

`ytd-summary`

`GRAND TOTAL`

`Product 1 sales`

Invalid range names	Reason
`Q1`	This is a valid cell address.
`Monthly sales summaries`	The name is more than 15 characters.
`*TOTAL`	The name starts with a mathematical operator.
`(YTD SALES)`	The name starts with a mathematical operator.

Figure 8-4 The rules for creating range names

How to use a range name for moving the cell pointer

Once you've set up the range names for a spreadsheet, you can quickly move the cell pointer to the one of the ranges by using the F5 (Goto) key. Two methods for doing this are illustrated in figure 8-7. After you press the F5 (Goto) key, *Lotus* waits for either a cell address or a range name. If you know the range name, you can type it and press the Enter key as summarized in method 1. *Lotus* then moves the cell pointer to the first cell in the named range.

If you can't remember the range name that you want the cell pointer moved to, you can use method 2 in figure 8-7. After you press the F5 (Goto) key, you press the F3 (Name) key to get a complete listing of the range names that have been created for the spreadsheet. Then, you can either type in the name of the range that you want or you can use the Arrow keys to highlight the range name. When you press the Enter key, *Lotus* moves the cell pointer to the first cell in the named range.

1. Enter the range name to be deleted as prompted by the control panel:

```
Enter name to delete:
MONTH-SUM   QTR-SUM   YTD-SUM
```

   You can use the Arrow keys to highlight the range name to be deleted, or you can type the name to be deleted. If you want a complete listing of all range names, you can press the F3 (Name) key.

2. Press the Enter key.

Figure 8-5 How to use the /Range Name Delete command to delete a range name

How to use a range name in a formula

You can use a range name in a formula whenever a range is called for. If, for example, you've used the range name BUDGET-ITEMS to refer to cells B6..B10, you can add together the cells in the range with this formula:

```
@SUM(budget-items)
```

In fact, *Lotus* substitutes the range names for the ranges in the formulas that you've already created as soon as you create new range names.

If you can't remember what the range name is as you're entering a formula, you can press the F3 (Name) key to display all of the range names for the spreadsheet. Then, you can either enter the name into the formula, or you can highlight the name and press the Enter key to enter it into the formula.

If you can't remember what range address a range name represents when the cell pointer is on a formula, you can press the F2 (Edit) key to display the formula in the third line of the control panel. This shows the range address instead of the range name. To end this display, you press the Enter key just as you do when you end an editing operation.

If you use a range name within a formula, you can still copy the formula to other cells. In this case, though, the range name is treated as a range address when it's copied. If you want the range copied as an absolute address instead of a relative address, you can precede the range name with a dollar sign when you enter it in the original formula. Thus, $BUDGET-ITEMS is an *absolute range name*.

When you use range names in a formula, the formula is often easier to understand. However, you have to take the time to create range names before you can use them. As a result, you won't increase your overall productivity by using range names in formulas alone.

1. Enter the range of cells that should receive the table of range names as prompted by the control panel:

   `Enter range for table:  BD81`

   You can enter the range by direct entry or the anchor-and-point method. You only have to identify the first cell in the range, but enough cells below and to the right of this cell should be empty so they can receive the table.

2. Press the Enter key. The table of range names is then generated in the range that you specified in step 1:

```
BD81: [W11] 'MONTH-SUM                                                    READY

          BD          BE          BF          BG          BH          BI          BJ
81   MONTH-SUM   Z41..BC80
82   QTR-SUM     F21..Y40
83   YTD-SUM     A1..E20
84
85
```

3. If necessary, use the /Worksheet Column Set-width command to increase the width of the first column in the table to 15 so all the characters in the range names are displayed.

Figure 8-6 How to use the /Range Name Table command to create a listing of the range names within the spreadsheet

How to use a range name in a command

You can use a range name in a command whenever the command asks for a range. If you can't remember what the range name is, you can use the F3 (Name) key as I described earlier to display the range name so you can select it for the command.

When you're working with a spreadsheet like the one in figure 8-1, for example, you can use a range name when you want to print a named range within the spreadsheet. If, for example, you want to print the quarterly summaries, you use the name QTR-SUM in the /Print Printer Range command. Similarly, when you want to print the year-to-date summary, you can use the name YTD-SUM. As you can see, using range names this way makes it easy to print just a portion of a large spreadsheet.

If you have already created range names for moving the cell pointer, it makes sense to use the range names in commands too. But don't create range names just so you can use them in commands. In general, that won't increase your productivity.

Method 1: When you know the range name

1. Press the F5 (Goto) key.
2. Type the range name for the range that you want to cell pointer moved to.
3. Press the Enter key.

Method 2: When you can't remember the range name

1. Press the F5 (Goto) key.
2. Press the F3 (Name) key to display the range names for the spreadsheet. Then, type the range name or use the Arrow keys to highlight the range name for the range that you want the cell pointer moved to.
3. Press the Enter key.

Figure 8-7 How to use range names with the F5 (Goto) key

Discussion

What I hope you've learned about range names is that they're primarily useful for working with large spreadsheets. Not only do they help you organize a large spreadsheet, but they make it easier for you to move the cell pointer from one portion of the spreadsheet to another. Although you can also use range names in formulas and commands, that doesn't always help you improve your efficiency.

Terms

range name
absolute range name

Objectives

1. Create, manage, and use range names when working with a large spreadsheet to move the cell pointer more efficiently.
2. Use the range names you've created in formulas and commands.

Chapter 9

How to protect areas of a spreadsheet

After you create a spreadsheet, it sometimes makes sense to delegate the work of keeping the spreadsheet up-to-date to someone else. For instance, you can use the spreadsheet in figure 9-1 for summarizing the expenses for each month of the year. For each month, only the shaded cells need to be changed. This is a job that can easily be delegated to someone else.

But what if the person you want to delegate the job to isn't a competent *Lotus* user? What if the person accidentally changes one or more of the formulas in columns D and E instead of the data in column C? Most likely, you'll be called upon to restore the formulas yourself, and that certainly isn't the way the art of delegation is supposed to work.

In this chapter, you'll learn how to protect areas of a spreadsheet so the data in those areas can't be changed. Obviously, protecting data in a spreadsheet is useful when you want to delegate spreadsheet work to someone else. It's also useful when you create a spreadsheet that's so complicated that you don't want to take the chance of accidentally replacing critical data.

How the *Lotus* protection feature works

Every cell in a *Lotus* spreadsheet has a *protection attribute*. The status of this attribute is either *protected* or *unprotected*. If a cell is protected and the *Lotus* protection feature is turned on, the contents of the cell can't be changed. If a cell is unprotected or the *Lotus* protection feature isn't on, the contents of the cell can be changed.

The spreadsheet in figure 9-1 shows what happens when you try to enter data into a protected cell after the protection feature has been turned on. Here, someone tried to enter the number 60000 into a protected cell (B6). As a result, *Lotus* displayed the ERROR indicator at the top right corner of the screen along with this message in the lower left corner of the screen:

```
Protected cell
```

Before you can continue, you have to press the Esc key and move to another cell.

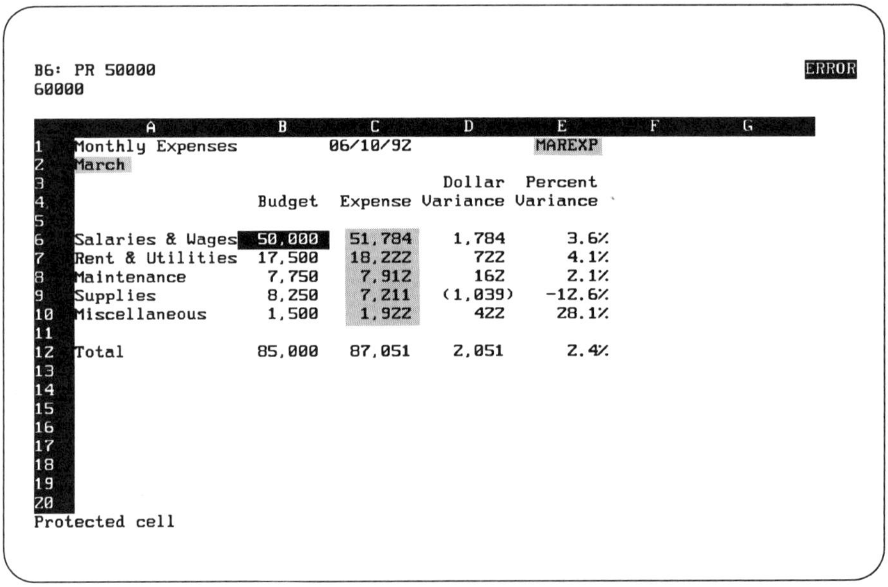

Figure 9-1 A spreadsheet with protected cells and the error message that you get when you try to enter data into a protected cell

When the protection feature is on, *Lotus* displays the contents of unprotected cells differently from the contents of protected cells. As a result, you can easily see the unprotected cells. If you have a color monitor, *Lotus* uses a different color to display the contents of the unprotected cells. If you have a monochrome monitor, *Lotus* uses boldfaced characters to display the contents of the unprotected cells.

You can also identify protected and unprotected cells by looking at the first line of the control panel. If the protection feature is on, PR is displayed for protected cells, and U is displayed for unprotected cells. If you turn the protection feature off after it's been on, the U is still displayed for unprotected cells, but nothing is displayed for protected cells. In figure 9-1, you can see that PR is displayed for cell B6. This means that not only is the cell protected, but that the protection feature is on.

How to protect areas of a spreadsheet

Figure 9-2 summarizes the commands you use with the protection feature. The first two commands are used to turn the protection feature on and off. Since the *Lotus* default is off, you have to use the /Worksheet Global Protection Enable command to turn the protection feature on.

Command name	Option	Function
/Worksheet Global Protection	Enable	Activate the protection feature for the current spreadsheet. When activated, this feature protects all cells that haven't been unprotected by the /Range Unprotect command.
	Disable	Deactivate the protection feature for the current spreadsheet. When deactivated, any cell in the spreadsheet can be modified. (This is the default setting.)
/Range	Unprot Unprotect	Assign unprotected status to a range of cells so they can be modified even when the protection feature is activated.
	Prot Protect	Return a range of cells that have been unprotected to protected status. This reverses the effects of the /Range Unprotect command.
/Range Input		Restrict the movement of the cell pointer to unprotected cells only.

Figure 9-2 The commands for using the *Lotus* protection feature

When you enable the protection feature, the protection attribute for every cell is set to protected. As a result, the next step is to use the /Range Unprotect command to set the attributes to unprotected for those cells that you want to enter data into. To do that, you execute the command for each range in the spreadsheet that you want unprotected.

If you make a mistake as you use the /Range Unprotect command, you can use the /Range Protect command to reverse the mistake. Otherwise, you won't need to use the /Range Protect command. After you enable the protection feature and unprotect those ranges that are going to receive data, you're ready to work on the spreadsheet.

Incidentally, the command names for the /Range Unprotect and Protect commands were shortened to /Range Unprot and Prot starting with *Lotus* release 2.2. So don't be concerned by these minor differences in the wording of the command names. You still use the same keystrokes to access the commands.

1. Execute the /Range Input command and specify the input range. This range must include all of the cells that you want to enter data into:

    `Enter data input range: A1..A1`

2. Enter the new data and use the Arrow keys to move to the unprotected cells in the input range.
3. Press the Esc key to end the input session. *Lotus* then returns the cell pointer to normal operation.

Figure 9-3 How to use the /Range Input command to restrict the movement of the cell pointer to unprotected cells

How to restrict the movement of the cell pointer to unprotected cells

Lotus provides a command that you can use with the protection feature called the /Range Input command. By using this command, you can improve your efficiency when you enter data because this command restricts the movement of the cell pointer to unprotected cells only. Then, you can type an entry, press the Right arrow key, and *Lotus* automatically moves you to the next unprotected cell in the spreadsheet.

Figure 9-3 summarizes the use of the /Range Input command. In step 1, you start the /Range Input command and specify the *input range*. This range must include all of the cells that you want to enter data into. Since you'll only be able to move to unprotected cells after you execute this command, specifying the entire spreadsheet as the input range is often the most efficient option. In step 2, you use the Arrow keys to move to the unprotected cells and enter labels and values. In step 3, you press the Esc key to end the *input session*. (Pressing the Enter key without an entry has the same affect). After you end the session, the cell pointer returns to normal movement.

Unfortunately, *Lotus* doesn't save the input range with the spreadsheet. As a result, you must execute the /Range Input command for each input session. Because this requires additional effort, using this command is practical only when you need to enter a considerable amount of data into a spreadsheet.

Terms

protection attribute
protected
unprotected
input range
input session

Objective

1. Use the *Lotus* protection feature to protect the cells in a spreadsheet that shouldn't be changed.
2. Use the /Range Input command to improve your data entry efficiency.

Chapter 10

How to sort the data in a spreadsheet

After you use a spreadsheet to organize or summarize data, it sometimes makes sense to sort the data. If, for example, you develop a sales summary like the one in figure 10-1, you may want to sort the total sales row. Then, you can tell at a glance who had the highest sales total and who had the lowest.

Often, in fact, you'll find that sorting the data in a spreadsheet makes it easier to interpret. That's why you should learn how to use the *Lotus* sort feature. Because it's an easy feature to use, you should be able to master it quickly by reading this chapter. And once you know how to use the sort feature, you're likely to find many uses for it.

How to sort the data in a range of cells

Figure 10-2 summarizes the commands for sorting a range of cells. When you reach the /Data Sort menu, six options are displayed. If your release of *Lotus* supports the F6 (Window) key, you can display a Sort Settings screen like the one shown in figure 10-3. This screen helps you keep track of the settings you're using for the sort.

Figure 10-4 summarizes the sort procedure. First, you use the Data-Range option of the /Data Sort command to specify the range of cells that you want sorted. Second, you use the Primary-Key option to identify the column of data that the sort should be based on. Third, if you want to sort based on the data in more than one column, you use the Secondary-Key option to identify the second column of data that the sort should be based on. Fourth, you use the Go option to perform the sort. *Lotus* then returns you to the spreadsheet screen.

How to specify the data range The first step in any sort is to specify the range of cells that you want to sort. This range is called the *data range,* and you use the Data-Range option to specify it. You can use the direct entry method to specify the range of cells, but usually it's easier to use the anchor-and-point method.

A1: 'Monthly sales READY

	A	B	C	D	E	F	G
1	Monthly sales			APRSLS			
2	05/13/92						
3			Product	Product	Total	Commission	
4	First	Last	Group 1	Group 2	Sales	7%	
5	========	========	========	========	========	========	
6	Bob	Gomez	123,148	78,520	201,668	14,117	
7	Judy	Steadman	38,921	68,903	107,824	7,548	
8	Brenda	Rogers	210,010	105,482	315,492	22,084	
9	Lori	Anders	42,127	82,150	124,277	8,699	
10	Wendy	Jones	73,102	51,160	124,262	8,698	
11	Jack	James	38,197	76,511	114,708	8,030	
12	Lisa	Van Dyke	201,980	109,100	311,080	21,776	
13	John	Underwood	187,125	91,773	278,898	19,523	
14	Frank	Hart	123,015	87,321	210,336	14,724	
15	Bill	Lang	220,629	72,160	292,789	20,495	
16	Lee	Wong	116,439	21,576	138,015	9,661	
17	========	========	========	========	========	========	
18			1,374,693	844,656	2,219,349	155,354	
19							
20							

13-May-92 11:39 AM NUM

Figure 10-1 A spreadsheet with unsorted sales totals

When you specify the data range, you should include only the cells that contain the data that you want sorted. For the spreadsheet in figure 10-1, for example, you should include only the cells in rows 6 through 16. You shouldn't include the cells in the heading row or cells in the bottom row that return the total for each column.

Also, you should include all of the columns in each row in the data range. Otherwise, when you execute the sort, *Lotus* will sort some of the data in each row but not all of it. As a result, the sort will mix up the data in the spreadsheet. For the spreadsheet in figure 10-1, you should include columns A through F in the data range.

How to identify the primary sort key The second step in any sort is to identify the *primary sort key*. To do this, you select the Primary-Key option. Then, *Lotus* displays this prompt:

```
Primary sort key:
```

At this screen, you move the cell pointer to any cell in the column that you want to use as the primary sort key. If for example, you want to sort the data range in figure 10-1 by the data in the Total Sales column, you move the cell pointer to any cell in column E. Then, when you press the Enter key, *Lotus* displays this prompt:

```
Sort order (A or D):
```

Command name	Level	Function
/Data Sort F6 (Window)	Data-Range	Specify the range of cells to be sorted (the sort range)
	Primary-Key	Identify the primary column that you want the range of cells to be sorted by and specify the sort sequence (ascending or descending)
	Secondary-Key	Identify the secondary column (if any) that you want the range of cells to be sorted by and specify the sort sequence
	Go	Perform the sort
	Reset	Clear all sort settings
	Quit	Exit from the /Data Sort command

Figure 10-2 The commands for sorting a range of cells

```
A1: 'Monthly sales                                                    EDIT
Primary sort key: E6                      Sort order (A or D): D

     ------------------------ Sort Settings ---------------------------
     Data range:        A6..F16

     Primary key:
       Field (column)   E6..E6
       Sort order       Descending

     Secondary key:
       Field (column)
       Sort order
```

Figure 10-3 The Sort Settings screen for sorting the spreadsheet in figure 10-1

Here, you must type *A* or *D* to select either *ascending sort order* or *descending sort order*. When you press the Enter key, *Lotus* returns you to the /Data Sort menu.

How to identify the secondary sort key (if any) For most spreadsheet sorts, you'll use only a primary sort key. Occasionally, though, a *secondary sort key* is useful. When you use a secondary sort key, the sort is based on the data in two columns instead of one. To identify a secondary sort key, you select the

1. Start the /Data Sort command. Then, select the Data-Range option; identify the range of cells that you want to sort using the direct entry or anchor-and-point method; and press the Enter key. This returns you to the /Data Sort menu.
2. Select the Primary-Key option so *Lotus* displays this prompt:

   ```
   Primary sort key:
   ```

   To specify this key, type the address of a cell in the column that you want to sort by or move the cell pointer to a cell in the column that you want to sort by. Next, press the Enter key so *Lotus* displays this prompt:

   ```
   Sort order (A or D):
   ```

   Then, type A if you want to sort the data in ascending order or D if you want to sort it in descending order. Last, press the Enter key. This returns you to the /Data Sort menu.
3. If you want to sort by a secondary key too, select the Secondary-Key option. Then, specify the secondary sort key and its sort order in the same way that you did for the primary sort key.
4. Select the Go option to perform the sort that you've specified in steps 1-3. *Lotus* then returns to the spreadsheet screen and displays the sorted spreadsheet.

Figure 10-4 The procedure for sorting a range of cells by one or two keys

Secondary-Key option. After that, you identify the column and the sort order for the key just as you did for the primary sort key. I'll illustrate a sort using a secondary sort key in a moment.

How to run the sort After you have specified the data range and at least a primary sort key, you're ready to perform the sort. To do that, you use the Go option. *Lotus* then sorts the rows in the data range and returns you to the spreadsheet screen. To illustrate, figure 10-5 shows the spreadsheet in figure 10-1 after it has been sorted using the settings given in the Sort Settings screen in figure 10-3.

Sort orders

When you perform a sort based on columns that contain just letters or just numbers, the sort works the way you would expect. If you sort in descending order and the primary sort key is total sales, the numbers are sorted in descending numerical sequence as shown in column E of figure 10-5. Similarly, if you sort in ascending order and the primary sort key is employee last name, the names are sorted alphabetically just as you would expect.

When you sort based on sort keys that contain a mix of letters, numbers, and symbols, though, it's not as easy to predict the sorted order. Also, when you sort based on both a primary and a secondary key, it's not always easy to predict the sorted order.

A1: 'Monthly sales READY

	A	B	C	D	E	F	G
1	Monthly sales			APRSLS			
2	05/13/92						
3			Product	Product	Total	Commission	
4	First	Last	Group 1	Group 2	Sales	7%	
5	==========	==========	==========	==========	==========	==========	
6	Brenda	Rogers	210,010	105,482	315,492	22,084	
7	Lisa	Van Dyke	201,980	109,100	311,080	21,776	
8	Bill	Lang	220,629	72,160	292,789	20,495	
9	John	Underwood	187,125	91,773	278,898	19,523	
10	Frank	Hart	123,015	87,321	210,336	14,724	
11	Bob	Gomez	123,148	78,520	201,668	14,117	
12	Lee	Wong	116,439	21,576	138,015	9,661	
13	Lori	Anders	42,127	82,150	124,277	8,699	
14	Wendy	Jones	73,102	51,160	124,262	8,698	
15	Jack	James	38,197	76,511	114,708	8,030	
16	Judy	Steadman	38,921	68,903	107,824	7,548	
17	==========	==========	==========	==========	==========	==========	
18			1,374,693	844,656	2,219,349	155,354	
19							
20							

13-May-92 11:45 AM NUM

Figure 10-5 The spreadsheet in figure 10-1 after the Total Sales column has been sorted in descending order

Sorts that are based on mixed sort keys If you perform an ascending sort that is based on a column that contains both labels and values, all of the labels will come before all of the values. If you perform an ascending sort based on a column that contains just labels but the labels contain mixed combinations, this is the sort sequence:

empty cells
cells that start with a blank
cells that start with a digit
cells that start with a letter
cells that start with a symbol

When you sort in descending order, the entire sort order is reversed.

If you try a sort with mixed keys, you can see for yourself how the sort works. Normally, though, this isn't a problem because you either sort a column that contains numeric values or a column that contains alphanumeric labels. And those sorts usually work the way you want them too.

Sorts that are based on two or more sort keys Because it can be hard to visualize how a sort of more than one sort key is going to work, figure 10-6 shows a sort that uses both a primary sort key and a secondary sort key. Here, the primary key is the region name in ascending order, and the secondary key is sales in descending order. After the sort has finished, you can see that all of the rows for the East region precede those for the West. Also, the five rows for the East region are in descending sequence by sales, and the five rows for the West region are in descending sequence by sales.

If you look at the first row in the sorted data range, you can see that it is empty. The empty row is there because the unsorted spreadsheet had an empty row separating the rows for the West and East regions. To put the sorted spreadsheet in a more readable format, you can delete row 5 and insert a new row to separate the two regions.

Although you'll probably never need to perform a sort with more than two keys, *Lotus* release 3.X provides this capability. In fact, when you select the Extra-Key option of the /Data Sort command, you can identify as many as 253 extra keys. I won't illustrate the use of extra keys in this book, though, since I doubt that you will ever need to go beyond a secondary key.

Practical advice for using the sort feature

Because the sort feature is easy to use, you shouldn't have much trouble with it. But here are three ideas that may save you some extra work.

Use separate columns for the data that you want to use as sort keys If you think you will want to sort the data in a spreadsheet by some data item, be sure to create a separate column for that data item. If, for example, you want to be able to sort employee rows by employee last name, the last name has to be in a separate column. It can't be in the same column as the first name.

Don't put empty rows in your data range until after you've done the sort As you can see in figure 10-6, an empty row in a data range gets sorted along with the other rows. Then, you usually have to delete the old empty rows and insert new ones to get the data range back into a readable format. To avoid this extra work, just wait until you've done the sort before you put in the empty rows.

Don't save the sorted spreadsheet over the existing spreadsheet if you want to return it to the original sequence When you sort the data in a data range, it's usually difficult to return the data to its original sequence. So if you want to retain the data in its original sequence, be sure to save the spreadsheet to disk before you sort the data. Then, make sure that you don't save the sorted spreadsheet with the same name as the original spreadsheet. If you want to keep a copy of the sorted spreadsheet, save it with a new file name.

A spreadsheet before the data rows have been sorted

```
A1: [W9] 'Quarterly sales by product group                              READY

     A          B              C           D          E            F
1  Quarterly sales by product group                 QRTSLS       05/13/92
2  ==================================================================
3  Region    Product group    $ Sales
4  ==================================================================
5  West      Group A          164,491
6  West      Group B          171,297
7  West      Group C          115,335
8  West      Group D        1,220,039
9  West      Group E          274,149
10
11 East      Group A          592,989
12 East      Group B          607,714
13 East      Group C           44,972
14 East      Group D          463,862
15 East      Group E        1,876,107
16 ==================================================================
17                         $5,530,955
18
```

The Sort Settings screen for a two-key sort

```
A1: [W9] 'Quarterly sales by product group                              EDIT
Secondary sort key: C5                    Sort order (A or D): D

                          Sort Settings
   Data range:        A5..C15

   Primary key:
     Field (column)   A5..A5
     Sort order       Ascending

   Secondary key:
     Field (column)   C5..C5
     Sort order       Descending
```

The spreadsheet after the data have been sorted

```
A1: [W9] 'Quarterly sales by product group                              READY

     A          B              C           D          E            F
1  Quarterly sales by product group                 QRTSLS       05/13/92
2  ==================================================================
3  Region    Product group    $ Sales
4  ==================================================================
5
6  East      Group E        1,876,107
7  East      Group B          607,714
8  East      Group A          592,989
9  East      Group D          463,862
10 East      Group C           44,972
11 West      Group D        1,220,039
12 West      Group E          274,149
13 West      Group B          171,297
14 West      Group A          164,491
15 West      Group C          115,335
16 ==================================================================
17                         $5,530,955
18
```

Figure 10-6 A sort that uses both primary and secondary keys

Terms

data range
primary sort key
ascending sort order
descending sort order
secondary sort key

Objective

Use the *Lotus* sort feature to sort the data in a spreadsheet based on one or two sort keys.

Chapter 11

How to share data and link cells between spreadsheets

Starting with release 2.0, *Lotus* provided commands for sharing data between spreadsheets. If, for example, you want to copy a range of cells from one spreadsheet to another, *Lotus* release 2.0 provides commands for the task. As a result, you don't have to re-enter the range of cells in the second spreadsheet.

Then, *Lotus* release 2.2 provided a feature that lets you link cells in one spreadsheet to cells in another spreadsheet. If, for example, you want to link cells that contain the monthly totals from several monthly spreadsheets to cells that contain yearly totals in an annual spreadsheet, you can do so using the cell linking feature. That way, you can link data in two or more small spreadsheets instead of creating one large spreadsheet that contains all the data.

Finally, *Lotus* release 3.0 provided commands for creating more than one worksheet (spreadsheet) in a single spreadsheet file. It also provided commands that let you work on more than one spreadsheet file at a time. Using these commands makes it easier to link cells because all of the linked worksheets or spreadsheets are available to you at the same time.

In this chapter, you'll learn how to use *Lotus* commands and features to share and link data between spreadsheets. Then, you can decide whether any of these skills will benefit you. You can also decide whether you need to upgrade to a newer release of *Lotus* to get the improved features for linking cells between spreadsheets.

How to use the /File Xtract and Combine commands to share data between spreadsheets

Figure 11-1 summarizes the two commands that all releases of *Lotus* provide for sharing data between spreadsheets. With these commands, you can copy a range of cells in one spreadsheet to a range in another spreadsheet. If you

Command name	Function
/File Xtract	Copy a range of cells from the current spreadsheet to a spreadsheet file on disk
/File Combine	Copy a range of cells from a spreadsheet stored on disk into the current spreadsheet

Figure 11-1 The /File Xtract and the /File Combine commands

want to copy a range of cells from the current spreadsheet to a spreadsheet file on disk, you use the /File Xtract command. And if you want to copy a range of cells from a spreadsheet on disk to the current spreadsheet, you use the /File Combine command.

Figure 11-2 shows how to use the /File Xtract command. In step 1, you select the option that tells *Lotus* whether you want the cells extracted just as they are (the Formulas option), or whether you want the formulas converted to values before the data is extracted. If you select the Formulas option, you must be sure that the range of cells you extract includes both the formulas and the cells that the formulas refer to. In step 2, you enter a name for the file that the command will create. In step 3, you specify the range of cells that you want extracted.

Figure 11-3 shows you how to use the /File Combine command. In step 1, you move to the cell in the current spreadsheet where you want the combine operation to start. Then, you select one of these options: Copy, Add, Subtract. Usually, you want the Copy option because it tells *Lotus* that you want the cells copied from the spreadsheet on disk to the current spreadsheet. The other two options are difficult to use because they add or subtract the cells from the file on disk to or from the corresponding cells in the current spreadsheet.

In step 2, you select one of these two options: Entire-file or Named/Specified-Range. Generally, you select the Entire-File option to tell *Lotus* that you want the entire file copied. Otherwise, you have to be able to specify the range of cells you want combined with the current spreadsheet. In step 3, you enter the name of the file that you want copied into the current spreadsheet.

If you want to use the /File Combine command to copy the values in a few cells of another spreadsheet into the current spreadsheet, you'll often run into problems. That's because the /File Combine command copies the actual contents of a cell. Since the cells that have the values you want are often returned by formulas, the /File Combine command will copy the formulas into the spreadsheet and not the values you want.

1. Start the command and select one of these options from the control panel:

   Formulas   Values

   If you want the formulas converted to values before they are extracted from the file, select the Value option. If you want the formulas extracted the way they are, select the Formulas option. In this case, you should be sure to extract all of the cells that are in the ranges operated upon by the formulas.

2. Enter the name of the file that the range of cells should be extracted to:

   Enter name of file to extract to: D:\LTSDATA*.wk1
   1QSLS.WK1   2QSLS.WK1   3QSLS.WK1   4QSLS.WK1

   You can specify an existing file or create a new file. Then, press the Enter key.

3. Enter the range of cells that you want to extract from the current file:

   Enter extract range: A1..F6

   You can use the direct entry or the anchor-and-point method to specify the range. Then, when you press the Enter key, the range of cells is copied to the file that you specified in step 2.

Figure 11-2 How to use the /File Xtract command to extract a portion of the current spreadsheet and save it to a spreadsheet file on disk

1. Move to the cell in the current spreadsheet where you want the combine operation to start. Then, start the /File Combine command and select one of these options:

   Copy   Add   Subtract

   The Copy option copies a range from the spreadsheet on disk into the current spreadsheet at the location of the cell pointer. The Add and Subtract options add or subtract the cell values to or from the range in the spreadsheet on disk to the corresponding cell values in the current spreadsheet.

2. Select one of these options from the control panel:

   Entire-File Named/Specified-Range

   The Entire-File option copies the entire spreadsheet on disk. The Named/Specified-Range option copies just the range of cells from the spreadsheet on disk that you specify. To use this option, you have to know the name of the range or the range address before you start the command.

3. Enter the name of the file on disk that you want to combine with the current file:

   Enter name of file to combine: D:\LTSDATA*.wk1
   1QSLS.WK1   2QSLS.WK1   3QSLS.WK1   4QSLS.WK1

   After you specify the file name, you press the Enter key to complete the operation.

Figure 11-3 How to use the /File Combine command to copy a spreadsheet file from disk into the current spreadsheet

To overcome this problem, you can use the /File Xtract and /File Combine commands together. First, you use the /File Xtract command to copy a range of cells from one spreadsheet to a new file on disk. During this operation, you can select the Values option so the formulas in the range are converted to values. Then, you use the /File Combine command to copy the new spreadsheet into another spreadsheet.

How to link cells in one spreadsheet to cells in another spreadsheet (releases 2.2 and later)

Starting with release 2.2, *Lotus* provided a special type of formula that lets you *link cells* in one spreadsheet with cells in another. Figure 11-4 shows you a year-to-date spreadsheet that uses formulas that are linked to cells in quarterly spreadsheets. Here, the values in column C of the year-to-date spreadsheet are taken from another spreadsheet named Q1SLS.WK1, and the values in column D are taken from another spreadsheet named Q2SLS.WK1. This can be continued so the values in column E are taken from another spreadsheet, and the values in column F from yet another.

If you look at the formulas used to provide this linkage, you can see that they have this form:

```
+<<Q1SLS.WK1>>C4
```

Here, the plus sign is required to tell *Lotus* that the entry is a formula. Then, the file name is given between the << and >> symbols. Last, the address of the cell that should be linked to the current spreadsheet is given. In figure 11-4, for example, the value in cell C6 is taken from cell E6 in the file named Q1SLS.WK1, and the value in cell D6 is taken from cell E6 in the file named Q2SLS.WK1. *Lotus* assumes that both of these files are in the default directory. If they aren't, you have to include the correct path along with file name in the linking formulas.

When you retrieve a file with a formula that provides a link to another spreadsheet, *Lotus* automatically gets the data from the file on disk and updates the value in the linked cell in the current spreadsheet. This happens each time you retrieve the file. As a result, a change to the data in one spreadsheet automatically changes the data in the spreadsheet that it is linked to when that spreadsheet is retrieved.

If you link spreadsheets this way, you must be careful when you insert or delete rows or columns in the source spreadsheet. If you change cell addresses in the source spreadsheet that are referenced in the link, the linked spreadsheet won't work correctly. When that spreadsheet is retrieved, it will still get data from the source spreadsheet, but not from the right cells.

One way to get around this problem is to use a range name instead of a cell address for the linked cell in the source spreadsheet. In this case, the

The year-to-date spreadsheet

```
C6: (,0) [W10] +<<Q1SLS.WK1>>E6                                              READY

     A        B              C          D          E          F          G
1  Year-to-date sales summary                                         07/02/92
2  (SLS-SUM.WK1)
3                          1ST QTR    2ND QTR    3RD QTR    4TH QTR        YTD
4  Region  Salesperson       SALES      SALES      SALES      SALES     REGION
5  =========================================================================
6  West   Bob Gomez        201,668    221,754          0          0  1,272,950
7         Brenda Rogers    315,492    285,482          0          0
8         Lori Anders      124,277    124,277          0          0
9
10 North  Wendy Jones      124,262    152,178          0          0    557,333
11        Jack James       114,708    166,185          0          0
12
13 South  Lisa Van Dyke    311,080    251,445          0          0  1,511,758
14        John Underwood   278,898    249,663          0          0
15        Frank Hart       210,336    210,336          0          0
16
17 East   Bill Lang        292,789    292,789          0          0    861,608
18        Lee Wong         138,015    138,015          0          0
19 =========================================================================
20                       2,111,525  2,092,124          0          0  4,203,649
02-Jul-92  01:15 PM
```

The formulas used in the year-to-date spreadsheet

```
A1: [W6] 'Year-to-date sales summary                                         READY

     A        B                    C                         D
1  Year-to-date sales summary
2  (SLS-SUM.WK1)
3                                  1ST QTR                    2ND QTR
4  Region  Salesperson               SALES                      SALES
5  ================================================================
6  West   Bob Gomez        +<<Q1SLS.WK1>>E6      +<<Q2-SLS.WK1>>E6
7         Brenda Rogers    +<<Q1SLS.WK1>>E7      +<<Q2-SLS.WK1>>E7
8         Lori Anders      +<<Q1SLS.WK1>>E8      +<<Q2-SLS.WK1>>E8
9
10 North  Wendy Jones      +<<Q1SLS.WK1>>E10     +<<Q2-SLS.WK1>>E10
11        Jack James       +<<Q1SLS.WK1>>E11     +<<Q2-SLS.WK1>>E11
12
13 South  Lisa Van Dyke    +<<Q1SLS.WK1>>E13     +<<Q2-SLS.WK1>>E13
14        John Underwood   +<<Q1SLS.WK1>>E14     +<<Q2-SLS.WK1>>E14
15        Frank Hart       +<<Q1SLS.WK1>>E15     +<<Q2-SLS.WK1>>E15
16
17 East   Bill Lang        +<<Q1SLS.WK1>>E17     +<<Q2-SLS.WK1>>E17
18        Lee Wong         +<<Q1SLS.WK1>>E18     +<<Q2-SLS.WK1>>E18
19 ================================================================
20                               2,111,525               2,092,124
02-Jul-92  01:17 PM
```

Figure 11-4 A year-to-date sales spreadsheet with links to four quarterly spreadsheets (releases 2.2 and later) range name should represent only one cell. Then, you can use the range name in the formula that provides the linkage as in this example:

```
+<<Q1SLS.WK1>>TOTAL_SALES
```

When you use a range name like this, the cell address that it represents is automatically adjusted if columns or rows are added to or deleted from the source spreadsheet. If you're not already familiar with range names, you can learn how to use them in chapter 8.

How to use the *Viewer* add-in to create cell links (releases 2.3, 2.4 and 3.4) It's difficult to link spreadsheets when you can view only one spreadsheet at a time. First, you have to retrieve the source spreadsheet so you can note the addresses of the cells you want to link. Then, you have to retrieve the other spreadsheet and enter the appropriate formulas. To overcome this limitation, *Lotus* releases 2.3, 2.4 and 3.4 come with an add-in program called *Viewer*. This add-in lets you work with the source spreadsheet that you want to link from while you have the current spreadsheet open.

Figure 11-5 shows how you use *Viewer* to create links. In step 1, you move the cell pointer to the cell in the current spreadsheet that you want to use for a cell-linking formula. Then, you invoke *Viewer*. If you don't know how to invoke an add-in program, you can find out in chapter 14.

In step 2, you select the Link option from the *Viewer* menu. The screen shown in step 3 is then displayed. At this screen, you press the Up and Down arrow keys to highlight the spreadsheet file that you want to link to. In this example, the 3QSLS.WK1 spreadsheet is highlighted. *Viewer* displays this spreadsheet in the right portion of the screen as shown.

In step 4, you press the Right arrow key to move to the spreadsheet portion of the *Viewer* screen so you can specify the cell that you want to use for the link. Then, you use the Arrow keys to move the highlight to the cell you want. Finally, you press the Enter key. *Viewer* then returns you to the current spreadsheet and inserts the appropriate cell linking formula.

When to use the /File List or the /File Admin Table command If you develop a complicated spreadsheet with many links to other spreadsheets, you may have difficulty keeping track of the links. In that case, you can use the /File List command to display a list of the files that are linked to the current spreadsheet. Or, you can use the /File Admin Table command to store a list of the files that are linked to the current spreadsheet in one range of the spreadsheet. Both of these commands provide a Linked option for this purpose, and you can learn how to use these commands in chapter 13.

When to use the /File Admin Link-Refresh command As you use the *Lotus* menus, you may notice the /File Admin Link-Refresh command. Since the name suggests that it has something to do with updating the results of cell-links, you may wonder if you need to use it. Because this command has a

1. Move to the cell you want to use for a cell-linking formula and invoke *Viewer*.
2. Select the Link option from the *Viewer* menu that's displayed:

   Retrieve   Link   Browse

3. Then, *Viewer* displays this screen:

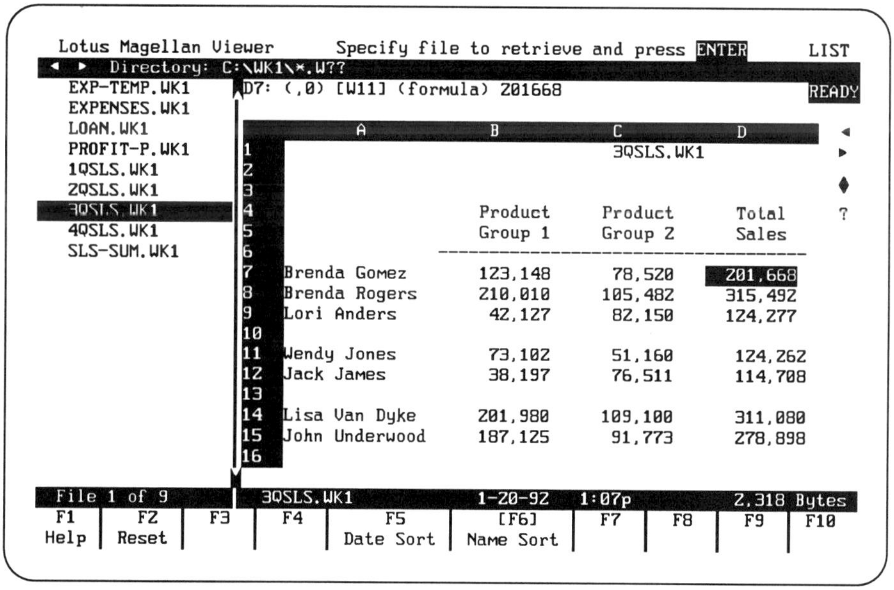

   Here, you use the Up and Down arrow keys in the file list to specify the spreadsheet that you want to link to. *Viewer* displays the highlighted spreadsheet in the right portion of the screen.

4. To specify the cell in the spreadsheet you want to use for the link, you use the Right arrow key to move from the file list to the spreadsheet. Then, you use the Arrow keys to highlight the cell you want, and you press the Enter key to complete your selection. *Viewer* then returns you to the current spreadsheet and inserts the appropriate cell linking formula.
5. To link other cells, you repeat steps 1-4 for each cell-linking formula you require.

Figure 11-5 How to use the *Viewer* add-in to define the cell-links in a spreadsheet (releases 2.3, 2.4, and 3.4)

slightly different purpose than you might expect, I'll take a moment to explain its use.

The /File Admin Link-Refresh command is intended for use when two or more people share spreadsheet files on a network. Although *Lotus* updates all links whenever you retrieve a file that uses linked cells, another *Lotus* user on the network can change the data in one of the spreadsheets that provides data to the spreadsheet that you're working on after you have retrieved the file. In that case, your spreadsheet won't have the most current data. To avoid this possibility, you can use the /File Admin Link-Refresh command to update all links after you have retrieved a file.

Unfortunately, this command refreshes the data from the linked files on disk. As a result, it doesn't get the current data if another person on the network is updating a linked file but hasn't yet saved it. This suggests that close communication is required between the people on a network that use linked files to make sure that the links are refreshed properly.

How to link cells in one worksheet of a multi-dimensional spreadsheet to cells in another worksheet (release 3.0 and later)

Starting with *Lotus* release 3.0, you can create a spreadsheet that contains more than one *worksheet* (another name for spreadsheet). *Lotus* calls these *multi-dimensional spreadsheets*. Sometimes, these multi-dimensional spreadsheets are called *3D spreadsheets*. Using this type of spreadsheet makes it easier to link cells because all of the linked worksheets are in the current spreadsheet.

Figure 11-6 summarizes the commands that you can use for working with multi-dimensional spreadsheets. To start, you use the /Worksheet Insert Sheet command to insert one or more worksheets before or after the first worksheet of a spreadsheet. Figure 11-7 shows you how to use this command. After you tell *Lotus* where you want the additional worksheets inserted, you specify how many worksheets you want inserted.

When the command is finished, the worksheets in the spreadsheet are identified by a letter followed by a colon in the upper left corner of the control panel. For example, *A:* identifies the first spreadsheet; *B:* identifies the second one; and so on. Only one of the worksheets is current, and it's always the one that's displayed. To move from one spreadsheet to another, you can use the first two keystroke combinations in figure 11-8. For instance, when you press the Alt+Page-up key combination, *Lotus* moves back one worksheet.

After you have created empty worksheets, you can use them to develop your spreadsheet application. Besides allowing for links that I'll explain in a moment, these multi-dimensional worksheets work just like any other spreadsheet. And if you find you've created too many worksheets, you can delete one or more of them by using the /Worksheet Delete Sheet command.

To make it easier for you to work with two or more worksheets, you can use the /Worksheet Window Perspective command to display three worksheets at a time as shown in figure 11-9. Then, you can use any of the first three keystroke combinations in figure 11-8 to move from one worksheet to another. If you want to expand a worksheet so it is displayed on the full screen, you can use the Alt+F6 keystroke combination. Then, you can use this

Command name	Next level	Function
/Worksheet Insert	Sheet	Insert one or more worksheets into a multi-dimensional spreadsheet
/Worksheet Delete	Sheet	Delete one or more worksheets from a multi-dimensional spreadsheet
/Worksheet Window	Perspective	Display three worksheets of a multi-dimensional spreadsheet as shown in figure 11-9
	Sync	Synchronize the scrolling of the worksheets in the windows
	Unsync	Stop the synchronized scrolling of the worksheets in the windows
	Clear	Clear the effect of the /Worksheet Window Perspective command

Figure 11-6 The commands for creating and using multi-dimensional spreadsheets (release 3.X)

1. Start the command and select one of these options from the control panel:

   `Before    After`

   This tells *Lotus* whether you want the worksheets inserted before or after the current worksheet.

2. Enter the number of worksheets to be inserted:

   `Enter number of worksheets to insert: 4`

   When you press the Enter key, the worksheets are inserted into the current spreadsheet.

Figure 11-7 How to use the /Worksheet Insert Sheet command to add worksheets to a multi-dimensional spreadsheet

key combination again, to return to the Perspective display. When you press the F6 (Window) key by itself, you move from one worksheet to another.

Once you establish the Perspective display, you can use any of the last three commands in figure 11-6. If you use the Sync option of the /Worksheet Window command, the worksheets in all three windows scroll in synchronization as you move the cell pointer. If you use the Unsync option, the synchronized scrolling is turned off. If you use the Clear option, the Perspective display is turned off.

Keystrokes	Function
Ctrl+Page-up	Move back one worksheet.
Ctrl+Page-down	Move forward one worksheet.
F6 (Window)	Move from one worksheet to another within the spreadsheet whether the worksheet is displayed in full size or in perspective size.
Alt+F6	Display the current worksheet at full size. Or, return it to perspective size so you can see more than one worksheet.

Figure 11-8 The keystroke combinations for moving from one worksheet to another within a multi-dimensional spreadsheet

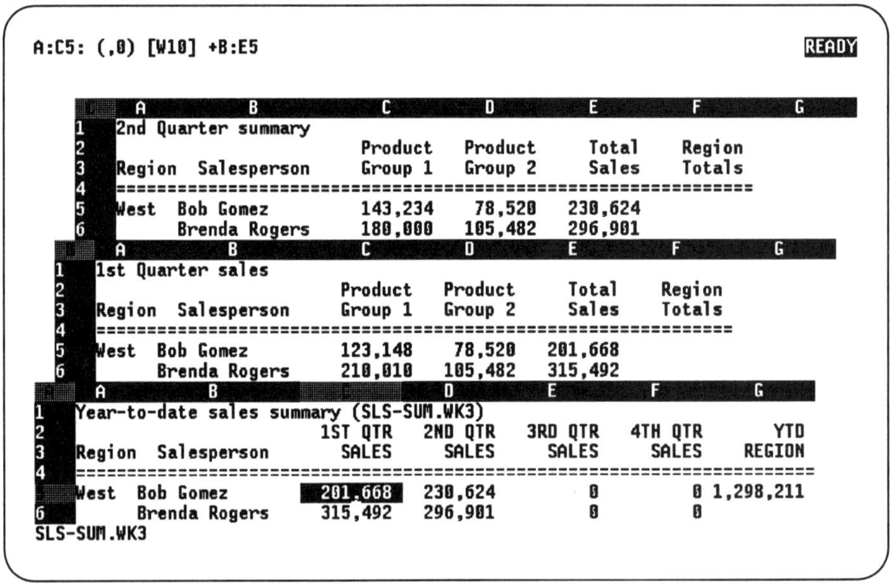

Figure 11-9 How the /Worksheet Window Perspective command displays a multi-dimensional spreadsheet that contains three worksheets

To link cells between the worksheets in a multi-dimensional spreadsheet, you use the notation shown in figure 11-10. In cell C6, for example, you can see this notation:

+B:E6

The plus sign is required to tell *Lotus* that the entry is a formula. Then, the B: identifies the worksheet, and the E6 identifies the cell that's linked to the current cell.

To enter a formula for linking cells like the ones in 11-10, you can use either the direct entry or the anchor-and-point method. With the anchor-and-point method, you type an operator like the plus sign to start the formula. Then, you use the keystroke combinations in figure 11-8 to move to the worksheet that has the cell that you want. Last, you move the cell pointer to the cell and press the Enter key.

If you compare this capability for linking cells to the one that started with *Lotus* release 2.2, you can see that there's less chance for error. Because it's easy to move from one worksheet to another, you can make sure that the cell references are correct. In addition, when you insert or delete rows or columns in a worksheet with cells that are linked to another worksheet, the cell addresses in that worksheet are automatically changed so they still refer to the right data. The cell linking feature provided by release 2.2 can't make this adjustment.

How to use two /File commands so you can work on more than one spreadsheet file at the same time (release 3.0 and later)

Sometimes, it isn't practical to put all of your related spreadsheets into one three-dimensional spreadsheet file. But you may still want to create links between the separate files. When you create these links, you can use the /File Open and /File New commands that release 3.X provides to open and use more than one spreadsheet file at a time. Using these commands can make it easier to create links between two spreadsheet files because you can easily view the spreadsheets that you want to use for a link.

To illustrate, figure 11-11 shows three different spreadsheet files after they have been loaded into *Lotus*. They are displayed using the perspective view that is provided by the /Worksheet Windows Perspective command. Here, the first spreadsheet is named SLS-SUM.WK3. It uses the cell linking formulas provided by releases 2.2 and later. The second spreadsheet is named Q1SLS.WK3, and it is the first quarter sales summary that the SLS-SUM.WK3 spreadsheet draws data from. The third spreadsheet is named Q2SLS.WK3, and it is the second quarter sales summary.

The /File Open command Figure 11-12 summarizes the procedure for using the /File Open command to open two or more spreadsheet files. In step 1, you use the /File Retrieve command to load the first file. In step 2, you execute the /File Open command and specify whether you want the next file to be opened before or after the current file. In step 3, you specify the name of the file you want to open. In step 4, you use the /Worksheet Window commands presented in figure 11-6 and the keystrokes for working with multiple spreadsheets presented in figure 11-8.

The year-to-date spreadsheet

```
A:A1: [W6] 'Year-to-date sales summary (SLS-SUM.WK3)                    READY

 A  A        B            C         D         E         F          G
1  Year-to-date sales summary (SLS-SUM.WK3)
2                       1ST QTR   2ND QTR   3RD QTR   4TH QTR        YTD
3  Region  Salesperson    SALES     SALES     SALES     SALES     REGION
4  =====================================================================
5  West  Bob Gomez       201,668   230,624         0         0 1,298,211
6        Brenda Rogers   315,492   296,901         0         0
7        Lori Anders     124,277   129,248         0         0
8
9  North Wendy Jones     124,262   158,265         0         0   570,068
10       Jack James      114,708   172,832         0         0
11
12 South Lisa Van Dyke   311,080   261,503         0         0 1,540,216
13       John Underwood  278,898   259,650         0         0
14       Frank Hart      210,336   218,749         0         0
15
16 East  Bill Lang       292,789   304,501         0         0   878,840
17       Lee Wong        138,015   143,536         0         0
18 =====================================================================
19                     2,111,525 2,175,809         0         0 4,287,334
20
SLS-SUM.WK3                                             NUM
```

The formulas used in the year-to-date spreadsheet

```
A:A1: (T) [W6] 'Year-to-date sales summary (SLS-SUM.WK3)                READY

 A  A        B            C         D         E         F          G
1  Year-to-date sales summary (SLS-SUM.WK3)
2                       1ST QTR   2ND QTR   3RD QTR   4TH QTR        YTD
3  Region  Salesperson    SALES     SALES     SALES     SALES     REGION
4  =====================================================================
5  West  Bob Gomez      +B:E5     +C:E5     +D:E5     +E:E5     1,298,211
6        Brenda Rogers  +B:E6     +C:E6     +D:E6     +E:E6
7        Lori Anders    +B:E7     +C:E7     +D:E7     +E:E7
8
9  North Wendy Jones    +B:E9     +C:E9     +D:E9     +E:E9       570,068
10       Jack James     +B:E10    +C:E10    +D:E10    +E:E10
11
12 South Lisa Van Dyke  +B:E12    +C:E12    +D:E12    +E:E12    1,540,216
13       John Underwood +B:E13    +C:E13    +D:E13    +E:E13
14       Frank Hart     +B:E14    +C:E14    +D:E14    +E:E14
15
16 East  Bill Lang      +B:E16    +C:E16    +D:E16    +E:E16      878,840
17       Lee Wong       +B:E17    +C:E17    +D:E17    +E:E17
18 =====================================================================
19                     2,111,525 2,175,809         0         0 4,287,334
20
SLS-SUM.WK3                                             NUM
```

Figure 11-10 A year-to-date sales worksheet with links to four quarterly worksheets in a multi-dimensional spreadsheet (release 3.X)

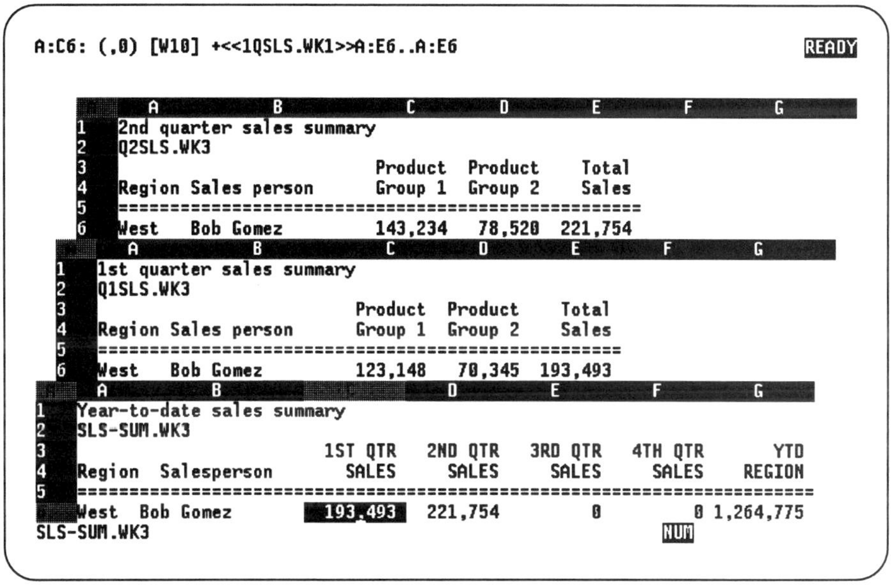

Figure 11-11 Three different spreadsheet files in a perspective display after they have been opened by the /File Retrieve and /File Open commands

When you load multiple files and then use the /File Save command, *Lotus* displays the following prompt:

`Enter name of file to save: [ALL MODIFIED FILES]`

To save all of the files, you just press the Enter key. *Lotus* then saves the files using their original names. Otherwise, can you press the Esc key once, then use the regular procedure for saving the current spreadsheet. To save each of the other files, you repeat the /File Save command and press the Esc key.

The /File New command As you can see in figure 11-13, the /File New command works like the /File Open command. The difference is that the /File New command lets you create a new spreadsheet file, while the /File Open command opens an existing file. In step 1, you tell the /File Open command whether you want the new spreadsheet before or after the current spreadsheet. In step 2, you specify a name for the new spreadsheet.

Discussion

When you link cells between spreadsheets or between the worksheets in a multi-dimensional spreadsheet, you can create two or more small spreadsheets or worksheets instead of one large one. This can help you simplify your development work. On the other hand, linking cells between

1. Retrieve the first file using the /File Retrieve command.
2. Start the /File Open command and select one of these options from the control panel:

   `Before    After`

   This tells *Lotus* whether you want the file opened before of after the current spreadsheet.
3. Specify the name of the spreadsheet file you want to open:

   ```
   Enter name of file to open: D:\WK3\*.WK*
   Q1SLS.WK3   Q2SLS.WK3   Q3SLS.WK3   Q4SLS.WK3   SLSSUM.WK3
   ```
4. Now, you can repeat the process to open more files. And you can use the /Worksheet Window commands presented in figure 11-6 and the keystrokes presented in figure 11-8 to view and move between the spreadsheets you have open.
5. When you're through working on your files, you can save them using the /File Save command. To save all of them at one time, press the Enter key at this prompt:

   ```
   Enter name of file to save: [ALL MODIFIED FILES]
   ```

   Otherwise, press the Esc key at this prompt. Then, use the regular procedure for saving each file you modified.

Figure 11-12 How to use the /File Retrieve and /File Open commands to open two or more spreadsheet files at the same time

two spreadsheets can also lead to inaccuracy and inefficiency. If, for example, you insert rows in a spreadsheet with linked cells when you're using *Lotus* release 2.4, you also have to change the addresses in the spreadsheet that provides the links. Otherwise, the links won't work correctly.

If you use *Lotus* 3.0 or later to link cells between two worksheets in a multi-dimensional spreadsheet, you reduce the chance for an error because *Lotus* automatically adjusts the addresses in the worksheet that provides the links. However, when you use this linking feature, all of the worksheets of the multi-dimensional spreadsheet are in internal memory at the same time. As a result, your PC may require more memory to accommodate the worksheets, and your PC may run more slowly.

Because each of these methods for linking cells has limitations, developing one large spreadsheet is occasionally the best way to work. That way, you can work efficiently because you won't have to use any new techniques or commands. You can be sure that the cell references from one portion of the spreadsheet to another are accurate. And you won't have to upgrade your release of *Lotus*.

However, some *Lotus* applications benefit from the use of linked cells. If your applications are in this category and you aren't already using *Lotus*

1. Start the /File New command and select one of these options from the control panel:

   ```
   Before    After
   ```

   This tells *Lotus* whether you want the new file inserted before or after the current spreadsheet.

2. Specify a name for the new spreadsheet file at the prompt and press the Enter key:

   ```
   Enter name of file to create: D:\WK3\*.WK*
   Q1SLS.WK3    Q2SLS.WK3    Q3SLS.WK3    Q4SLS.WK3    SLSSUM.WK3
   ```

Figure 11-13 How to use the /File New command to create a new file while you already have other spreadsheet files open

release 3.0 or later, you should consider an upgrade to release 3.4 because it provides the best linking features. Remember, though, that this release of *Lotus* requires a PC with at least a 286 processor and 1MB of internal memory. In addition, this release of *Lotus* runs considerably slower on a 286 than the 2.X releases run.

Terms

linking cells
worksheet
multi-dimensional spreadsheet
3D spreadsheet

Objectives

1. Decide if your applications will benefit from the *Lotus* features for sharing data and linking cells.
2. Use the sharing and linking features that are appropriate for your spreadsheets.
3. Decide whether it's worth upgrading to *Lotus* release 3.4 for its improved cell-linking features.

Chapter 12

How to import data from or export data to another program

If you switch to *Lotus* from another spreadsheet program, you probably will want to convert your old spreadsheet files to the *Lotus* format. Similarly, you may occasionally want to retrieve data that has been created by another program like a database program into a *Lotus* spreadsheet. And you may occasionally want to convert the data from a *Lotus* spreadsheet into a form that can be used by another program like a word processing program.

When a program retrieves data from another program and converts it into its own format, it can be referred to as *importing* the data. When a program can save its own data in a form that can be used by another program, it can be referred to as *exporting* the data. In this chapter, you will learn how to use the import and export functions that *Lotus* provides, but you will also learn how to take advantage of the functions that other programs provide.

How to transfer data to or from programs that have *Lotus* import and export functions

Because *Lotus* is the most widely-used spreadsheet program, many other programs provide import and export functions that are specifically designed for use with *Lotus*. For instance, *Quattro Pro* is a DOS-based spreadsheet program that can import a *Lotus* spreadsheet just as though it were a *Quattro Pro* spreadsheet. All you have to do is retrieve the *Lotus* spreadsheet. Similarly, if you want to export a *Quattro Pro* spreadsheet to *Lotus*, you just save it with the extension WK1 instead of WKQ. This automatically saves the spreadsheet in the format required by *Lotus*.

Many other spreadsheet programs provide similar import and export functions for *Lotus* files. As a result, when you want to import a spreadsheet from one of these programs, you can use the export function of that program, instead of the import function of the *Lotus* program. You should realize,

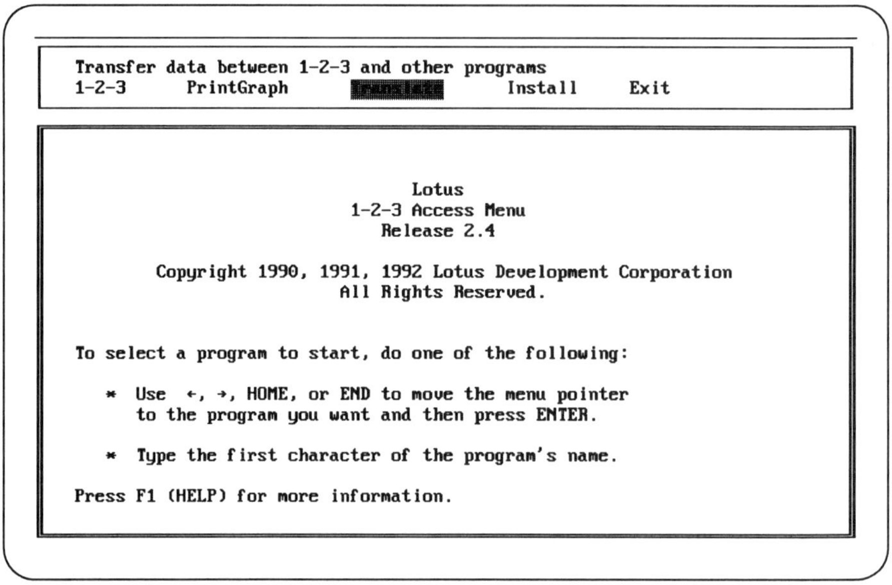

Figure 12-1 The *Lotus* Access System menu

though, that the export function may not provide for the advanced features of the program. If, for example, you've used the macro or graphics functions of another spreadsheet program, they may not be usable after the spreadsheet has been converted to a *Lotus* spreadsheet.

Besides spreadsheet programs, many other programs provide import and export functions for *Lotus* files. For instance, database programs often provide these functions. Then, you can use the import function of the database program to retrieve a *Lotus* spreadsheet in the format of the database. And you can use the export function of the database program to save the database in the *Lotus* format. So when you want to import data from another program into a *Lotus* spreadsheet or export data from a *Lotus* spreadsheet into the format required by another program, you should start by checking the import and export functions of the other program. That may make the job easy for you.

How to use the Translate utility to convert data to or from *Lotus* format

Lotus provides a Translate utility that provides for a variety of conversions to and from the *Lotus* format. To start the Translate utility, you select the Translate option from the Access System menu shown in figure 12-1. To start *Lotus* with the Access System menu instead of the spreadsheet screen, you usually enter *lotus* instead of *123* at the DOS command prompt as in this example:

```
C:>cd \123
C:\123>lotus
```

If you don't start *Lotus* from the command prompt, your PC should provide another way for displaying the Access System menu.

When you select Translate from the Access System menu, *Lotus* displays the first screen in figure 12-2. Here, you can see the file formats that are supported by the Translate utility that comes with *Lotus* release 2.4, but the formats vary somewhat from one release to another. To translate a file that has any one of the formats listed in figure 12-2, you select the appropriate format. Then, *Lotus* displays a screen like the second one in this figure. This screen shows the conversions that are available for the format you selected on the first screen. In figure 12-2, you can see that the Translate utility lets you convert a *Lotus* 2.4 spreadsheet to any one of eight other formats.

When you reach the second screen in figure 12-2, *Lotus* gives you information that helps you complete the conversion. If, for example, you are trying to convert a *Lotus* spreadsheet into a database format, the help information tells you how the spreadsheet needs to be formatted for the conversion to work right. And if the file that you're trying to convert doesn't have the right format, *Lotus* displays an appropriate message.

The dBase II and III options on this list specify the file formats used by the *dBase* program. Many database programs support these formats even if they don't store their files in them by default. As a result, you can probably use one of the dBase formats to transfer data into *Lotus* even if you are using another database program. After you export the data from your database program into the dBase format, you can use the Translate utility to convert it to *Lotus* format. When the translation is complete, you can use the /File Retrieve command to load the new file.

The *DIF* format is a standard format that's short for Data Interchange Format. Since many application programs support this format, you can also use this format to help you get data from one program to another. If, for example, you use the Translate utility to convert a *Lotus* spreadsheet to a DIF file, another program that supports this format can import the data from the DIF file into the format that it requires.

How to use text files to export or import data

If the application program that you want to import data from or export data to doesn't provide an appropriate function and if the *Lotus* Translate utility doesn't provide one either, you can usually use *text files* (also know as *ASCII text files* or *ASCII files*) to get the job done. Text files are general-purpose files, and most programs provide for both exporting and importing them. Often, though, working with text files takes more time than using specific import or export functions, and the conversion isn't as thorough as you would like it to be.

The most useful type of text file is a *delimited text file*. This type of file contains one or more *records*, and the end of each record is marked by the code for the Enter key. In addition, each record is usually divided into two or more *fields* by *delimiters*. The delimiters are the comma, the semicolon, the colon, and one or more spaces. When you import this type of file, each record in the file becomes one row in a spreadsheet, and each field in a record becomes one cell in the row.

The other type of text file can be called a *nondelimited text file*, but most people refer to them as just *text files* or as *ASCII files*. This type of file contains lines of text with no delimiters, and each line of text ends with the code for the Enter key. When you import this type of file, each line (or record) in the file becomes one cell in the spreadsheet. As a result, this type of file is more difficult to work with.

To export or import text files, you use the *Lotus* commands that are summarized in figure 12-3. You can use the /Print File command to export a range within a spreadsheet as a nondelimited text file. You can use the /File Import command to import either a text file or a delimited text file into a spreadsheet.

How to export data from *Lotus* to a nondelimited text file One of the best uses of a text file is for transferring a *Lotus* spreadsheet to a word processing program. Then, the word processing program can use the spreadsheet data in a document like a report. Although some word processing programs provide import functions for *Lotus* files, you can usually use a nondelimited text file for this purpose too.

To save a portion of a spreadsheet as a text file, you use the /Print File command that's summarized in figure 12-3. This command directs the output of the /Print command to a text file instead of a printer. Otherwise, the command works like the /Print Printer command. Before you select the Go option, you should be sure that you have identified the range that you want exported. Then, when you select the Go option, *Lotus* prompts you for the file name that you want to use for the text file. After the file has been saved in this format, you can use your word processing program to retrieve the text file into a document. If, for example, you're using *WordPerfect*, you use the Text In command to retrieve the text file.

When *Lotus* "prints" a spreadsheet to a text file, it creates spaces for the left margin, and it puts in empty lines for the top and bottom margins. If, for example, the left margin for a print job is set to 4, *Lotus* puts four spaces at the beginning of every line in the file. And if the top margin is set to 2, *Lotus* puts two blank lines at the top of the file. Usually, though, you want to use your word processing program to format the report that contains the spreadsheet. That's why it's best to set the left, top, and bottom margins to zero before you save the range to a text file.

The first screen of the Translate utility for *Lotus* 2.4

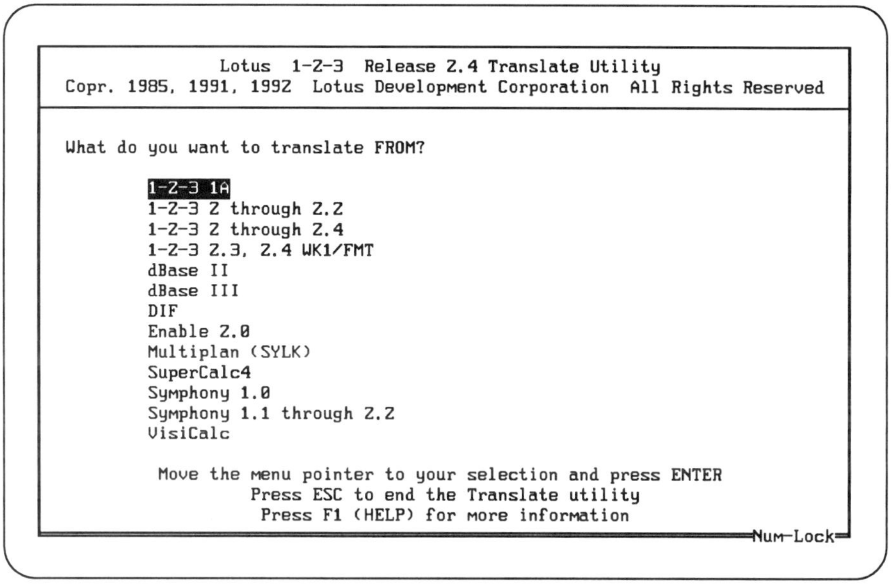

The second screen of the Translate utility when you want to transfer from *Lotus* 2.4 to another format

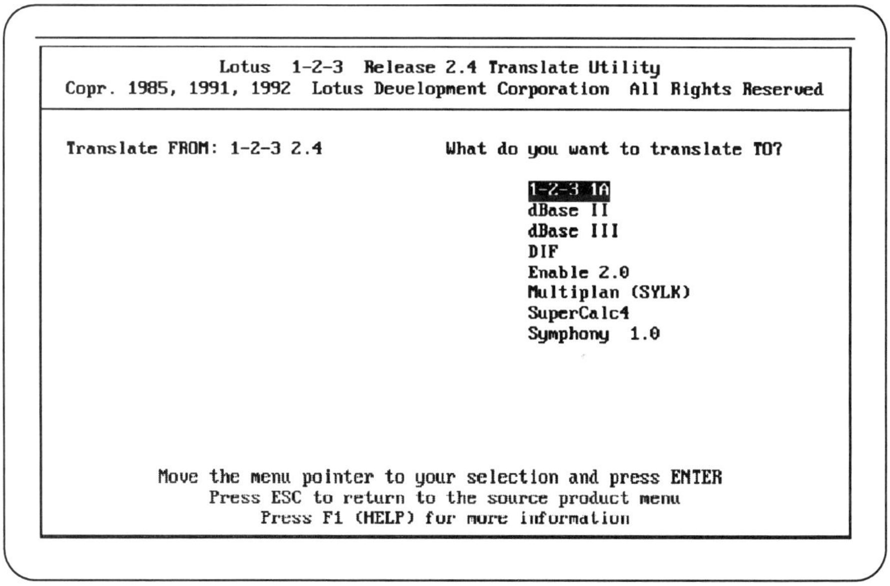

Figure 12-2 Two screens of the Translate utility for *Lotus* 2.4

Command name	Next level	Function
/Print File F6 (Window)		Transfer the contents of the print range to a nondelimited text file with one row in the print range as one line in the text file
/File Import	Text	Transfer the contents of a nondelimited text file into column A of the current spreadsheet with one line of the text file in each row (cell)
	Numbers	For a nondelimited text file, transfer just the values in the file into one column of the current spreadsheet with one line of the text file in each row (cell)
		For a delimited text file, transfer the contents of the file into the current spreadsheet with one record in the file in each row and with one field in each record in each column

Figure 12-3 The *Lotus* commands for exporting or importing text files

How to import a delimited text file Figure 12-4 shows you how to import a delimited text file into *Lotus* using the /File Import Numbers command that is summarized in figure 12-3. In this example, the text file contains two records, and each record contains four fields. Although the numeric fields aren't in quotation marks, the alphanumeric fields have to be in quotation marks.

When you start the /File Import Numbers command, *Lotus* asks for the name of the file that you want to import. Then, *Lotus* imports each record of the file into a row, and it puts each field in a separate cell. It also imports the numeric fields as values and the alphanumeric fields as labels.

If you purchase a database that has been created by another a company, you can usually get it in the delimited text format. In addition, most database programs have the ability to save data to a delimited text file. As a result, you can usually use a delimited text file to transfer the data from a database into a *Lotus* spreadsheet. Most databases and database programs also support one of the *dBase* formats, though. In that case, you have to decide which format is easier to use for the conversion: the dBase format or the delimited text format.

When you use some database programs to save the data in delimited text format, both the numeric and the alphanumeric fields are enclosed in quotation marks. Then, when you use the /File Import Numbers command to import the file, both the numeric and alphanumeric fields are imported as labels. Unfortunately, though, that usually isn't what you want because you can't perform arithmetic operations on labels. As a result, for database

The contents of a delimited text file

```
100,"John Smith",12905,32890
101,"Beverly Ryan",18330,39511
```

The codes used in a delimited text file

Code	**Use**
,	Field delimiter
;	Field delimiter
:	Field delimiter
" "	Enclose alphanumeric fields (labels)
one or more spaces	Field delimiter

The file after it has been imported into *Lotus* (the data is in columns A through D with one record of the text file as one row of the spreadsheet and with one field of each record in each cell)

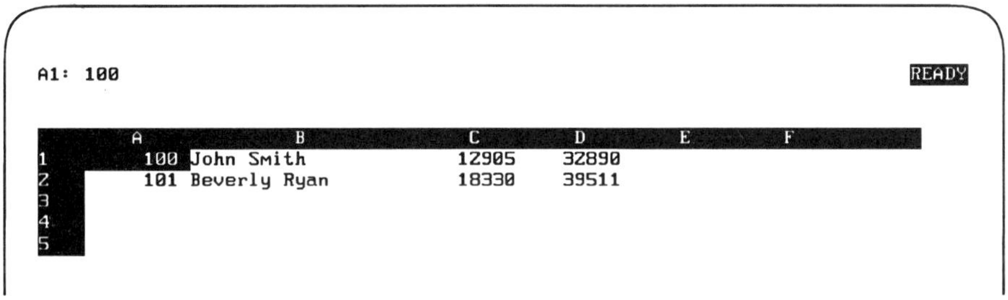

Figure 12-4 How a delimited text file is imported into *Lotus* by the /File Import Numbers command

programs that work this way, you're usually better off using the dBase format than the delimited text format as the transfer format.

How to import a nondelimited text file Figure 12-5 shows you how to import a nondelimited text file into *Lotus* using the /File Import Text command that is summarized in figure 12-3. In this example, the text file contains two lines of information.

When you start the /File Import Text command, *Lotus* asks for the name of the file that you want to import. If you don't specify the extension, *Lotus* assumes an extension of PRN, but you can override this assumption by typing the correct extension. Then, when *Lotus* imports the file, it treats each line in the text file as a single label in the spreadsheet. In figure 12-5, for example, the first line of the text file is stored in cell A1 of the spreadsheet; the second line in cell A2.

Because most programs have the ability to save a file as a text file, you can use this method for transferring data from most programs to *Lotus*. You should consider this a last resort, though, because all of the data in each line of the text file is stored in a single cell. As a result, you can't operate on the separate portions of data within each cell. Before you can do that, you must use the /Data Parse command.

If you want to import just the numeric data from a text file, you can use the /File Import Numbers command. This works the same way that /File Import Text command works, but only the numbers are imported. All other characters are ignored.

When you use the /File Import Numbers command, *Lotus* assumes that spaces are meant to delimit fields. In other words, *Lotus* assumes that the file is delimited if a record contains one or more spaces. As a result, any numbers that are separated by spaces are put in separate cells. Sometimes, this works the way you want it to so you can operate upon the individual fields without using the /Data Parse command. Often, though, it doesn't work quite right so you end up having to use this command.

In an ASCII file like the one in figure 12-5, the items of data (fields) within the lines (records) are aligned. That means that the fields have the same length. For instance, the first three characters in each record probably represent one numeric field. The next twenty characters probably represent one alphanumeric field. And the next ten characters probably represent one or more numeric fields. Because the fields have fixed lengths as opposed to variable lengths, a file like this is sometimes referred to as a *fixed ASCII file*. When you're working with a nondelimited file, you want it to be a fixed file because that makes it easier for you to separate the data into fields by using the /Data Parse command.

How to parse the data in a text file after it has been imported into a spreadsheet

Figure 12-6 summarizes the use of the /Data Parse command. The purpose of this command is to divide up the data that is stored in one cell and copy it into separate cells. This function can be referred to as *parsing*. When you use this command, you usually are trying to parse the data that is stored in one column of a spreadsheet into separate columns. For instance, you can use this command to parse the data in column A in figure 12-5 into separate columns.

To parse the data in a column, you follow the procedure given in figure 12-7. In step 1, you move the cell pointer to the top row in the column that is to be parsed and start the /Data Parse Format-Line Create command. This inserts a new row at the top of the data to be parsed. It also creates a *format*

The contents of a nondelimited text file

```
100John Smith           1290532890
101Beverly Ryan         1833039511
```

The file after it has been imported into *Lotus* (all of the data is in column A with one line of the text file as one row of the spreadsheet)

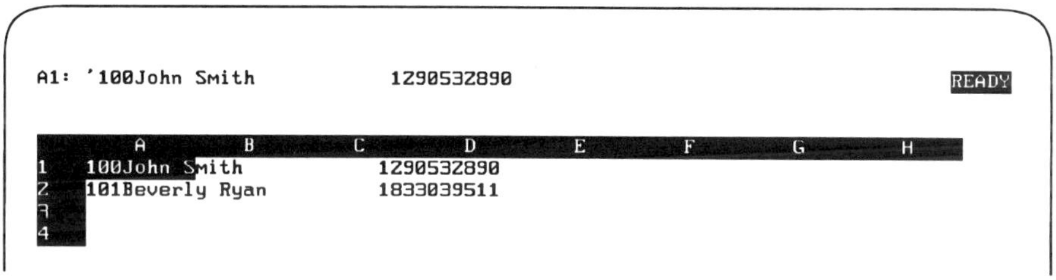

Figure 12-5 How a nondelimited text file is imported into *Lotus* by the /File Import Text command

line as shown in figure 12-7. The format line contains the codes given in figure 12-6, and *Lotus* automatically creates the initial format line based on the data in the first cell below the format line.

Sometimes, *Lotus* makes the right assumptions so you don't have to edit the format line. More often, though, the format line isn't quite right so you have to edit it in step 2. To do that, you use the Edit option of the /Data Parse Format-Line command. As you edit, you can use the codes and keystrokes in figure 12-6 in addition to the normal editing keystrokes.

In step 3, you use the Input-Column option of the /Data Parse command to identify the range of cells that you want to parse. This range must include the format line. Then, in step 4, you use the Output-Range option to identify the range that should receive the parsed data. In general, the output range should be in a different area of the spreadsheet than the input column is in. That way, you can parse the data over again if the command doesn't work the way you expected it to. After you set the output range, you use the Go option to parse the data. When the parsing is complete, you can use the Quit option to exit from the command and return to the spreadsheet.

If the parsing doesn't work the way you want it to, you can edit the format line by using the /Data Parse Format-Line Edit command. Then, you can parse the data again. Sometimes, you have to parse different portions of the data column with different format lines. Eventually, though, you should be able to get the text data in a form that you can use.

Command name	Next level	Function
/Data Parse F6 (Window)	Format-Line	Create or edit the format line that shows how the data in the column is to be parsed (separated) into other cells
	Input-Column	Identify the range of cells to be parsed including the cell that contains the Format line
	Output-Range	Identify the range of cells that is going to receive the parsed data
	Reset	Clear all parse settings
	Go	Parse the data
	Quit	Exit from the /Data Parse command

The codes that you can use in the format line

Code	Meaning
`L`	The start of a label
`V`	The start of a value
`D`	The start of a date
`T`	The start of a time
`S`	The start of characters to be skipped
>	Continuation of the label, value, date, time, or skip
*	A space that should be skipped

The keystrokes you can use as you edit a format line in addition to the normal editing keystrokes

Keystroke	Meaning
Up arrow	Scroll the labels to be parsed up one row so you can see how the format line matches up with the data
Down arrow	Scroll the labels to be parsed down one row
Page-up	Scroll the labels to be parsed up one page
Page-down	Scroll the labels to be parsed down one page
Esc	Erase the format line so you can start over

Figure 12-6 The options, codes, and keystrokes for the /Data Parse command

A screen that shows the format line, input column, and output range for a parsing operation

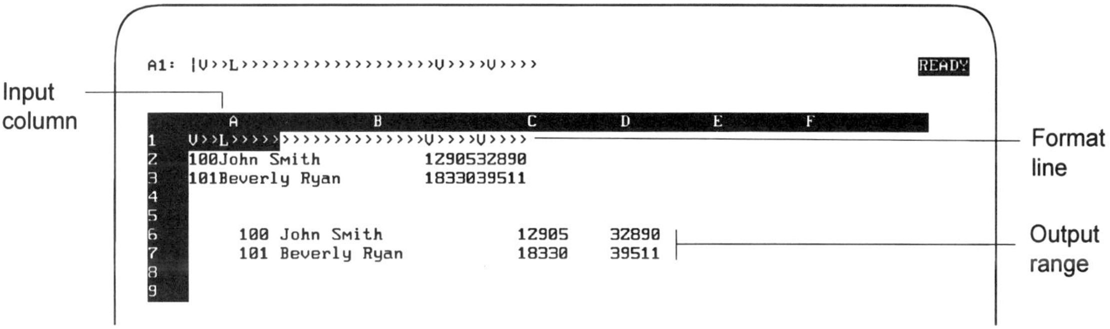

How to use the /Data Parse command to parse the labels in a column

1. Move the cell pointer to the top of the column that you want to parse, and start the /Data Parse Format-Line Create command. This inserts a new row at the top of the column and creates a format line in this row that is based on the data in the first cell to be parsed.
2. If you need to modify the format line, use the Format-Line Edit option of the /Data Parse command. As you edit, you can use any of the codes or keystrokes in figure 12-6 in addition to the normal editing keystrokes.
3. Use the Input-Column option to identify the cells that you want to parse. Be sure to include the cell that contains the format line.
4. Use the Output-Range option to identify the range of cells that should receive the parsed data.
5. Use the Go option to perform the parsing operation.
6. Use the Quit option to exit from the command and return to the spreadsheet screen.

Figure 12-7 A screen that shows the operation of the /Data Parse command

Discussion

If you need to import data from another program to *Lotus* or export data from *Lotus* to another program, you can probably do it without too much trouble. That's because most programs provide their own facilities for using *Lotus* data. Before you use the *Lotus* import and export functions, then, you should check the import and export functions that are provided by the other program. If those functions don't provide an obvious solution to your problem, you can check the options that are offered by the *Lotus* Translate utility. And if all else fails, you can usually use a delimited or nondelimited text file for importing or exporting the data.

Terms

importing
exporting
DIF
text file
ASCII text file
ASCII file
delimited text file
record
field
delimiter
nondelimited text file
fixed ASCII file
parsing
format line

Objectives

1. Decide which functions are most efficient for importing data from or exporting data to a specific program: the functions of the other program, the *Lotus* functions, or a combination of the two.
2. Use the Translate utility for performing any of the file conversions that it provides for.
3. Use the /Print File and /File Import commands for exporting or importing text files.
4. Use the /Data Parse command for parsing data that has been imported from a nondelimited text file.

Chapter 13

How to manage *Lotus* files

As you use *Lotus*, you create and save spreadsheet files to disk storage. Before long, you can have dozens of spreadsheets in several different directories. Eventually, you need to manage these files. In other words, you need to erase files that you no longer need. You need to copy or move files from one drive or directory to another. You need to find the files you want to use. And so on.

Lotus provides several commands and features to help you manage your files, and you'll learn how to use these commands and features in this chapter. But you should know right from the start that there are some file management tasks that you can't do with *Lotus*. For instance, you can't copy files or create directories with *Lotus*. Instead, you must do these and other tasks using DOS. Furthermore, it's often easier to use DOS for a file management task than it is to use the command that *Lotus* provides for the task.

As a result, you may want to skip this chapter if you already know how to use DOS to manage your files. If, on the other hand, you don't know how to use DOS, you'll benefit from knowing the commands presented here. Eventually, though, you'll have to know how to use DOS to do the tasks that you can't do with *Lotus*.

How to use the *Lotus* commands for managing files

Figure 13-1 presents the three commands that *Lotus* provides for managing files. All releases of *Lotus* provide the first two commands for deleting and listing files. But only releases 2.2 and later provide the third command for creating a file table.

The /File Erase command Figure 13-2 shows you how to use the /File Erase command to delete a file from disk storage. In step 1, you specify the type of file you want to erase. The Worksheet option lists spreadsheet files. The Print option lists text files that use the PRN extension. The Graph option lists *Lotus* graph files. And the Other option lists all the files in a directory.

Command	Function
/File Erase F3 (Name)	Erase the file you specify from disk storage.
/File List	Display a list of *Lotus* files. You can list spreadsheet, print, graph, or all files. With releases 3.0 and later, you can list the files that are loaded in memory. And with releases 2.2 and later, you can list the files that are linked to the current spreadsheet.
/File Admin Table	Create a table of the files in a directory in the current spreadsheet. This table can include spreadsheet, print, graph or all files. With releases 3.0 and later, you can include files that are loaded in memory. And with releases 2.2 and later, you can include files that are linked to the current spreadsheet.

Figure 13-1 The commands *Lotus* provides for managing files

After you select the option for the type of file you want to erase, *Lotus* displays a file list in the third line of the control panel as shown in step 2. Then, you can press the F3 (Name) key to display a list of all of the files in the directory. Next, you specify the file you want to erase by highlighting it or by typing its name. If the file you want to erase isn't in the current directory, you can press the Esc key to clear the path specification so you can type a new specification. After you specify the file you want to erase, you press the Enter key.

In step 3, you respond to the prompt *Lotus* displays. If you're sure that you want to delete the file, you select Yes. Otherwise, you can cancel the command by selecting No.

The /File List command Figure 13-3 shows you how to use the /File List command to list all the files in a directory. This listing is equivalent to the one that you get when you press the F3 (Name) key when you're using the /File Retrieve, Save, or Erase command. As you will see, this command is most useful when you only want to list certain types of files.

In step 1 in figure 13-3, you specify the type of file that you want to list by specifying one of the options that's displayed. The Worksheet option lists spreadsheet files. The Print option lists text files that use the PRN extension. The Graph option lists *Lotus* graph files. And the Other option lists all files in the current directory. If you have release 3.X, you can specify the Active option to list all of the files that are currently loaded into memory. And if you have release 2.2 or a later, you can specify the Linked option to list all spreadsheets that are linked to the current spreadsheet.

In step 2, *Lotus* displays the selected files. Then, you can use the Arrow keys to move from one file to another in the listing. In the second line of the

1. When you select the /File Erase command, *Lotus* displays the following options:

   Worksheet   Print   Graph   Other

   You select Worksheet to display spreadsheet files; Print to display text files that use the PRN extension; Graph to display graph files; and Other to display all of the files in the current directory.

2. Specify the file you want to erase from disk storage at the next prompt:

   Enter name of file to erase: D:\WK1*.wk?
   EXP-TEMP.WK1   EXPENSES.WK1   LOAN.WK1   PROFIT-P.WK1

   Here, you can either highlight the file you want to erase, or you can type the file name. After you specify the file you want to erase, press the Enter key.

3. Respond to the warning prompt that *Lotus* displays next:

   No Yes
   Cancel command – Do not erase the file

   You select Yes to erase the file or No to cancel the command.

Figure 13-2 How to use the /File Erase command to delete a *Lotus* file from disk storage

1. When you select the /File List command, *Lotus* 3.X displays the following options:

   Worksheet   Print   Graph   Other   Active   Linked

   Select Worksheet to list spreadsheet files; Print to list text files that use the PRN extension; Graph to list graph files; Other to list all of the files in the current directory; Active (*Lotus* 3.0 and later) to list all of the files loaded into internal memory; and Linked (*Lotus* 2.2 and later) to list all the files that are linked to the current spreadsheet.

2. *Lotus* then displays a file list like the one it uses for other /File operations when you press the F3 (Name) key. Here, you can use the Arrow keys to move the highlight, and you can change directories by highlighting one in the list and pressing the Enter key.
3. To exit from the command, you press the Esc key.

Figure 13-3 How to use the /File List command to view the files in the current directory

control panel, *Lotus* displays information about the highlighted file including the date and time that the file was last saved and its size in bytes. After you find the file that you're looking for, you can cancel the command by pressing the Esc key as summarized in step 3.

The /File Admin Table command (releases 2.2 and later) You can use this command to create a table of the files in a directory. This table contains the file name, the date and time that the file was last saved, and size of the file in bytes. Then, you can print the table if you want to keep a hard copy of this information.

Figure 13-4 shows you how to use the /File Admin Table command. In step 1, you specify the type of file you want included in the table. Like the /File List command, the options are Worksheet, Print, and so on.

In step 2, you specify the directory that contains the files that you want included in the table. By default, *Lotus* displays the current directory. If you want to use this directory, you just press the Enter key. Otherwise, you can use the Esc key to clear the current directory so you can enter the appropriate one.

In step 3, you specify the range in the current spreadsheet that you want to use for the table. If the current spreadsheet is blank, you can specify cell A1 for the range. But if the current spreadsheet contains data, be sure to specify a blank range. Otherwise, the table will overwrite existing data in the spreadsheet.

In step 4, *Lotus* creates the table in the current spreadsheet. The name of each file is in the first column. The date value is in the second column. The time value is in the third column. And the file size in bytes is in the fourth column.

In step 5, you can make the table more useful by adjusting the widths of the columns using the /Worksheet Column Set-Width command. In addition, you can use the /Range Format command to apply date and time formats to the date and time columns. You may also want to enter a label that identifies the directory that the files are in if you want to print the table.

If you use linked spreadsheets, the /File Admin Table command is particularly useful. When you specify the Linked option, the command creates a table of all of the files that are linked to the current spreadsheet. This makes it easier to keep track of the links that are used in a spreadsheet. (If you want to learn more about how to link data between spreadsheets, you should read chapter 11.)

How to use the *Viewer* add-in program for finding and retrieving files (release 2.3, 2.4, and 3.4)

Lotus 1-2-3 releases 2.3, 2.4, and 3.4 come with an *add-in program* called *Viewer*. This add-in program uses its own screen, and it displays a file list that's similar to the list displayed by one of the /File commands. When you move the highlight to one of the files in this list, however, *Viewer* automatically displays a portion of the spreadsheet that's stored in the file. This helps you find the file you want to use.

1. When you execute the /File Admin Table command, *Lotus* displays the following options:

   ```
   Worksheet  Print  Graph  Other  Active  Linked
   ```

   You select Worksheet to select spreadsheet files for a table; Print to select files that use the PRN extension; Graph to select graph files; Other to select all of the files in the current directory; Active (releases 3.0 and later) to select all of the files loaded into memory; and Linked (releases 2.2 and later) to select all the files that are linked to the current spreadsheet.

2. Next, you specify the directory you want to use for the table:

   ```
   Enter directory: C:\WK1\*.wk?
   ```

   By default, *Lotus* displays the current directory. But you can specify any other drive or directory. This directory prompt is not displayed for the Active and Linked options.

3. At the next prompt, you specify the range you want to use for the table:

   ```
   Enter range for table: A1
   ```

   If you are using a blank spreadsheet, you can specify a range starting a cell A1 of the spreadsheet. But if you're using an existing spreadsheet, you must specify a range that won't affect existing portions of the spreadsheet.

Figure 13-4 How to use the /File Admin Table command to create a table of the files in a directory (part 1 of 2)

To illustrate, figure 13-5 shows you how to use *Viewer*. In step 1, you invoke this add-in program. If you don't know how to do this, chapter 14 explains the procedure in detail. Once invoked, *Viewer* asks whether you want to use the Retrieve, Link, or Browse option. The Retrieve option lets you view and then retrieve a file. The Link option lets you view a file and then create links to the current spreadsheet file as explained in chapter 11. And the Browse option just lets you view a file.

Step 2 shows the screen that *Viewer* uses once it has been invoked. In this example, the Retrieve option was selected in step 1. As you can see, the file list appears on the left side of the screen. In this example, the list is for the spreadsheet files in the \WK1 directory on the C drive. Since the highlight is on EXP-TEMP.WK1, that spreadsheet is displayed on the right side of the screen. Even though the entire spreadsheet isn't displayed, you can see enough of it to identify it. Then, to retrieve the file once you've identified it, you press the Enter key.

Although *Viewer* can be useful for finding files, it does have one drawback that you should be aware of. Just like all add-in programs, it requires internal memory. And that means that less memory is available for your spreadsheets. So if internal memory limitations are a problem, I

4. *Lotus* then creates a table of information on the files you specified like the one shown here:

A1: 'EXP-TEMP.WK1 READY

	A	B	C	D	E	F	G	H
1	EXP-TEMP.	33623	0.546608	2318				
2	EXPENSES.	33557	0.600254	2322				
3	LOAN.WK1	32995	0.594756	11744				
4	PROFIT-P.	33018	0.582974	6331				
5	Q1SLS.WK1	33066	0.564641	3201				
6	Q2SLS.WK1	33787	0.548877	4081				
7	Q3SLS.WK1	33787	0.549317	3919				
8	Q4SLS.WK1	33787	0.549398	3891				
9	SLS-SUM.W	33787	0.550115	4243				
10								

The file names are in the first column, the date values are in the second column, the time values are in the third column, and the file sizes are in the fourth column.

5. To make the table more useful, you can use the /Worksheet Column Set-Width command to increase the width of some of the columns. And you can use the /Range Format command to apply date and time formats to the second and third columns as shown here:

A1: [W14] 'EXP-TEMP.WK1 READY

	A	B	C	D	E	F	G
1	EXP-TEMP.WK1	01/20/92	01:07 PM	2318			
2	EXPENSES.WK1	11/15/91	02:24 PM	2322			
3	LOAN.WK1	05/02/90	02:16 PM	11744			
4	PROFIT-P.WK1	05/25/90	01:59 PM	6331			
5	Q1SLS.WK1	07/12/90	01:33 PM	3201			
6	Q2SLS.WK1	07/02/92	01:10 PM	4081			
7	Q3SLS.WK1	07/02/92	01:11 PM	3919			
8	Q4SLS.WK1	07/02/92	01:11 PM	3891			
9	SLS-SUM.WK1	07/02/92	01:12 PM	4243			
10							

Figure 13-4 How to use the /File Admin Table command to create a table of the files in a directory (part 2 of 2)

recommend that you only attach and invoke *Viewer* when you need it for a function that you can't do easily without it. For instance, you'll want to use *Viewer* when you can't remember what spreadsheets the file names in a directory refer to. And you'll want to use it when you're linking spreadsheets. On the other hand, you shouldn't need it for the routine retrieval of spreadsheet files.

1. Invoke the *Viewer* add-in program as described in chapter 14. *Lotus* then displays the following prompt:

   Retrieve Link Browse

   The Retrieve option lets you view and retrieve a file. The Link option lets you view and create links between files. And the Browse option just lets you view files.

2. After you select an option, *Lotus* displays a screen like this:

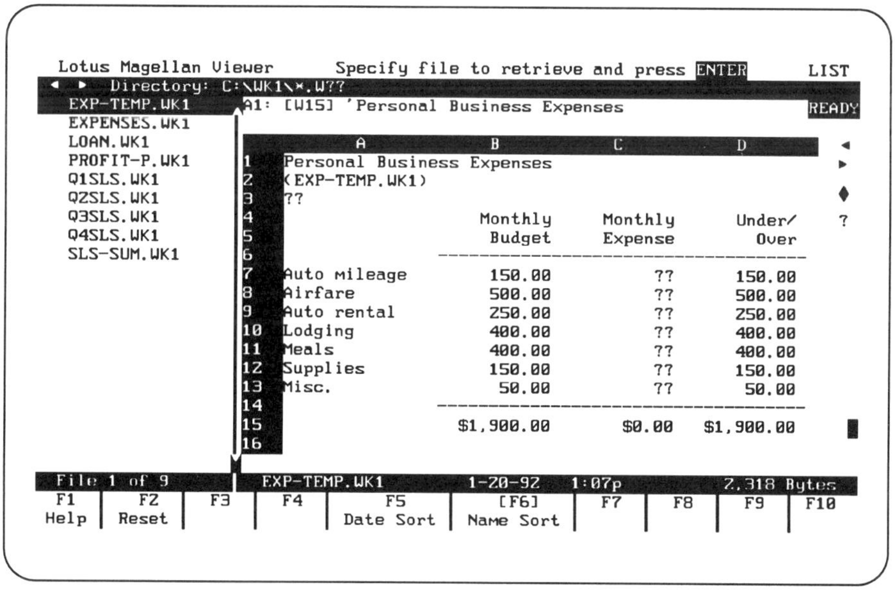

At this screen, you use the Up and Down arrow keys to highlight the files that you want to view so you can identify them.

Figure 13-5 How to use the *Viewer* add-in program to manage files

Why you should occasionally use DOS or a shell program to manage your *Lotus* files

If you're familiar with the DOS commands for managing files and directories, you know that the *Lotus* commands are limited. They only let you delete one file at a time. They don't let you copy or move files from one directory to another. They don't let you create or remove directories. And so on. That's why you occasionally need to use the DOS commands for managing your files.

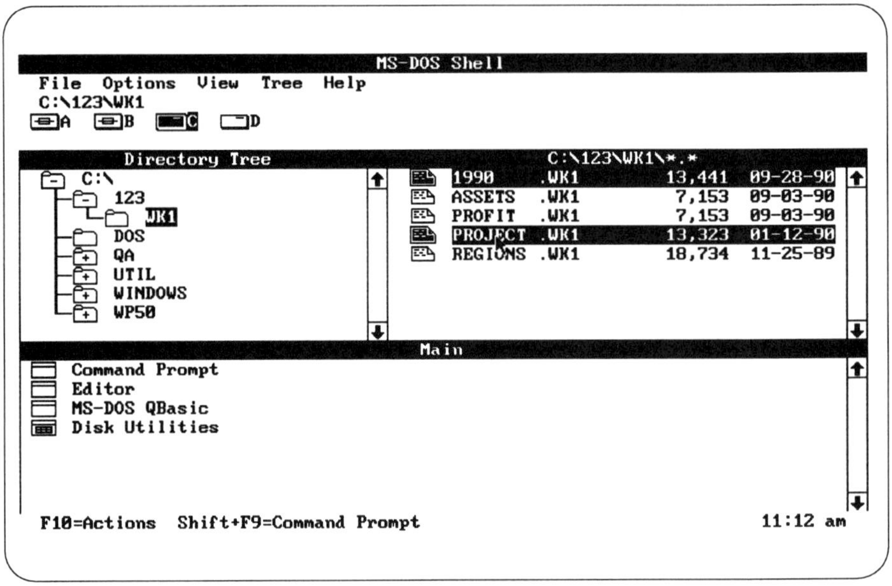

Figure 13-6 The DOS shell that comes with DOS 5.0

Often, the easiest way to use the DOS commands is through a *shell program*. For instance, figure 13-6 shows the shell program that comes with DOS 5.0 as it is used to display the files in the WK1 directory that is subordinate to the 123 directory. Here, two of the files in the directory are highlighted. After you highlight one or more files, you can pull down menus that make it easy for you to copy, move, or delete the files. Similarly, the shell makes it easy for you to add or remove directories from a hard disk.

If you want to learn more about the DOS commands for file management and about the DOS shell program, you can learn what you need to know from a companion book to this one. It is called *The Least You Need to Know About DOS*. It will help you keep your files under control when the commands provided by *Lotus* are no longer adequate for that purpose.

Terms

add-in program
shell program

Objectives

1. Use the /File commands that *Lotus* provides for managing files.
2. If you have the *Viewer* add-in program, use it for finding and retrieving files that you can't identify by their names.
3. Explain the need for the file management capabilities provided by DOS or a DOS shell.

Chapter 14

How to use add-in programs to enhance *Lotus 1-2-3*

An *add-in program* provides features or capabilities that *Lotus* itself doesn't provide. For instance, *Sideways* is an add-in program that lets you print a spreadsheet sideways (landscape mode) instead of vertically (portrait mode). Until *Lotus* release 3.X, you couldn't print a spreadsheet in landscape mode without using an add-in program.

Today, many add-in programs are available for use with *Lotus*, and you get a few of them when you buy *Lotus*. Because some of these may be useful for your applications, this chapter starts by showing you how to use add-in programs. Next, it introduces you to the add-in programs that are included with *Lotus* releases 2.4 and 3.4. Then, it introduces you to the types of add-in programs that are available from other vendors. Finally, it introduces you to two other types of products that you can buy to enhance *Lotus* applications.

As you read this chapter, keep in mind that I used release 2.4 for the examples. So unless you're using the same release, what you see on your screen may differ slightly from the screens in this chapter.

How to work with an add-in program

Before you can use an add-in program, it must be installed on the hard disk of your PC. Once an add-in program is installed, you can use *Lotus* commands to load it into memory and invoke it. Once it's invoked, you can use it with your spreadsheet. Then, when you're through using it, you can use other *Lotus* commands to remove it from internal memory.

Figure 14-1 summarizes the *Lotus* commands that you can use when you're working with an add-in program. In the descriptions that follow, I'll refer to the commands in this summary.

How to install an add-in When you install *Lotus 1-2-3*, you can *install* some or all of the add-in programs that come with your release of *Lotus*. If you decide later that you want to install an add-in that you omitted during the *Lotus* installation, you can perform part of the installation procedure over again using the *Lotus* diskettes.

If you're installing an add-in program that didn't come with *Lotus*, you follow the instructions that come with the program. Often, you just copy the add-in program files into the *Lotus* directory, but sometimes you can install the add-in program in a directory other than the *Lotus* directory.

How to attach an add-in program After the add-in program is installed on your hard disk, you have to load it into internal memory before you can use it. In *Lotus* terminology, you *attach* the program. To do this, you access the *Lotus* Add-in menu. If you're using release 2.2 through 2.4, the Add-in menu is an option on the Main menu, so you access the /Add-in menu by pressing /a. However, you can also press the Alt+F10 key combination to access this menu. If you're using *Lotus* release 3.X, though, you have to use the Alt+F10 key combination to access the Add-in menu.

Figure 14-2 shows how to attach an add-in program. In step 1, you select the Attach (2.X) or the Load (3.X) command from the Add-in menu. Then, the control panel displays the names of the add-in programs that have been installed in the *Lotus* program directory. To get a complete listing of all of the available add-in programs in that directory, you can press the F3 (Name) key. And if an add-in program is stored in another directory, you can change the default directory just as you can when retrieving a file.

In step 2, you specify the name of the program that you want to attach. Then, in step 3, you have the option of assigning an Alt+Function key combination that you can use later to invoke the program. For programs that you want to use intermittently, like *Auditor* or *Viewer*, you should assign a function key. But for programs that you want to use continuously, like *WYSIWYG*, you should select the No-Key option.

When an add-in program is attached, it is stored in internal memory. As a result, it is ready for use. However, this also means that less internal memory is available for the spreadsheet you're working on. Although a small add-in program may take only a few thousand bytes of internal memory, a large add-in program can take hundreds of thousands of bytes of memory.

How to invoke an add-in program When you're ready to use the add-in program that you've attached, you *invoke* the program. To do that, you can use the Invoke command from the Add-in menu. Or, if you assigned a function key to the program when you attached it, you can invoke it using the Alt+Function key combination. If, for example, you assign the number 7 to an add-in program when you attach it, you can invoke it by pressing the Alt+F7 key combination.

Figure 14-3 shows you how to invoke a program from the Add-in menu. In step 1, you select the Invoke option. Then, in step 2, the control panel displays the names of the add-in programs that have been attached to *Lotus*.

Command	Next level	Next level	Next level	Function
/Add-in (2.X) Alt+F10 (2.X, 3.X)	Attach (2.X) Load (3.X)			Load an add-in program into internal memory
	Invoke			Invoke an add-in program that has already been attached
	Detach (2.X) Remove (3.X)			Detach an attached add-in program by removing it from internal memory
	Clear			Detach all add-in programs by removing them from internal memory
/Worksheet Global Default (2.X)	Other	Add-in	Set	Set up an add-in program so it gets auto-attached each time you start *Lotus 1-2-3*
			Cancel	Cancel the auto-attach function for a program
	Update			Save the auto-attach setting as the default setting for *Lotus*
Alt+F10 (3.X)	Settings	System	Set	Set up an add-in program so it gets auto-attached each time you start *Lotus 1-2-3*
			Cancel	Cancel the auto-attach function for a program
			Update	Save the auto-attach setting as the default setting for *Lotus*
	Settings	File	Set	Set up an add-in program so it gets auto-attached each time you retrieve a specific spreadsheet file
			Cancel	Cancel the auto-attach function for a spreadsheet

Figure 14-1 The *Lotus* commands for working with add-in programs

1. Select the Attach (2.X) or the Load (3.X) command from the Add-in menu.
2. Specify the name of the add-in program that you want to attach as prompted by the control panel:

   ```
   Enter add-in to attach: C:\123\*.ADN
   AUDITOR.ADN   BSOLVER.ADN   ICONS.ADN   MACROMGR.ADN   VIEWER.ADN
   ```

   If more than five add-in programs are available, you can press the F3 (Name) key to get a complete listing of the add-ins. After you type or highlight the name of the add-in that you want to attach, you press the Enter key.

3. Select the function key that you want to use for invoking the add-in program as prompted by the control panel:

   ```
   No-Key  7  8  9  10
   ```

   If, for example, you select number 7, you can invoke the add-in program later using the Alt+F7 key combination. If you don't want to assign a function key to the program, select the No-key option.

Figure 14-2 How to attach an add-in program

At this screen, you specify the program that you want to invoke. When you press the Enter key, the program starts.

When you invoke an add-in program, it usually displays its own menu. However, the menus and commands of an add-in program usually work much like those of *Lotus* so most add-in programs are relatively easy to use. If you want to get Help information about how to use the add-in program, you press the F1 key. And when you're through using it, you press the Esc key to return to the spreadsheet screen.

How to cancel an add-in program When you're through using an add-in program, you can *detach* it from internal memory. To do that, you use the Detach (2.X) or the Remove (3.X) command. After you access the command, you highlight the add-in program that you want to remove and press the Enter key. If you want to remove all of the attached add-in programs from memory, you can use the /Add-in Clear command.

How to auto-attach and auto-invoke an add-in program If you use an add-in program all the time, you can set up *Lotus* so the add-in program is loaded into internal memory whenever you start *Lotus*. This can be referred to as *auto-attaching* an add-in program. You can also set up *Lotus* so the add-in program is invoked during the startup procedure. This can be referred to as *auto-invoking* an add-in program.

Although the commands for auto-attaching and auto-invoking are different for releases 2.X and 3.X, the basic procedures for auto-attaching an

1. Select the Invoke command from the Add-in menu:

   `Attach   Detach   Invoke   Clear   Quit`

2. Specify the name of the add-in program that you want to invoke:

   `Enter add-in to invoke: AUDITOR`
   `AUDITOR`

   After you type or highlight the name of the add-in program that you want to invoke, press the Enter key.

Figure 14-3 How to invoke an add-in program

add-in are similar. They are summarized in figure 14-4. If you're using release 2.X, you use the /Worksheet Global Default Other Add-in command and the /Worksheet Global Default Update command. If you're using release 3.X, you use the Alt+F10 key combination to activate the Add-in menu. Then, you use the Settings System Set command and the Settings System Update command.

As you perform one of the procedures in figure 14-4, a screen is displayed that shows which add-in programs are going to be auto-attached and which ones are going to be auto-invoked. Although the screens are slightly different for releases 2.X and 3.X, both screens are easy to work with.

If you're using one of the 3.X releases, you can auto-attach and auto-invoke one or more add-in programs when you retrieve a spreadsheet, instead of when you start *Lotus*. To do that, you use the Settings File commands, which work just like the Settings System commands. If you auto-attach or auto-invoke an add-in program that has already been attached or invoked, *Lotus* just ignores the command so this works the way you want it to. When you're through working with the spreadsheet, however, the add-in program remains attached to *Lotus* so you have to detach it if you no longer want it attached.

Although it's tempting to auto-attach all of your favorite add-ins when you start *Lotus*, remember that each add-in requires internal memory. As a result, the attached add-in programs can limit the size of the spreadsheets that you can develop. In some cases, your PC may not have enough memory for all of the add-ins that you want to attach even before you start working on a spreadsheet. In practice, then, it makes sense to limit the number of add-ins that you auto-attach. In fact, it often makes sense to avoid using the auto-attach feature altogether.

The add-in programs that come with *Lotus* releases 2.4 and 3.4

Lotus release 2.4 comes with six add-in programs: *Auditor*, *Viewer*, *Macro Library Manager*, *WYSIWYG*, *SmartIcons*, and *Backsolver*. All but the *SmartIcons*

***Lotus* release 2.X**

1. Start the /Worksheet Global Default Other Add-in Set command to get this prompt:

```
1  2  3  4  5  6  7  8
Select auto-attach add-in setting
```

   At this point, a screen is displayed so you can see what the current settings are for auto-attached and auto-invoked programs. This screen is changed to reflect the entries that you make in the steps that follow. To start, select the number that you want to use for the program that you want to auto-attach.

2. After you select a number, *Lotus* displays this prompt:

```
Enter name of add-in:  C:\123\*.ADN
AUDITOR.ADN   BSOLVER.ADN   ICONS.ADN   MACROMGR.ADN   VIEWER.ADN
```

   Here, you specify the program that you want to auto-attach. To get a complete listing of all the add-in programs in the directory, you can press the F3 (Name) key.

3. If you want to invoke the add-in program using an Alt+Function key combination, select the function key from the numbers listed:

```
No-Key  7  8  9  10
```

   Otherwise, select the No-Key option.

4. Select the option that says whether or not you want the program auto-invoked.

```
No   Yes
Automatically invoke this add-in whenever you start 1-2-3?
```

5. To save the new default setting, use the Update option of the /Worksheet Global Default command.

Figure 14-4 How to auto-attach and auto-invoke an add-in program (part 1 of 2)

program are also provided with *Lotus* release 3.4, but *SmartIcons* is included in *WYSIWYG* for that release. In addition, release 3.4 provides an add-in program called *Solver*. Since these seven programs are representative of the types of add-in programs that are available for *Lotus*, and since it's likely that one or more of them are installed on your PC, I'll introduce you to them now.

Auditor Chapter 2 shows how you can use the *Auditor* add-in program to find circular references in formulas. When you invoke this program, the screen in figure 14-5 is displayed. The menu at the top of this screen provides commands for tracing the references in formulas to make sure that the formulas use the right data. When you develop large spreadsheets with lengthy formulas, this program can help you manage those formulas. But it's most useful for consultants or PC resource people who need to check the spreadsheets that other people have created.

***Lotus* release 3.X**

1. Start the Add-in menu by pressing the Alt+F10 key combination. Then, select the Settings System Set command. At this point, a screen is displayed so you can see what the current settings are for auto-attached and auto-invoked programs. This screen is changed to reflect the entries that you make in the steps that follow.
2. Specify the name of the program that you want to attach as prompted by the control panel:

```
Enter add-in to read into memory automatically:  C:\123\*.ADN
AUDITOR.ADN  BSOLVER.ADN  ICONS.ADN  MACROMGR.ADN  VIEWER.ADN
```

   To get a complete listing of all the add-in programs in the directory, you can press the F3 (Name) key.

3. Select the option that says whether or not you want the program auto-invoked.

```
Yes  No
Automatically start this application when it is read into memory
```

4. If you want to invoke the add-in program using an Alt+Function key combination, select the function key from the numbers listed:

```
No-Key  1  2  3
```

   Otherwise, select the No-Key option.

5. To save the new default setting, select the Update option of the Settings System command.

Figure 14-4 How to auto-attach and auto-invoke an add-in program (part 2 of 2)

Viewer Chapter 13 shows how you can use the *Viewer* add-in program to find and retrieve your *Lotus* files. After you invoke this program and select the Retrieve function, the screen in figure 14-6 is displayed. Here, the cursor is on the EXP-TEMP.WK1 file, and the top left portion of this spreadsheet is displayed on the right panel of the screen. Then, if the spreadsheet is the one that you want to retrieve, you just press the Enter key to retrieve it. Since this program lets you view a portion of the spreadsheet before you retrieve it, you can be sure that you're retrieving the right file.

If you link cells between spreadsheets, the *Viewer* is particularly useful. Not only can you use it to view the source spreadsheet, but it also creates the appropriate cell linking formulas so you don't have to enter them directly. This use of the *Viewer* is covered in detail in chapter 11.

Macro Library Manager The *Macro Library Manager* makes it easier for you to use macros. If you're not already familiar with macros, you can learn how to create and use them in chapter 19. When you invoke the *Macro Library Manager*, it displays a menu like the one in step 1 of figure 14-7. Then, when

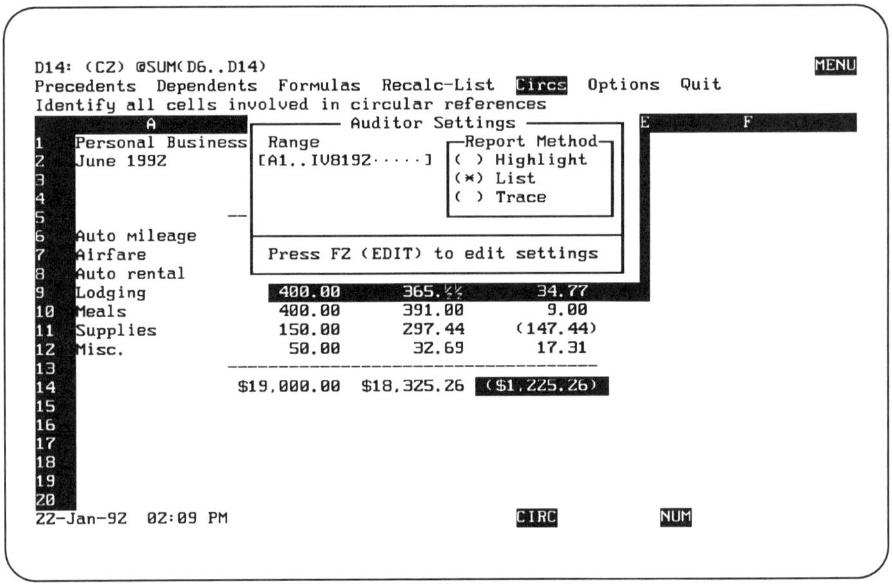

Figure 14-5 The first screen of the *Auditor* program after it has been invoked

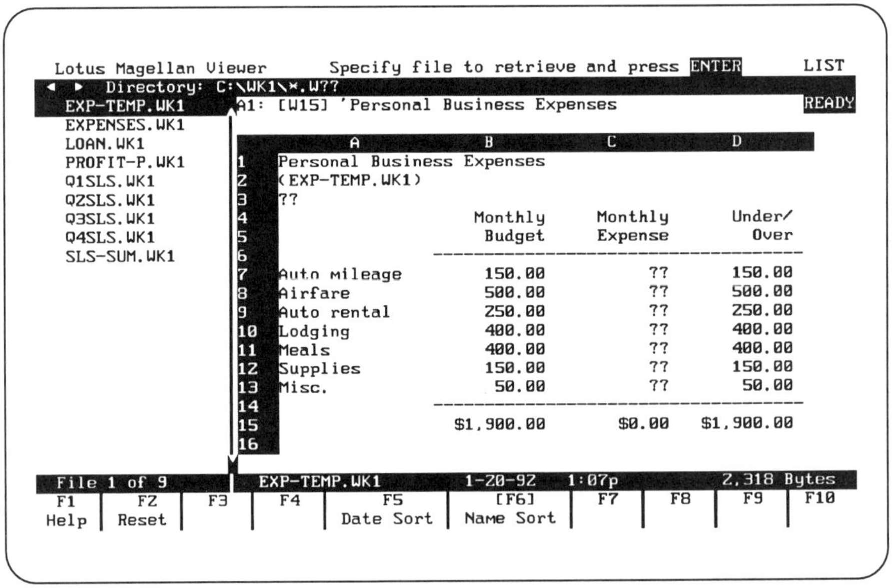

Figure 14-6 How the *Viewer* lets you select and display a spreadsheet file

1. Select the Load function from the *Macro Library Manager*'s menu:

   ```
   Load   Save   Edit   Remove   Name-List   Quit
   ```

2. Specify the name of the macro library to load as prompted:

   ```
   Enter name of macro library to load: C:\123\DATA\*.MLB
   AUTOLOAD.MLB  STANDARD.MLB
   ```

   You can type the name or use the Arrow keys to highlight it. When you press the Enter key, the macro library is available to any of the spreadsheets that you work on during your *Lotus* session.

Figure 14-7 How to use the *Macro Library Manager* to load a macro library

you select the Load option, the program displays a list of the macro libraries that are available as shown in step 2. After you select one of these libraries and press the Enter key, you are returned to the spreadsheet screen. After that, you can use the macros in the macro library that you've selected without entering the macros into the current spreadsheet file.

WYSIWYG Chapter 18 shows you how to use the *WYSIWYG* add-in program for business presentations. When you invoke this program, a screen like the one in figure 14-8 is displayed. To activate its menu, which has the same form as the *Lotus* menu, you press the colon (:). Then, you can use its commands to change the typefaces used in portions of the spreadsheet. You can also use its commands to add shading, boxes, lines, spacing, boldfacing, and other effects to the spreadsheet.

When you're ready to print the spreadsheet, you can be sure that the printed spreadsheet is going to look like the one on the screen as shown in figure 14-8. That accounts for the name of this program: What You See Is What You Get. When you install *Lotus* releases 2.4 and 3.4, *WYSIWYG* is auto-attached and auto-invoked by default, but it requires more than 100,000 bytes of internal memory. If this isn't what you want, you can detach it using the appropriate commands in figure 14-1.

SmartIcons The *SmartIcons* program comes with *Lotus* release 2.4, but not with release 3.4. However, release 3.4 provides a *SmartIcons* capability that is built into its *WYSIWYG* program. When you invoke both *WYSIWYG* and *SmartIcons* when using release 2.4, a bar of *icons* is displayed to the right of the spreadsheet as shown in figure 14-9. If *SmartIcons* is invoked, but *WYSIWYG* isn't, the icons are displayed but in a form that is hard to interpret. As a result, it's usually best to use *SmartIcons* with *WYSIWYG*. Like the *WYSIWYG* program, *SmartIcons* is auto-attached and auto-invoked by default when you install *Lotus*, so you need to change that if that isn't what you want. The name of the *SmartIcons* program on the system is just *Icons*.

The spreadsheet screen

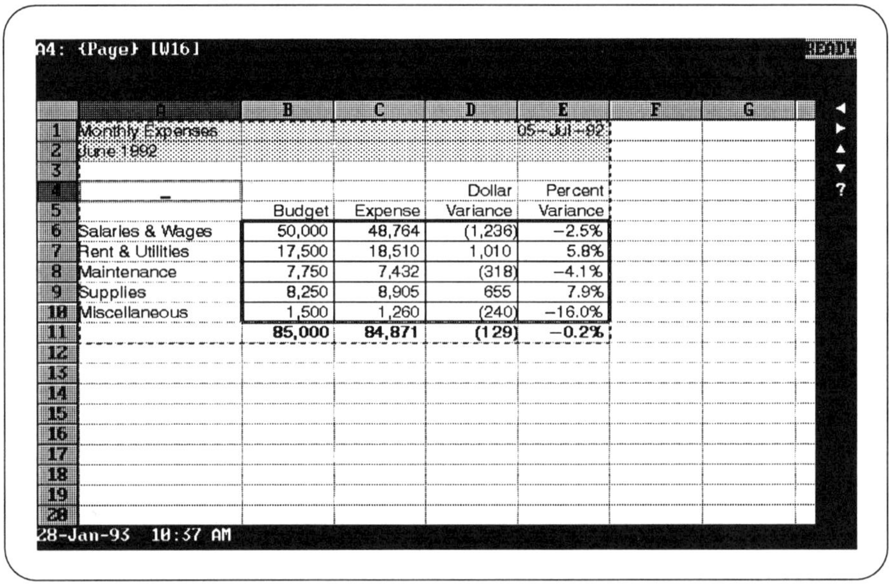

The printed spreadsheet

Monthly Expenses 05–Jul–92
June 1992

	Budget	Expense	Dollar Variance	Percent Variance
Salaries & Wages	50,000	48,764	(1,236)	−2.5%
Rent & Utilities	17,500	18,510	1,010	5.8%
Maintenance	7,750	7,432	(318)	−4.1%
Supplies	8,250	8,905	655	7.9%
Miscellaneous	1,500	1,260	(240)	−16.0%
	85,000	**84,871**	**(129)**	**−0.2%**

Figure 14-8 A spreadsheet report after it has been enhanced by using *WYSIWYG*

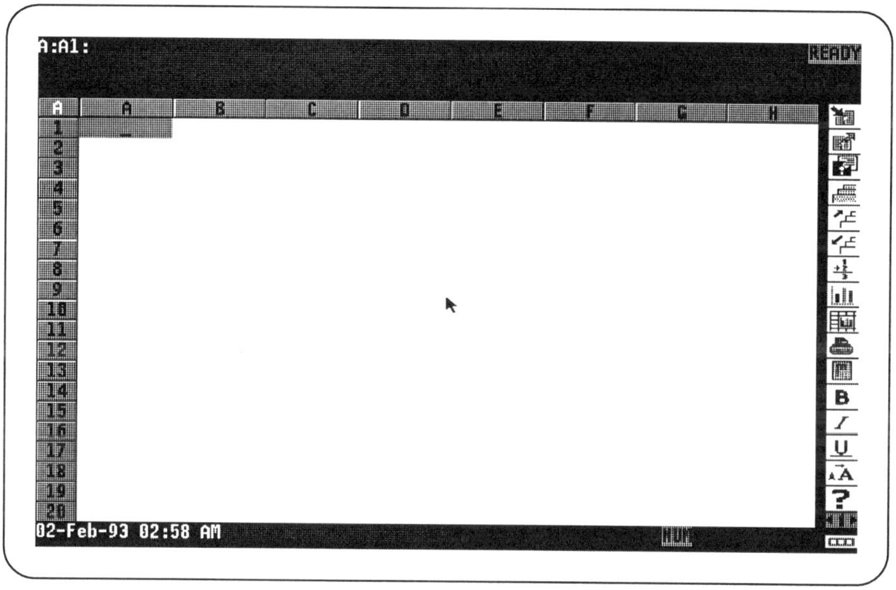

Figure 14-9 The icon bar that's displayed by the *SmartIcons* program

When you move the mouse pointer and click on one of the icons that's displayed by the *SmartIcons* program, *Lotus* executes the command or function that's assigned to the icon. For example, the first icon in figure 14-9 starts the command that saves the current spreadsheet to disk. As a result, clicking on this icon is the same as pressing /fs to start the /File Save command.

In total, the *SmartIcons* feature provides seven (2.X) or eight (3.X) icon bars, and the bottom icon on each bar shows the bar number. To display the other icon bars, you click the mouse on the arrow characters to the left or right of the number. If, for example, you click on the right arrow on icon bar 1, *Lotus* replaces that icon bar with icon bar 2.

In general, using the icons doesn't help you improve your efficiency. However, a few of the icons are helpful. For instance, the third icon down in figure 14-9 is the Sum icon. When you click the mouse on this icon when the cell pointer is below a column of numbers, *Lotus* automatically creates an @SUM function that sums the numbers in the column. This can be far more efficient than entering the @SUM function using the anchor-and-point method. So if you have a mouse on your system and you want to learn how to make the best use of the icons, please read chapter 21.

Backsolver This add-in was first supplied with *Lotus* release 2.4, and the name of the file that you use to attach and invoke it is *Bsolver*. This add-in lets you find the variable that's required to make the result of a formula equal to a value you specify. For example, you can use *Backsolver* with a proforma model to find the exact number of unit sales that are required to reach the break-even point for a product. As a result, this add-in program can be quite useful for what-if analysis.

Figure 14-10 shows you an example of how you can use *Backsolver* to find the break-even point for a new product. In step 1, you invoke *Backsolver*. In step 2, you select the Formula-Cell option. Then, you specify the cell that contains the formula that you want to return a target value. In step 3, you select the Value option and specify the value you want the formula in the Formula-Cell to return. In step 4, you select the Adjustable option and specify the value in the spreadsheet that you want adjusted to solve for the target value. In step 5, you select the Solve option to solve the problem.

After you've used *Backsolver* to solve the problem for one set of variables, you can change one or more of them to see "what will happen if...." For instance, you can run *Backsolver* on the data in column D in figure 14-10 to see how a unit price of $20.00 affects the result. If you experiment with this add-in program, I think you'll quickly see whether or not it is going to be useful for the types of what-if analysis that you do.

Solver This add-in was first supplied with *Lotus* release 3.1+. The plus sign after the 3.1 just meant that this release included several add-in programs that weren't included with releases 3.0 or 3.1. *Solver* was one of these add-ins.

Like *Backsolver*, *Solver* is designed to help you do what-if analysis. However, *Backsolver* requires only 27,000 bytes of disk storage when it's installed, while *Solver* requires more than 700,000 bytes. That gives you some idea of the relative size and complexity of these two programs.

When you use *Solver*, you start by defining the scope of your what-if analysis. To do that, you identify (1) the spreadsheet cells that contain the values that can be varied by *Solver* (the *adjustable cells*) and (2) the cells that contain logical formulas that limit the variation of other cells (the *constraint cells*). Then, you ask *Solver* to solve the problem. If *Solver* can't derive a solution, it displays messages that ask you to supply guesses for one or more of the adjustable cells. If *Solver* derives at least one solution, you can display or print the answer or answers when *Solver* is finished with its calculations.

Because of its size and complexity, *Solver* isn't for everybody. In fact, most *Lotus* users can do a better job of what-if analysis by adjusting their own variables than they can by defining the variables so *Solver* can do the adjusting. That's why I'm not going to illustrate the use of *Solver* in this chapter. For most *Lotus* users, figuring out how this add-in works is going to be more trouble than it's worth.

In this spreadsheet, *Bsolver* was used to determine the number of units that have to be sold to reach the break-even point.

```
C15: [W15] +C7-C13                                                       READY

          A              B           C           D          E
1   Proforma profit model for a new product
2   ==========================================================
3   Units                              10,225       9,063
4   Unit price                          18.00       20.00
5   Unit cost                            2.25        2.25
6   ==========================================================
7   Sales                          184,049.08  181,268.88
8
9   Cost of goods sold              23,006.13   20,392.75
10  Variable indirect costs   6.0%  11,042.94   10,876.13
11  Fixed marketing expense        150,000.00  150,000.00
12                              ----------------------------
13  Total expense                  184,049.08  181,268.88
14
15  Profits                              0.00        0.00
16
```

How to use *Backsolver* to determine the break-even point for one column of data

1. Invoke the *Bsolver* add-in to display the following menu:

   `Formula-Cell  Value  Adjustable  Solve  Quit`

2. Select the Formula-Cell option and specify the cell that contains the formula you want to return a target value at the following prompt:

   `Enter the range address or name of the formula cell: C15`

3. Select the Value option and enter the value you want the formula to return when *Bsolver* displays the following prompt:

   `Enter the desired result value: 0`

4. Select the Adjustable option and specify the value in the spreadsheet that you want adjusted:

   `Enter the range address or name of the adjustable cell(s): C3`

5. Select the Solve option to solve the problem and display the results.

Figure 14-10 How to use the *Backsolver* program to solve for a specific value

Five of the most popular types of add-in programs

You can buy many different add-in programs for *Lotus*. In fact, if you think you need a feature or capability that *Lotus* doesn't provide, you can probably find an add-in program that provides it. Five of the most popular types of add-in programs are summarized in figure 14-11, and I'll introduce you to each type now.

Print enhancement add-ins The programs in the first group in figure 14-11 let you enhance the printing of a spreadsheet. As I mentioned earlier, *Sideways* lets you print in landscape mode. In contrast, *Allways* and *Impress* provide the same types of features that *WYSIWYG* provides. *Allways* was included with *Lotus* release 2.2, and *Impress* was included with *Lotus* release 3.0 for a while, so you are likely to have one of these programs on your PC if you're using one of these releases.

View and documentation add-ins The programs in the second group in figure 14-11 let you view and document spreadsheets. *SeeMore* uses small display modes so you can view large portions of a spreadsheet on the screen at one time. *Noteworthy* and *Note-It Plus* let you put notes on individual cells in a spreadsheet to document and explain what you've done.

Consolidation add-ins The programs in the third group in figure 14-11 let you view and share the data in spreadsheets. The sharing features of these programs work much like the sharing features of *Lotus* releases 2.2 through 3.4 that I presented in chapter 11. So even if you're still using *Lotus* release 2.0, you can share data between spreadsheets by using one of these add-ins.

General utility add-ins The programs in the fourth group in figure 14-11 provide general utilities that can make *Lotus* faster or easier to use. For instance, *3-2-1 Blastoff* speeds up *Lotus* calculations. *@Ease* provides a collection of @functions that can make it easier for you to perform some calculations. And *Sqz! Plus* lets you compress spreadsheet files so they take less space on disk.

Special purpose add-ins The programs in the last group in figure 14-11 provide special purpose capabilities. For instance, *The Budget Express* provides special features for creating financial spreadsheets. And *Project Calc* provides special features for using *Lotus* to help manage projects. Although I've only listed three programs in this group, dozens of special purpose add-ins are available for *Lotus* users.

Program	Vendor	Added capability
Print enhancement add-ins		
Sideways	Funk Software	Print wide spreadsheets in landscape mode
Allways	Funk Software	Enhance the graphics presentation of a spreadsheet (like *WYSIWYG*)
Impress	PC Publishing	Enhance the graphics presentation of a spreadsheet (like *WYSIWYG*)
View and documentation add-ins		
SeeMore	Personics	View large portions of a spreadsheet by using small display modes
Noteworthy	Funk Software	Place a note on a cell and have it displayed whenever you move the cell pointer to the cell
Note-It Plus	Symantec	Place a note on a cell and have it displayed whenever you move the cell pointer to the cell
Consolidation add-ins		
Look&Link	Personics	View and share data between two or more spreadsheets
XYZ Consolidate	Intex Solutions	Share data between two or more spreadsheets
General utility add-ins		
3-2-1 Blastoff	Intex Solutions	Faster calculations
Worksheet Utilities	Funk Software	Improved formula editor, search and replace features, and so on.
@Ease	Intex Solutions	Additional @functions that eliminate rounding errors, calculate subtotals, and so on.
Sqz! Plus	Symantec	Compressed spreadsheet files that take less disk space
Special purpose add-ins		
The Budget Express	Symantec	Special features for creating financial spreadsheets
What-if Analyst	Intex Solutions	Special features for performing what-if analysis
Project Calc	Intex Solutions	Special features for managing projects

Figure 14-11 The most popular add-in programs

Two other types of enhancement products

To complete your introduction to programs and products that are available for use with *Lotus*, I'll introduce you to add-on programs and commercial template packages.

Add-on programs An *add-on program* doesn't run at the same time that *Lotus* does. However, an add-on program uses the data in a *Lotus* spreadsheet. Many of these programs are designed to provide printing or graphics capabilities that go beyond those that *Lotus* provides.

Figure 14-12 lists four of the most popular add-on programs. *Report Writer* lets you print reports and mailing labels from the data in a *Lotus* spreadsheet. *Smart Forecasts II* lets you use the data in a spreadsheet for financial forecasting. And *Harvard Graphics* and *Lotus Freelance* let you use the data in a *Lotus* spreadsheet for preparing graphs, charts, and other business presentations. These last two programs are useful with or without *Lotus* because the data they use doesn't have to come from a *Lotus* spreadsheet.

Template packages As I explained in chapter 5, you can create *template spreadsheets* (or just *templates*) so you don't have to start your spreadsheets from scratch. In some cases, though, you can save time by buying a commercial template package that includes all of the templates you need for a group of applications. Often, a commercial template package comes with several large, complex spreadsheets that include sophisticated macros. As a result, a template package in combination with *Lotus* can provide the same capabilities as a specialized program.

Figure 14-13 lists three popular template packages. The first one, *101 Macros Plus*, is a template that provides 101 macros that you can use with *Lotus*. *Inventory Analyst* provides a series of templates that can become a complete inventory management system when used with *Lotus*. And *Ready-to-Run Accounting* provides a series of templates that can become a complete accounting system.

Keep in mind, though, that template packages aren't programs. They consist of spreadsheets that you can use with *Lotus*. As a result, a template package is likely to be more difficult to use than an add-in program or an add-on program that provides a menu system for using its features. It can also be difficult to find template packages that are suitable for your purposes. That's why you are often better off if you develop your own templates for your spreadsheet applications.

Discussion

Today, hundreds of enhancement products are available for use with *Lotus*. In general, though, you should proceed with caution when you're considering the purchase of enhancement products. Not all of the enhancement products are good ones. Even the good ones aren't right for everyone. And that's particularly true for template packages.

Program	Vendor	Function
Lotus Report Writer	Lotus Development Corporation	Prepare and print reports and mailing labels from *Lotus* data
Smart Forecasts II	Smart Software	Prepare financial forecasts from *Lotus* data
Harvard Graphics	Software Publishing	Prepare and print graphs, charts, and other business presentations from *Lotus* data
Lotus Freelance	Lotus Development Corporation	Prepare and print graphs, charts, and other business presentations from *Lotus* data

Figure 14-12 Four popular add-on programs

Program	Vendor	Function
101 Macros Plus	Individual Software	101 macros for use with *Lotus*
Inventory Analyst	Intex Solutions	A complete inventory management system that runs in *Lotus*
Ready to Run Accounting	Intex Solutions	A complete accounting system that runs in *Lotus* and includes general ledger, payables, receivables, billing, and inventory

Figure 14-13 Three popular template packages

Also, you should try to keep your *Lotus* environment simple and manageable just as you should try to keep your spreadsheets simple and manageable. That means that: (1) you should avoid using an enhancement product unless it's just right for your requirements; (2) you should keep the number of enhancement products that you use to a minimum; and (3) you shouldn't buy an enhancement product that uses *Lotus* to perform a function that *Lotus* was never intended for.

To some extent, this same advice applies to the add-in programs that come with *Lotus*. Just because they're free doesn't mean that you have to use them. As a result, you should only use one of the *Lotus* add-ins if it helps you work better or faster. If you're like most *Lotus* users, that means you can probably make effective use of the *Viewer* and *WYSIWYG* add-ins from time to time, but you probably won't ever need the *Auditor*, *Macro Library Manager*, *Backsolver*, or *Solver* add-ins.

Terms

add-in program
install
attach
invoke
detach
auto-attach
auto-invoke
icon
add-on program
template spreadsheet
template

Objectives

1. Describe the characteristics of add-in programs, add-on programs, and template packages.
2. Decide whether any of the add-in programs described in this chapter can help you work more productively.
3. Attach, invoke, and use any of the add-in programs that are already installed on your PC and that are appropriate for your spreadsheet applications.

Chapter 15

Setup, printing, networking, and range commands for occasional use

This chapter presents a collection of commands that don't logically fit into any of the other chapters in this book. These commands let you perform setup, printing, networking, and range operations that you will use occasionally, if at all. Nevertheless, you should at least know that these commands are available.

Because all of the commands in this chapter are easy to use, you can go through this chapter quickly. If you just review the headings and the figures, you can probably tell whether you need any of these commands. Then, if you decide that you do need one or more of them, you can read the related text.

How to set up *Lotus* so it works the way you want it to

If *Lotus* works just the way you want it to on your PC, you don't need to review the commands for setting *Lotus* up. Otherwise, you can review the commands that follow to see how they affect the operation of *Lotus*.

How to set up the default printer Figure 15-1 summarizes the commands for setting up the default printer for *Lotus*. Chapter 3 has already introduced the commands for setting margins and the page length. The other commands can be used for changing the default printer or making minor adjustments to its operation.

To change the default printer, you use the Interface and Name options of the /Worksheet Global Default Printer command. The first procedure in figure 15-3 summarizes the steps for using these options. As you can see, you use the Interface option to identify the *printer port* that the printer is attached to, and you use the Name option to identify the name of the printer. If

Command	Next level	Next level	Next level	Function
/Worksheet Global Default F6 (Window)	Printer F6 (Window)	Interface	1-8	Select the printer port for the default printer.
		AutoLF	Yes No	Set the printer codes for automatic line feed if your printer requires it.
		Left Right Top Bottom		Set the default values for the print margins.
		Pg-Length		Set the default value for the page length. For 8-1/2 by 11 paper, this is usually 66 for a dot-matrix printer and 60 for a laser printer.
		Wait	No Yes	Set the printer codes so the printer waits between pages if your printer requires this for single sheet feeding.
		Setup		Set the default setup string for your printer if it requires one (see chapter 4).
		Name	1-8	Select the printer driver for the default printer.
	Update			Update the default settings so they become permanent defaults.

Figure 15-1 The commands for setting up the default printer

possible, then, you should know which port the printer is connected to and the name of the printer before you start using this command. Otherwise, you have to experiment with the selections until your printer works right.

When you use the Name option to set up a new printer as the default printer, the correct printer name may not be available to *Lotus*. Then, you have to use the *Lotus* Install program to install the proper *printer driver* for your printer. Once the driver is installed, the correct name will appear when you use the Name option of the /Worksheet Global Default Printer command.

The Setup option of the /Worksheet Global Default Printer command lets you specify a default code that determines the size and style of the printing that is done for each new spreadsheet that you create. In chapter 4, you can learn how to make an appropriate specification for this option. With some printers, this option is worth setting because otherwise the size and type of printing depends on how the buttons are set on the printer. With other printers, there's no need to set this option.

Normally, the AutoLF and Wait options work the way you want them to, so you don't have to set them. But if your printer is double spacing when you don't want it to, try turning the AutoLF option off; and if it isn't skipping lines properly, try turning this option on. Similarly, if your printer isn't working properly when you're using single sheets, you can experiment with the Wait option.

When you've got the printer set up the way you want it, be sure to use the /Worksheet Global Default Update option to save the setup. Otherwise, the defaults will be reset when you exit from *Lotus*.

How to set the other global defaults Figure 15-2 summarizes the other default options that you can set. You should already know how to set the Directory option to the one that you store your spreadsheets in. Similarly, you should already know how to use the Status option to display a summary of the default settings. If you're using one of the 2.X releases, though, you can just press the F6 (Window) key to display the default settings.

If you look at the Other options, you may see a few that you want to change. The International options let you set the character that's used for decimal punctuation, the sign that's used for currency, and the formats for the date, time, and negative values. The Clock options let you change the formats for the date and time that are displayed at the bottom of the *Lotus* screen. If you want to, you can use the Clock Filename option to replace the date and time with the file name of the spreadsheet you're working on. And you can use the Beep option to turn the beeper on or off.

The Help option tells *Lotus* how you want the Help facility to work. Assuming that you use a hard-disk PC, this should be set to Instant so *Lotus* keeps the Help file open instead of closing it after each use. This can improve the speed at which *Lotus* accesses the Help information.

The Undo option turns the Undo feature off or on. If the feature is on, you can restore the last change that you made to a *Lotus* spreadsheet by pressing the Alt+F4 key combination. If, for example, you delete a row by mistake, you can press Alt+F4 to restore the row and its data. Obviously, this can be useful, but it also slows *Lotus* down. So whether or not you keep this feature on depends on your PC and your working preferences.

The Add-In, Graph, and Autoexec options are related to add-in programs, graphing capabilities, and macros. So you need to read the related chapters to decide how you want to set these options.

Command	Next level	Next level	Next level	Function
/Worksheet Global Default F6 (Window)	Directory			Set the default directory for spreadsheet files.
	Status			Display the default settings screen.
	Update			Update the default settings so they become permanent defaults.
	Other	International	Punctuation Currency Date Time Negative	Set the formats for decimal punctuation, currency, date, time, and negative values so they're appropriate for your country or environment.
		Help	Instant Removable	Set the Help feature for Instant or Removable access. On a hard-disk system, the Instant setting keeps the Help files open to improve access speed.
		Clock	Standard International None Clock Filename	Set the format for the clock display at the bottom of the *Lotus* screen. Also, specify whether you want the clock or the current file name to be displayed at the bottom of the *Lotus* screen.
		Undo	Enable Disable	Turn the *Lotus* Undo feature on or off. If Undo is on, you can restore the last spreadsheet change by pressing Alt+F4.
		Beep	Yes No	Turn the beeper on or off.
		Add-In (2.X)	Set Cancel	Automatically start one or more add-in programs when *Lotus* is started (see chapter 14).

Figure 15-2 A summary of the /Worksheet Global Default commands (part 1 of 2)

Command	Next level	Next level	Next level	Function
/Worksheet Global Default F6 (Window)		Expanded-Memory (2.3, 2.4)	Standard Enhanced	Specify how you want expanded memory to be used. The Enhanced option provides for larger spreadsheets than the Standard option.
		Graph (3.X)	Columnwise Rowwise Metafile PIC	Set the defaults for working with graphs (see chapters 16 and 17).
		Temp (3.X)		Set the default directory for temporary files.
		Ext (3.X)	List Save	Specify the default extension to be used when you list or save files.
	Autoexec	Yes No		Automatically execute a macro named \0 (zero) when a file containing that macro is retrieved (see chapter 19).

Figure 15-2 A summary of the /Worksheet Global Default commands (part 2 of 2)

The Temp option lets you set the default directory for the temporary files that *Lotus* 3.X creates as you work on spreadsheets. Although these files should be deleted by *Lotus* when you exit from it properly, a power failure or an operator error can lead to an improper exit. Then, the files aren't deleted so they remain in the *Lotus* directory. However, if you use this option to set up a special directory for the temporary files, you can delete them yourself. For most *Lotus* users, though, this type of housekeeping isn't necessary.

The Ext option lets you specify the default extension that you want *Lotus* to assume when you list or save files with release 3.X. For instance, you can set this option so *Lotus* 3.4 only lists files with WK1 extensions. Normally, though, you don't need this option.

The last option in figure 15-2 is the Expanded-Memory option for releases 2.3 and 2.4 only. Normally, you should leave this option set to Standard. But if you're working on a large spreadsheet, you can set this option to Enhanced so *Lotus* will let you create the largest spreadsheet possible by taking full advantage of expanded memory.

Here again, when you've got the options set the way you want them, be sure to use the /Worksheet Global Default Update option to save the setup. Otherwise, the defaults will be reset when you exit from *Lotus*.

How to switch from one printer to another

If two or more printers are attached to your PC or if you're working on a network that offers two or more printers, you need to know how to switch from one printer to another. The two procedures for doing that are summarized in figure 15-3. The first one can be used with either release 2.X or 3.X. The second one can only be used with release 3.X.

How to use the /Worksheet Global Default Printer command (2.X and 3.X) The first procedure in figure 15-3 shows you how to use the /Worksheet Global Default Printer command to switch to another printer. This is the same procedure that you use for establishing the default printer for a PC. In this case, though, you don't use the Update option unless you want to establish the new printer as the permanent default printer.

How to use the /Print Printer Options Advanced Device command (3.X) The second procedure in figure 15-3 shows you how to switch from one printer to another temporarily when you're using release 3.X. When you use this procedure, the printer change is saved with the spreadsheet. When you start a new spreadsheet, though, the default printer becomes the active printer again.

How to use background printing

Background printing refers to printing that is done independently (or in the background) of *Lotus* operations. As a result, you can continue *Lotus* operations while the spreadsheet is being printed. If you frequently print lengthy spreadsheets, this feature can help you get more done.

If you're using release 2.X, you use a separate utility program for background printing, and you use special commands for sending print jobs to this utility. If you're using release 3.0 or 3.1, though, background printing takes place automatically. As a result, you don't have to use any special commands to take advantage of it. Unfortunately, this feature slows down printing when it's done on a network. As a result, *Lotus* dropped it from release 3.4 and replaced it with the printing utility and commands that are used by release 2.X.

How to use the *BPrint* utility for large print jobs (2.X and 3.4) Figure 15-4 shows you how to use background printing with releases 2.X and 3.4. Before you start *Lotus*, you start the *BPrint* utility from DOS. To do that, you change the directory to the *Lotus* directory and execute the *bprint* command. Then, you can start *Lotus*.

How to use the /Worksheet Global Default Printer command to switch from one printer to another (2.X and 3.X)

1. Start the command and select Interface.
2. *Lotus* displays a prompt like this:

   ```
   1  2  3  4  5  6  7  8
   Parallel 1
   ```

   As you move the cursor from one number to the next, the message in the third line of the control panel describes the port. Select the number of the port for the printer you want to use.

3. This returns you to the options for the Default Printer command. Select Name.
4. *Lotus* displays this prompt:

   ```
   1  2  3  4
   HP LaserJet 4 No Cartridge
   ```

   One number is listed for each print driver that has been installed. As you move the cursor from one number to the next, the message in the third line of the control panel describes the printer. Select the number of the printer you want to use.

How to use the /Print Printer Options Advanced Device command to switch from one printer to another (3.X)

1. Start the command and select Device.
2. *Lotus* displays this prompt:

   ```
   Name  Interface
   ```

   Select Interface.

3. *Lotus* displays a prompt like this:

   ```
   1  2  3  4  5  6  7  8
   Parallel 1
   ```

   As you move the cursor from one number to the next, the message in the third line of the control panel describes the port. Select the number of the port for the printer you want to use.

4. Select the Device command again, and this time select Name from the prompt in step 2.
5. *Lotus* displays this prompt:

   ```
   1  2  3  4
   HP LaserJet 4 No Cartridge
   ```

   One number is listed for each print driver that has been installed. As you move the cursor from one number to the next, the message in the third line of the control panel describes the printer. Select the number of the printer you want to use.

Figure 15-3 How to switch from one printer to another

When you want to print a job from *Lotus* in the background, you use the /Print Background command instead of the /Print Printer command. This command creates an *encoded file* with an extension of ENC and sends it to the *BPrint* utility. After you use the /Print Background command, you use the Range, Align, Go, and Page commands to finish sending the job to the print utility. This starts the job printing in the background so you can return to your work on the *Lotus* screen.

If you want to save an encoded file for later printing by the *BPrint* utility, you can use the /Print Encoded command as summarized in the third procedure in figure 15-4. But this command doesn't start the printing of the file. Then, after you exit from *Lotus*, you can print the file by entering *bprint* at the DOS prompt followed by the file name of the encoded file. Normally, though, you don't need this capability.

If you're using a *network printer*, you don't need to use background printing because the network should have its own facility for that. As a result, this background printing feature only works for a printer that's attached to your PC (called a *local printer*). In addition, this background printing feature may not work while you're logged on to the network even though you're using your local printer. Although this feature isn't as easy to use as it ought to be by today's software standards, it is adequate for an occasional long print job.

How to use the /Print Printer command to control background printing (3.0 and 3.1) As I said earlier, *Lotus* releases 3.0 and 3.1 provide automatic background printing. As a result, you don't have to use any commands to benefit from it. However, these releases do provide commands that let you control the print jobs that are printing in the background.

Figure 15-5 summarizes the commands for controlling background printing. If you review them, you're likely to decide that you don't need any of them. If you start a lengthy print job, though, you may occasionally want to cancel it, so the Cancel command can be useful. And if you want to make sure that a short job prints ahead of a lengthy job that hasn't starting printing yet, the Priority options can be useful. But for most *Lotus* users, these commands are unnecessary.

Three printing skills for special purposes

Figure 15-6 presents three printing skills that are useful occasionally. The first two can help you relate the data in the spreadsheet to the cells that contain the data. The third skill lets you print two or more ranges at the same time (3.X only).

How to print a spreadsheet with cell formulas instead of values The first procedure in figure 15-6 shows you how to print the cell formulas of a spreadsheet instead of the values in the cells. This is useful when you want to

How to start the *BPrint* utility from the DOS prompt before you start *Lotus*

1. Use the Change-directory command to change to the *Lotus* directory as in this example:

```
C:\>cd \123
```

2. Enter *bprint* at the command prompt as in this example:

```
C:\123>bprint
```

How to print a job in the background from *Lotus*

1. Start the /Print Background command.
2. *Lotus* displays a prompt like this:

```
Enter name of background print file: C:\123\MMA\*.ENC
```

   Type the name that you want to use for the encoded file and press Enter. *Lotus* automatically adds ENC as the extension of the file name.

3. Use the Range, Align, Go, and Page options as needed to send the print job to the *BPrint* utility for background printing.

How to save an encoded file for later printing by the *BPrint* utility

1. Start the /Print Encoded command.
2. *Lotus* displays a prompt like this:

```
Enter name of encoded file: C:\123\MMA\*.ENC
```

   Type the name that you want to use for the encoded file and press Enter. *Lotus* automatically adds ENC as the extension of the file name.

3. Use the Range, Align, Go, and Page options as needed to save the encoded file so it can be printed.

How to print an encoded file from the DOS prompt

1. If necessary, use the Change-directory command to change to the *Lotus* directory as in this example:

```
C:\>cd \123
```

2. Enter *bprint* at the command prompt followed by the name of the encoded file that you want to print as in this example:

```
C:\123>bprint c:\123\mma\marexp.enc
```

Figure 15-4 How to use the *BPrint* utility for background printing (2.X and 3.4)

Command	Next level	Function
/Print	Suspend	Suspend all background print jobs including the one that's printing.
	Resume	Restart all background print jobs.
	Cancel	Cancel all background print jobs including the one that's printing.
/Print Printer Options Advanced Priority	Default	Assign a mid-level priority to a print job.
	High	Assign a high-level priority to a print job.
	Low	Assign a low-level priority to a print job.

Figure 15-5 The commands for controlling automatic background printing (3.0 and 3.1)

check the formulas to make sure that the calculations are being done correctly. In figure 15-7, you can see an example of this type of printing.

The problem with this form of printing is that it is difficult to relate the formulas to the spreadsheet. One way to improve upon this form is to use the /Range Format Text command to display the formulas in the cells themselves. To display the complete formulas, you may have to increase the widths of some of the columns. Then, you can print out the spreadsheet in a form that is easier to interpret.

How to print a spreadsheet with a frame (3.X) The second procedure in figure 15-6 shows you how to print a spreadsheet with a row and column frame around it. This form is illustrated by the second printing example in figure 15-7. If you print a spreadsheet in both of the forms shown in figure 15-7, you can more easily relate the cell formulas to the spreadsheet.

How to print two or more ranges with a single /Print Printer command (3.X) The third procedure in figure 15-6 shows you how to print two or more ranges with a single command. All you have to do is put a semi-colon (;) after each range when you use the /Print Printer Range command.

How to use the /File Admin Reservation command to reserve a network file

If you're using spreadsheet files that are stored on a disk drive that's available to other users of the network, you sometimes need to make sure that no one else updates a file while you're using it. To do that, you reserve the file as

How to print a spreadsheet with cell formulas instead of values

1. Start the /Print Printer Options Other command.
2. *Lotus* displays this prompt:

   `As-Displayed   Cell-Formulas   Formatted   Unformatted`

   Select Cell-Formulas.
3. Use the /Print Printer Range, Go, and Page commands as needed to print the spreadsheet.

How to print a spreadsheet with a frame (3.X)

1. Start the /Print Printer Options Borders command.
2. *Lotus* displays this prompt:

   `Columns   Rows   Frame   No-Frame`

   Select Frame.
3. Use the /Print Printer Range, Go, and Page commands as needed to print the spreadsheet.

How to print two or more ranges with a single /Print Printer command (3.X)

1. Start the /Print Printer Range command. At the prompt, specify the first range that you want to print as in this example:

   `Enter print range:   A:A1..A:D15`
2. Press the semi-colon (;) key and specify the next range you want to print as in this example:

   `Enter print range:   A:A1..A:D15;A:G50..A:K60`

   Repeat this step for each range you want to include in the print job. Then, press the Enter key to complete the command.
3. Use the /Print Printer Go command to print the ranges.

Figure 15-6 Three printing skills for special purposes

summarized in figure 15-8. Until you release your reservation, other *Lotus* users on the network can retrieve the file, but they can't save it. This protects the file from inadvertent error.

If another user retrieves the file while you have the reservation for it, an RO (Read Only) indicator is displayed at the bottom of that user's screen. This means that the file can't be saved. To update the file, the other user has to wait until you release it. Then, that user should retrieve the file again, update it, and save it.

The data range of a spreadsheet as printed with cell formulas

```
A:B6: [W9] 50000
A:C6: [W9] 51784
A:D6: [W9] +C6-B6
A:E6: (P1) +D6/B6
A:B7: [W9] 17500
A:C7: [W9] 18222
A:D7: [W9] +C7-B7
A:E7: (P1) +D7/B7
A:B8: [W9] 7750
A:C8: [W9] 7912
A:D8: [W9] +C8-B8
A:E8: (P1) +D8/B8
A:B9: [W9] 8250
A:C9: [W9] 7211
A:D9: [W9] +C9-B9
A:E9: (P1) +D9/B9
A:B10: [W9] 1500
A:C10: [W9] 1922
A:D10: [W9] +C10-B10
A:E10: (P1) +D10/B10
A:B12: [W9] @SUM(B6..B10)
A:C12: [W9] @SUM(C6..C10)
A:D12: [W9] @SUM(D6..D10)
A:E12: (P1) +D12/B12
```

The entire spreadsheet printed with a frame (3.X)

```
 A          A               B         C          D         E
 1    Monthly Expenses             01/28/93               MAREXP
 2    March
 3                                             Dollar   Percent
 4                        Budget   Expense   Variance  Variance
 5
 6    Salaries & Wages    50,000    51,784      1,784      3.6%
 7    Rent & Utilities    17,500    18,222        722      4.1%
 8    Maintenance          7,750     7,912        162      2.1%
 9    Supplies             8,250     7,211    (1,039)    -12.6%
10    Miscellaneous        1,500     1,922        422     28.1%
11
12    Total               85,000    87,051      2,051      2.4%
```

Figure 15-7 A spreadsheet printed with cell formulas and with a frame

How to reserve a network file (release 2.X)

Use the /File Retrieve command to retrieve the file. If you're using release 2.X, a file is automatically reserved if you're the first one to retrieve it.

How to reserve a network file (release 3.X)

1. Use the /File Retrieve command to retrieve the file. If you're using release 3.X, the file is automatically reserved if you're the first one to retrieve it and the Setting option for the file is Automatic.
2. If the Setting option for the file is Manual, use the /File Admin Reservation Get command to reserve the file that you have retrieved.

How to change the Setting option for a file (release 3.X)

1. Retrieve the file.
2. Start the /File Admin Reservation Setting command.
3. *Lotus* displays this prompt:

   ```
   Automatic  Manual
   ```

   Select Automatic if you want the file to be reserved automatically for the first person who retrieves it. Select Manual if you don't want the file to be reserved automatically. Then, you have to use the /File Admin Reservation Get command to get the reservation for the file after you have retrieved it.
4. Save the file.

Four ways to release a reserved file

1. Use the /File Admin Reservation Release command.
2. Use the /Worksheet Erase command to erase the file that you reserved.
3. Use the /File Retrieve command to retrieve a file into internal memory so it replaces the file that you reserved.
4. Exit from *Lotus*.

Figure 15-8 How to reserve and release network files

If you're using *Lotus* release 2.X, you automatically reserve a file when you're the first person to retrieve it. If you're using release 3.X and the Setting option for the file is Automatic, you automatically reserve the file when you're the first person to retrieve it. But if the Setting option for the file is Manual, you have to use the /File Admin Reservation Get option to reserve the file after you've retrieved it.

Figure 15-8 summarizes four ways to release a reserved file. Once you're through with the file so it is removed from internal memory, it is automatically released by *Lotus*. But if you want to continue to use the file after you've updated it, you can release it to other users by using the /File Admin Reservation Release command.

Three more /Range commands

All but three of the /Range commands are presented in other chapters of this book. These three are easy to use, and I think you'll find them useful because of the way they let you manipulate labels, values, columns, and rows.

How to use the /Range Justify command to divide a long label into two or more rows Figure 15-9 illustrates the use of the /Range Justify command. In the first spreadsheet, cell A14 contains a long label that extends off the screen to the right. I then used the /Range Justify command to justify the label in cell A14 into the range from A14 through E20. You can see the result in the second spreadsheet in this figure. This command is useful when you want to add lengthy comments to a spreadsheet as efficiently as possible.

How to use the /Range Transpose command to convert the columns in a range of cells to rows The /Range Transpose (or Trans) command converts rows to columns and columns to rows as illustrated by the spreadsheet in figure 15-10. This is useful when you start developing a spreadsheet and realize along the way that it will work better if the rows and columns are transposed. This is also useful when you want to sort data by its row values, but you can't do that because the /Data Sort command can only sort data by its column values. After you transpose the rows and columns, you can use the /Data Sort command that's presented in chapter 10.

How to use the /Range Search command to search and replace specific characters in a range of cells The /Range Search command lets you search the formulas and values in a range for a specific *character string*. If you use the Find option, the command just moves the cursor to the next cell in the range that contains the character string. If you use the Replace option, the command finds each occurrence of the first character string that you specify and replaces it with the second character string that you specify.

Figure 15-11 illustrates the use of the Replace option of the /Range Search command. Here, I used the command to search all labels in the range from A6 through A10 for this character string: *expenses*. And I replaced each occurrence of it with this character string: *costs*. If you've ever used the search-and-replace feature of a word processor, you won't have any trouble using this command.

The spreadsheet before the label in cell A14 has been justified

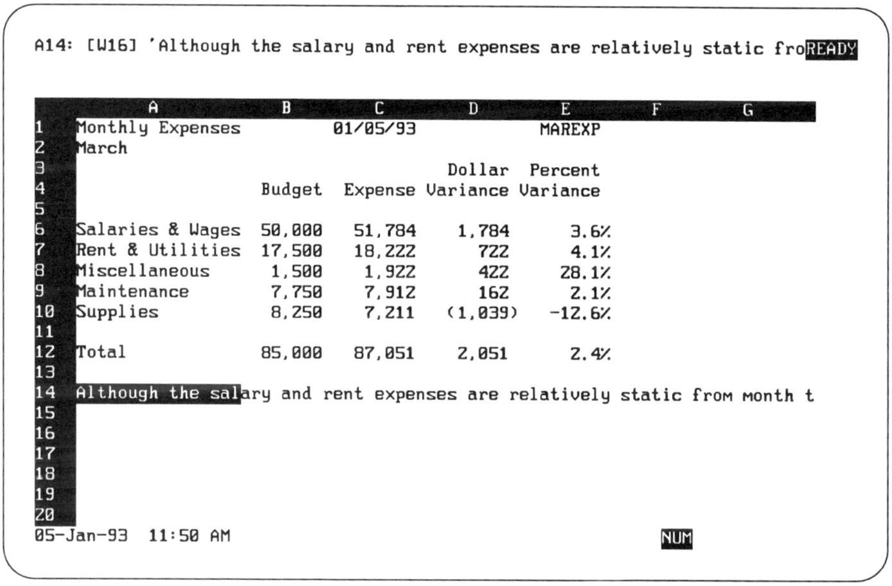

The spreadsheet after the label has been justified into the range from A14..E20

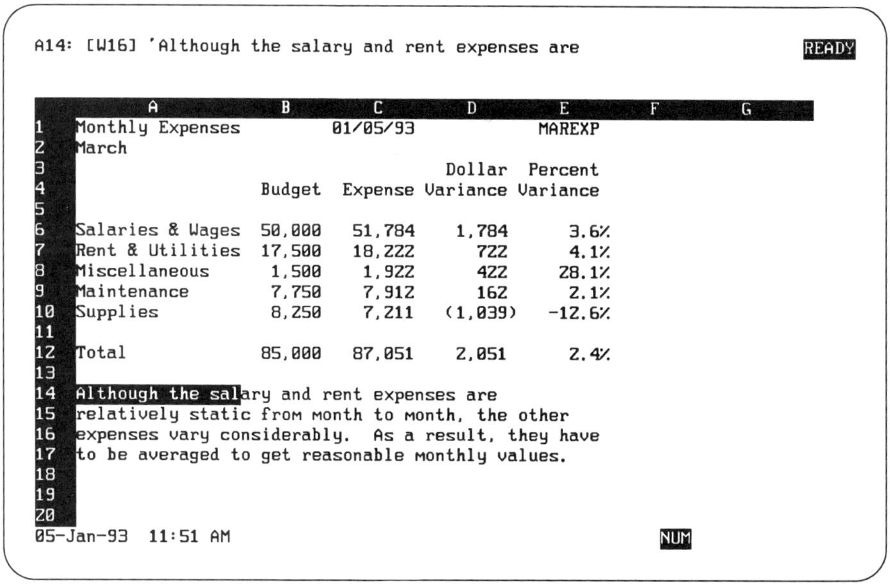

Figure 15-9 The operation of the /Range Justify command

The rows and columns in the range from A3..E8 are transformed into the range starting with A10

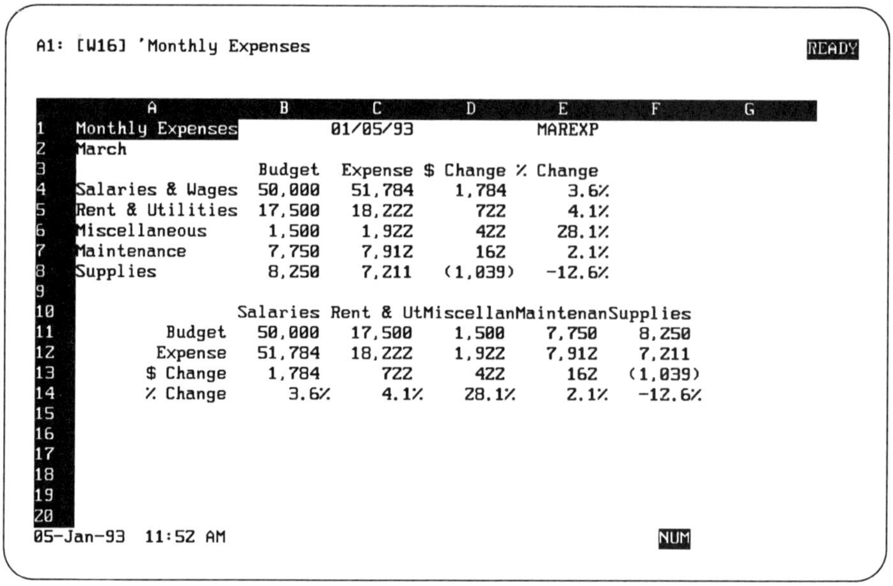

Figure 15-10 The operation of the /Range Transpose command

Discussion

If you use *Lotus* much, one of the commands in this chapter will eventually come in handy. You don't have to try to memorize these commands, though, because you probably won't need them often. Just refer to this chapter when you need one of them.

Terms

printer port
printer driver
background printing
encoded file
network printer
local printer
character string

Objective

Remember the types of operations that are available through the commands and skills presented in this chapter so you can refer back to it when you need to.

The spreadsheet before the search and replace operation

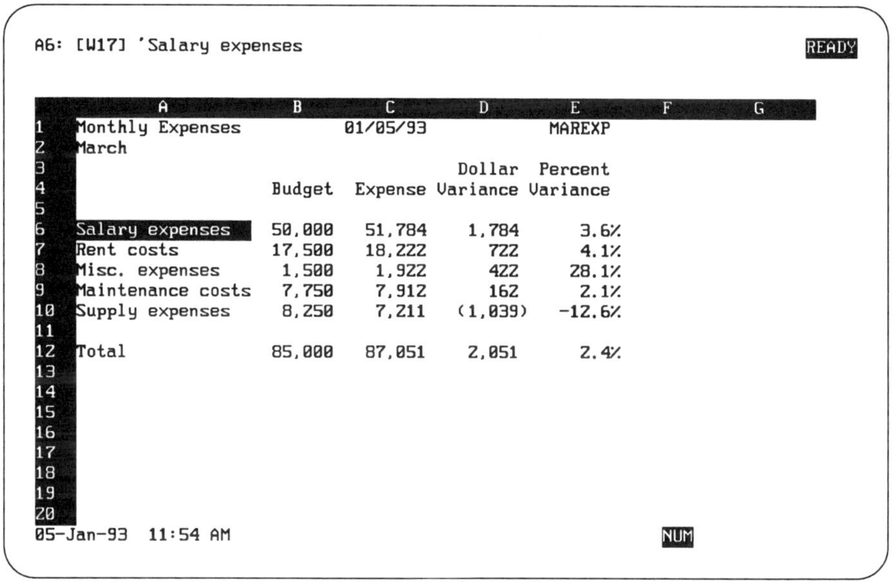

The spreadsheet after the character string *expenses* has been replaced by *costs* in the range from A6 through A10

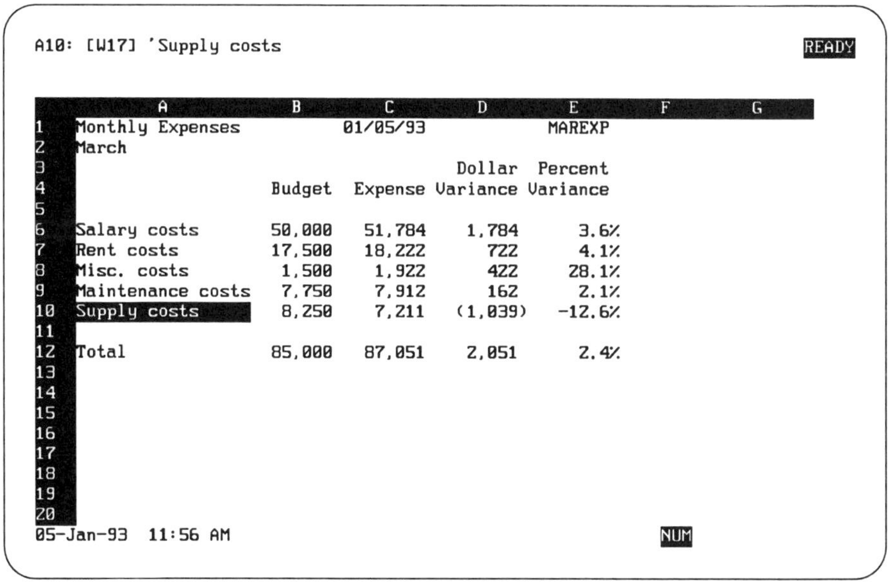

Figure 15-11 The operation of the /Range Search command

Section 3

Lotus 1-2-3 skills for business presentations

The chapters in this section present the skills that you need for making effective business presentations. In chapter 16, you'll learn how to graph the data in a *Lotus* spreadsheet. Then, you can print both the spreadsheet data and its related graphs for your presentations. In chapter 17, you'll learn how to use the enhanced graphing and printing features that are available with the *Lotus* releases from 2.3 and 3.4. In chapter 18, you'll learn how to use the *WYSIWYG* add-in program for enhancing the appearance of spreadsheet data.

If you want to learn how to use *WYSIWYG* and you're not interested in the *Lotus* features for graphing, you can read chapter 18 without reading the other two chapters in this section. Otherwise, it's best to read the chapters in this section in sequence.

Chapter 16

How to graph the data in a spreadsheet

The numbers in *Lotus 1-2-3* refer to its three major capabilities: spreadsheet, graphics, and database. Most of this book focuses on *Lotus 1-2-3*'s spreadsheet capability because that's the most useful one. But *Lotus 1-2-3*'s graphing capability shouldn't be overlooked. Often, graphing the data in a spreadsheet presents a picture of the data that makes it easier to understand.

Figure 16-1, for example, presents a simple spreadsheet and the bar graph that has been printed from it. Here, the graph shows the sales levels for four different types of business over the period from 1988 through 1992. You can create a bar graph like this in just a few minutes when you use any one of the *Lotus* releases. And you can create graphs with more elaborate graphic effects when you use *Lotus* release 3.X.

In this chapter, you'll learn how to use *Lotus* releases 2.X and 3.X to define the five types of graphs that are most useful for business applications. Next, you'll learn how to define and save more than one type of graph for a single spreadsheet. Last, you'll learn how to print a graph using either release 2.X or release 3.X.

If you're using *Lotus* release 3.X, you'll find that some of your displays are slightly different than those in the illustrations. In the bar chart in figure 16-1, for example, release 3.X displays the values on the left side of the chart in thousands instead of in millions. The patterns used in the bars are also different. As you will see, though, these release variations are trivial.

The commands for defining, modifying, and saving graphs

Figure 16-2 summarizes the /Graph commands that you use for defining, modifying, and saving graphs. As you will see in a moment, all but a few of these commands are used to define graphs. For instance, you use the /Graph Type command to identify the type of graph that you're defining. You use the /Graph A command to define the first range of data that should be graphed.

To enhance a graph, you use the /Graph Options command. This command is summarized in figure 16-3, and it lets you define options like

The spreadsheet

```
A1: 'Sales by type                                                   READY

     A             B          C          D          E          F
1  Sales by type                                              SLSTYPE
2
3                 1988       1989       1990       1991       1992
4  Retail      472,077    833,634  1,101,755  1,144,799  1,319,306
5  College     300,586    263,661    299,971    292,105    360,759
6  Trade       400,116    823,512    960,521    890,949    880,819
7  Foreign      54,097     88,331    130,144    179,091    198,685
8
9            1,226,876  2,009,138  2,492,391  2,506,944  2,759,569
10
```

The bar graph

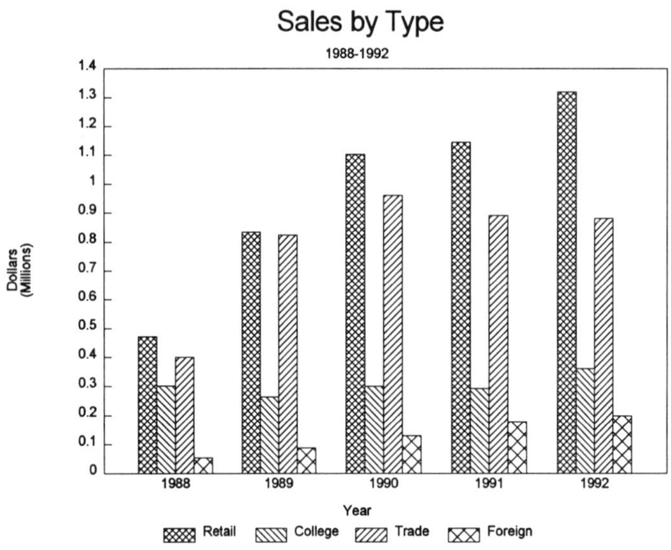

Figure 16-1 A spreadsheet and the bar graph derived from it

those shown in figure 16-4. For instance, the /Graph Options Titles command lets you define the first, second, X-axis, and Y-axis *titles* for a graph, and the /Graph Options Legend command lets you define the *legends* for the ranges of data that are graphed. Note in figure 16-4 that the *X-axis* is the horizontal line at the bottom of a graph; the *Y-axis* is the vertical line on the left of a graph.

Command	Next level	Next level	Function
/Graph F6 (Window) F10 (Graph)	Type	Line Bar Stack-Bar XY Pie HLCO Mixed	Set the graph type. The first five types are valid for all releases of *Lotus*. The last two types are only valid with release 3.X; they are presented in the next chapter.
	X		Set the range of cells to be used to identify the data on the X-axis.
	A-F		Set from one to six ranges of data (A through F) that should be graphed.
	Reset		Reset one or more of the settings for a graph (see figure 16-12).
	View		Display the graph for the current graph settings. You can also use the F10 (Graph) key to view the current graph when you're in Ready mode at the spreadsheet screen.
	Save F3 (Name)		Save the graph so it can be used by another program. For releases, 2.0 through 2.4, you have to save a graph before it can be printed by the *PrintGraph* menu.
	Options		Set the options that can be used with the graph such as the legends, data formats, titles, and data labels (see figure 16-3).
	Name	Use F3 (Name)	Switch to the settings for a named graph.
		Create F3 (Name)	Assign a graph name to the current graph settings.
		Delete F3 (Name)	Delete a graph name for the current spreadsheet.
		Reset	Delete all the graph names for the current spreadsheet.

Figure 16-2 The commands for defining, modifying, naming, and saving graphs (part 1 of 2)

Command	Next level	Next level	Function
/Graph F6 (Window) F10 (Graph)	Group	Columnwise	Set the ranges for the X-axis (X) and for the data that should be graphed (A-F) in a single command by getting the data from successive columns.
		Rowwise	Set the ranges for the X-axis (X) and for the data that should be graphed (A-F) in a single command by getting the data from successive rows.
	Quit		Return to the spreadsheet screen.

Figure 16-2 The commands for defining, modifying, naming, and saving graphs (part 2 of 2)

If you're using *Lotus* releases 2.2 through 2.4 or release 3.4, you can use the F6 (Window) key to display a Graph Settings screen whenever you're working with the /Graph command. To illustrate, figure 16-5 shows the Graph Settings screen and the spreadsheet screen for the graph in figure 16-4. As you can see, this screen displays all of the ranges and settings that you've defined for a graph. As a result, the F6 key makes it easier to use the graphing feature. Although the arrangement of the Graph Settings screen varies from one release of *Lotus* to another, all of these screens present the same information so you shouldn't have any trouble relating the screens in this chapter to the ones for your release. Unfortunately these screens aren't available when you use *Lotus* release 3.0 or 3.1, or any release before 2.2, which makes these releases more difficult to work with.

Whenever you want to see the graph on the screen, you can use the /Graph View command to display it. You can also display the graph for a spreadsheet by pressing the F10 (Graph) key. This key works whenever you're at the spreadsheet screen so you can quickly see how a change in the spreadsheet data affects the related graph. To return to the spreadsheet screen when the graph is displayed, you can press any other key.

If you want to change some or all of the settings for a graph, you use the /Graph Reset command. If you want to define more than one graph for a spreadsheet, you use the /Graph Name command. If you want to save a graph so it can be used by another program or so it can be printed by *Lotus* release 2.X, you use the /Graph Save command. After I show you how to define a graph, I'll show you how to use these commands.

Command	Next level	Next level	Function
/Graph Options F6 (Window)	Legend	A-F	Set the legend for any one of the six data ranges that are graphed.
	Format	Graph	For Line and XY graphs only. Specify whether lines, symbols, or both should be used for all of the ranges in the graph.
		A-F	For Line and XY graphs only. Specify whether lines, symbols, or both should be used for any of the six ranges in the graph.
	Titles	First	Set the top line of the title for the graph.
		Second	Set the second line of the title for the graph.
		X-axis	Set the title for the X-axis.
		Y-axis	Set the title for the Y-axis.
	Grid	Horizontal Vertical Both Clear	Specify whether horizontal, vertical, or both types of grid lines should be used in the graph. If none of these options is specified, grid lines aren't used.
	Scale	Y-scale	Specify whether the scale of the Y-axis should be set manually or automatically. If you specify Manual, you can use the Lower and Upper options to set the lower and upper limits of the scale. You can also use this command to format the numbers used in the scale and to suppress the display of the scale indicator.
		X-scale	For XY graphs only, which require numeric X-scales. This option lets you set the scale for the X-axis just as you can for the Y-axis.
	Color		Display the graph in color if your PC has a color graphics monitor.

Figure 16-3 The commands for setting the options for a graph (part 1 of 2)

Command	Next level	Next level	Function
/Graph Options F6 (Window)	B&W		Display the graph in monochrome even if your PC has a color graphics monitor. You should use this setting when you're going to print a graph on a printer that doesn't support colors.
	Data-Labels	A-F	Set the data label for any one of the six data ranges that are graphed.
	Quit		Return to the /Graph menu.

Figure 16-3 The commands for setting the options for a graph (part 2 of 2)

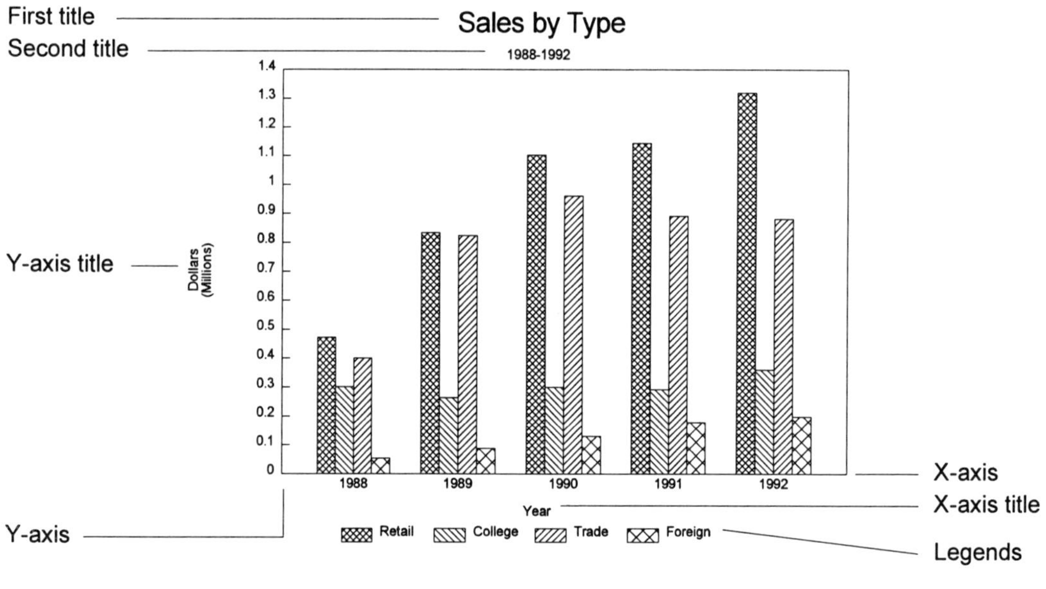

Figure 16-4 The X-axis, Y-axis, and the primary options for a *Lotus* graph

The spreadsheet

```
A1: 'Sales by type                                                   READY

          A          B          C          D          E          F
1   Sales by type                                              SLSTYPE
2
3                    1988       1989       1990       1991       1992
4   Retail        472,077    833,634  1,101,755  1,144,799  1,319,306
5   College       300,586    263,661    299,971    292,105    360,759
6   Trade         400,116    823,512    960,521    890,949    880,819
7   Foreign        54,097     88,331    130,144    179,091    198,685
8
9               1,226,876  2,009,138  2,492,391  2,506,944  2,759,569
10
```

The Graph Settings screen

```
A1: 'Sales by type                                                     MENU
Type  X  A  B  C  D  E  F  Reset  View  Save  Options  Name  Group  Quit
Line  Bar  XY  Stack-Bar  Pie
---------------------------------- Graph Settings ----------------------
 Type: Bar                      Titles: First  Sales by Type
                                        Second 1988-1992
 X: B3..F3                              X axis Year
 A: B4..F4                              Y axis Dollars
 B: B5..F5
 C: B6..F6                                     Y scale:       X scale:
 D: B7..F7                              Scaling    Automatic  Automatic
 E:                                     Lower
 F:                                     Upper
                                        Format     (G)        (G)
 Grid: None        Color: No            Indicator  Yes        Yes

    Legend:                   Format:   Data labels:          Skip: 1
 A  Retail                    Both
 B  College                   Both
 C  Trade                     Both
 D  Foreign                   Both
 E                            Both
 F                            Both
27-Jul-92  10:35 AM                                       NUM
```

Figure 16-5 The spreadsheet and Graph Settings screen for the bar graph in figure 16-4

How to define the five most useful types of graphs

Lotus releases 2.0 through 2.2 let you create five types of graphs, and releases 2.3 through 3.4 let you create two more. Of these, the line graph, XY graph, bar graph, stacked bar graph, and pie chart are the most useful for business applications. So in this chapter, you'll learn how to define only these types of graphs.

Since the bar graph is probably the most commonly used type of graph, I'll start by showing you how to define one of those. Next, I'll show you how to define a line and stacked bar graph because they are closely related to bar graphs. Then, I'll show you how to define a pie chart.

How to define a bar graph Figure 16-6 gives a procedure for defining a *bar graph* like the one in figure 16-4. A graph like this is also known as a *bar chart*. The spreadsheet and the Graph Settings screen for this graph are shown in figure 16-5. Please refer to these figures as well as to the command summaries in figures 16-2 and 16-3 as you read about the procedure for defining a bar chart.

In step 1 of figure 16-6, you use the /Graph Type command to select Bar for the type of graph. In step 2, you use the /Graph X command to set the range for the cells that provide the labels that are used below the X-axis. In this case, the labels are the numbers for the years 1988 through 1992 that are stored in cells B3 through F3. Often, though, the range of cells for the X-axis contains alphabetic labels.

In step 3, you use the /Graph A command to set the first data range. In this case, this range is cell B4 through F4 because this range contains the data for retail sales for the years 1988 through 1992. Then, in step 4, you repeat the process for the second (college), third (trade), and fourth (foreign) data ranges. To set these ranges, you use the /Graph B, C, and D commands.

In step 5, you can use the /Graph View command to see what the graph looks like at this point of definition. Since all of the critical ranges have already been set, the graph should look like the one in figure 16-4 without the titles and legends. Then, to return to the /Graph menu, you can press any key.

In step 6, you use the /Graph Options Titles command to set the titles for the graph. As you can see in the summary in figure 16-3, the four options for this command are First, Second, X-axis, and Y-axis. All four of these are shown in the graph in figure 16-4 and in the Graph Settings screen in figure 16-5. To enter a title, you type the label that you want and press the Enter key.

In step 7, you use the /Graph Options Legend command to set the legends for data ranges A through D. Here again, these legends are shown in figure 16-4 and in the Graph Settings screen in figure 16-5. To enter the legend for a data range, you type the label and press the Enter key.

In step 8, you can use the /Graph View command to view the graph again. If it looks the way you want it to, the graph is finished. Then, you can save the graph settings, print the graph, or both.

1. Use the /Graph Type command to select Bar for the type of graph.
2. Use the /Graph X command to set the range for the cells to be used to label the X-axis at the bottom of the graph. In this case, the range should be B3..F3 so the years 1988 through 1992 are used to identify the groups of bars.
3. Use the /Graph A command to set the range for the first data range. In this case, the range should be B4..F4 so the Retail values are taken for the years 1988 through 1992.
4. Use the /Graph B through D commands to set the range for the next three data ranges. Here, the ranges are B5..F5, B6..F6, and B7..F7 so the College, Trade, and Foreign values are taken for the years 1988 through 1992.
5. Use the /Graph View command to view the graph to make sure it is being developed correctly. It should look like the one in figure 16-4 without the titles and legends. Press any key to return to the /Graph menu.
6. Use the /Graph Options Titles command to set the titles for the graph. Use the First option to enter "Sales by Type" as the first line in the title for the graph. Use the Second option to enter "1988-1992" as the second line in the title. Use the X-axis option to enter "Year" as the title for the X-axis. And use the Y-axis option to enter "Dollars" as the Y-axis title.
7. Use the /Graph Options Legend command to set the legend for each data range in the graph. Use the A option to enter "Retail" as the legend for the first data range. Similarly, use the B through D options to set the legends for the other three data ranges.
8. Use the /Graph View command to view the graph to make sure it is correct. It should look like the one in figure 16-4.

Figure 16-6 The procedure for creating a bar graph like the one in figure 16-4

The only required settings for a bar chart are the entries for the X range and the A range, but you can have up to six data ranges from A through F. If the X range and the data ranges are in consecutive rows or columns, you can speed up the entry process by using the /Graph Group command that's summarized in figure 16-2. In figure 16-6, for example, the X range and the four data ranges are in consecutive rows 3 through 7. As a result, you can use the /Graph Group Rowwise command to enter in all five ranges with a single command instead of using five separate commands.

How to define a line or stacked bar graph Figure 16-7 shows a *line graph* and a *stacked bar graph* (also known as a *stacked bar chart*). Both of these graphs were generated from the spreadsheet in figure 16-5. And both graphs share all but one of the settings shown on the Graph Settings screen in figure 16-5. The difference in the settings is the Type setting. You select /Graph Type Line for the line graph and /Graph Type Stack-Bar for the stacked bar graph.

If you study the graphs in figure 16-4 and 16-7, you can see how closely related line, bar, and stacked bar graphs are. All three have just two required entries, the X range and the A range, but you can specify up to six data ranges for any one of these graphs. Then, to change from one type of graph to another, all you have to do is change the Type setting.

How to define a pie chart Figure 16-8 shows the spreadsheet screen and the Graph Settings screen for the *pie chart*, or *pie graph*, shown in figure 16-9. Since the procedure for defining a pie chart is much like the one for defining a bar chart, I won't go through the exact steps that you must follow to define this type of graph. Instead, I'm going to focus on the graph settings that are required for a pie chart.

In the Graph Settings screen, you can see that the Type setting is Pie. You can also see that the First and Second titles indicate that the pie chart is going to show the sales by type for the year 1992. You define those settings just as you do for any other graph.

The X and the A settings for a pie chart, though, have different meanings than they do for line, bar, or stacked bar graphs. For a pie chart, the X setting gives the range of cells that contain the labels that identify the segments of the pie. In this example, the range is cells A4..A7 because this range contains the Retail, College, Trade, and Foreign labels that are applied to the pie segments. Then, the A setting identifies the range of cells that contain the values for each of the pie segments. Here, the range is F4..F7 because this range contains the sales values for the year 1992 for each of the pie segments.

The only settings you have to define to create a pie chart are the X and A settings. In addition, though, you'll probably want to define the B setting to make the chart more effective. When you omit the B setting, the pie segments don't contain patterns; they are blank. Also, you have to define a B setting if you want to have an *exploded segment* like the Foreign segment in figure 16-9.

To define the B setting, you enter a code number for the type of pattern and type of segment into the spreadsheet. In figure 16-8, you can see these codes in column G. Then, you use the /Graph B command to establish the range for the B setting. For the spreadsheet in figure 16-8, the range is G4..G7. The numbers 1 through 9 represent nine different pattern numbers, so you can have up to nine segments in a pie without repeating a pattern. If a pattern number is preceded by 10, the segment is also exploded. Cell G8, for example, contains the number 104. As a result, the Foreign segment uses pattern 4, and it's exploded.

Note in figure 16-9 that a percent is given in parentheses for each of the segments in the pie. That's the percent of the total pie that the segment represents. *Lotus* automatically calculates and displays these percentages as part of its graphing capability.

How to define an XY graph Figure 16-10 shows the spreadsheet screen and the *XY graph* derived from it. Here, cells A4..A16 are the X range, and

Line graph

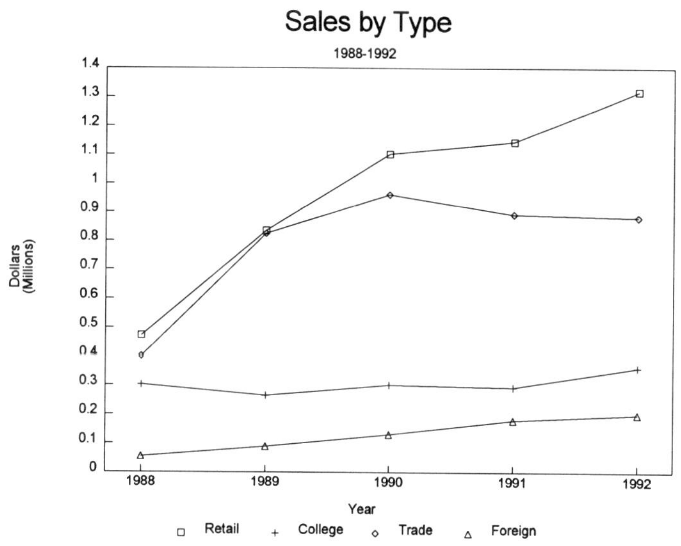

Stacked bar graph

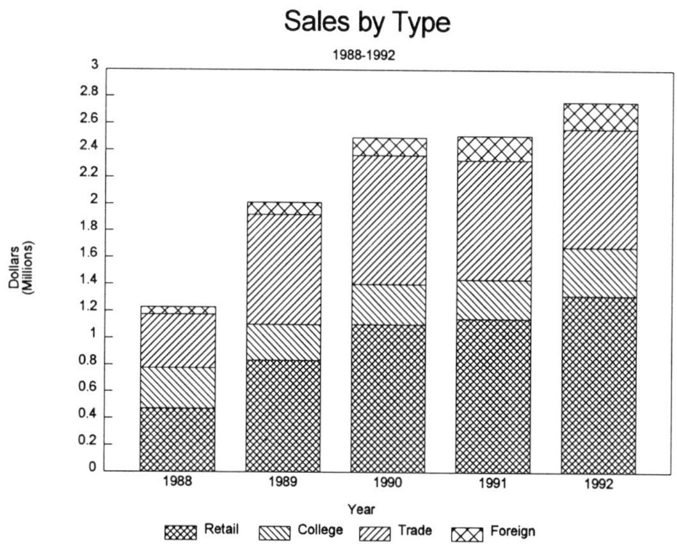

Figure 16-7 The line and stacked-bar graphs with the same graph settings as in figure 16-5, except for the Type setting

The spreadsheet

```
A1: 'Sales by type                                                  READY

     A           E          F           G          H          I
1  Sales by type           SLSTYPE
2
3                  1991        1992
4  Retail     1,144,799   1,319,306          1
5  College      292,105     360,759          2
6  Trade        890,949     880,819          3
7  Foreign      179,091     198,685        104
8
9             2,506,944   2,759,569
10
```

The Graph Settings screen

```
A1: 'Sales by type                                                            MENU
Type  X  A  B  C  D  E  F  Reset  View  Save  Options  Name  Group  Quit
Line  Bar  XY  Stack-Bar  Pie
                                    Graph Settings
 Type: Pie                          Titles: First  Sales by Type
                                            Second 1992
 X: A4..A7                                  X axis
 A: F4..F7                                  Y axis
 B: G4..G7
 C:                                                      Y scale:        X scale:
 D:                                         Scaling      Automatic       Automatic
 E:                                         Lower
 F:                                         Upper
                                            Format       (G)             (G)
 Grid: None          Color: No              Indicator    Yes             Yes

    Legend:                      Format:    Data labels:                 Skip: 1
 A                               Both
 B                               Both
 C                               Both
 D                               Both
 E                               Both
 F                               Both

27-Jul-92  10:39 AM                                                 NUM
```

Figure 16-8 The spreadsheet and Graph Settings screen for the pie chart in figure 16-9

cells B4..B16 are the A range. Beyond that, titles have been entered for the First title, X-axis title, and Y-axis title.

Although an XY graph looks like a line graph, there are some differences. Most important, the data in the X range of an XY graph has to be numeric. Then, *Lotus* decides what values to display on the X-axis. In figure 16-10, for example, the X range covers values from 40 through 100, but *Lotus* uses

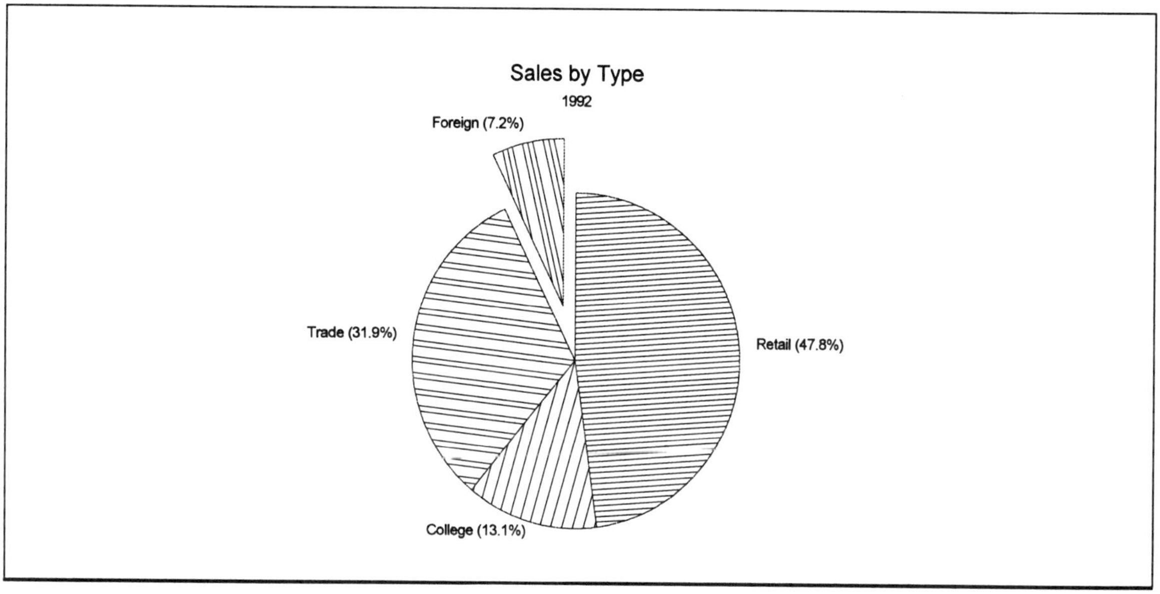

Figure 16-9 The pie chart derived from the spreadsheet in figure 16-8

values from 40 through 110 on the X-axis in the graph. In contrast, the data on the X-axis in a line graph is taken directly from the X range, and that data doesn't have to be numeric.

Note also in figure 16-10 that the data in the X range is in descending sequence (from 100 to 40), but the values on the graph are in ascending sequence. In fact, when you define an XY graph, the values in the X range don't have to be in sequence. *Lotus* figures out what the range of values is and puts an appropriate range in sequence on the X-axis. In that case, though, the lines connecting the nodes on the graph don't make sense so you usually print only the symbols for the nodes, which I'll show you how to do in a moment. When an XY graph is printed without lines, it is usually referred to as a *scatter graph*, or *scatter diagram*.

I have presented this type of graph last because you will probably use it infrequently, if at all. Occasionally, it makes sense to use an XY graph to show the relationships between two sets of values such as marketing costs and sales, but even then the graph is likely to be difficult to interpret. And for simple XY graphs like the one in figure 16-10, you can get the same result by using a line graph.

The spreadsheet data

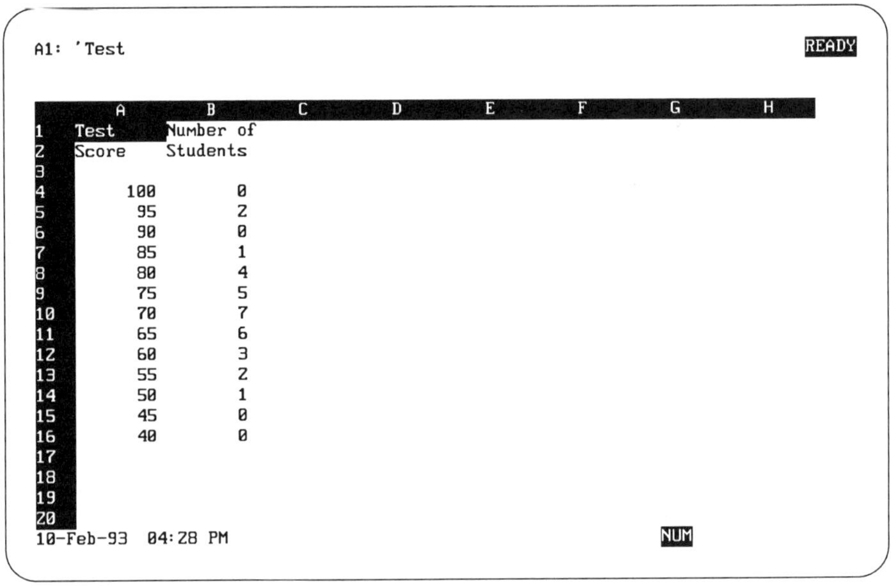
A1: 'Test READY

	A	B	C	D	E	F	G	H
1	Test	Number of						
2	Score	Students						
3								
4	100	0						
5	95	2						
6	90	0						
7	85	1						
8	80	4						
9	75	5						
10	70	7						
11	65	6						
12	60	3						
13	55	2						
14	50	1						
15	45	0						
16	40	0						
17								
18								
19								
20								

10-Feb-93 04:28 PM NUM

The XY graph

Figure 16-10 The spreadsheet data and graph for an XY graph

When and how to enhance a graph by using other options

In general, an effective graph is both simple and complete. As a result, you should use the Titles and Legend options to make your graph complete, but you should avoid options that make it cluttered or complicated. That's why I recommend that you avoid using the Grid, Scale, and Data-labels options summarized in figure 16-3 unless they make your graph more effective.

To illustrate what can happen when you use too many options on a graph, figure 16-11 shows the line graph in figure 16-7 after it has been enhanced. Figure 16-11 also shows the Graph Settings screen for the enhanced graph. As you can see, both horizontal and vertical lines have been added to the graph in figure 16-11. The scale for the Y-axis has been manually changed, and the values for the Y-axis have been formatted with two decimal places. Finally, data labels have been placed on the four lines of the graph.

With figure 16-11 for reference, I'll introduce you to the options in figure 16-3 that I haven't already presented. If you experiment with them, you'll see that most are easy to use. Too often, though, they don't make a graph any easier to understand.

The Format option can be used for an XY graph or a line graph like the one in figure 16-7. This option can be used to specify whether the graphed values should be identified by connecting lines only, by symbols only, or by connecting lines with symbols on the lines as in figure 16-7. Normally, you want to use both lines and symbols for a line graph so you just accept the default option of Both. But if you're defining an XY graph that looks like a scatter diagram, you should use symbols only. When you change this option, you can change it for all of the lines in the graph (Graph) or one or more of the individual lines (A-F).

The Grid option can be used to put *grid lines* on an XY, line, bar, or stacked bar graph. These lines can be horizontal, vertical, or both as shown in figure 16-11. If you look at figure 16-11, you can see that the grid lines clutter the graph without improving its clarity.

The Scale option lets you change the *scale* for the Y-axis in an XY, line, bar, or stacked bar graph. It also lets you change the scale for the X-axis in an XY graph. If you don't use this option, the scales are set automatically to provide for the minimum and maximum values in the ranges that are graphed. In the line graph in figure 16-7, for example, you can see that the Y scale was automatically set from 0 to 1.4 million. In contrast, you can see that the Y scale for the graph in figure 16-11 was manually set from 0 to 2 million. In figure 16-11, increasing the range of the Y scale flattened out the graph lines. This makes it harder to see small increases and decreases in the graphed data.

You can also use the Scale option to format the numbers in the scale and to omit the indicator (the word *millions* on the Y scale in figure 16-11). In figure 16-11, for example, the format for the Y scale has been set to Fixed format with two decimal places. As a result, the numbers in the Y scale in this figure have a different format than those formatted with the default format in

The Graph Settings screen

```
A1: 'Sales by type                                                    MENU
Type  X  A  B  C  D  E  F  Reset  View  Save  Options  Name  Group  Quit
Line  Bar  XY  Stack-Bar  Pie
                                 Graph Settings
  Type: XY                       Titles: First  Sales by Type
                                         Second 1988-1992
  X: B3..F3                              X axis Year
  A: B4..F4                              Y axis Dollars
  B: B5..F5
  C: B6..F6                                         Y scale:    X scale:
  D: B7..F7                              Scaling    Manual      Automatic
  E:                                     Lower      0
  F:                                     Upper      2000000
                                         Format     (F2)        (F0)
  Grid: Both         Color: No           Indicator  Yes         No

     Legend:                     Format: Data labels:           Skip: 1
  A  Retail                      Both    [A] B4..F4
  B  College                     Both    [B]
  C  Trade                       Both    [R]
  D  Foreign                     Both    [A]
  E                              Both
  F                              Both
10-Feb-93  04:30 PM                                         NUM
```

The line graph

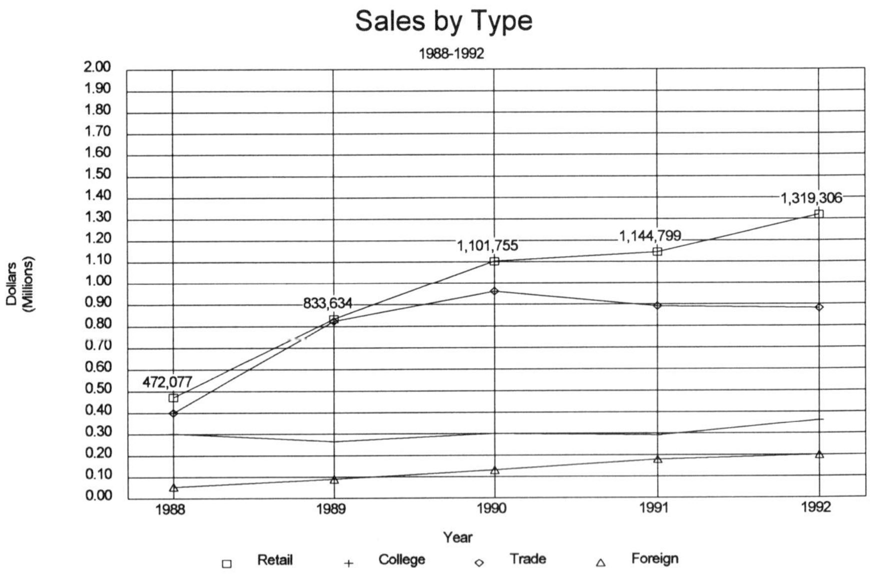

Figure 16-11 The line graph in figure 16-7 after grid lines and data labels have been added and the Y-axis has been scaled and formatted

Command	Next level	Function
/Graph Reset	Graph	Reset all the current graph settings and return to the default settings.
	X	Reset the range for the X-axis.
	A-F	Reset the range for one of the six data ranges.
	Ranges	Reset all the ranges.
	Options	Reset all the options.

Figure 16-12 The commands for resetting graph settings

figure 16-7. Normally, though, you won't need to change the scale formats, and you will want the scale indicators to show.

If you use the /Graph Color command to turn the Color option on, the graph will be displayed in color if your PC has a color monitor. The default, though, is the B&W option. This option displays a graph in one color even if you have a color monitor. If you don't have a color printer, and you're going to print a graph, you should make sure the B&W option is on when you save the graph for printing or when you print the graph. If you leave the Color option on, many of the colors will be printed in black, and that's not what you usually want.

The last option in figure 16-3 is the Data-labels option. This lets you put *data labels* on one or more of the lines or bars of a graph. In figure 16-11, for example, a range of cells is specified for the data labels for the A range so values are printed over each of the nodes in the top line of the graph. After you identify a data label range, you select Center, Left, Above, Right, or Below to position the data label in relation to the line or bar. It usually takes a few tries to get the data labels in the right position.

How to reset the settings for a graph

To reset some or all of the settings for a graph, you use the /Graph Reset command as summarized in figure 16-12. You can use this command when you want to modify the graph you are working on. You can also use this command when you want to start another graph for the spreadsheet you're working on.

How to save more than one group of graph settings for a spreadsheet

When you use the /File Save command to save a spreadsheet to disk storage after you've defined a graph for it, the graph settings are saved along with the spreadsheet. Then, when you retrieve the spreadsheet the next time, you get both the spreadsheet and its graph.

Sometimes, though, you want to define and save more than one graph for a spreadsheet. To do that, you use the /Graph Name command as summarized in figure 16-13. The Create option of this command lets you name the settings for one graph. The result is a *named graph*. After you name a graph, you can use the /Graph Reset command to change the graph settings and start another graph.

To select a named graph, you use the Use option of the /Graph Name command as shown in figure 16-13. When you start the command, the list of named graphs for the spreadsheet is displayed in the third line of the control panel. You can then type the name of the graph you want to use or highlight the name in the control panel. When you press the Enter key, the current graph gets changed to the one you specified.

If you want to modify the settings for a named graph, you use the /Graph Name Use command to access the named graph. Next, you modify its graph settings. Then, you use the Create option to save the current graph settings with the original graph name.

If you want to delete one named graph, you use the Delete option of the /Graph Name command. And if you want to delete all of the named graphs for a spreadsheet, you use the Reset option.

How to save a graph so it can be printed by *Lotus* release 2.X or used by another graphics program

When you use *Lotus* release 2.X without the *WYSIWYG* add-in program, you have to use the /Graph Save command to save a graph to a *PIC file* before you can print it. When you use release 3.X or when you use *WYSIWYG*, you don't have to save a graph in order to print it. However, if you want to use a program like *Lotus Freelance* or *Harvard Graphics* to enhance the graph, you do have to use the /Graph Save command to save the file for use by the other program.

Figure 16-14 shows you how to use the /Graph Save command with release 2.X or 3.X. When you use release 2.X, all of the saved files have the PIC extension. When you start the command, the names of all the saved graphs can be accessed on the third line of the control panel. If you want a complete display of the names of all of the saved graphs, you can press the F3 (Name) key. If you want to save a graph using one of the old graph names, you can use the Arrow keys to highlight the name. Otherwise, you can type the name that you want to use for the graph file. Then, when you press the Enter key, the graph (not the spreadsheet) is saved to the PIC file.

Command	Next level	Function
/Graph Name	Create F3 (Name)	Assign a name to the current graph settings so you can use them again without having to specify each setting again. You can use up to 15 characters in the name.
	Use F3 (Name)	Select a named graph that you have saved for use with the current spreadsheet.
	Delete F3 (Name)	Delete a named graph for the current spreadsheet.
	Reset	Delete all the named graphs for the current spreadsheet.

How to save a graph setting

1. Start the /Graph Name Create command.
2. Type the name to be used for the current graph settings at this prompt:

   ```
   Enter graph settings name:
   ```

   The name can be up to 15 characters long, and it can consist of any combination of letters, digits, or symbols with the exception of <<.

3. Press the Enter key to save the named graph settings.

How to retrieve a graph setting

1. Start the /Graph Name Use command.
2. From the list of named graph settings that appears after the prompt, select the name you want by highlighting it or by typing it:

   ```
   Enter graph settings name to use:
   BAR                STACK                PIE
   ```

3. Press the Enter key to complete your selection.

Figure 16-13 The commands for saving and retrieving the graph settings that apply to a spreadsheet

How to save a graph to a PIC file (release 2.X)

1. Start the /Graph Save command.
2. Type the file name for the current graph as prompted by *Lotus*:

```
Enter graph file name: C:\123\DATA\*.pic
5YRBAR.PIC       5YRLINE.PIC      1992PIE.PIC
```

   Or, if you want the current graph to be saved in an old file, type or highlight the name of the file that's displayed in the third line of the control panel.

3. Press the Enter key to save the graph.

How to save a graph to a metafile (CGM file) or a PIC file (release 3.X)

1. If necessary, use the /Worksheet Global Default Graphics command to set the default to Metafile (CGM) or PIC file. If you want the default to be permanent, use the /Worksheet Global Default Update command after you set this default.
2. Start the /Graph Save command.
3. Type the file name for the current graph as prompted by *Lotus*:

```
Enter graph file name: C:\123\DATA\*.cgm
5YRBAR.CGM       5YRLINE.CGM      1992PIE.CGM
```

   Or, if you want the current graph to be saved in an old file, type or highlight the name of the file that's displayed in the third line of the control panel. However, if the default is set to Metafile, only files with CGM extensions are listed. If the default is set to PIC, only files with PIC extensions are listed. To override the default, type the extension that you want along with the file name.

4. Press the Enter key to save the graph.

Figure 16-14 How to save a graph to a PIC or CGM file

When you use the /Graph Save command with release 3.X, a saved file can have either a PIC or a CGM extension. These extensions represent two different graphic formats, and the CGM format can also be referred to as the *metafile* format. When you save a file for use with another program, you should make sure that you're using the right format for that program. To set the default for either PIC or CGM format, you can use the /Worksheet Global Default Graph command as summarized in step 1 of figure 16-14. Then, when you use the /Graph Save command, only the files with the default extension are listed. If you want to save a file with the other extension, though, you can override the default by typing the extension along with the file name.

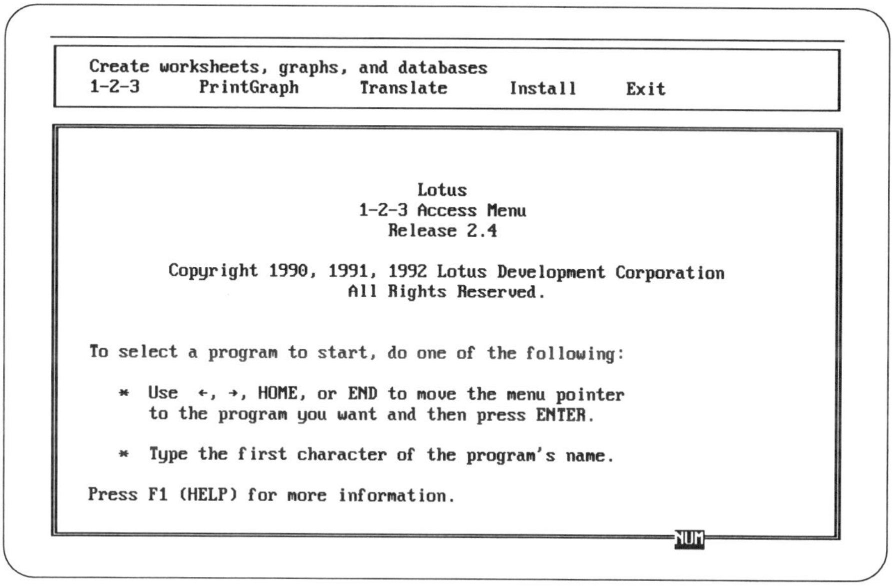

Figure 16-15 The *Lotus 1-2-3* Access System menu (release 2.X)

How to print a saved graph using *Lotus* release 2.X

When you use *Lotus* release 2.X without *WYSIWYG*, you have to use the *PrintGraph* menu to print a graph after you've saved it to a PIC file. To get to the *PrintGraph* menu, though, you must first get to the Access System menu shown in figure 16-15. If you used this Access System menu to start *1-2-3*, you get back to this menu by using the /Quit command to exit from *1-2-3*. Otherwise, you have to exit from *1-2-3* and restart *Lotus* in another way.

Perhaps your PC is set up so there's an easy way to start the Access System menu after you exit from *1-2-3*. If not, you can start this menu from the DOS prompt. First, you change to the drive and directory that contains the *Lotus 1-2-3* program files. If, for example, *Lotus* is stored in the 123 directory on the C drive, you start by entering this command at the DOS prompt:

```
C:>cd \123
```

Then, you enter this command:

```
C:\123>lotus
```

to start the Access System menu.

When you select *PrintGraph* from the Access System menu, *Lotus* displays a screen like the one in figure 16-16. At the top of this screen you can see the *PrintGraph* menu. It gives you access to the commands that you need for printing a graph that's stored in a PIC file. These commands are summarized

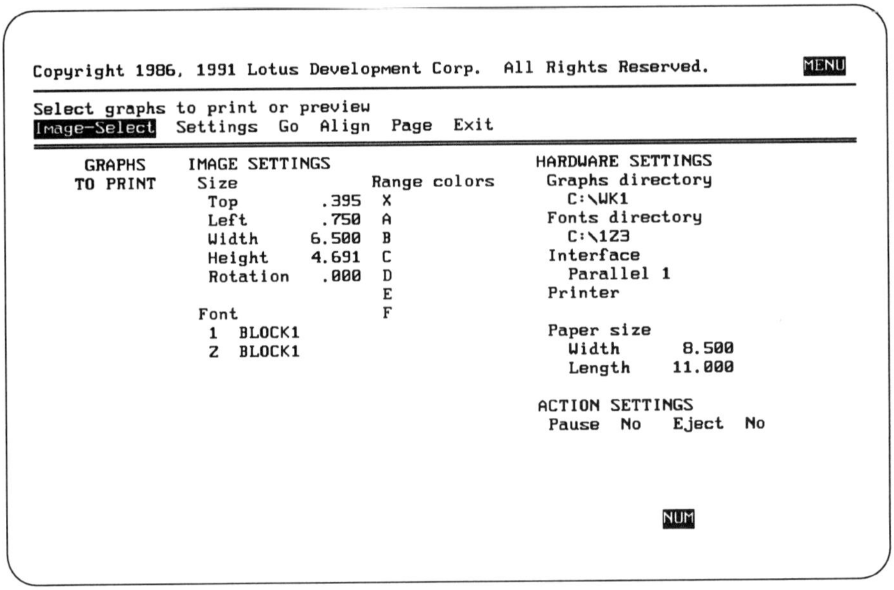

Figure 16-16 The *PrintGraph* menu (release 2.X)

in figure 16-17. Then, to print a graph, you use a procedure like the one in figure 16-18.

In step 1 in figure 16-18, you use the Settings commands to change any settings that are given in the *PrintGraph* screen like the one in figure 16-16. For instance, you can use the Settings Image Size command to set the size for your graphs to either half page or full page. You can also use the Settings Hardware Graphs-Directory command to set the graphs directory to the one that contains your PIC files. If you're the only one who uses *Lotus* on your PC, you can use the Settings Save command to save the current settings so they become the permanent defaults. If you want to change the current *PrintGraph* settings, you can use the Settings Reset command.

In step 2, you select the Image-Select command so you can select the graphs that you want to print. *Lotus* then displays a screen like the one shown in figure 16-18. This screen lists the PIC files in the graphs directory. Then, to select a file for printing, you use the Arrow keys to highlight the file name, and you press the Spacebar. When you do that, *Lotus* displays a number sign (#) next to the file as shown in the figure. After you select one or more files, you press the Enter key to finish the Image-select command. *Lotus* then returns to the *PrintGraph* menu.

In step 3, you select the Go option to print all of the graphs that you selected. In step 4, you select the Page option to skip to the top of the page after the last graph has been printed. These commands and the Align command work just as they do when you're printing a spreadsheet. Printing a

Command	Next level	Next level	Function
Image-Select			Select one of the graph files that you saved for a spreadsheet.
Settings	Image	Size	Select the size setting for the printed graph: full, half, or manual. If you select manual, you must enter the top, left, width, and height settings for the printed graph.
	Hardware	Graphs-Directory	Set the default directory for the graph files.
		Fonts-Directory	Set the default directory for the font files; normally, this is the same as the *Lotus* directory.
	Save		Save the current *PrintGraph* settings as the permanent default settings.
	Reset		Reset the current *PrintGraph* settings.
Go			Print the selected graph.
Align			If necessary, tell *Lotus* that the paper is aligned properly.
Page			Skip to the top of the next page.
Exit			Exit from the *PrintGraph* menu.

Figure 16-17 The commands for printing a graph from the *PrintGraph* menu (release 2.X)

graph, though, can take much longer than printing a spreadsheet. So don't be alarmed if it takes several minutes to print each graph on a dot-matrix printer.

How to print a graph using *Lotus* release 3.X

Lotus release 3.X makes it much easier than release 2.X to print a graph when you aren't using *WYSIWYG*. Because you use the /Print Printer command just as you do when you're printing a spreadsheet, you don't have to save a graph in a PIC file, exit from *Lotus*, and use the *PrintGraph* menu to print your graph. Instead, you just select the graph that you want to print and print it.

Figure 16-19 summarizes the commands you use to print a graph. And figure 16-20 shows you how to use those commands to print a graph. In step 1, you use the /Print Printer Image command to select the graph that you want to print. It can be either the current graph or a named graph. In step 2,

1. Use the Settings menu to change any of the settings that aren't appropriate for your graphs:

   Image **Hardware** **Action** **Save** **Reset** **Quit**

   The first time you print graphs, for example, you may have to use the Hardware Graphs-Directory command to change the directory to the one you have saved your PIC files in. You may also want to use the Image Size command to change the size for your graphs from full to half page.

2. Use the Image-Select command in the *PrintGraph* menu to select one or more graphs for printing:

```
Copyright 1986, 1991 Lotus Development Corp.  All Rights Reserved.          POINT
Select graphs to print

    GRAPH FILE  DATE      TIME      SIZE
    ----------------------------------        Space bar marks or unmarks selection
    EXP-R       05-25-92  8:56      3002      ENTER selects marked graphs
    EXPENSE     05-25-92  8:56      6678      ESC exits, ignoring changes
  # PROFIT      09-26-92  12:46     2850      HOME moves to beginning of list
                                              END moves to end of list
                                              ↑ and ↓ move highlight
                                                List will scroll if highlight
                                                moved beyond top or bottom
                                              GRAPH (F10) previews marked graph
```

   To select a graph, move the highlight to it and press the Spacebar. To return to the *PrintGraph* menu after you've selected one or more graphs, press the Enter key.

3. Use the Go option in the *PrintGraph* menu to print the selected graphs.

4. Use the Page option in the *PrintGraph* menu to skip the form to the top of the next page.

Figure 16-18 How to use the *PrintGraph* menu to print a PIC file (release 2.X)

you select Go to print the graph that you've selected. In step 3, you select Page to skip to the top of the next page if that's necessary. Printing a graph can take much longer than printing a spreadsheet, though, so don't be alarmed if it takes several minutes to print a graph on a dot-matrix printer.

Discussion

In this chapter, I've shown you how to define the most useful types of graphs that you can use with all releases of *Lotus*. I've also shown you how to use the most useful graphing options with these five types of graphs. If you limit your use to those options and those five types of graphs, you can develop useful graphs in a minimum of time.

You should realize, though, that *Lotus* releases 2.3 through 3.4 provide extended capabilities for graphing and for printing graphs. These capabilities are the subject of the next chapter. In addition, you should know that the later

Command	Next level	Next level	Function
/Print Printer	Image	Current	Select the current graph settings.
		Named-Graph	Select the settings for a named graph.
	Go		Print the selected graph.
	Align		If necessary, tell *Lotus* that the paper is aligned properly.
	Page		Skip to the top of the next page.
	Quit		Exit from the /Print Printer menu.

Figure 16-19 The commands for printing a graph using release 3.X

1. Start the /Print Printer command. Then, select the Image option to select a graph for printing:

   ```
   Current   Named-Graph
   ```

   If you select the Current option, the current graph will be printed. If you select the Named-Graph option, you can select one of the named graphs at this prompt:

   ```
   Enter name of graph to print:
   BAR                LINE                PIE                STACK
   ```

   After you type or highlight the named graph, press the Enter key to return to the /Print Printer menu.

2. Select Go command to print the selected graph.

3. If necessary, select the Page command to skip the form to the top of the next page.

Figure 16-20 How to print a graph using release 3.X

releases of *Lotus 1-2-3* come with an add-in program that is designed for graphic presentations. Release 2.2 comes with a program called *Allways*, and releases 2.3, 2.4, 3.1, and 3.4 come with a program called *WYSIWYG*. Releases 2.4 and 3.4 also come with a *SmartIcons* feature that can help you develop some graphs and graphic presentations more efficiently. In chapter 18, you can learn how to use the *WYSIWYG* add-in program, and you can learn how to use a mouse and the *SmartIcons* in chapter 21. If your PC has a laser printer, *WYSIWYG* and the extended capabilities of release 3.X make it possible to develop and print graphs at the high level of quality that is sometimes referred to as *presentation graphics*.

Terms

title
legend
X-axis
Y-axis
bar graph
bar chart
line graph
stacked bar graph
stacked bar chart
pie chart
pie graph
exploded segment
XY graph
scatter graph
scatter diagram
grid line
scale
data label
named graph
PIC file
metafile
presentation graphics

Objective

Use your release of *Lotus* to define, save, and print any one of these five types of graphs: line, bar, stacked bar, pie, or XY.

Chapter 17

How to use the enhanced graphing and printing features of releases 2.3 through 3.4

In the last chapter, you learned a practical set of skills for preparing graphs from spreadsheets. Those skills can be used with any of the releases of *Lotus* from release 2.01 to the current releases. In the last chapter, you also learned how to print a graph using either a 2.X or a 3.X release. If you're like most *Lotus* users, those graphing and printing skills are going to be more than you'll ever need for your graphics requirements.

If those skills don't cover all of your graphing requirements, though, this chapter presents the enhanced graphing and printing features of *Lotus* releases 2.3, 2.4, and 3.0 through 3.4. With few exceptions, these enhancements are easy to learn so I'll go through them quickly. When you finish this chapter, you can decide for yourself whether you should use any of these enhanced capabilities.

A summary of the enhancement commands that started with *Lotus* releases 2.3 and 3.0

Figure 17-1 summarizes the commands and features that were added to new releases of *Lotus*. In column 4 of this table, you can see the first 2.X or 3.X release that provided a new capability. For instance, the capability for displaying a graph horizontally became available with releases 2.3 and 3.0. And the capability for displaying a graph with a three-dimensional effect became available with releases 2.3 and 3.4. That means that this feature wasn't available with releases 3.0 or 3.1. If you study this summary, you can see that some of the capabilities still aren't available for any of the 2.X releases.

When you first start using the enhanced capabilities of figure 17-1, you are likely to have trouble remembering the menu path to the feature or option

Command	Next level	Next level	First 2.X and 3.X releases	New capability
/Graph Type	HLCO Mixed		2.3, 3.0	Two more graph types
	Features	Vertical Horizontal Stacked 100% 2Y-Ranges Y-Ranges Frame Drop Shadow 3D-Effect Table	2.3, 3.0 2.3, 3.0 2.3, 3.0 2.3, 3.0 N/A, 3.0 N/A, 3.0 2.3, 3.4 N/A, 3.4 2.3, 3.4 N/A, 3.4	Enhancement features for the seven graph types
/Graph Options	Format	Area	2.3, 3.4	Apply hatch patterns to the areas below the lines in a line graph
	Titles	2Y-Axis Note Other-Note	N/A, 3.0 N/A, 3.0 N/A, 3.0	Identify the second Y-axis of a 2Y graph and add footnotes to a graph
	Grid	Y-Axis	N/A, 3.0	Identify the Y-axis in a 2Y graph that you want the grid to apply to
	Scale	2Y-Scale	N/A, 3.0	Set the scale for the second Y-axis in a 2Y graph
	Advanced	Text Hatches	N/A, 3.0 N/A, 3.0	Specify the styles and sizes for the text in a graph or specify the hatch patterns to be used in the areas of a graph
/Print Printer Options	Advanced	Image	N/A, 3.0	Specify the printing size and orientation (vertical or horizontal) for a graph
		Fonts	N/A, 3.0	Specify the fonts to be used for portions of a spreadsheet
/Worksheet	Window	Graph	N/A, 3.0	Display a spreadsheet and a graph at the same time

Figure 17-1 A summary of the commands for enhancing graphs and spreadsheets

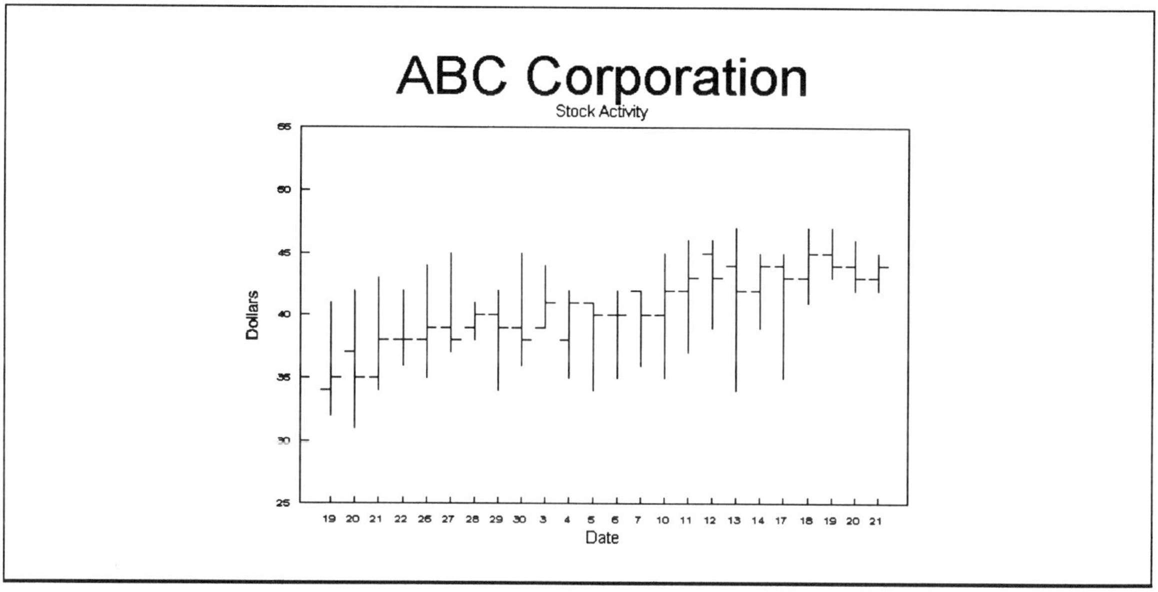

Figure 17-2 An HLCO graph (2.3 and 3.0)

that you want to use. That's why you may want to refer to this summary frequently when you start using the new features. If, for example, you want to specify the styles and sizes for the text used in a graph, you can see that you have to use the /Graph Options Advanced Text command. And if you want to display a graph horizontally, you can see that you have to use the /Graph Type Features Horizontal command. Because the menu paths aren't always logical, a summary like the one in figure 17-1 can help you work more efficiently.

Two more graph types

All of the *Lotus* releases starting with release 2.3 and 3.0 provide for two more graph types.

The HLCO graph Figure 17-2 presents an *HLCO graph* (High, Low, Close, Open). Here, the long vertical lines indicate the range of prices from high to low; the short horizontal mark to the right of each line shows the closing price; and the short horizontal mark to the left of each line shows the opening price. When you define an HLCO graph, the A, B, C, and D data ranges should contain the high prices, the low prices, the closing prices, and the opening prices. If you have anything to do with the trading of stocks or other commodities, you may have use for this type of graph. Otherwise, you probably won't ever need it.

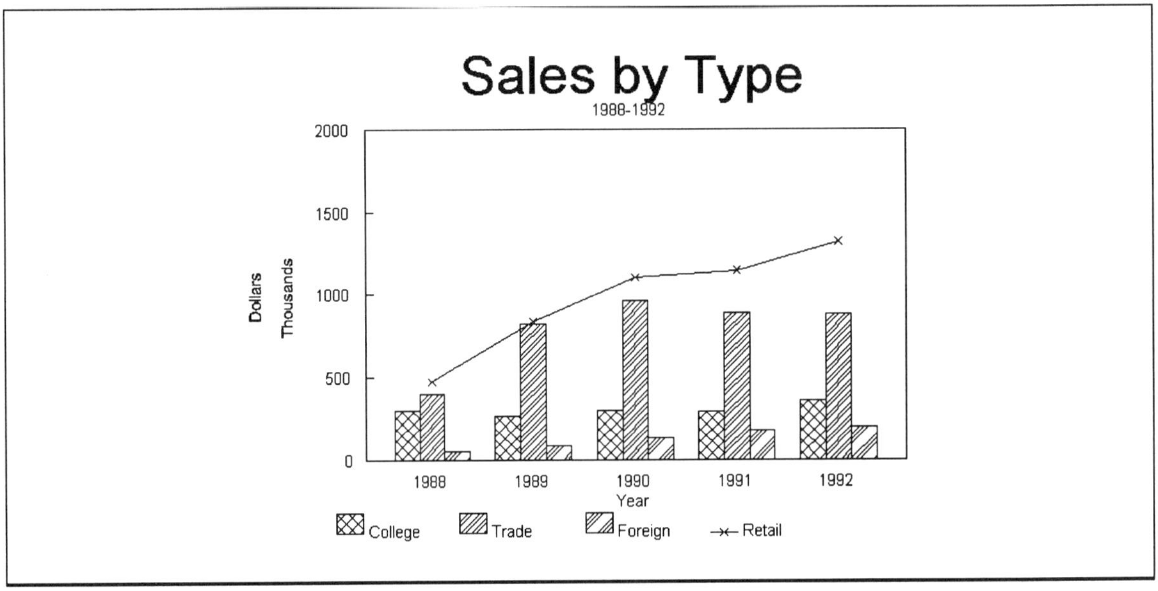

Figure 17-3 A mixed graph (2.3 and 3.0)

The Mixed graph Figure 17-3 presents a *mixed graph.* As you can see, a mixed graph is a mix of a bar chart and a line graph. When you define a mixed graph, the A, B, and C data ranges are for the bar graph; the D, E, and F data ranges are for the line graph. If you have already defined a bar chart and you change it to a mixed graph, the A, B, and C ranges stay as bars, but the D, E, and F ranges change to lines. In the graph in this figure, there are no E and F ranges.

The enhancement options of the /Graph Type Features command

Figure 17-4 summarizes ten enhancement features of the /Graph Type Features command. The first six of these features are supported by releases 2.3 and 2.4, and all of them are supported by release 3.4. Note, however, that releases 3.0 and 3.1 provide for only six of the features, and these six are somewhat different from those provided by releases 2.3 and 2.4. In the explanations that follow, the headings include release numbers that identify the first 2.X and 3.X release that offered the feature.

Vertical and Horizontal (2.3 and 3.0) The default option for a graph is Vertical. Occasionally, though, the Horizontal feature makes a graph easier to read. In figure 17-5, you can see a graph with this feature on, but I think this graph is easier to read in its Vertical form. To change from one orientation to the other, you just select Vertical or Horizontal. *Lotus* does the rest.

Command	Next level	First 2.X and 3.X releases	Function
/Graph Type Features	Vertical (Vert)	2.3, 3.0	Create a graph with a vertical Y-axis and horizontal X-axis
	Horizontal (Horiz)	2.3, 3.0	Create a graph with a horizontal Y-axis and vertical X-axis
	Stacked	2.3, 3.0	Create a line graph with stacked values
	100%	2.3, 3.0	Show each range as a percent of the whole instead of its actual value
	Frame	2.3, 3.4	Identify the portions of the frame that should be put around the graph: left, right, top, or bottom
	3D-Effect (3D)	2.3, 3.4	Add a three-dimensional effect to a graph
	2Y-Ranges	N/A, 3.0	Identify the ranges that relate to the second Y-axis in a 2Y graph
	Y-Ranges	N/A, 3.0	Identify the ranges that relate to the first Y-axis in a 2Y graph
	Drop-Shadow	N/A, 3.4	Add a three-dimensional effect to a graph
	Table	N/A, 3.4	Add a data table beneath a graph

Figure 17-4 The options of the /Graph Type Features command

Stacked (2.3 and 3.0) Figure 17-6 shows a line graph with the Stacked feature on. This is like a stacked bar chart, but in the form of a line graph. As you will see later, you can use the /Graph Options Format command to apply hatch patterns to the areas below the lines. But even then, a stacked bar chart is usually a more effective presentation than a stacked line graph.

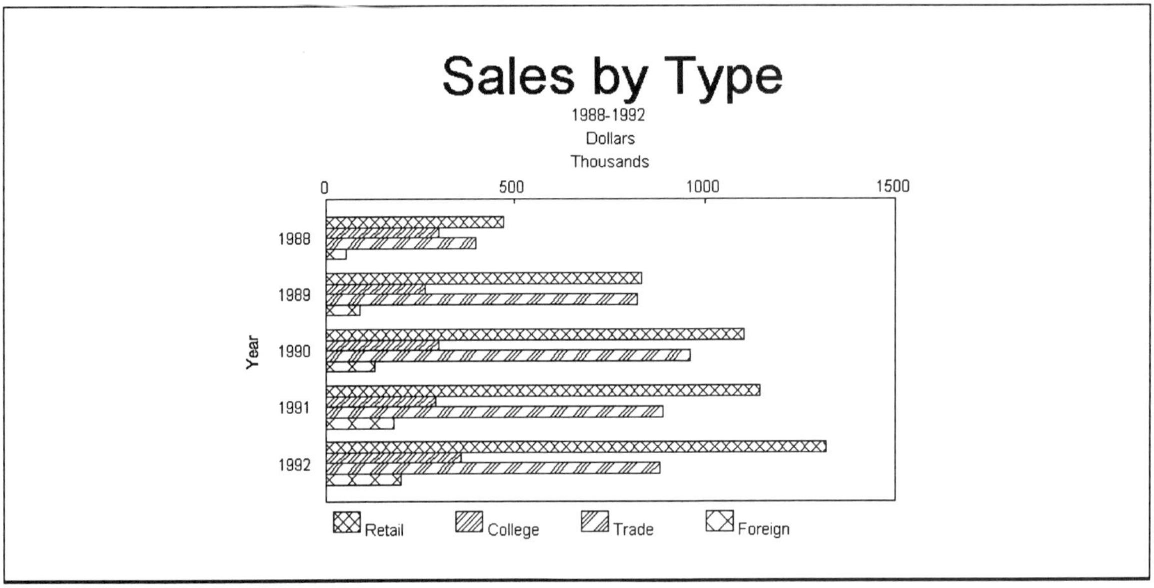

Figure 17-5 A bar chart that uses the Horizontal option (2.3 and 3.0)

100% (2.3 and 3.0) Figure 17-7 shows a stacked bar graph that uses the 100% feature. For each year, the sales categories are treated as a percent of the total sales for that year. This feature is occasionally useful because it gives you a different perspective on your data. To get the graph in this form, you just select the 100% feature, and *Lotus* does the rest. If you have used a title for the Y-axis, though, you should probably change it to something like "Percent," as shown in this example.

Frame (2.3 and 3.4) The default for this feature is to display a complete frame around a graph as illustrated by all the graphs so far. However, this command lets you remove one or more sides of the frame. Since there's usually no point in doing that, I'm not going to illustrate a graph with a partial frame or with no frame at all.

3D-Effect or 3D (2.3 and 3.4) Figure 17-8 shows a graph that uses the 3D-Effect feature of release 2.3 and another graph of the same data that uses the 3D feature of release 3.4. As you can see, this feature adds a depth perspective to a graph. Although this effect is frequently used today, it usually makes a graph harder to understand. That's why I recommend that you use this feature with restraint. In particular, you should avoid using the form illustrated by the chart for release 3.4.

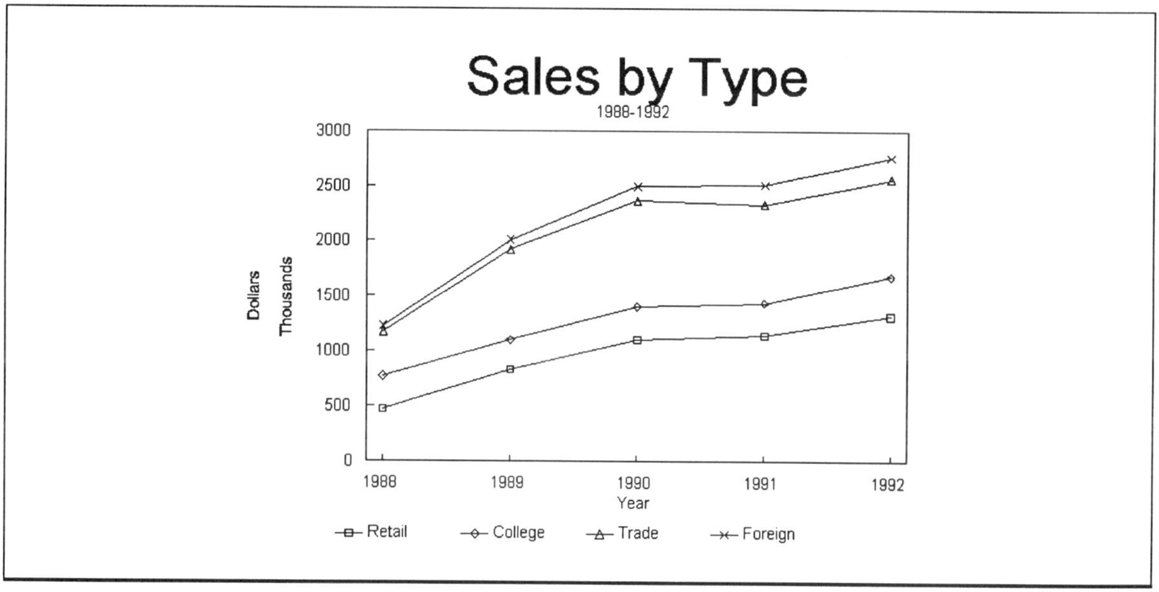

Figure 17-6 A line graph that uses the Stacked option (2.3 and 3.0)

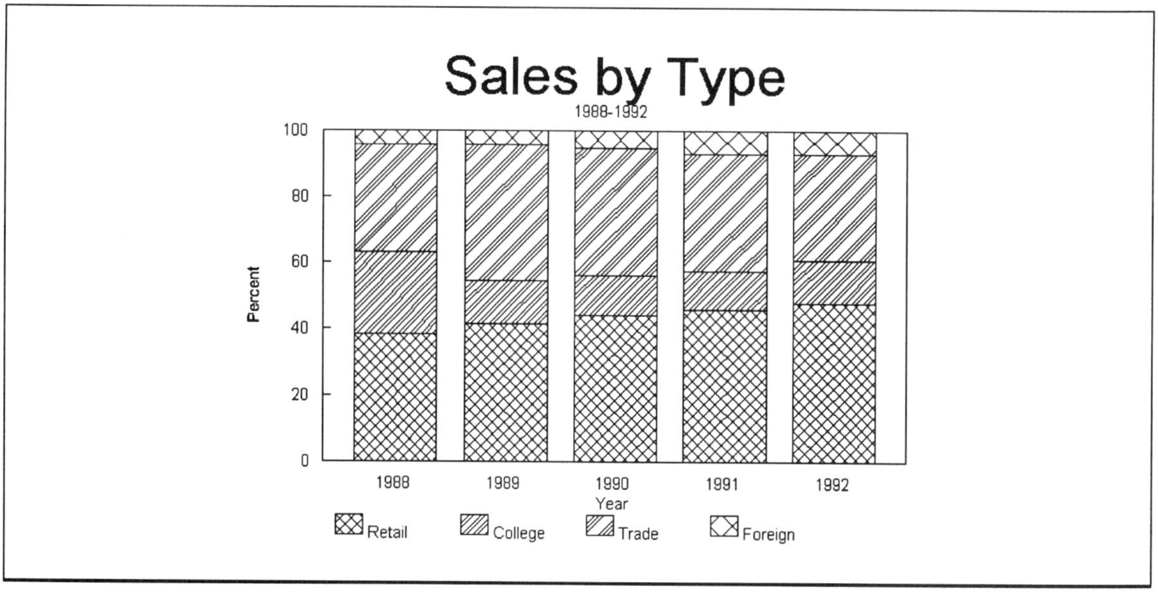

Figure 17-7 A stacked bar chart that uses the 100% option (2.3 and 3.0)

If you try this effect with different types of graphs, you can see that it varies from graph to graph. If, for example, you use the 3D feature for release 3.4 on a stacked bar chart, it gives you the type of effect shown in figure 17-8 for release 2.3. And if you use it on a line graph, it gives you an effect that I think you'll definitely want to avoid.

2Y-Ranges and Y-Ranges (3.0) Figure 17-9 presents a mixed graph that uses two different scales for the Y-axis. On the left side of the graph, you can see that a scale of dollars from one to three million is used. On the right side, you can see that a scale of percentages from zero to 12 percent is used.

To develop a graph with two Y-axes, you use the 2Y-Ranges option to identify those data ranges from A through F that should relate to the second Y-axis. Although you normally don't need to use the Y-Ranges option, you use that if you want to switch a range back to the first Y-axis after you've assigned it to the second Y-axis. Once you've assigned the ranges, you use the /Graph Options command to enhance the graph so it makes sense. I'll explain this in more detail in a moment when I present the enhanced options of that command.

Although you can use the 2Y-Ranges feature on bar charts and line graphs, it is often most dramatic on a mixed graph like the one in figure 17-9. On the other hand, this isn't a feature that you'll frequently find a need for.

Drop-Shadow (3.4) For a bar chart like the one in figure 17-8, this feature provides a depth perspective like the 3D-Effect shown for release 2.3. For a stacked bar chart, this feature and the 3D feature provide the same effect. So here again, you need to experiment with this feature to see how it affects different types of graphs. And again, you should use this feature with restraint.

Table (3.4) Figure 17-10 shows a stacked bar chart after the Table feature has been applied to it. As you can see, this feature creates a table below the graph that displays all of the data that went into a graph. As I see it, this is the most useful new graphing feature of release 3.4.

The graph enhancement options of the /Graph Options command

Figure 17-11 summarizes the enhancement options of the /Graph Options command that became available with *Lotus* releases 2.3 and 3.0. As you can see, only the first option is available for a 2.X release. The others are available only with a 3.X release. Now, I'll present these options in the context of the functions that they relate to.

A bar chart with the 3D-Effect feature of release 2.3

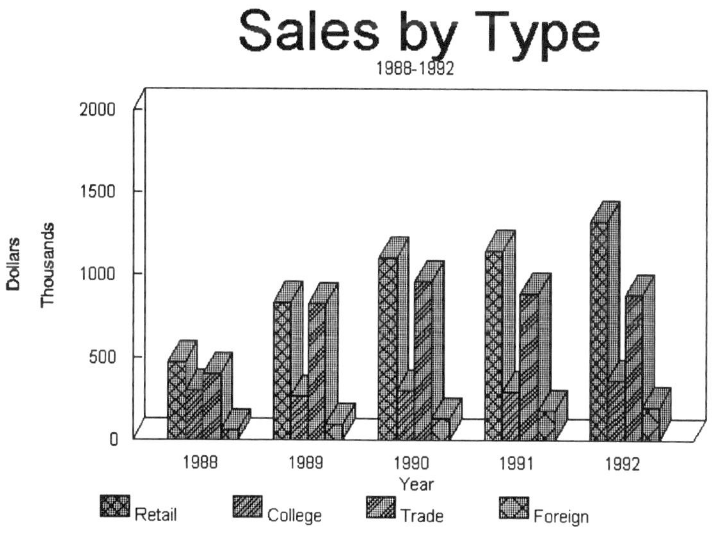

A bar chart with the 3D feature of release 3.4

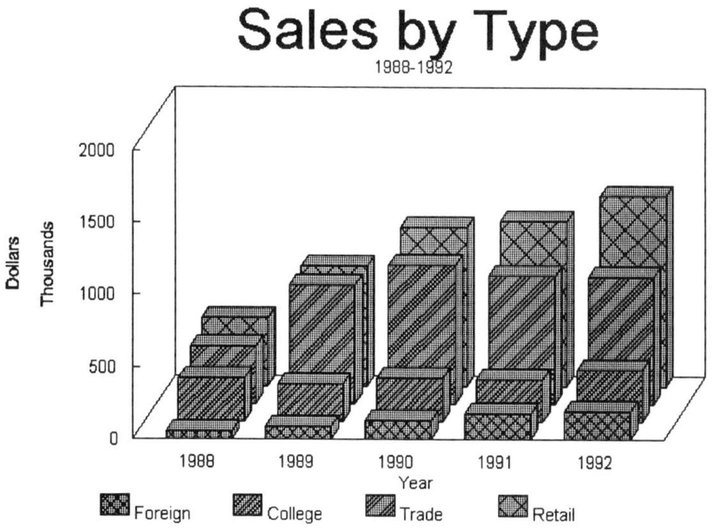

Figure 17-8 Two bar charts that use the 3D option (2.3 and 3.4)

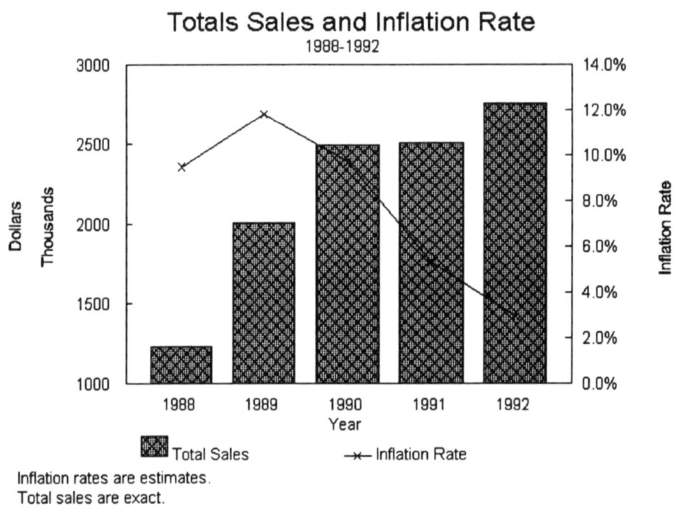

Figure 17-9 A graph with two Y-axes (3.0)

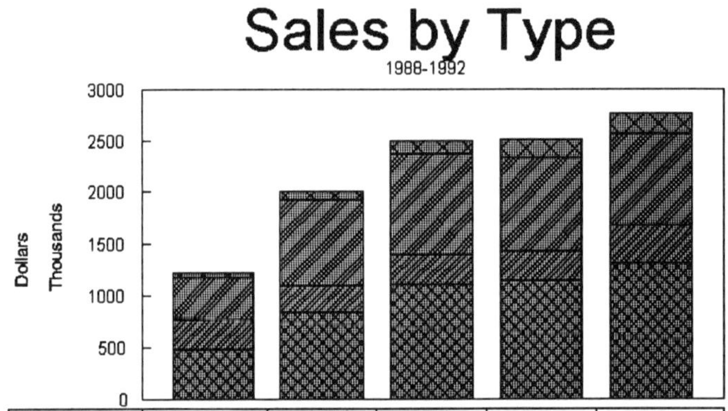

Year	1988	1989	1990	1991	1992
Retail	472,077	833,634	1,101,755	1,144,799	1,319,306
College	300,586	263,661	299,971	292,105	360,759
Trade	400,116	823,512	960,521	890,949	880,819
Foreign	54,097	88,331	130,144	179,091	198,685

Figure 17-10 A graph that uses the Table option (3.4)

Command	Next level	Next level	Next level	First 2.X and 3.X releases	New capability
/Graph Options	Format	Graph A B C D E F	Area	2.3, 3.0	Apply hatch patterns to the areas below the lines in a line graph
	Titles	2Y-Axis Note Other-Note		N/A, 3.0 N/A, 3.0 N/A, 3.0	Identify the second Y-axis of a 2Y graph and add footnotes to a graph
	Grid	Y-Axis		N/A, 3.0	Identify the Y-axis in a 2Y graph that you want the grid to apply to
	Scale	2Y-Scale		N/A, 3.0	Set the scale for the second Y-axis in a 2Y graph
	Advanced	Text Hatches		N/A, 3.0 N/A, 3.0 N/A, 3.0	Specify the text styles and sizes and the hatch patterns to be used in a graph

Figure 17-11 A summary of the commands for enhancing graphs and spreadsheets

How to fill in the areas below the lines in a line graph (2.3 and 3.0) Figure 17-12 presents a line graph with the areas below the lines filled in. To get this effect, you use the /Graph Options Format command to apply the Area option to one or more data ranges of a graph. In this case, the option has been applied to all of the data ranges. Although this effect is interesting, I doubt that it makes a graph easier to understand, so you can easily get along without it.

How to enhance a graph with two Y-axes (3.0) If you look back to figure 17-9, you can see a graph with two Y-axes. To develop a graph like this, you use a procedure like the one that's summarized in figure 17-13. After you develop the graph for the first Y-axis, you use the /Graph Type Features 2Y-Ranges command to tell *Lotus* which data ranges should apply to the second axis. Then, in step 3, you use the /Graph Options Titles command to identify the second Y-axis. In step 4, you use the /Graph Options Scale

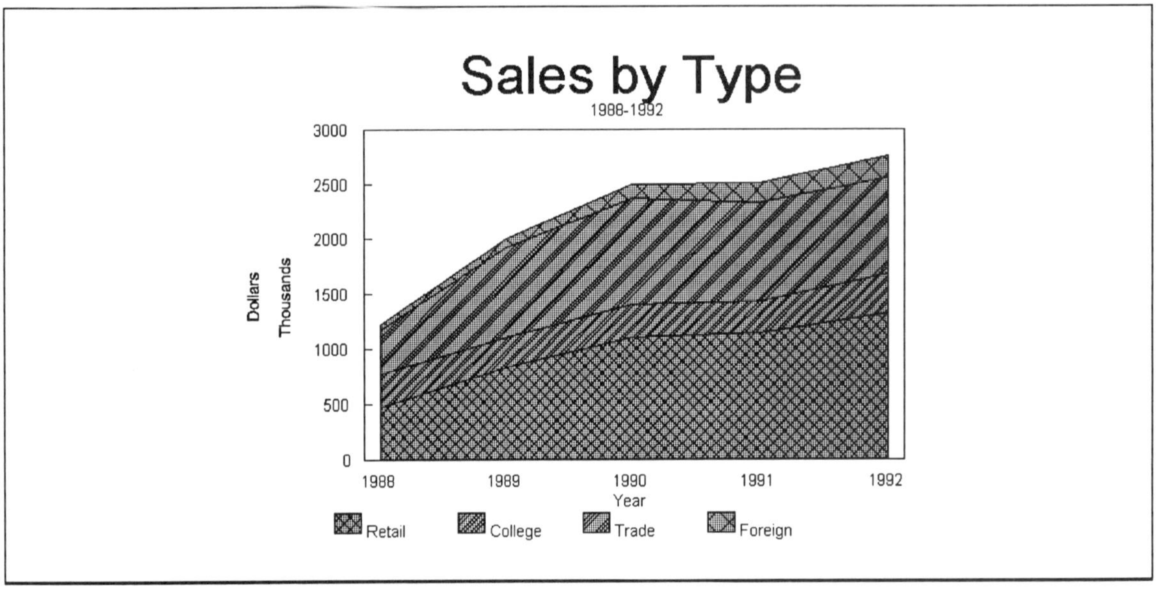

Figure 17-12 A line graph with filled-in areas below the lines (2.3 and 3.0)

command to set the scale for the second Y-axis. And in step 5, you can use the /Graph Options Grid command to tell *Lotus* which Y-axis the grid should be applied to. However, you're usually better off not using a grid.

How to add notes to a graph (3.0) With the 3.X releases, the /Graph Options Titles command provides a Note and an Other-Note option. You enter these just as you enter a First title or Second title, and they're displayed at the bottom of a graph as shown in figure 17-9.

How to specify the style and size for the text that is used in a graph (3.0) Figure 17-14 presents a procedure for changing the style and size of the text that is used in a graph. In step 1, you start the /Graph Options Advanced Text command. Then, you select the level of the text items that you want to modify. The First level represents just the First title of the graph; the Second level represents the Second title, the titles of the axes, and the legends; and the Third level represents all the other text in the graph.

In step 2, you select Font if you want to specify the style of the text that you've selected or Size if you want to specify the size. In either case, *Lotus* displays a list of numbers like this:

```
Default  1  2  3  4  5  6  7  8
```

For Font, the numbers represent the eight styles that can be used for the text in a graph. For Size, the numbers 1 through 9 represent a range from the

1. Develop the graph just as though all of the data ranges are going to apply to the first Y-axis.
2. Use the /Graph Type Features 2Y-Ranges command to identify the ranges that apply to the second Y-axis. If you make a mistake, use the /Graph Type Features Y-Ranges command to identify the ranges that apply to the first Y-axis.
3. Use the /Graph Options Titles 2Y-Axis command to label the second Y-axis.
4. Use the /Graph Options Scale 2Y-Scale command to set the scale for the second Y-axis.
5. If necessary, use the /Graph Options Grid command to tell *Lotus* that the grid is supposed to be based on the values in the second Y-axis, but you normally don't want to use a grid in a graph like this.

Figure 17-13 How to develop a graph with two Y-axes (3.0)

1. Start the /Graph Options Advanced Text command, which displays this prompt:

   `First   Second   Third   Quit`

   Select First to set the text options for the First title in the graph; select Second to set the text options for the Second title, the titles for the axes, and the legends; and select Third to set the text options for all other text in the graph.

2. *Lotus* displays this prompt:

   `Color   Font   Size   Quit`

   Select Font to specify the style of the type that you want to use for the text that you have selected, or select Size to specify the size of the type that you want to use.

3. *Lotus* displays a prompt like this:

   `Default   1   2   3   4   5   6   7   8`

   Select the number of the font or size that you want to use for the text that you have selected. For font, the numbers refer to eight style options. For size, 1 is the smallest size and 9 is the largest.

Figure 17-14 How to use the /Graph Options Advanced Text command to specify the style and size of the text used in a graph (3.0)

smallest size to the largest size. To get a listing of the styles and sizes that these numbers represent when you're using releases 3.0 or 3.1, you can use the /Print Printer Sample command followed by the Go command. If you're using release 3.4, however, you don't have this command. Then, you can just experiment with the numbers to see what each represents. When you select one of the numbers in step 3 of the procedure, the related style or size is used for the level of text that you selected in step 1.

Normally, though, you don't need to use this command because *Lotus* uses appropriate styles and sizes for the text in a graph. All of the graphs in this chapter, for example, use the default styles and sizes, and I don't think that you can improve them much by experimenting with other styles and sizes. In fact, this type of enhancement usually takes more time than it's worth so it reduces your productivity.

How to specify the hatch patterns that are used in a graph (3.0)

Figure 17-15 presents a procedure for changing the hatch patterns that are used in a graph. Occasionally, it makes sense to do this because the hatch patterns cause an effect that is disturbing to the eye (called the moire effect). As you move the cursor to the number in the prompt in step 2 of the procedure, *Lotus* displays a brief description of the pattern. Then, after you select a pattern, you can press the F10 (Graph) key to see how the selection has affected the graph. The trouble is that *Lotus* doesn't provide hatch patterns that make it easy for you to avoid the moire effect, so experimenting with the hatch patterns may not help.

The enhancement options of the /Print Printer command (3.0)

Figure 17-16 summarizes the enhancement options of the /Print Printer command that became available with release 3.0. The options of the /Print Printer Options Advanced Image command apply to a graph, and the options of the /Print Printer Options Advanced Fonts command apply to the spreadsheet. None of these options are currently available with any of the 2.X releases. But as you will see, none are that valuable.

How to print a spreadsheet and graph on the same page One of the more useful enhancements to the /Print Printer command is the ability to print both a spreadsheet and a graph on the same page when you're using a laser printer. This capability, however, isn't done by using one of the commands in figure 17-16. Instead, you use the procedure in figure 17-17.

Before you can use this feature, you have to name the graph you want to print as summarized in step 1 of figure 17-17. Then, in step 2, you use the /Print Printer Range command to identify the range of the spreadsheet that you want to print, but don't press the Enter key. Instead, type a semicolon (;), an asterisk (*), and the name of the graph that you want to print. If you want to print other ranges or named graphs, you can type another semicolon and continue the list. You can even start a list with a named graph. When you press the enter key to finish the Range command, you can use the Go command to print the ranges and graphs that you've listed.

1. Start the /Graph Options Advanced Hatches command, which displays this prompt:

   ```
   A  B  C  D  E  F  Quit
   ```

   Select the data range that you want to set the hatch pattern for.

2. *Lotus* displays this prompt:

   ```
   1  2  3  4  5  6  7  8  Range
   Solid
   ```

   Select the number of the hatch pattern that you want to use for the data range that you've selected. As you move the cursor from one number to the next, you can see a description of the hatch pattern that the number represents in the third line of the control panel.

Figure 17-15 How to use the /Graph Options Advanced Hatches command to specify the hatch patterns for the data ranges in a graph (3.0)

How to control the orientation, size, and print quality of a graph when it's printed When you start the /Print Printer Options Advanced Image command that's summarized in figure 17-16, you get three options: Rotate, Image-Sz, and Density. If you select Rotate, *Lotus* offers two options: No or Yes. The No option means you don't want the graph rotated when printed so it is printed in the normal vertical (portrait) orientation. The Yes option means you want the graph rotated when printed so it's printed in a horizontal (landscape) orientation. Unfortunately, though, the landscape option doesn't work on dot-matrix printers or on all laser printers. If you do use the landscape orientation, you usually need to use the Image-Sz option to adjust the size of the graph to this orientation.

When you select the Image-Sz option of the /Print Printer Options Advanced Image command, *Lotus* offers three options. If you select Margin-Fill, the graph will be sized so it fills the area between the left and right margin settings. As a result, the margins you set before you execute this command control the width of the graph. If you select Length-Fill, *Lotus* displays a prompt that asks for the length that you want to fill. Your response to this prompt should be in lines. A value of 44 will take up roughly two-thirds of a page when printed on a dot-matrix printer. Using this option is usually the most efficient way to adjust the size of a graph. If you select Reshape, *Lotus* prompts you for both a width and a length value. Here, the width value should be in characters. A value of 40 represents four inches if you're using a dot-matrix printer that is printing at ten characters per inch. And the length value should again be in lines.

The Image-Sz command is most useful when you want to print a graph on the same page as a spreadsheet. But this command is also useful when you

Command	Next level	Next level	Next level	Next level	Function
/Print Printer Options	Advanced	Image	Rotate	No	Print the graph in a vertical orientation
				Yes	Print the graph in a horizontal orientation
			Image-Sz	Margin-Fill	Print the graph so it fills the print margins from side to side
				Length-Fill	Print the graph so it is the length of the value that you supply
				Reshape	Print the graph in a new shape based on the width and length values that you supply
			Density	Draft	Print the graph in draft mode
				Final	Print the graph in letter quality mode
		Fonts	Range		Select the font style (but not the size) for the entire print range
			Header/Footer		Select the font style for the header and footer of a spreadsheet
			Border		Select the font style for the borders of a spreadsheet

Figure 17-16 A summary of the /Print Printer Advanced Options for enhancing graphs and spreadsheets (release 3.X)

1. Define a graph and save it using the /Graph Name Create command.

   `Enter graph name: PROFIT`

2. Execute the /Print Printer Range command and specify the spreadsheet range you want to print.

   `Enter print range: A:A1..A:F20`

   Type a semi-colon (;), type an asterisk (*), and type the name of the graph you want to print as shown in the following prompt:

   `Enter print range: A:A1..F20;*PROFIT`

   You can continue this list with other ranges and graph names. And you can start the list with a graph name. To complete the command, press the Enter key.

3. Use the /Print Printer Go command to start the print job.

Figure 17-17 How to print a spreadsheet and graph on the same page (3.0)

size a graph for landscape orientation. In either case, the Length-Fill option provides an efficient way to make sure that the graph fits properly on the page. If the length is too short, though, the text in the graph becomes too large in proportion to the graph. This detracts from the graph's appearance.

The /Print Printer Options Advanced Image command is designed for working with dot-matrix printers. When you start this command, *Lotus* offers two options. If you select Draft, the graph is printed with draft quality so the graph is printed more quickly. If you select Final, the graph is printed with the best quality that is available for the printer.

How to control the fonts used in a spreadsheet If you look again at the summary in figure 17-16, you can see that the /Print Printer Options Advanced Fonts command lets you select the fonts that you want to use in a spreadsheet. When you use this command, you can select a font for the entire print range, the header or footer of the spreadsheet, or the borders of the spreadsheet. Then, *Lotus* offers these selections:

`1 2 3 4 5 6 7 8`

Here, the numbers apply to eight different type styles. As you move the cursor from one number to the next, *Lotus* gives a description of the style in the third line of the control panel. On my PC, for example, you can choose from Regular Serif, Bold Serif, Italic Serif, and so on. Unfortunately, this command doesn't let you change the size of the type that is used for printing the spreadsheet.

Because changing type styles without changing type sizes doesn't improve the graphics of a spreadsheet, I'm not even going to illustrate the use of this command. Instead, I recommend that you avoid using it altogether. If you want to enhance a spreadsheet by changing both the style and size of selected portions of type, you need to use an add-in program like *WYSIWYG*, which is presented in the next chapter.

How to use the /Worksheet Window Graph command to view a graph and spreadsheet at the same time (3.0)

Figure 17-18 shows a portion of a spreadsheet and a graph that are displayed at the same time. To create a display like this one, you define the graph first. Then, you move the cell pointer to the right of the spreadsheet data that you want to display and execute the /Worksheet Window Graph command. That puts the spreadsheet in one vertical window and the current graph in the other. From that time on, you can see what happens to the graph as you change data in the spreadsheet without pressing the F10 (Graph) key. To clear the graph window, you execute the /Worksheet Window Clear command.

Discussion

If preparing graphic presentations is an important part of your job, you most likely have a need for some of the capabilities presented in this chapter. But if you're like most *Lotus* users, you don't need any of these enhanced capabilities. In either case, though, you should be aware that experimenting with graphic features can waste hours of your time. So use the features that you need for making effective presentations, but don't let the joy of graphing interfere with your productivity.

If the enhanced capabilities presented in this chapter still don't meet your requirements for graphic presentations, perhaps the capabilities provided by *WYSIWYG* will fill the gap. In addition, the *SmartIcons* feature that goes along with *WYSIWYG* in releases 2.4 and 3.4 can help you develop some graphs and graphic presentations more efficiently. You can read about *WYSIWYG* in the next chapter and about mouse support and *SmartIcons* in chapter 21.

Another option for developing graphic presentations from *Lotus* spreadsheets is to use a graphics program like *Lotus Freelance* or *Harvard Graphics*. In general, these programs are easier to use and provide more features than *Lotus 1-2-3*. In addition, they accept *Lotus* spreadsheet data without any difficulties.

Terms

HLCO graph

mixed graph

Objectives

1. Decide whether you need any of the enhanced graphing or printing capabilities presented in this chapter.
2. Use the capabilities presented in this chapter that are appropriate for your graphics requirements.

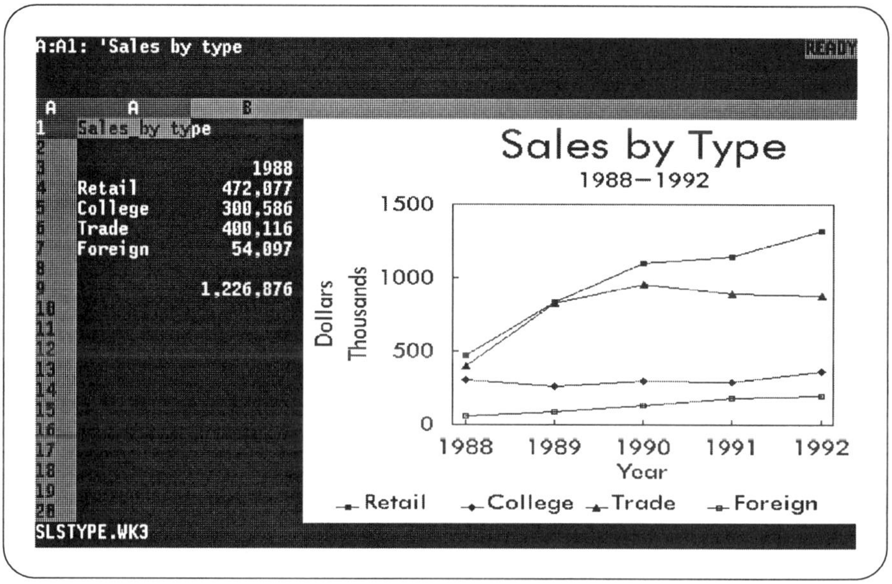

Figure 17-18 A spreadsheet and graph displayed at the same time by using the /Worksheet Window Graph command (3.0)

Chapter 18

How to use the *WYSIWYG* add-in program

WYSIWYG is an *add-in program* that comes with *Lotus* releases 2.3, 2.4, 3.1, and 3.4. This program lets you enhance the appearance of a spreadsheet by specifying the fonts to be used for portions of the spreadsheet, by adding lines to a spreadsheet, by adding shading and shadows to a spreadsheet, and so on. Some of these enhancements are illustrated by the spreadsheet in figure 18-1.

As you enhance a spreadsheet with *WYSIWYG*, the enhancements appear on the screen. Then, when you print the spreadsheet, the printed spreadsheet looks like the one on the screen as shown in figure 18-1. This accounts for the name of this add-in program: *WYSIWYG*, or What You See Is What You Get. You can pronounce its name like this: wis'-ee-wig.

Besides letting you enhance the appearance of a spreadsheet, *WYSIWYG* lets you put a graph in a spreadsheet and then print it. If you're using one of the 2.X *Lotus* releases, this makes it easier for you to print a graph because you don't have to create a PIC file first. And if you're using one of the 3.X releases, this makes it easier for you to print a spreadsheet and a graph on a single page.

Although *WYSIWYG* has other features, these are the most important ones. So if you need to enhance the appearance of a spreadsheet for formal presentations, you'll probably find *WYSIWYG* useful. And if you need to print graphs from one of the 2.X releases, you'll definitely find it useful. After I show you how to use *WYSIWYG* for these purposes, I'll introduce you to some of its other capabilities.

Before you start learning about *WYSIWYG*, though, you need to know how to start an add-in program. So if you haven't already read chapter 14, you should read that chapter first. Also, you should realize that *WYSIWYG* requires a large amount of internal memory (from 105,000 to 165,000 bytes depending on which release of *Lotus* you're using) so you may not be able to use it for large spreadsheets if your PC has a limited amount of memory.

How to use the *WYSIWYG* menu system

When you attach and invoke *WYSIWYG* as described in chapter 14, *WYSIWYG* replaces the *Lotus* display with its own display. That's why the *WYSIWYG* screen shown in figure 18-1 looks different than the regular *Lotus* screen. However, you still access the *Lotus* menu system by pressing the slash (/) key.

Although *WYSIWYG* uses menus that are similar to those of *Lotus*, you access its menus by using the methods shown in figure 18-2. If you're using the keyboard, you press the colon (:) key to display the *WYSIWYG* main menu that's shown in the figure. If you're using a mouse, you move the mouse cursor to the control panel to display the *Lotus* menu. Then, you press the right mouse button to display the *WYSIWYG* menu. To return to the *Lotus* menu, you press the right mouse button again.

Once the *WYSIWYG* menu is displayed, you access its commands just as you do the *Lotus* commands. If you're using a keyboard, either press the first letter of the selection, or move the cursor to the selection and press the Enter key. If you're using a mouse, just move the mouse cursor to the selection and click the left mouse button. To escape from a command, press the right mouse button (the equivalent of pressing the Esc key).

I mention using the mouse in this chapter because *WYSIWYG* is designed to be used with a mouse. In addition, *WYSIWYG* for *Lotus* releases 2.4 and 3.4 supports the use of *SmartIcons*. It was also designed to be used with a mouse. So if you're going to use *WYSIWYG* and *SmartIcons* much, I recommend that you read chapter 21. It explains using the mouse and using *SmartIcons* in more detail.

Since the *WYSIWYG* and *Lotus* menus are similar in appearance, at first you may find it a bit confusing to tell them apart. So remember that the mode indicator in the top right corner of the screen displays MENU when the *Lotus* menu system is active and WYSIWYG when the *WYSIWYG* menu system is active. In addition, if you have a color monitor, the highlight for the *Lotus* menu is a different color than the one for the *WYSIWYG* menu. Beyond that, of course, the two menus have different options.

Since you use the colon to access the *WYSIWYG* menu system from the keyboard, I'll use the following form to refer to *WYSIWYG* commands in the remainder of this chapter:

```
:Format Bold
```

This means you press the colon key to activate the main *WYSIWYG* menu, followed by *f* for the Format option, and *b* for the Bold option. This is the same form that I have been using for *Lotus* commands, except they begin with a slash instead of a colon.

A spreadsheet printed from *WYSIWYG*

Yearly Expenses				BUDGET93 01/05/93
	1992 Budget	1992 Expense	Variance	1993 Budget
Salaries & Wages	600,000	645,780	(45,780)	650,000
Rent & Utilities	210,000	212,420	(2,420)	215,000
Insurance	15,000	17,600	(2,600)	18,000
Maintenance	93,000	94,512	(1,512)	90,000
Supplies	99,000	112,364	(13,364)	115,000
Miscellaneous	12,000	16,651	(4,651)	17,500
Total	$1,029,000	$1,099,327	($70,327)	$1,105,000

The same spreadsheet on the *WYSIWYG* screen

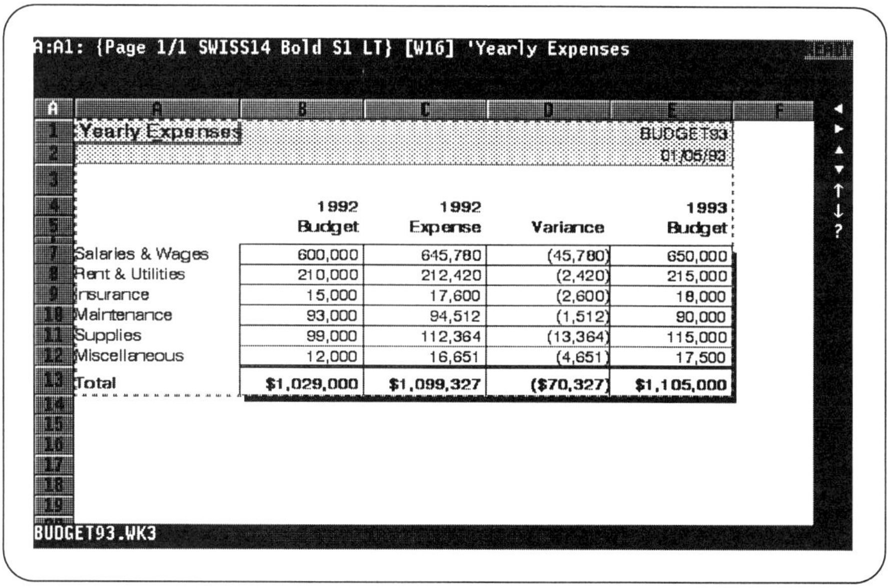

A:A1: {Page 1/1 SWISS14 Bold S1 LT} [W16] 'Yearly Expenses

A	A	B	C	D	E
1	Yearly Expenses				BUDGET93
2					01/05/93
3					
4		1992	1992		1993
5		Budget	Expense	Variance	Budget
7	Salaries & Wages	600,000	645,780	(45,780)	650,000
8	Rent & Utilities	210,000	212,420	(2,420)	215,000
9	Insurance	15,000	17,600	(2,600)	18,000
10	Maintenance	93,000	94,512	(1,512)	90,000
11	Supplies	99,000	112,364	(13,364)	115,000
12	Miscellaneous	12,000	16,651	(4,651)	17,500
13	Total	$1,029,000	$1,099,327	($70,327)	$1,105,000

BUDGET93.WK3

Figure 18-1 A *WYSIWYG* spreadsheet

The *WYSIWYG* main menu

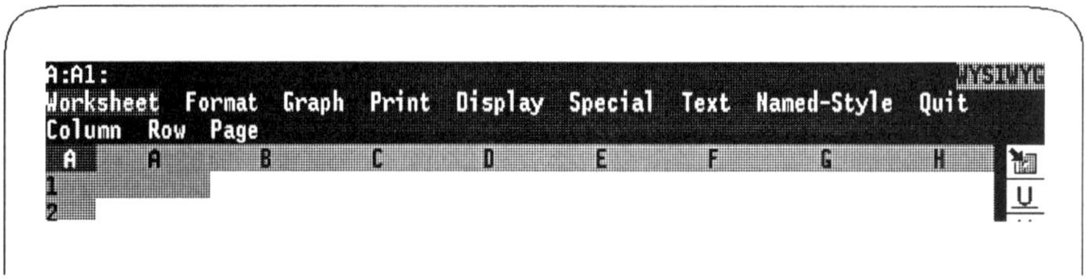

How to access the *WYSIWYG* menu from the keyboard

Press the colon (:) key.

How to access the *WYSIWYG* menu with a mouse

1. Display the *Lotus* menu by moving the mouse cursor to the control panel of the spreadsheet.
2. Press the right mouse button to toggle between the *Lotus* and *WYSIWYG* menus.

Figure 18-2 How to access the *WYSIWYG* menu

How to use *WYSIWYG* to improve the appearance of a spreadsheet

Figure 18-3 summarizes the two commands you'll use most often when you improve the appearance of a spreadsheet. The :Format command lets you change the appearance and size of the fonts used for the spreadsheet. It also lets you add lines, shading, and shadows to a spreadsheet. The :Worksheet command lets you adjust the widths of columns and the heights of rows so they can accommodate the changes made by the :Format command. This command also lets you put page breaks in a spreadsheet.

Before you start improving the appearance of a spreadsheet, you may want to take out any lines that you've put in it by using hyphens, equals signs, or underscores across a cell. Similarly, you may want to take out any empty rows that you've used for spacing. As you will see, *WYSIWYG* makes it easy for you to provide lines and spacing in other ways.

If you study the commands in figures 18-3 and 18-5, you can probably use most of them without any further help. Here, though, are some specific ideas that may help you use them.

How to specify the fonts for a spreadsheet The first procedure in figure 18-4 shows you how to specify the font for a range of cells. In step 1, when you start the :Format Font command, a screen like the one in this figure

Command	Next level	Next level	Next level	Function
:Worksheet	Column	Set-Width Reset-Width		Set or reset the width of a column. Works like the /Worksheet Column Set-Width command.
	Row	Set-Height Auto		Set the height of a column in points. Otherwise, the height of a column is set automatically based on the size of the fonts used in the row.
	Page	Row Column Delete		Insert or delete a page break in a spreadsheet; the break can occur before either a row or a column.
:Format	Font	1-8		Apply one of the eight fonts in the current font set to a range of cells.
		Replace		Replace one of the eight fonts in the current font set with another font and change the font for the related ranges in the spreadsheet.
		Default	Restore Update	Restore the default font set as the current font set, or Update the default font set by replacing it with the current font set.
		Library	Retrieve Save Erase	Save the current font set in the font library; Retrieve a font set from the font library so it becomes the current font set; or Erase a font set from the font library.

Figure 18-3 A summary of the :Worksheet and :Format commands (part 1 of 2)

Command	Next level	Next level	Next level	Function
:Format	Bold Italics Underline	Set Clear		Set or clear the boldfacing, italics, or underlining on a range of cells.
	Lines	Outline Left Right Top Bottom All Double Wide Clear Shadow		Apply various line effects to a range of cells or clear the effects. See figure 18-5.
	Shade	Light Dark Solid Clear		Apply light, dark, or solid shading to a range of cells or clear the shading.
	Reset			Remove all formatting for a range of cells and restore the default formatting.

Figure 18-3 A summary of the :Worksheet and :Format commands (part 2 of 2)

is displayed. In the control panel, you can see the options that are available. Below the control panel, you can see the fonts that selections 1 through 8 refer to. This set of eight fonts is called the *current font set*.

In the current font set, the names Swiss, Dutch, and Xsymbol are the names of *font families*. Each family represents a font style. Then, the numbers after the names give the font sizes. These sizes are measured in *points*, and there are 72 points to the vertical inch. As a result, a size of 10 or 12 points is appropriate for most spreadsheet data; a size of 14 points or more is appropriate for headings; and a size of 8 points or less is appropriate for footnotes. If you look back to figure 18-1, you can see that I used Swiss 14 point for the spreadsheet title, Dutch 12 point for the column headings, and Swiss 12 point for everything else.

In step 2, you type a number from one to eight to indicate your font selection. If you're not sure what the font is going to look like, you will see it displayed in the spreadsheet as soon as you complete this command. Then, in step 3, you identify the range that the font should be applied to. If you don't

The Font Selection panel for the :Format Font command

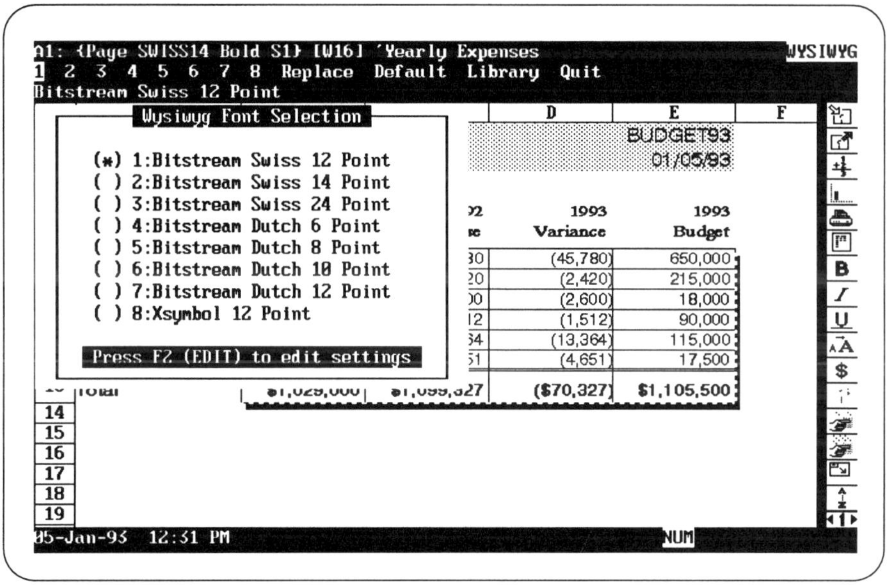

How to select the font for a range of cells

1. Start the :Format Font command to display the screen shown above.

2. Type a number from 1 through 8 indicating your font selection.

3. *Lotus* displays a prompt like this:

   `Change the attributes of range: A:A1..A:A1`

   Here, you can type the range address or use the anchor-and-point method to highlight the range. When you press the Enter key, the font is applied to the range.

Figure 18-4 How to specify the fonts in an spreadheeet (part 1 of 2)

like the way the font looks when the command is completed, you can select a different font for the range by repeating the command.

If you want to use a font that isn't in the current font set, you can use the second procedure in figure 18-4 to replace one of the fonts in the current set. In steps 1 and 2 of this procedure, you start the :Format Font Replace command. In step 3, you select the font that you want to replace by number. In step 4, you select the font family that you want to use. And in step 5, you

How to replace a font in the current font set

1. Start the :Format Font command to display the screen shown above.

2. Select Replace.

3. *Lotus* displays a prompt like this:

   ```
   1  2  3  4  5  6  7  8  Quit
   ```

   Select the number of the font that you want to replace.

4. *Lotus* displays a prompt like this:

   ```
   Swiss  Dutch  Courier  Xsymbol  Other
   ```

   Select the font family that you want. If you select Other, more font families are listed so you can select from them too.

5. *Lotus* displays a prompt like this:

   ```
   Font size in points (3..72): 24
   ```

   Type the size you want and press Enter. This changes the font in the current font set. It also changes the font for all ranges that have that font number applied to it.

Figure 18-4 How to specify the fonts in a spreadsheet part 2 of 2)

specify the point size that you want to use. When you complete this command, the new font replaces the old font in the current font set. However, the new font also replaces the old font in all the ranges that you have already applied the old font to.

If you look back to the summary in figure 18-3, you can see that the :Format Font command also offers Default and Library options. The Default option lets you replace the current font set with the default set (Restore), and it lets you establish the current font set as the new default set (Update). The Library option lets you Save a font set for use with other spreadsheets, and it lets you Retrieve a font set that you saved previously for use with the current spreadsheet. So after you use the Replace command to get the current font set the way you want it, you can use the Default command to establish it as the default font set or the Library command to save it for use in another spreadsheet.

How to boldface, italicize, or underline the data in a range To boldface, italicize, or underline the data in a range of cells, you use the :Font Bold, :Font Italics, or :Font Underline command. To apply an effect to a range of cells, you use the Set option. To remove the effect, you use the Clear option. Normally, though, you won't want to use the Underline command because

Command	Option	Function
:Format Lines	Outline	Create a line around the range you specify.
	Left	Create a line at the left side of each cell in the range you specify.
	Right	Create a line at the right side of each cell in the range you specify.
	Top	Create a line at the top of each cell in the range you specify.
	Bottom	Create a line at the bottom of each cell in the range you specify.
	All	Create a grid throughout the range you specify.
	Double	Create double lines. When you select this option, another menu is displayed that has the first six options in this figure in it.
	Wide	Create wide lines. When you select this option, another menu is displayed that has the first six options in this figure in it.
	Clear	Remove the lines in the range you specify.
	Shadow	Create a shadow effect that's to the right and below the range you specify.

Figure 18-5 The options of the :Format Lines command

you can add lines to a spreadsheet using other *WYSIWYG* commands. If you look back to figure 18-1, you can see that I used boldfacing for the spreadsheet title, the column headings, and the total line.

How to add lines and shadows to a range If you look back to figure 18-1, you can see that I added lines and shadows to the spreadsheet. I outlined the title portion of the spreadsheet with a single line. I applied a grid of lines to the numerical data in the spreadsheet and added a shadow effect to the grid. And I used a double line before the total line in the grid to separate the data from the totals.

Figure 18-5 presents the options that are available with the :Format Lines command. The Outline option creates a line around the range you specify as illustrated by the heading in figure 18-1. The All option creates a box for each cell in the range you specify as illustrated by the grid in figure 18-1. The Double option creates a double line and the Wide option creates a heavier line for the range you specify. When you select either of these options, *WYSIWYG* displays another menu that lets you select Outline, Left, Right, Top, Bottom, or All. The Clear option removes the lines in the range you specify. And the Shadow option creates a shadow effect to the right and below the range you specify.

How to add shading to a range If you look back to the summary in figure 18-3, you can see that the :Format Shade command provides four options. In figure 18-1, I used the Light option to apply light shading to the title range of the spreadsheet. This is the option you'll use most often because the Dark option assigns a dark shade to a range that makes it harder to read the data in the range. And the Solid option assigns a solid shade to a range that completely blacks out any characters or lines in the range. To remove shading from a range, you use the Clear option.

How to adjust column width, row heights, and page breaks If you refer back to the summary in figure 18-3, you can see that the :Worksheet commands let you adjust column widths, row heights, and page breaks. Because the :Worksheet Column command works the way the /Worksheet Column Set-Width command works, you shouldn't have any trouble using that command. Similarly, the :Worksheet Page command works the way the /Worksheet Page command works so you shouldn't have any trouble using that command. However, the *WYSIWYG* command not only lets you set page breaks at rows, but also at columns. Also, the *WYSIWYG* command doesn't insert a row or column into a spreadsheet to mark the page break; it just identifies the page break location on the screen with a dotted line. To remove the page breaks, you use the :Worksheet Page Delete command.

Unlike *Lotus*, *WYSIWYG* lets you adjust the height of the rows in a spreadsheet. In fact, it automatically adjusts the height of a row to accommodate the size of the largest font that has been used in the row. In addition, you can use the :Worksheet Row Set-Height command to increase or decrease the height of a row. In figure 18-1, for example, you can see that I used this command to increase the height of row 3 and to decrease the height of row 6. I did this to improve the vertical spacing of the spreadsheet. When you use this command, you can use the Up and Down arrow keys to decrease or increase the height of the row that is highlighted. Or, you can specify the height that you want for the row in points.

How to use a graph in a *WYSIWYG* spreadsheet

Figure 18-6 shows a spreadsheet after a graph has been added to it. As you can see, the graph is in the range from cell B11 to F20. Once a graph has been added to a spreadsheet, you can use the *WYSIWYG* print command to print it by itself or with the spreadsheet. This is one of the main benefits that you get from adding a graph to a spreadsheet.

Figure 18-7 summarizes the :Graph commands. With few exceptions, these commands are easy to use once you figure out what each command does. Although the last command in this summary, the :Graph Edit command, isn't easy to use, you probably won't ever need it. As a result, I'll present this command later in this chapter. For now, I'll just show you how to use the most important functions of the :Graph command.

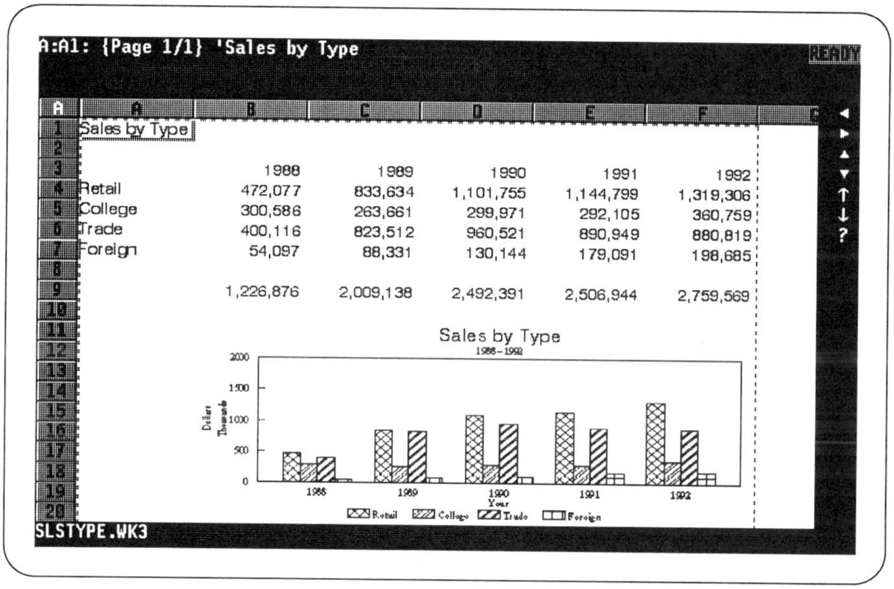

Figure 18-6 A *WYSIWYG* spreadsheet after the current graph has been added to it

How to add a graph to a spreadsheet Figure 18-8 presents a procedure for adding a graph to a spreadsheet. In step 1, you start the :Graph Add command. In step 2, you select the type of graph that you want to add. Current and named graphs are already a part of the spreadsheet that you're working on, so it's easy to add them to a graph. PIC and Metafile (or CGM) graphs are not a part of the spreadsheet; they are graph files that you create by using the /Graph Save command. If you want to reserve space for a graph but you don't want to select the graph, you can select Blank in step 2.

If you selected Current or Blank in step 2, you skip step 3 in the procedure in figure 18-8. Otherwise, you select the graph that you want to add to the spreadsheet in step 3. If you selected Named in step 2, you can select the graph from a list of the named graphs for the spreadsheet. If you selected PIC or Metafile in step 2, you can select from a list of PIC or CGM files. If necessary, you can change the directory to the one that contains the PIC or CGM file that you want to use.

Once you've selected the graph, *Lotus* prompts you for the range in the spreadsheet that the graph should be added to. That's step 4 in the procedure. Then, when you identify the range, the graph is moved into it.

If you specify a range that's too small, the graph won't look right in the range. This is illustrated by the graph in figure 18-6. Here, the graph range is so small that the graph is out of proportion, and you can't read the legends or

Command	Next level	Next level	Function
:Graph	Add		Add a graph to the current spreadsheet.
	Remove		Remove a graph from the current spreadsheet.
	Goto		Move the cell pointer to the next graph in the current spreadsheet.
	Settings	Graph	Replace a graph in the spreadsheet with another graph.
		Range	Reset the range for a graph in the spreadsheet.
		Sync	Automatically redraw the current or named graphs in the spreadsheet whenever they are changed; this doesn't work for PIC or CGM graphs. If this option is turned off, a current or named graph isn't automatically redrawn.
		Display	Display the graphs in the spreadsheet. This option is normally on. If it is off, the graphs in the spreadsheet aren't displayed.
		Opaque	Display a graph so it blocks out any cells that it overlays. This option is normally on, but you don't normally add a graph to a range of cells that contain data.
	Move		Move a graph from one range of cells to another.
	Zoom		Make the graph larger so you can inspect it more closely.
	Compute		Redraw a current or named graph when the :Graph Settings Sync option isn't on. Or, redraw a PIC or CGM graph when an updated PIC or CGM file is available.
	View		View a PIC or CGM file that hasn't been added to the spreadsheet.
	Edit		Edit a graph in a *WYSIWYG* spreadsheet. See figure 18-16.

Figure 18-7 A summary of the :Graph commands

How to add a graph to a spreadsheet in *WYSIWYG*

1. Start the :Graph Add command.

2. *Lotus* displays this prompt:

   `Current   Named   PIC   Metafile   Blank`

   Select the type of graph that you want to add to the spreadsheet. Metafile means a graph with the CGM extension. And Blank means that you're just reserving the space for a graph, but you're not going to select it now.

3. If you selected Current or Blank in step 2, skip to step 4. Otherwise, *Lotus* displays the graph names for the type of graph that you selected. If, for example, you selected Named, a prompt like this is displayed:

   `BAR               LINE               2Y`

   Here, select the graph that you want to add to the spreadsheet. To get a complete listing, you can press the F3 key. For PIC or Metafile graphs, you can change the directory to the one that contains the graph that you want.

4. *Lotus* displays a prompt like this:

   `Enter the graphic display range: A:B12`

   Type or highlight the range that you want to put the graph in, and press the Enter key.

5. If the graph doesn't look right in the range that you've selected, use the :Graph Settings Range command to resize the graph by changing its range.

Figure 18-8 How to add a graph to a spreadsheet

the axis titles. Then, you can use the :Graph Settings Range command to resize the graph.

How to move the cell pointer to a graph in a spreadsheet Whenever you want to perform a function on a graph, the cell pointer must be somewhere within it. One way to move the cell pointer to the graph is to use the :Graph Goto command. This just jumps the cell pointer to the next graph in the spreadsheet. Otherwise, you can use the Arrow keys to move the cell pointer to a graph.

How to change the range of the graph If you study figure 18-7, you can see that you use the :Graph Settings Range command to change the range for a graph that you've added to a spreadsheet. After you move the cell pointer to the graph, you start this command and identify the range that you want to use for the graph. This has the effect of resizing the graph.

How to remove, change, or move a graph If you refer again to figure 18-7, you can see that you use the :Graph Remove command to remove a graph from a spreadsheet. If you want to replace a graph in a spreadsheet with another graph, you use the :Graph Settings Graph command. This puts the new graph in the same range as the old graph. And if you want to move a graph, you use the :Graph Move command. Before you start any of these commands, you should move the cell pointer to the related graph.

How to redraw a current or named graph The :Graph Settings Sync command turns the recalculation (or redraw) feature on or off. If this feature is on, a current or named graph is automatically redrawn when any of its values or graphing options are changed. As a result, you don't have to press the F10 (Graph) key to see how a change affects the graph. When the recalculation feature is turned off, however, you have to use the :Graph Compute command to redraw the graph. Normally, though, the recalculation feature is on.

How to redraw a PIC or CGM graph A PIC or CGM graph is no longer related to a spreadsheet; it is independent. As a result, the graph can't be automatically redrawn when the data in the spreadsheet that it was derived from is changed. However, if a new PIC or CGM file is saved after the spreadsheet is changed, you can use the :Graph Compute command to redraw the graph in the spreadsheet. This doesn't actually redraw the graph, though. It just replaces the PIC or CGM graph in the spreadsheet with the graph in the new PIC or CGM file of the same name.

How to print a *WYSIWYG* spreadsheet

If you use *WYSIWYG* to enhance a spreadsheet or add a graph to a spreadsheet, you have to use the *WYSIWYG* Print command to print the enhancements or the graph. If you use the *Lotus* /Print Printer command, none of the *WYSIWYG* enhancements are printed.

Figure 18-9, 18-11, and 18-12 summarize the many commands and options of the *WYSIWYG* Print command. For many print jobs, you only need to use the Range and Go commands, but you should know that the other commands and options are there if you need them. After I show you how to use the Range and Go commands for a simple print job, I'll describe the Layout, Config, and Settings options.

How to specify the print range and start the print job Figure 18-10 presents a typical procedure for a simple print job. In step 1, you use the :Print Range command to identify the print range. This range can consist of spreadsheet only, graphs only, or both spreadsheet and graphs. After you use this command, *WYSIWYG* displays a dashed line around the print range as

Command	Next level	Function
:Print	Go	Start the print job.
	Range	Specify the print range.
	File	Save the print job as an encoded file (ENC) for background printing (see chapter 15).
	Background	Save the print job for background printing and start it printing (see chapter 15).
	Config	Set the printer configuration (see figure 18-12).
	Settings	Set the options for the print job (see figure 18-12).
	Layout	Define the margins and other options for the page layout (see figure 18-11).

Figure 18-9 A summary of the :Print commands

illustrated in figure 18-1 so you can tell what the print range is the next time you use the :Print command.

In step 2, you use the :Print Go command to print the range. When you use this command, you don't have to issue another command to skip to the next form or align the page as you do with the *Lotus* /Print Printer command. *WYSIWYG* does these functions automatically.

You should know, however, that a *WYSIWYG* print job is likely to take considerably longer than a *Lotus* print job. That's because *WYSIWYG* prints in graphics mode instead of character mode. As a result, it takes about as long to print a *WYSIWYG* spreadsheet as it does to print a graph. If you're using a dot-matrix printer, these printing delays can be frustrating.

Although it's usually more trouble than it's worth, you can use the :Print File and :Print Background commands to print a *WYSIWYG* job in the background. These *WYSIWYG* commands are analogous to the /Print Printer File and Background commands that are explained in chapter 15.

How to specify the page layout for a spreadsheet Figure 18-11 presents the options that are provided by the :Print Layout command. Here, the Paper-Size option lets you specify the size of paper you'll use for printing a spreadsheet. If you use just one size of paper, you only need to set this option once. Then, you can use the :Print Layout Default Save command to save the current settings as the default settings.

The Margins option lets you set the left, right, top, and bottom margins, but you specify these margins in inches instead of characters and lines like you do in *Lotus*. The Titles option lets you define headers and footers for a spreadsheet just as you do when you use *Lotus*. And the Borders option lets you define top or left borders just as you can do with the /Print Printer

1. Use the :Print Range command to specify the range for the print job.
2. Use the :Print Go command to start the job. Page alignment and skipping are automatic with *WYSIWYG*.

Figure 18-10 A typical procedure for printing a *WYSIWYG* spreadsheet

Options Borders command. The *Lotus* equivalents of these options are explained in chapter 4, so you can refer to that chapter if you need help with these *WYSIWYG* options.

The Compression option lets you compress the printing in a job. Usually, you'll only want to do this when you're trying to fit a spreadsheet on a single page. In that case, you use the Automatic option if you want *Lotus* to automatically select the compression ratio that you need. Otherwise, you can use the Manual option to specify the compression ratio that you want for a print job.

The Default and Library commands help you manage page layout settings. If you want to save the current page layout settings as the default settings, you use the Update option of the Default command. If you want to restore the default settings after you've modified them for a spreadsheet, you use the Restore option of the Default command.

If you want to use several sets of page layout settings, you can use the Save option of the Library command to save the current layout settings with a settings name. Then, when you're working on another spreadsheet, you can use the Retrieve option of this command to replace the current settings with a named group of settings.

How to specify other print options Figure 18-12 summarizes the options of the :Print Config and :Print Settings commands. Here, you can see that the *WYSIWYG* Print options go way beyond those of *Lotus*.

If you look at the Config options in figure 18-12, you can see that you use the Printer and Interface options to specify the type of printer and the printer port that you're using. The first time you use *WYSIWYG*, you can use these options to identify the printer that you're going to be using. You use also use these options when more than one printer is available to your PC and you want to switch from one printer to another.

The other options of the :Print Config command may or may not apply to your printer. The Orientation option of the Config command lets you specify whether the spreadsheet should be printed in portrait or landscape mode, but landscape printing won't work on all printers. The Resolution option (not available for 2.X releases) lets you specify whether you want the printing to be done in Draft or Final mode. The Bin option lets you specify the bin that you want paper to be fed from. And if your printer provides for one or more

Command	Next level	Next level	Function
:Print Layout	Paper-Size		Specify one of the standard paper sizes, or define a custom paper size.
	Margins	Left Right Top Bottom	Set the left, right, top, and bottom margins using inches as the unit of measurement.
	Titles	Header Footer Clear	Define a header or a footer for a spreadsheet using the same special characters that you use for *Lotus* headers or footers.
	Borders	Top Left Clear	Define top or left borders just as you can do with the /Print Printer Options Borders command.
	Compression	None Manual Automatic	Automatically compress a spreadsheet so it fits on one page, or manually set the compression ratio.
	Default	Restore Update	Restore the default page layout settings as the current settings, or Update the default page layout settings by replacing them with the current settings.
	Library	Retrieve Save Erase	Save the current page layout settings in a library of layout settings; Retrieve a named group of page layout settings so they become the current settings; or Erase a named group of settings.
	Quit		Return to the :Print menu.

Figure 18-11 A summary of the :Print Layout command

cartridges, the 1st and 2nd-Cart options let you specify the cartridges that are available for font selection.

If you look at the Settings options in figure 18-12, you can see that these options apply to the spreadsheet that you're working on. You can use these options to specify the pages to be printed, the number that should be used for the first printed page, the number of copies to be printed, whether or not the grid lines should be printed, and so on. To reset these options, you use the :Print Settings Reset command. But for most documents, you won't need any of these options.

Command	Next level	Next level	Function
:Print	Config	Printer	Select the printer that you're going to use.
		Interface	Select the printer port.
		1st-Cart	Identify the first font cartridge that's used by the printer.
		2nd-Cart	Identify the second font cartridge that's used by the printer.
		Orientation	Select Portrait or Landscape orientation.
		Resolution	Select Final or Draft printing.
		Bin	Select the bin that the paper should be fed from.
	Settings	Begin	Specify the first page that should be printed.
		End	Specify the last page that should be printed.
		Start-Number	Specify the number that should be used on the first printed page.
		Copies	Specify the number of copies that should be printed.
		Wait	Specify whether the printer should wait between the printing of pages.
		Grid	Specify whether the grid lines should be printed.
		Frame	Specify whether a frame that identifies the rows and columns of the spreadsheet should be printed.
		Reset	Reset the Settings options.

Figure 18-12 A summary of the :Print Config and Settings commands

Other *WYSIWYG* commands

The commands that I've presented to this point in this chapter are probably all that you'll ever need for your spreadsheet presentations. In general, those commands are easy to master and use. And you can quickly enhance a spreadsheet so it's appropriate for a formal presentation using just those commands.

However, *WYSIWYG* offers many commands besides those I've already presented. Although I'm going to introduce you to those other commands now, I recommend that you use them with restraint. In general, using these commands won't improve your spreadsheet presentations. Worse, many of these commands aren't easy to use so you can waste a lot of time by experimenting with them.

The :Text commands The :Text commands are summarized in figure 18-13. Although these commands are probably the most useful of the remaining commands, they don't offer any dramatic new features. For instance, the :Text Edit command lets you edit text in the spreadsheet, but you can get the job done without this command by using the F2 key to edit the text in the control panel. Similarly, the :Text Reformat command lets you reformat a long label so it fits within a range of cells, but you can also do this by using the /Range Justify command that's described in chapter 15.

Of the five commands in figure 18-13, the most useful one is probably the :Text Align command. This lets you align the text in a range of cells relative to the entire range. If, for example, you want to center "Sales by Type" in cell A1 in figure 18-6 over the six columns of the spreadsheet, you use the :Text Align Center command with a range of A1..F1. When you use the Even option of this command, the size of the text is adjusted so it spreads across the entire range.

The :Display commands Figure 18-14 summarizes the :Display commands. These commands set the options for the *WYSIWYG* display on the screen. Otherwise, they don't have any effect on the spreadsheet or the way the spreadsheet is printed.

If you experiment with these options, you'll find that they're easy to use. If, for example, you want to display the spreadsheet in a larger size so it's easier to read, try the :Display Zoom Large command. Or if you want to see what the other Frame displays look like, try the :Display Options Frame command. Once you get the display options set the way you want them, you can use the Update option of the Default command so the display will look the same the next time you use *WYSIWYG*. Then, you can stop experimenting with these options and get back to productive work.

The :Special and :Named-Style commands Figure 18-15 summarizes the :Special and :Named Style commands. These commands are designed to make it easier for you to use standard formatting options. For instance, the :Special Copy and Move commands let you copy or move the formatting options from one range of cells to another.

The :Special Import and Export commands are useful when you want to make sure that you use the same formats in a new spreadsheet that you've used in an old spreadsheet. You use the Export command to save the *WYSIWYG* formats that you've used in a spreadsheet and the Import command to retrieve the formats. Note in figure 18-15, though, that the

Command	Next level	Next level	Function
:Text	Edit		Edit text in the range of cells itself, not in the control panel. Press the F3 key to display some additional editing features.
	Align	Left Right Center Even	Align the text in a range of cells, not in a single cell. The Even option expands the text so it fills the entire range from left to right.
	Reformat		Reformat a long label from a single cell into a range of cells. Works like the /Range Justify command presented in chapter 15.
	Set		Specify the range to be used for one of the :Text commands before you start the command.
	Clear		Clear the :Text settings for a range.

Figure 18-13 A summary of the :Text commands

Import command has four options. The Fonts option retrieves just the fonts from another file, the Graphs option retrieves just the graphs, and the All option retrieves both the fonts and graphs and applies them to the same cells in the new spreadsheet that they were applied to in the old spreadsheet. I'll cover the fourth option in a moment.

When you use the :Special Import command, you can import fonts and graphs from a file that you've saved with the :Special Export command. But you can also use the Import command to import fonts and graphs from any spreadsheet that has been enhanced by *WYSIWYG* and saved. That's possible because *Lotus* actually saves a *WYSIWYG* enhanced spreadsheet in two files. For release 2.X, the *Lotus* part is saved in a file with a WK1 extension, and the *WYSIWYG* part is saved in a file with an FMT extension. For release 3.X, the *Lotus* part is saved with a WK3 extension, and the *WYSIWYG* part is saved with an FM3 extension. So if you use the :Special Import command, *Lotus* will not only display a listing of exported files, but also files with FMT and FM3 extensions. In addition, the :Special Import command can import from files with ALL extensions (files prepared by the *Allways* add-in program) and FMS extensions.

The :Named-Style Define command lets you treat the formats that have been applied to the range as a *named style*. When you use this command, you assign a number from one through eight, a style name, and a description to

Command	Next level	Next level	Function
:Display	Mode	Graphics Text	Display the spreadsheet in graphics (*WYSIWYG*) mode or text (*Lotus*) mode.
		B&W Color	Display the spreadsheet in black and white on a color monitor or in color.
	Zoom	Tiny Small Normal Large Huge Manual	Display the spreadsheet in a smaller or larger size.
	Colors		Select the colors for components of the screen display like the background, the text, the frame, and the cell pointer.
	Options	Frame	Select the style of the screen frame.
		Grid	Display or not display grid lines in the spreadsheet area.
		Page-Breaks	Display or hide page break symbols in the spreadsheet.
		Cell-Pointer	Display the cell pointer as an outline or solid block.
		Intensity	Increase the intensity of the colors used in *WYSIWYG* mode.
	Fonts-Directory		Set the directory for the *WYSIWYG* fonts.
	Rows		Specify the number of rows that should be displayed on the screen (from 16 through 60).
	Default	Restore Update	Restore the default display settings as the current settings or Update the default settings by replacing them with the current settings.

Figure 18-14 A summary of the :Display commands

the named style. Later, you can apply the formats of a named style to another range of cells by using the :Named-Style command. After you start this command, you type the number of the named style that you want to use.

By using named styles, you make sure that you're using consistent styles for all of your spreadsheets. Also, if you decide to change the formats for one

Command	Next level	Next level	Function
:Special	Copy		Copy the *WYSIWYG* formats from one range of cells to another.
	Move		Move the *WYSIWYG* formats from one range of cells to another.
	Import	All Named-Styles Fonts Graphs	Import the styles, formats, or graphs from another file into the current spreadsheet.
	Export		Export the *WYSIWYG* formats to another file.
:Named-Style	1-8		Apply one of eight named styles to a range of cells.
	Define		Create a named style by applying the formats of the current range of cells to the style number.

Figure 18-15 A summary of the :Special and :Named-Style commands

of the named styles after you've enhanced a spreadsheet, all of the cells that the style has been applied to are changed too. So if you intend to use *WYSIWYG* frequently to enhance your spreadsheets, I recommend that you take the time to set up the eight named styles and use them for all your spreadsheets. To save them with a name like STYLES, you can use the :Special Export command. To import them for use in another spreadsheet, you use the Named-Styles option of the :Special Import command.

The :Graph Edit commands Figure 18-16 summarizes the :Graph Edit commands. These commands let you enhance a graph that you've added to a spreadsheet by adding text or lines to it, by rotating it, and so on. With few exceptions, though, these enhancements aren't going to improve a graphic presentation. In addition, the :Graph Edit commands are relatively difficult to use so they are likely to reduce your productivity considerably.

Occasionally, though, it makes sense to point out a highlight in a graph by adding objects like text, a line, or an arrow to the graph. To do that, you need only the first three commands in figure 18-16. If you use a mouse with these commands, you should be able to make simple enhancements to a graph without too much trouble. But if you need to do more than that, you should probably be using a true graphics program, not *WYSIWYG*.

Command	Next level	Function
:Graph Edit	Add	Add text, lines, arrows, rectangles, ellipses, and so on to a graph.
	Select	Select the object that you want to edit, transform, or rearrange. The object can be the entire graph or one of the objects that you've added to the graph.
	Edit	Edit text, change fonts, change line styles, and so on.
	Transform	Resize, rotate, or turn selected objects in a graph.
	Rearrange	Delete, restore, move, copy, or protect selected objects in a graph.
	View	Zoom in or zoom out on a graph.
	Options	Display a grid pattern, change the cursor size, or magnify fonts.

Figure 18-16 A summary of the :Graph Edit commands

Discussion

If preparing formal presentations is an important part of your job, you most likely have a need for some of the capabilities presented in this chapter. In particular, *WYSIWYG* makes it easy for you to improve the presentation graphics of a spreadsheet. It also makes it easy for you to combine a spreadsheet with one or more graphs.

Remember, though, that improving the appearance of a spreadsheet doesn't change the data. As a result, working to improve the appearance of a spreadsheet can quickly become counterproductive. So use the features that you need for making effective presentations, but don't let it get out of control.

Because *WYSIWYG* was designed to be used with a mouse, you may find that you can use *WYSIWYG* more efficiently with a mouse. In addition, the *SmartIcons* feature that goes along with *WYSIWYG* in releases 2.4 and 3.4 can help you use *WYSIWYG* more efficiently. If you're interested, you can learn how to use a mouse and the *SmartIcons* in chapter 21.

Should *WYSIWYG* be active all the time? That depends on your PC and your working style. If your PC doesn't have enough internal memory, you may not be able to keep *WYSIWYG* active when you're working on large spreadsheets. On the other hand, if your PC has enough memory and you like using the *SmartIcons*, you may want to keep *WYSIWYG* active all the time. To help you keep your perspective, I recommend that you use *Lotus* without *WYSIWYG* whenever you're creating or updating a spreadsheet. That way, you can concentrate on the data. Then, if you need to improve the appearance of a spreadsheet for a formal presentation, you can activate *WYSIWYG* and concentrate on the presentation.

Terms

add-in program
current font set
font family
point
named style

Objectives

1. Decide whether you need any of the *WYSIWYG* capabilities presented in this chapter.
2. Use the capabilities presented in this chapter that are appropriate for your presentation requirements.

Section 4

Three *Lotus 1-2-3* features for limited use

This section presents three *Lotus* features that aren't for everybody. If you have the time, though, it's worth reading about these features to see whether they're right for you. For ease of use, each chapter in this section is treated as an independent module so you can read the chapters in whatever sequence you prefer.

In chapter 19, you'll learn how to create and use macros. If you're a typical *Lotus* user, you probably won't want to create your own macros. But if someone else in your company has created some that are useful, this chapter will show you how to take advantage of them.

In chapter 20, you'll learn how to use the *Lotus* database feature. Today, better products are available for creating and using most databases, but this feature is occasionally useful for small databases. Also, you can use a few of its commands for manipulating spreadsheet data that isn't in a database. Last, you can use one of its commands for working with external databases that have been created by programs like *dBase IV* and *Paradox*.

In chapter 21, you'll learn how to use a mouse with *Lotus* and how to use the *SmartIcons* feature of releases 2.4 and 3.4. If you like using a mouse, this chapter will show you how to make the best use of one with *Lotus*. If *SmartIcons* are available to you, this chapter will show you how you can benefit from them.

Chapter 19

The macro feature

The macro feature of *Lotus* lets you perform a series of keystrokes or commands with just one keystroke combination. For instance, you can create a *macro* named \d that will put the @NOW function in a cell and format the cell with a date format. Then, you can access those functions just by holding down the Alt key while you press the letter *d*.

You can also create macros that perform functions that are far more extensive than that. In fact, the *Lotus* macro writing capabilities are like a programming language that you can use to develop custom *Lotus* applications. In the mid-80s, for example, I used the *Lotus* macro feature to develop complete accounting systems.

Today, however, you probably shouldn't bother with macros. Often, you'll take more time creating the macros than you'll ever save by using them. And if you need to develop a custom application, you should probably use a database program.

Nevertheless, some people love macros. The author of one *Lotus* book, for example, described macros as "one of the most exciting capabilities of 1-2-3." Although I disagree, I'm presenting macros in this chapter so you'll know what they can do. In addition, there are some occasions when it does make sense to use macros. If, for example, you're developing a spreadsheet for someone else, you can use macros to make the spreadsheet easier to use.

In this chapter, then, I'll introduce you to the *Lotus* macro feature as quickly as possible. First, I'll show you how to create, use, and debug simple keystroke macros. Next, I'll introduce you to the more complicated Command Language macros. When you complete this chapter, you'll be able to decide for yourself whether or not macros make sense for your spreadsheets.

How to create and use keystroke macros with one-letter names

A *keystroke macro* is a macro that performs a series of keystrokes. This type of macro is relatively easy to create and use. To illustrate, figure 19-1 presents three simple keystroke macros. The first one is named \f, and it is stored in cell J24. The second one is named \m, and it is stored in J27..J30. The third one is named \d, and it is stored in J32..J33.

```
J24: '/wgf,0~                                                        READY

      I        J         K         L         M         N         O         P
21  Worksheet macros
22  Name      Keystroke macro                          Description
23
24  \f        /wgf,0~                                  Set global format to comma
25                                                     with zero decimal places
26
27  \m        "JAN{right}"FEB{right}"MAR{right}        Enter the abbreviations for
28            "APR{right}"MAY{right}"JUN{right}        the twelve months in the
29            "JUL{right}"AUG{right}"SEP{right}        twelve columns starting
30            "OCT{right}"NOV{right}"DEC{right}        with the current cell
31
32  \d        @now~                                    Enter and format the date
33            /rfd4~                                   in the current cell
34
35
```

Figure 19-1 Three typical keystroke macros

The labels shown in column I in figure 19-1 are not a part of the macros and have nothing to do with the operation of the macros. They are there simply to help the spreadsheet user keep track of the names and locations of the macros. Similarly, the descriptions in columns N through P have nothing to do with the operation of the macros. They are there to help the spreadsheet user remember the purpose of each macro.

To use the \f macro in figure 19-1, you hold down the Alt key while you press the letter *f*. This starts the series of keystrokes that are stored in the macro:

```
/wgf,0~
```

Here, the slash starts the *Lotus* menu system. Then, the *w* accesses the Worksheet menu; the *g* accesses the Global menu; the *f* accesses the Format menu; the comma (,) selects Comma format; the zero (0) specifies zero decimal places; and the tilde (~), which is equivalent to the Enter key, completes the command. In other words, this macro sets the global format for a spreadsheet to Comma format with zero decimal places.

To use the \m macro in figure 19-1, you hold down the Alt key while you press the letter *m*. And to start the \d macro, you hold down the Alt key while you press the letter *d*. In other words, the name of the macro determines the keystroke combination that you use to start the macro. If someone has created macros for you, all you have to do to use them is press the correct letter for each macro while you hold down the Alt key. When you use a macro, it can be referred to as *running a macro*, *invoking a macro*, or *executing a macro*.

When *Lotus* performs a macro, it starts with the first cell of the macro. When it finishes the keystrokes in this cell, it looks at the cell below it. If the cell is empty, the macro is over. Otherwise, *Lotus* continues with the keystrokes in the cells below the starting cell. As a result, the first macro in figure 19-1 consists of only one cell. The second macro starts with cell J27 and continues until the end of the keystrokes that start in cell J30. And the third macro starts with cell J32 and finishes with cell J33.

To create a keystroke macro, you use a procedure like the one in figure 19-2. In step 1, you move to a cell in an area of the spreadsheet that won't be affected by other spreadsheet operations. That's why the macro area starts in cell I21 in figure 19-1, and the first macro starts in cell J24.

In step 2, you start the macro with an apostrophe (') to tell *Lotus* that you're entering a label. Then, you enter the keystrokes of the macro. When you need to enter the keystroke for a control or function key, you use the equivalents that are summarized in figure 19-3. Here, you can see that you use the tilde (~) for the Enter key, {down} for the Down arrow, and so on. You can see how the keystroke equivalent of the Right arrow key is used in the second macro in figure 19-1. If you need more than one cell for the keystrokes, you continue with the cell below the starting cell. You can continue with as many cells as you need, but make sure that an empty cell is below the last cell in the macro so *Lotus* can tell where the macro ends.

Although step 3 is optional, it is recommended. To identify each macro, you can enter its name in the cell to the left of its starting cell. That makes it easier for you to locate your macros later on. Here, you must start the name entry with an apostrophe to tell *Lotus* that you're entering a label. Otherwise, *Lotus* treats the backslash as the repeating label prefix. In this step, you can also enter a description of the macro in the cells to its right.

In step 4, you name the macro. To do that, you move the cell pointer to the first cell of the macro. Then, you use the /Range Name Create command to name the cell. This command is described in more detail in chapter 8. When this command asks for the name, you enter the backslash (\) followed by a letter. If possible, select a letter that helps you remember what the macro does. In figure 19-1, for example, the first macro uses the letter *f* because it formats the spreadsheet; the second uses the letter *m* because it enters the 12 months of the year; and so on.

If you want to name several macros at the same time, you can use the /Range Name Labels Right command. In this case, though, the macro names and the macros have to be set up as shown in figure 19-1. Then, when the command asks you for the range, you specify cells I24..I32. The names in column I are then applied to the cells in column J.

Now, can you tell how the second and third macros in figure 19-1 work? The second one just enters abbreviations for the 12 months of the year into twelve consecutive columns with the labels right aligned in their cells. As a

How to create a keystroke macro with a one-letter name

1. Move the cell pointer to a portion of the spreadsheet that won't be affected by other spreadsheet operations.

2. Start the macro entry with an apostrophe to identify it as a label. Then, enter the keystrokes of the macro in the cell. The first macro in figure 19-1, for example, requires these keystrokes:

   `/wgf,0~`

   If you need more than one cell, continue with the cells below. *Lotus* knows that a macro ends when it encounters an empty cell. To put the keystrokes for control and function keys into a macro, use the keystrokes given in figure 19-3.

3. This is an optional step that helps you manage your macros, but it has no effect on the operation of the macro. To identify the macro in the spreadsheet, you can enter the macro name in the cell to the left of the first cell in the macro. In figure 19-1, for example, \f is entered as a label in cell I24 to identify the macro to its right. Similarly, \m and \d are entered as labels in cells I27 and I32 to identify the macros to their right. To further identify the macro, you can enter a description to the right of the macro as shown in columns N through P in figure 19-1.

4. Move the cell pointer to the first cell in the macro. Then, start the /Range Name Create command so *Lotus* asks for the name:

   `Enter name:`

   Type a name that consists of the backslash followed by one letter. Then, press the Enter key so *Lotus* asks for the range:

   `Enter name: \f                    Enter range: J24`

   Move the cell pointer to the first cell in the macro if it isn't already there, and press the Enter key. The macro is now ready for use.

How to run a keystroke macro with a one-letter name

1. Move the cell pointer to a cell that's appropriate for the macro that you're going to use.

2. Hold down the Alt key while you press the letter that's in the macro's name. For instance, the Alt+f keystroke combination starts the macro named \f.

How to display the names of all the macros that are available

1. Press Alt+F3 to list up to five macro names. To get a full-screen listing of the names, press the F3 (Name) key.

2. To run one of the macros that is displayed, move the cell pointer to its name and press the Enter key.

Figure 19-2 How to create and use keystroke macros with one-letter names

Keyboard key	Macro entry
Enter	~
Down arrow	{down}
Up arrow	{up}
Left arrow	{left}
Right arrow	{right}
Page-up	{pgup}
Page-down	{pgdn}
Home	{home}
End	{end}
Tab	{bigright}
Shift+Tab	{bigleft}
Delete	{delete}
Insert	{insert}
Backspace	{bs}
Esc	{esc}
F2	{edit}
F3	{name}
F4	{abs}
F5	{goto}
F6	{window}
F9	{calc}
F10	{graph}

Figure 19-3 The macro entries for the common control and function keys

result, you must move the cell pointer to an appropriate cell before you start this macro. Note that the keystrokes in the macro extend into the three columns to the right of the starting column, but that doesn't affect the operation of the macro.

The third macro in figure 19-1 starts by entering the @NOW function into the current cell. Those are the keystrokes in cell J32. Then, *Lotus* moves to cell J33 and performs these keystrokes:

```
/rfd4~
```

This starts the /Range Format Date command, selects the fourth date format, and executes the command.

If you can't remember the name of a macro when you want to run it, you can press the Alt+F3 key combination to list the first five macro names. If more than that are available, you can press the F3 (Name) key to get a full-screen display of names. Then, you can run one of the macros by moving the cell pointer to its name and pressing the Enter key. This procedure is summarized near the bottom of figure 19-2.

How to create and use keystroke macros with longer names

In the early releases of *Lotus*, you had to use one-letter names for macros. Starting with release 2.2, though, this limitation was removed. Now, you can use any valid range name for a macro so the name can be up to fifteen characters long.

To run a macro that doesn't have a one-letter name, you have to use the method that's summarized at the bottom of figure 19-2. First, you press Alt+F3 to display the first five macros that are available. Next, if necessary, press the F3 (Name) key to get a full-screen display of the macro names. Then, move the cell pointer to the macro that you want to run and press the Enter key.

How to record a keystroke macro

Entering a lengthy macro into a spreadsheet can be a painstaking and tedious job. To make this easier, *Lotus* provides a feature for *recording a macro* starting with release 2.2. When you use this feature, you just perform the functions that you want the macro to perform. While you perform the functions, *Lotus* records the keystrokes that you're using for use in the macro. Because this works somewhat differently for the 2.X releases and the 3.X releases, I'll present the recording procedure for each release separately.

Using release 2.X Figure 19-4 presents the procedure for recording a macro when you're using one of the 2.X releases. In step 1, you start the /Worksheet Learn Range command and specify the range you want to use for the macro. This is called the *learn range*.

In steps 2 and 3, you move the cell pointer to another portion of the spreadsheet and activate the Learn feature by pressing Alt+F5. *Lotus* then displays the LEARN indicator at the bottom of the spreadsheet screen to show that the Learn feature is active. That means that any key you press is going to be recorded as part of the macro that gets stored in the learn range.

In step 4, you perform the functions that you want recorded. If, for example, you want to record the \d macro in figure 19-1, you type the

1. Start the /Worksheet Learn Range command. At the prompt that follows, you can either type the address of the first cell of the macro that you're going to record or move the cell pointer to that cell:

   ```
   Enter learn range: J24
   ```

   Then, press the Enter key.

2. Move the cell pointer to the cell that you want to start recording the macro in. You should choose the starting cell so the keystrokes that follow won't affect the cells in which the macro is going to be recorded.

3. Press Alt+F5 to activate the Learn feature. This displays the LEARN indicator at the bottom of the spreadsheet screen.

4. Make the entries and perform the commands that you want recorded in the macro. When you're finished, press Alt+F5 to turn the Learn feature off.

5. Move to the learn range. If you've done this procedure correctly, the keystroke macro will now appear in the range.

6. To identify the macro in the spreadsheet, you can enter the macro name in the cell to the left of the macro. To further identify the macro, you can enter a description of the macro.

7. Use the /Range Name Create command to name the macro. Or use the /Range Name Labels Right command to name more than one macro.

Figure 19-4 How to record a keystroke macro (release 2.X)

@NOW function and press the Enter key. Then, you perform the /Range Format Date command to format the cell. When you're finished, you press Alt+F5 again to turn the Learn feature off.

In step 5, you move the cell pointer to the learn range. This range should now have the macro in it. Then, in step 6, you can enter information that identifies the macro. And in step 7, you can use the /Range Name command to name one or more macros.

Using release 3.X Figure 19-5 presents the procedure for recording a macro when you're using one of the 3.X releases. In step 1, you move the cell pointer to the cell that you want to start recording the macro in. You should select a cell so the keystrokes that follow won't affect the cells in which the macro is going to be stored later on.

1. Move the cell pointer to the cell that you want to start recording the macro in. You should choose the starting cell so the keystrokes that follow won't affect the cells in which the macro is going to be stored later on.

2. Press Alt+F2 to display this menu:

   `Playback  Copy  Erase  Step`

   Select the Erase function to erase the record buffer.

3. Make the entries and perform the commands that you want recorded in the macro. This records the keystrokes in the record buffer.

4. Press Alt+F2 to display this menu again:

   `Playback  Copy  Erase  Step`

   Select the Copy function to copy the keystrokes from the record buffer to a cell in the spreadsheet. When you select this function, this prompt is displayed:

   `Press TAB to anchor cursor, then highlight keystrokes to copy: /wgf,0~`

   Here, you move the cursor to the first keystroke that you want to store in the macro, press the Tab key, move the cursor to the last keystroke that you want to store in the macro, and press the Enter key. *Lotus* then displays this prompt:

   `Select range to copy TO: A:J24`

   Here, you can either type the address of the first cell of the range in which you want the macro stored, or you can move the cell pointer to that cell. When you press the Enter key, the highlighted keystrokes in the record buffer are copied into the range that starts with the cell you identified.

5. To identify the macro in the spreadsheet, you can enter the macro name in the cell to the left of the macro. To further identify the macro, you can enter a description it.

6. Use the /Range Name Create command to name the macro. Or use the /Range Name Labels Right command to name more than one macro.

Figure 19-5 How to record a keystroke macro (release 3.X)

In step 2, you press Alt+F2 to activate the macro menu. Then, you select the Erase function to erase the contents of the *record buffer*. This buffer will be used to record the keystrokes that you want for the macro you will create.

In step 3, you perform the functions that you want recorded. If, for example, you want to record the \d macro in figure 19-1, you type the @NOW function and press the Enter key. Then, you perform the /Range Format Date command to format the cell. This records your keystrokes in the record buffer.

1. Move the cell pointer to an appropriate cell for testing the macro. Then, press Alt+F2 to activate the Step function. This displays the STEP indicator at the bottom of the spreadsheet screen.
2. Start the macro that you want to debug.
3. Press the Spacebar each time that you want one more keystroke in the macro to be tested.
4. When you find the error, you can press Ctrl+Break to stop the test. Then, you can move the cell pointer to the macro, press the F2 key, and edit the macro.
5. To deactivate the Step function, press Alt+F2.

Figure 19-6 How to debug a keystroke macro (release 2.X)

In step 4, you press Alt+F2 to activate the macro menu, and you select the Copy function. This function lets you copy the keystrokes from the record buffer to the cell or cells that you want to use for the macro. When *Lotus* displays the contents of the record buffer, you highlight the keystrokes that you want to copy and press the Enter key. When *Lotus* asks you for the range that you want the keystrokes copied to, you specify the range that you want to use for the macro.

Then, in step 5, you can enter information that identifies the macro. And in step 6, you can use the /Range Name command to name one or more macros.

How to test and debug a keystroke macro

After you create a macro, you need to test it by running it. Then, if it doesn't work the way you expected, you have to *debug* it. This just means that you have to find and correct the errors in the macro. To make this easier, *Lotus* provides a debugging feature starting with release 2.2. Because this feature works somewhat differently for the 2.X releases and the 3.X releases, I'll present the procedure for each release separately.

Using release 2.X Figure 19-6 presents the procedure for debugging a keystroke macro when you're using one of the 2.X releases. In step 1, you press the Alt+F2 key combination. *Lotus* then displays the STEP indicator at the bottom of the screen to show that the Step function has been activated.

In step 2, you start the macro that you want to debug. Then, in step 3, you press the Spacebar once to run each keystroke in the macro. As a result, you control the speed at which the macro is executed. That makes it easy for you to see at which keystroke the macro went wrong.

When you find the error, you can press the Ctrl+Break key combination as summarized in step 4. This cancels the execution of the macro. Then, you

1. Move the cell pointer to an appropriate cell for testing the macro. Then, press Alt+F2 to activate this menu:

   ```
   Playback  Copy  Erase  Step
   ```

   Here, you select the Step function. This displays the STEP indicator at the bottom of the spreadsheet screen.

2. Start the macro that you want to debug. This displays the SST indicator.

3. Press the Spacebar each time that you want one more keystroke in the macro to be tested.

4. When you find the error, you can press Ctrl+Break to stop the test. Then, you can move the cell pointer to the macro, press the F2 key, and edit it.

5. To deactivate the Step function, press Alt+F2 to activate the macro menu and select Step.

Figure 19-7 How to debug a keystroke macro (release 3.X)

can edit the macro to correct it. When you're through testing the macro, you press Alt+F2 again to deactivate the Step function.

Using release 3.X Figure 19-7 presents the procedure for debugging a keystroke macro when you're using one of the 3.X releases. In step 1, you activate the macro menu by pressing the Alt+F2 key combination. Then, when you select the Step function, *Lotus* displays the STEP indicator at the bottom of the screen to show that the Step function has been activated.

In step 2, you start the macro that you want to debug. Then, in step 3, you press the Spacebar once to run each keystroke in the macro. As a result, you control the speed at which the macro is executed. That makes it easy for you to see at which keystroke the macro went wrong.

When you find the error, you can press the Ctrl+Break key combination as summarized in step 4. This cancels the execution of the macro. Then, you can edit the macro to correct it. When you're through testing the macro, you press Alt+F2 again to display the macro menu, and you select Step to deactivate the Step function.

How to use keystroke macros in more than one spreadsheet

One of the limitations of the macro feature for some releases of *Lotus* is that a macro can only be used in the spreadsheet that it's stored in. But if you take the time to create macros like those in figure 19-1, you would like to be able to use them in more than one spreadsheet. In fact, you would like to have a collection of your most useful macros available to you as you work on all your spreadsheets. Depending on the release of *Lotus* that you're using, there are four practical ways to make macros available to the spreadsheet you're working on.

Use a template spreadsheet that contains the macros In chapter 5, I recommended that you use a template spreadsheet as the basis for starting a new spreadsheet. If you do that, you can include the macros of your macro library in the template spreadsheet. Then, when you retrieve the template spreadsheet as the start of a new spreadsheet, its macros are available to you.

Open the spreadsheet that contains the macros while you're working on another spreadsheet (release 3.X) If you're using one of the 3.X releases of *Lotus*, you can use macros without including them in the current spreadsheet. To do that, you use the /File Open command to retrieve the spreadsheet that contains your macros as a second spreadsheet. The use of this command is explained in chapter 11. When more than one spreadsheet file is open, the macros in one spreadsheet are available while you're working on another spreadsheet.

Use the *SmartIcons* feature (release 2.4 and 3.4) If you use *WYSIWYG* with *Lotus* release 2.4 or 3.4, you can also use the *SmartIcons* feature that is described in chapter 21. With this feature, you can assign up to 12 macros to *icons* that are displayed on the right side of the spreadsheet screen. Then, to run one of these macros, you just move the mouse pointer to the icon that represents the macro that you want to run and click the left mouse button. Using *SmartIcons* is easiest way to make macros available to all your programs, and this feature is described in detail in chapter 21.

Use the *Macro Library Manager* add-in program If you're using *Lotus* release 2.3, 2.4, or 3.4, you probably have an *add-in program* on your system called the *Macro Library Manager*. This program makes it relatively easy for you to make the macros in a spreadsheet available to you while you're working on other spreadsheets. Using the terminology of *Macro Library Manager*, a spreadsheet that contains macros is stored in a file called a *macro library*.

When you use the *Macro Library Manager*, both the add-in program and the active macro libraries are in internal memory along with the spreadsheet that you're working on. This means that less memory is available for your spreadsheet. So if your PC has limited memory, you may not be able to use the *Macro Library Manager* with your larger spreadsheets.

If you don't already know how to use an add-in program, chapter 14 will teach you what you need to know. Then, when you invoke the *Macro Library Manager*, a menu is displayed that offers the functions summarized in figure 19-8.

To start, you need to use the Save function to save the macros from a spreadsheet into a macro library file. The extension for this type of file is MLB. When you save a macro library, the macros in the file are also loaded into internal memory so they are available to you while you work on other spreadsheets.

Once you've created one or more macro library files, you can use the Load function to load one or more of them into internal memory. Once they're loaded, their macros are available to you. Then, you can press Alt+F3 to display a list of the available macros just as you can when you're not using the *Macro Library Manager*.

The other three functions in figure 19-8 let you edit the macros in a macro library, remove a macro library from internal memory, or copy a list of the macro names from a macro library into the current spreadsheet. Because all of the commands of the *Macro Library Manager* are easy to use, you shouldn't have any trouble using this add-in program.

If you want to use the macros in a macro library each time you start a *Lotus* session, you can put them in a library named AUTOLOAD.MLB. Then, you can set up *Lotus* so the *Macro Library Manager* is automatically attached and invoked whenever you start *Lotus*. This procedure is explained in chapter 14. When this add-in program is invoked, it automatically loads the AUTO-LOAD macro library so its macros are available in internal memory. As a result, you can go right to work on a spreadsheet using the macros in the AUTOLOAD library as soon as *Lotus* finishes this start-up procedure.

How to automatically run a macro when you retrieve a file

Although I didn't mention it before, you can name a macro \0 (zero). Then, you can run the macro just as you run a macro with a one-letter name by pressing the zero key while you hold down the Alt key. In addition, you can set *Lotus* up so the \0 macro is automatically executed when you retrieve the file that it is in. To turn this option on, you start the /Worksheet Global Default Autoexec command and select Yes.

An introduction to Command Language macros

Now that you know how to create and use simple keystroke macros, I want to introduce you to *Command Language macros*. When you create this type of macro, you can use any of the commands in the *Lotus Command Language*. To give you some idea of how varied and complex these commands can be, you can use the Help facility to look up the Macro commands that are available for your release of *Lotus*. For instance, release 2.3 provides more than 50 commands.

Function name	Function
Load	Load a macro library (a spreadsheet that contains macros) into internal memory so you can use its macros while you're working on other spreadsheets.
Save	Save a range of cells that contains macros from the current spreadsheet into a macro library file so it can be used by the *Macro Library Manager*. This also loads the range of cells into internal memory so the macros can be used while you're working on other spreadsheets.
Edit	Copy a macro library from internal memory into the current spreadsheet so you can edit its macros.
Remove	Remove a macro library from internal memory.
Name-List	Copy all the macro names from a macro library in internal memory into the current spreadsheet.
Quit	Exit from the *Macro Library Manager*.

Figure 19-8 The functions of the *Macro Library Manager* add-in program

When you use the Command Language, you can develop macros of great complexity. In fact, you can develop entire business applications with menus that access functions within the applications. To use this language, though, requires the logic and skills of a computer programmer. That's why entire books have been written on the proper use of this language.

With that as background, most *Lotus* users shouldn't make any attempt to learn the Command Language or to create Command Language macros. Work at this level should be done by *Lotus* experts only. And even experts should question whether they should be using *Lotus* for developing an application. Most likely, some other program is better suited for that application than *Lotus* is.

Why you should limit your use of macros

Although it's relatively easy to create a keystroke macro, some of the limitations of the macro feature should be obvious. The primary limitation is that it can easily take more time to create a macro than you'll ever save by using it. If, for example, you create a macro for a function that takes only a few keystrokes in the first place, it's hard to justify the development of the macro. If you doubt this, take the time to create a few simple macros like those in figure 19-1. Then, you'll see how easy it is to waste a few hours creating macros that save you seconds. Beyond that, if you want to use a macro in more than one spreadsheet, you have to take the extra time to create a template spreadsheet, to retrieve a second spreadsheet file, to assign macros to *SmartIcons*, or to use the *Macro Library Manager* add-in program.

Because of these limitations, you may want to avoid using macros altogether. Occasionally, though, it makes sense to develop a small set of keystroke macros for use in a series of spreadsheets. This makes even more sense if the macros are going to be used by more than one person in many different spreadsheets. In general, the more macros are used, the more sense it makes to create them.

Before you start creating a set of macros, though, you may want to check the software catalogs to see whether macro libraries are already available for the functions you're interested in. If, for example, you're thinking about developing a set of macros for accounting or statistical functions, you can probably find a macro library that includes the macros that you need. Often, buying a macro library can pay for itself many times over by saving you dozens of hours of development time.

Terms

macro
keystroke macro
running a macro
invoking a macro
executing a macro
recording a macro
learn range
record buffer
debug
add-in program
icon
macro library
Command Language macro
Command Language

Objectives

1. In general terms, describe the capabilities and limitations of the *Lotus* macro feature.
2. Whenever practical, create and use a keystroke macro.

Chapter 20

The database feature

The numbers in the name *Lotus 1-2-3* refer to its three major capabilities: spreadsheet, graphics, and database. Most of this book, of course, focuses on *Lotus*'s spreadsheet capabilities because those are its most useful capabilities. However, section 3 presents *Lotus*'s graphics and business presentation capabilities. And in this chapter, I'll introduce you to its database capabilities.

If you're like most *Lotus* users, though, you probably won't use the database capabilities much. Although these capabilities were okay several years ago when simple database programs weren't available, that's no longer true. Today, if you have serious database requirements, you're better off with a program like *Q&A* or *Paradox*. As a result, the *Lotus* database features are most likely to be useful when your database requirements are limited.

If you're using one of the 3.X releases of *Lotus*, you may be interested to know you can use the *Lotus* database commands to access some external databases. If, for example, your company uses a *Paradox* database for an application, you can use *Lotus* release 3.4 to retrieve the information from that database into a spreadsheet. Then, you can analyze the data in that database using the other *Lotus* commands.

In this chapter, then, I'll introduce you to the *Lotus* database feature. First, you'll learn how to set up a simple database. Next, you'll learn how to extract data from it. Then, you'll learn about the other commands and @functions that you can use with a database. Last, you'll learn how you can use *Lotus* release 3.X to access the data in an external database. When you complete this chapter, you'll be able to decide for yourself whether or not the *Lotus* database feature is going to be valuable for your applications.

How to set up a database

Figure 20-1 shows the structure of a *Lotus* database. Here, the first row is called the *field name row*. It contains a series of field names, one for each column of the spreadsheet. Then, each row after the field name row represents one *record* in the *database*. And each column in a record (each cell) is called a *field*.

To create a database like this one, you start with the field name row. In figure 20-1, this row starts in cell A1, but the database can be started in any

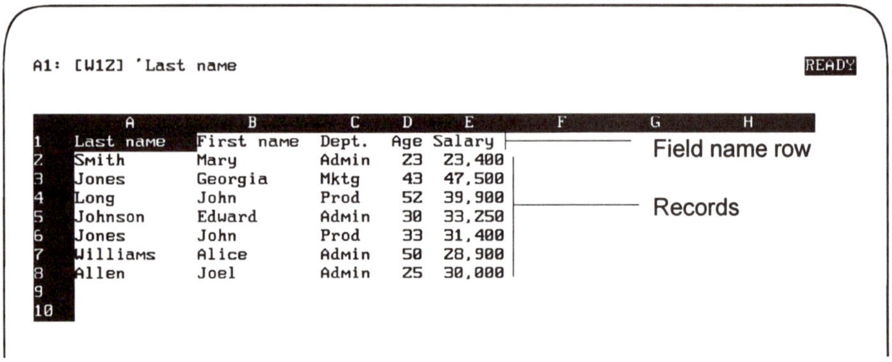

A1: [W12] 'Last name READY

	A	B	C	D	E	F	G	H
1	Last name	First name	Dept.	Age	Salary			
2	Smith	Mary	Admin	23	23,400			
3	Jones	Georgia	Mktg	43	47,500			
4	Long	John	Prod	52	39,900			
5	Johnson	Edward	Admin	30	33,250			
6	Jones	John	Prod	33	31,400			
7	Williams	Alice	Admin	50	28,900			
8	Allen	Joel	Admin	25	30,000			
9								
10								

Figure 20-1 The structure of a *Lotus* database

open range of a spreadsheet. After you enter the field name row, you enter the records of the database directly under the field names. You should enter these records with no empty rows to separate them.

After you've set up a database, you can sort the records by using the /Data Sort command that's described in chapter 10. For instance, you may want to keep a database like the one in figure 20-1 in last-name order. That will make it easier for you to find the records in the database.

If you want to add records to a database, you can add them at the end of the database, or you can insert rows for the new records. If you want to delete records, you just delete the rows that contain the records. In short, you don't need to learn any new skills to set up, sort, and maintain a database.

How to use the /Data Query command to query a database

After you create a database, you can use the /Data Query command to search for records in the database that contain specific items of information. For instance, you can search a database like the one in figure 20-1 for all the records that have Mktg in the Dept. field. Then, you can extract copies of those records to another portion of the spreadsheet. To do that you have to know how to set up the query ranges for a database, how to use the /Data Query command to query the database, and how to use logical and relational operators to specify selection criteria.

How to set up the query ranges for a database Before you can use the /Data Query command to query a database, you need to set up three *query ranges* in the spreadsheet as illustrated in figure 20-2. Here, the *input range* is just another name for the database that you've already established, so you don't have to do anything with it. But to set up the *criteria range*, you copy the field name row from the input range to another portion of the spreadsheet.

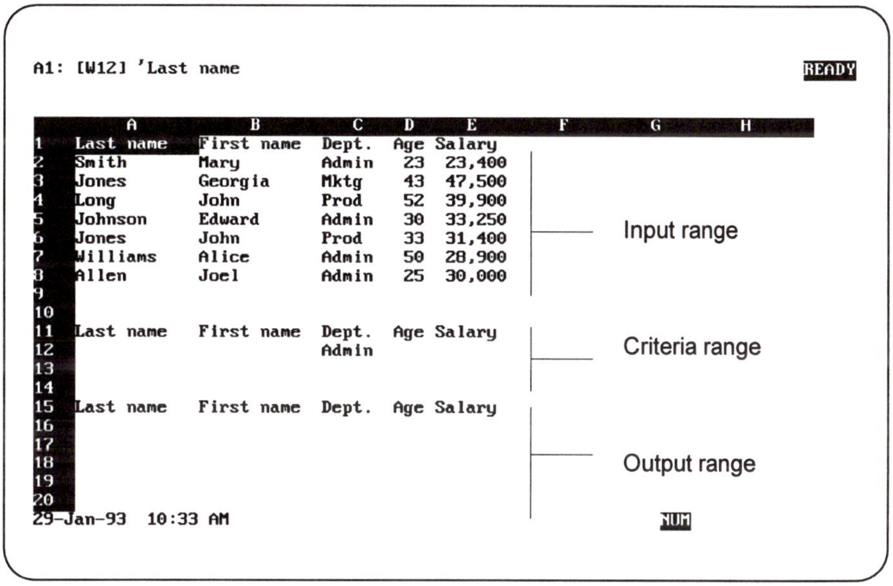

Figure 20-2 The ranges that *Lotus* requires for a query function

And to set up the *output range*, you copy the field name row again to a third range of the spreadsheet.

In figure 20-3, the three ranges are set up with one range below the other, but they don't have to be. They just have to be separate ranges of the spreadsheet. In fact, it often makes more sense to put the three ranges in a diagonal pattern in the spreadsheet. Then, you can insert or delete rows or columns in one of the ranges without affecting the rows or columns in the other ranges.

In figure 20-3, all three ranges have the same number of columns, but that's not necessary either. The criteria range only has to include those columns that are going to be used as the basis for queries. And the output range only has to include those columns that are supposed to be transferred there as the result of the query.

How to query a database Once you've set up the three query ranges, you're ready to find and extract records from a database. To do that, you start by entering data into one or more fields of the criteria range. If, for example, you want to find or extract all of the records in the database that have Admin in the Dept. field, you enter Admin into the criteria range as shown in figure 20-2. If you want to find or extract the records for all people whose names start with the letter J, you enter J* in the Last-name field. And if you want to find or extract the records for people over 40, you enter >40 in the Age field. You'll learn more about making entries like these in a moment.

Command	Next level	Function
/Data Query F6 (Window) F7 (Query)	Input	Specify the range of cells in the database (the input range)
	Criteria	Specify the range of cells in the criteria range
	Output	Specify the range of cells to be used for the query output (the output range)
	Find	Highlight a record in the input range that meets the criteria given in the criteria range
	Extract	Copy all records in the input range that meet the criteria in the criteria range to the output range
	Unique	Copy all records in the input range that meet the criteria given in the criteria range to the output range, but don't include duplicate records
	Delete	Delete all records in the input range that meet the criteria given in the criteria range
	Reset	Clear all query settings
	Quit	Exit from the /Data Query command

Figure 20-3 The /Data Query commands

After you've set up the criteria range, you use the /Data Query command that is summarized in figure 20-3 to perform the query that you want. To start, you use the Input, Criteria, and Output options to identify the three query ranges. If your release of *Lotus* provides for the use of the F6 (Window) key, you can use it to display the Query Settings screen as shown in figure 20-4.

When you use the /Data Query Output command to specify the output range for a query, you can do it in two ways. First, you can specify a range large enough for all records that meet the specifications in the criteria range. That's the way it's done in figure 20-4. Second, you can specify a one-row range that covers just the field name row. Then, the output records are written in the rows below the field name row in the output area. When you use this method to specify the output range, you should make sure that no data is below the range that could get replaced by output records.

Once you've used the /Data Query command to define the three query ranges, you can use the Find, Extract, or Unique options to search for the records that meet the criteria in the criteria range. In figure 20-4, for example, you can see the results of the Extract command. Here, the records that have

```
A1: [W12] 'Last name                                                        MENU
Input  Criteria  Output  Find  Extract  Unique  Delete  Reset  Quit
Specify range that contains records to search
┌──────────────────────────── Query Settings ────────────────────────────┐
│  Input range:        A1..E8                                            │
│                                                                        │
│  Criteria range:     A11..E13                                          │
│                                                                        │
│  Output range:       A15..E21                                          │
└────────────────────────────────────────────────────────────────────────┘
7   Williams    Alice       Admin   50  28,900
8   Allen       Joel        Admin   25  30,000
9
10
11  Last name   First name  Dept.   Age Salary
12                          Admin
13
14
15  Last name   First name  Dept.   Age Salary
16  Smith       Mary        Admin   23  23,400
17  Johnson     Edward      Admin   30  33,250
18  Williams    Alice       Admin   50  28,900
19  Allen       Joel        Admin   25  30,000
20
10-Feb-93  04:43 PM                                           NUM
```

Figure 20-4 The operation of the /Data Query Extract command

Admin in the Dept. field have been copied from the input range to the output range.

If you want to repeat a query with the same input, criteria, and output ranges, you can just press the F7 key to repeat the last /Data Query command. Between successive executions of the command, though, you usually change the specifications in the criteria range. And if you're using the Extract function, you usually erase the data in the output command so the new data won't write over it.

How to use logical operators, relational operators, and special symbols in the criteria range Figure 20-5 summarizes the operators and special symbols you can use in the queries that you specify in the criteria range. This should give you some idea of how complex you can make your queries. For most applications, though, your queries are likely to be relatively simple.

You can use the *relational operators* for both numeric fields (values) and alphanumeric fields (labels) as shown in the examples in figure 20-5. If, for example, you put >30 in the Age field in the criteria range, the /Data Query command will select those records in which the Age value is greater than 30. Similarly, if you put >=M in the Dept. field in the criteria range, the command will select those records that have department names that start with the letters M through Z.

The *logical operators* in figure 20-5 are *and*, *or*, and *not*. These operators let you combine two or more conditions that contain relational operators. Although the *and* and *or* operators are occasionally useful, you probably won't ever need the *not* operator. In most cases, you can express a *not* condition without using that operator.

The criteria range in figure 20-6 illustrates the use of the *and* operator. In the control panel at the top of the screen, you can see the expression that's stored in cell E12:

```
+E2>30000#AND#E2<=50000
```

This means that the Salary field must be greater than 30,000 *and* less than or equal to 50,000 for a record to be selected. Note that each relational condition in an expression like this must address the first field in the database that the condition is to be applied to. In this case, both the first relational condition

```
E2>30000
```

and the second condition

```
E2<=50000
```

address cell E2, which is the first Salary field in the database. However, the conditions that are combined by a logical operator can address different fields as in this example:

```
+D2>30#AND#E2<40000
```

If you relate this to the database in figure 20-6, it means that the Age field must be greater than 30 and the Salary field must be less than 40,000 for a record to be selected.

Because a logical expression is considered to be a formula, you usually have to start one with a plus or minus sign. Otherwise, *Lotus* thinks you're trying to enter a label. This also explains why the formula in figure 20-6 isn't displayed in cell E12. Instead, the value zero is displayed. When a formula consists of a logical expression, a value of 1 is displayed if the expression is true; a value of zero if the expression is false. In figure 20-6, the expression in E12 is false for the first record in the database so zero is displayed.

When you're working with fields that contain labels, you can use the special symbols that are summarized in figure 20-5. If you already know how to use the DOS wildcards, you shouldn't have any trouble with the * and ? symbols. And the tilde symbol (~) just means that the condition that follows should *not* be true.

If you look at the implied *and* and *or* conditions at the bottom of figure 20-5, you can see why you don't need to use the logical operators more frequently. If you put a label, value, or relational condition in two or more fields in the criteria range, all of the conditions must be true for a record to be selected. In other words, *and* relationships are implied. If you put a label in

Relational operators

Operator	Meaning	Example
<	Less than	`<30000`
>	Greater than	`>Admin`
<=	Less than or equal to	`<=M`
>=	Greater than or equal to	`>=20`
=	Equal to	`=555`
<>	Not equal to	`<>Mktg`

Logical operators

Operator	Meaning	Example
#AND#	Both conditions must be true	`+D2>30#and#D2<=40`
#OR#	Either condition must be true	`+D2<30#or#D2>=40`
#NOT#	The condition must not be true	`+D2<30#and##not#E2>40000`

Special symbols for label fields

Symbol	Meaning	Example
~	Not	`~Admin`
*	Any characters can be in the remainder of the field	`A*`
?	Any character can be in this position	`A?min`

Implied AND relationships in the criteria range — **Selection criteria**

```
Last name   First name Dept. Age Salary        Last name = Jones and
Jones                  Mktg                    Dept. = Mktg.

Last name   First name Dept. Age Salary        Age > 30 and
                             >30 <40000        Salary < 40,000
```

Implied OR relationships in the criteria range — **Selection criteria**

```
Last name   First name  Dept.  Age Salary      Dept. = Admin or
                        Mktg                   Dept. = Prod
                        Prod
```

Figure 20-5 The relational operators, logical operators, and special symbols that can be used in a query

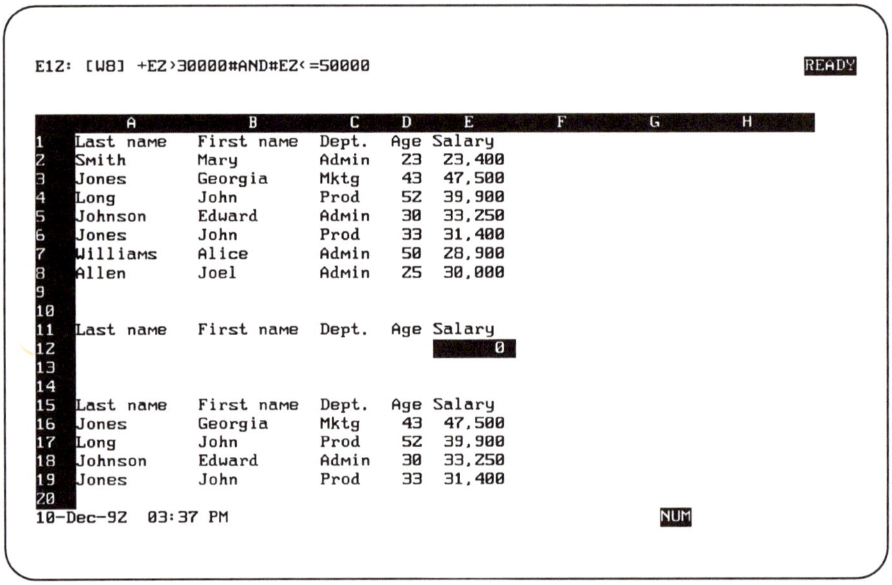

Figure 20-6 The operation of the /Data Query Extract command when relational and logical operators are used in the query

two successive rows for a field in the criteria range, records are selected that contain either one of the labels. In other words, an *or* relationship is implied.

With this as background, you should be able to set up the criteria range so the /Data Query command performs the correct selections. But if you still have doubts about how the queries work, just set up a simple database like the one in figure 20-6 and experiment with it. You'll soon see how easy it is to perform complex selections. And remember that you can use the F7 key to execute the /Data Query command each time that you change the data in the criteria range.

How to use the database @functions

Figure 20-7 summarizes the @functions that can be used with databases. These perform functions that are like those of their non-database counterparts: @COUNT, @SUM, @AVG, and so on. However, the database @functions require three *arguments*. The first argument identifies the range of the database. The second argument identifies the field in the database that the function is to be performed on. The third argument specifies the criteria range that should be used for identifying the records that the function should be performed upon.

The syntax of a database @function

```
@Dxxxxx(print-range,field-offset,criteria-range)
```

Argument	Meaning
`input-range`	The range that contains the database including the field name row
`field-offset`	An offset number starting with zero that identifies the field that the function is to be performed on (0 represents the first field; 1 represents the second field; and so on)
`criteria-range`	The range that contains the criteria for the records that should be included when the function is performed

The database functions

Function name	Function
`@DCOUNT`	Count the cells that aren't empty
`@DSUM`	Get the total
`@DAVG`	Get the average
`@DMIN`	Get the lowest value
`@DMAX`	Get the highest value
`@DVAR`	Get the variance
`@DSTD`	Get the standard deviation

An example that relates to the database in figure 20-6

Function	Meaning
`@DAVG(A1..E8,3,A11..E13)`	Get the average of the database fields in the fourth column in the input range (A1..E8), but only for those records that meet the criteria in the criteria range (A11..E13)

Figure 20-7 The database @functions

Command	Next level	Function
/Data	Fill	Fill a range of cells with numeric values (see chapter 1)
	Table	Calculate a table of values based on the variation of one or two values
	Sort	Sort the records in a database (see chapter 10)
	Distribution	Derive a frequency distribution for a range of cells
	Matrix	Invert a matrix, or multiply the columns in one matrix by the rows in another matrix to derive a third matrix
	Regression	Perform a regression analysis
	Parse	Parse the data in a column (see chapter 12)

Figure 20-8 The other /Data commands for internal databases

If you want to perform a function on all the records in a database, though, you don't need to use the database @functions. Instead, you can use their non-database counterparts. Similarly, if you use the /Data Query Extract command to extract the records that you want to perform the functions on, you can perform the functions on the records in the output area. So again, you don't need to use the database @functions. That's why you probably won't ever need to use the database @functions.

How to use the other /Data commands for working with internal databases

Figure 20-8 summarizes the other /Data commands that are available for working with internal databases. Three of these commands are presented in other chapters of this book, and they are only loosely associated with databases as described in this chapter. The /Data Fill command can be used to fill a range of cells with a sequence of values as described in chapter 1. The /Data Sort command can be used to sort the rows in a spreadsheet as described in chapter 10, whether or not you think of those rows as records in a database. And the /Data Parse command can be used to divide the data in a single field into two or more fields as described in chapter 12.

Of the remaining commands in figure 20-8, three are intended for advanced mathematical and statistical work. These are the /Data Table, Matrix, and Regression commands. If you like to work with tables of data, you can use the Table command for preparing what-if tables based on variations in other values. If you know what matrix math or regression analysis is, you can most likely figure out how to use the Matrix or Regression

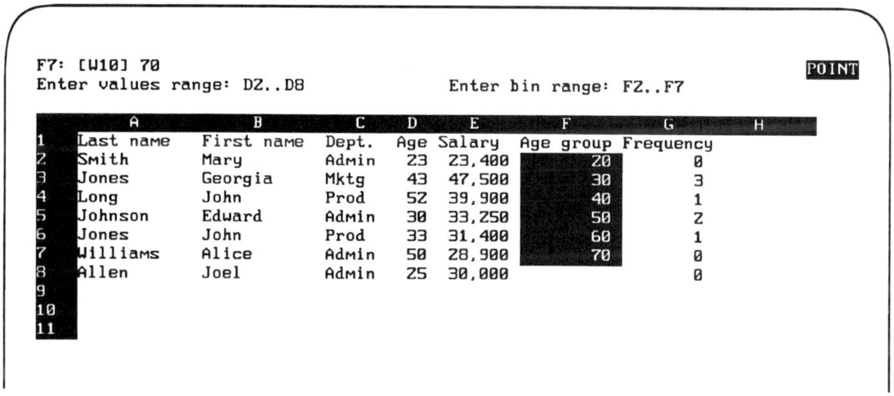

Figure 20-9 The operation of the /Data Distribution command

commands with just the aid of the Help facility. But these are not commands for the average *Lotus* user.

That leaves the /Data Distribution command that can be used to derive a frequency distribution. This can be quite useful for analyzing the data in some business spreadsheets. As a result, the operation of this command is illustrated in figure 20-9. Before you start this command, you can use the /Data Fill command to create a sequence of values like those in cells F2 through F7. This range of cells is known as the *bin range*. Then, when you start the /Data Distribution command, it asks you to identify the input range as well as the bin range as shown in the control panel in figure 20-9.

When *Lotus* executes the /Data Distribution command, it keeps a count of each value in the input range that relates to one of the values in the bin range. Then, it puts these counts in the cells to the right of the bin range. In figure 20-9, these counts are put in cells G2 through G8. In this case, the first count means that zero records had a value of 20 or less in the Age field; the second count means that 3 records had a value of from 21 through 30; the third count means that 1 record had a value of from 31 through 40; and so on. Note that there is one more count than there are values in the bin range. The count in cell G8 means that all of the records fell into one of the categories represented by the bin values. Thus, zero records were unaccounted for.

When you use the /Data Distribution command, the values in the bin range have to be in sequence, but they don't have to represent equal steps. For instance, the values in column F in figure 20-9 could be 20, 25, 30, 32, 35, 40, 60, and 80. In most cases, though, equal steps make the most sense so you can use the /Data Fill command for entering them. This is particularly true if you're going to graph the frequency distribution later on.

How to use the /Data External command to work with an external database

Figure 20-10 summarizes the /Data External command. This command lets you treat an *external database* like a *Paradox* or *DBase IV* database as though it is the input area for a /Data Query command. Then, you can use the /Data Query command to retrieve data from the external database into a *Lotus* spreadsheet. Once you do that, you can use the other *Lotus* commands to help you analyze the data in the database.

With *Lotus* release 3.4, you get three *datalens drivers* that make it possible for you to extract data from three types of external databases: *Paradox*, *dBase IV*, and *SQL Server* databases. In the future, you can expect that other datalens drivers will become available, either from *Lotus* or the companies that develop the database programs. It is likely, in fact, that datalens drivers will be developed for the databases of large mainframe computers, not just for PC databases. Although the /Data External Other Translation command lets you specify a character set for translating data between *Lotus* and the database, you shouldn't have to bother with that command if the datalens driver works the way it ought to.

When you work with an external database, you should know that it can contain one or more *database tables*. If the database contains only one table, the database name usually refers to the one table that it contains too. However, if a database contains two or more tables, each table has a unique name. When you use the /Data External command to set up a connection between *Lotus* and an external database, you need to know the name of the table that you want to access.

If you review the commands in figure 20-10, you can see that the Create command lets you create the structure for a new table in an external database. The Delete command lets you delete a table in an external database. And the Other Command lets you send a command to the database program. In general, though, you should only use the database program itself for changing the structure or data in a database. That helps maintain the integrity of the data in the database. That's why the database administrator for an external database is likely to put restrictions on it that disable the use of the *Lotus* Create and Delete commands. And that's why I'm not going to present these commands in this book. Instead, I'll just show you how to retrieve an external database into a *Lotus* spreadsheet.

How to establish a connection between an external database and *Lotus* Figure 20-11 presents a procedure for establishing a connection between an external database and *Lotus*. To do that, you start the /Data External Use command in step 1. Then, in step 2, you select the *datalens driver* for the type of database that you're going to get data from. If, for example, you're going to get data from a *Paradox* database, you use the *ParaLens* driver. If you're going to get data from a *dBase IV* database, you use that driver.

Command	Next level	Next level	Function
/Data External	Use		Establish a connection between a *Lotus* spreadsheet and a table in an external database.
	List	Tables	List the tables in an external database.
		Fields	List the fields in the database that has been attached to *Lotus* by the Use command.
	Create		Set up the structure for a new table in an external database.
	Delete		Remove a table from an external database.
	Other	Refresh	Set the Automatic and Interval options so the last /Data Query command will be executed automatically at specified time intervals to refresh the data that has been extracted from an external database.
		Command	Send a command to an external database program.
		Translation	Select the character set that should be used by the datalens driver to translate data that is extracted from an external database or copied to one.
	Reset		Disconnect an external database.

Figure 20-10 The /Data External commands for working with external databases

In step 3, you specify the directory that contains the database that you want to use. Then, in step 4, you select the database table that you want to use. And in step 5, you specify the range name that you want to use for the database table. If you're not familiar with range names, they are presented in detail in chapter 8. When you complete this command, you can think of the range name as the table in the external database.

How to retrieve data from an external database into a *Lotus* spreadsheet after the connection has been established Figure 20-12 presents a procedure for retrieving data from an external database once you've established a connection with it. And figure 20-13 shows four screens that illustrate how data is retrieved from a small database.

1. Start the /Data External Use command.

2. *Lotus* displays a prompt like this:

```
Enter name of table to use:
dBase_IV                  ParaLens                  SQL_Server
```

Select the datalens driver that you want to use.

3. *Lotus* displays a prompt like this:

```
Enter name of table to use: ParaLens
C:\123\MMA
```

If the directory that's displayed contains the database that you want, press the Enter key. Otherwise, type the appropriate directory specification and press the Enter key.

4. *Lotus* displays a prompt like this:

```
Enter the name of table to use: Paralens C:\PARADOX\MMA
EMPLOYEE        STOCK
```

Highlight the table that you want to use, and press the Enter key.

5. *Lotus* displays a prompt like this:

```
Enter range name for table: EMPLOYEE
```

Press enter if you want to use the table name for the range name. Otherwise, type the range name that you want to use and press Enter. This establishes the connection between *Lotus* and the external database. From this point on, you can think of the range name that you specified as the external database. You can also think of the range name as the Input range for a /Data Query command that gets records from the external database.

Figure 20-11 How to use the /Data External Use command to establish a connection between *Lotus* and an external database

In step 1 in figure 20-12, you use the /Data External List command to list the fields in the table of the external database. In the first screen in figure 20-13, a field table has been copied into the range starting with cell A1. Column A in this table lists the field names in the external database. The other columns give information about the fields.

Since you don't need the other field information, you can erase the data in columns B through F in the field table. That's step 2 in figure 20-12. Then, in step 3, you can use the /Range Transpose command to transpose the field names in the column into a row as illustrated by the second screen in figure 20-13. This row thus becomes the field name row for the external database. In step 4, you delete the field names below this row.

1. Use the /Data External List Fields command to list the fields in the external database. When you start this command, *Lotus* displays a prompt like this:

   ```
   Enter name of range whose fields are to be listed:
   EMPLOYEE
   ```

   Highlight the range name, and press the Enter key so *Lotus* displays this prompt:

   ```
   Enter range where field names will be copied: A1
   ```

   Move the highlight to the first cell in the range, and press the Enter key. This copies the table of fields into *Lotus* as illustrated by the first screen in figure 20-13.

2. Use the /Range Erase command to erase all field information except the field names in the first column of the table.

3. Use the /Range Transform command to move the field names from the column into a row as illustrated by the second screen in figure 20-13.

4. Use the /Range Erase command to delete the field names below the row that contains the field names.

5. Use the /Copy command to copy the field-name row to a row below it as illustrated by the third screen in figure 20-13.

6. At this point, you can retrieve some or all of the records from the external database into *Lotus* by using the /Data Query command. To do that, use the range name that you established with the /Data External Use command as the Input range. Use the top field row in the spreadsheet as the first row in the Criteria range. And use the next field row as the first row in the Output range. Then, use the Extract or Unique option of the /Data Query command to extract records from the external database into the spreadsheet as illustrated by the fourth screen in figure 20-13.

7. If you've extracted records from an external database that is continuously being updated by other users on a network, you can use the /Data External Other Refresh command to set the database up so the last /Data Query command is automatically re-executed at specified intervals. This keeps the data in the Output range up-to-date.

Figure 20-12 How to retrieve an external database into a *Lotus* spreadsheet

In step 5, you copy the field name row to a row at least two rows below it. Then, you can think of the upper field-name row as the first row in the criteria range and the lower field-name row as the first row in the output range. This is illustrated by the third screen in figure 20-13.

The field table generated by the /Data External List Fields command

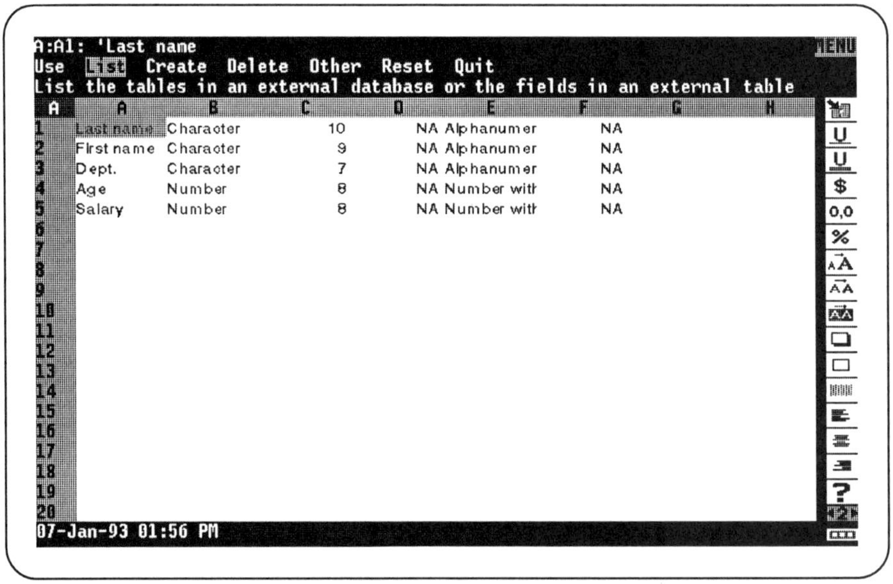

The first column of the field table after it has been transposed by the /Range Transpose command

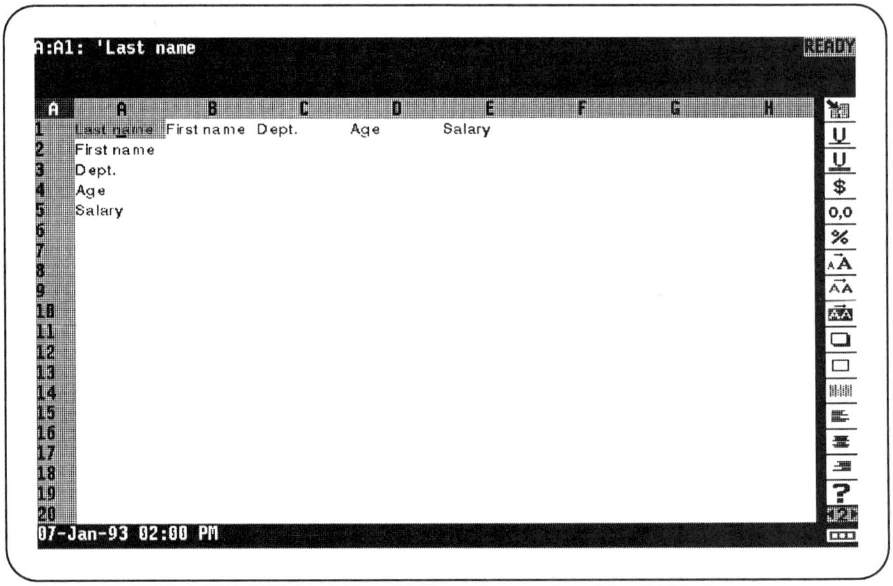

Figure 20-13 Four spreadsheet screens that show how data from an external database can be retrieved into a *Lotus* spreadsheet (part 1 of 2)

The field name row after it has been copied to another row

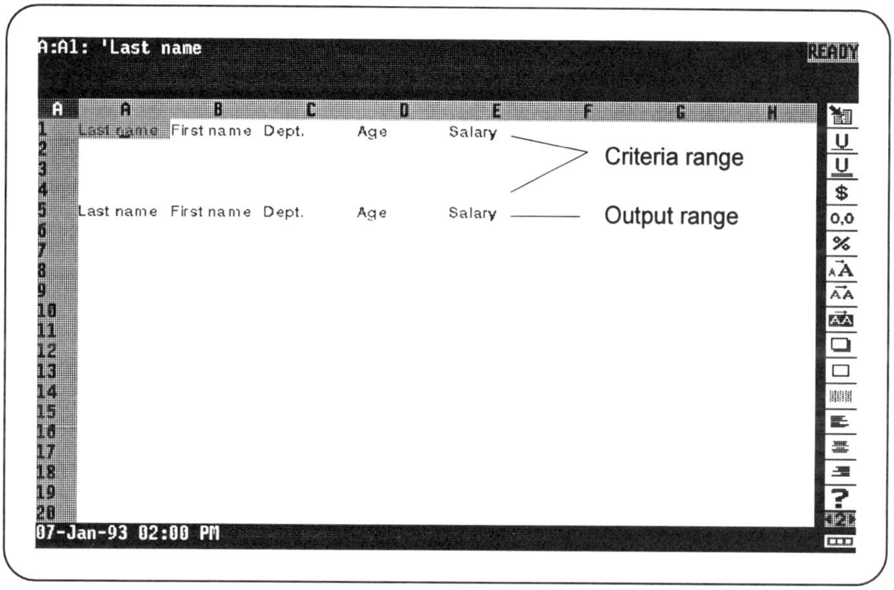

The criteria and output ranges after data has been retrieved from the external database

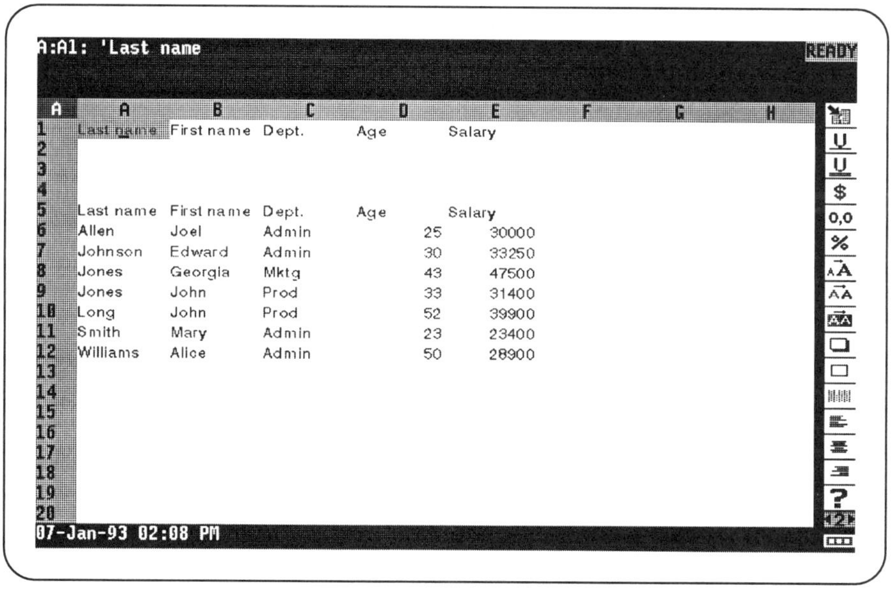

Figure 20-13 Four spreadsheet screens that show how data from an external database can be retrieved into a *Lotus* spreadsheet (part 2 of 2)

In step 6, you use the /Data Query command to retrieve the records from the database. For the Input range, use the range name that you used for the external database when you established the connection with it. For the Criteria and Output ranges, use ranges starting with the two field name rows. If you don't know how many records the command is going to retrieve, just use the second field-name row as the output range so all the records will be retrieved after that row. If you want to retrieve certain types of records only, enter the proper specifications in the criteria range. Then, use the /Data Query Extract or Unique command to retrieve the records from the external database into the spreadsheet as illustrated by the fourth screen in figure 20-13.

If you're using an external database that's on a network and it's continuously being updated by other users on the network, you can use the /Data External Other Refresh command to help keep the data in the output range of the spreadsheet up-to-date. When you use this command, you can specify Automatic updating along with the timed interval in seconds that should take place between updates. Once you've set these options, the last /Data Query command is automatically re-executed at the end of each timed interval.

When to use *Lotus* for working on an external database Once you've retrieved the external data into *Lotus*, you can use any of the other *Lotus* commands to summarize the data and to operate upon it arithmetically. This is valuable when you know how to use the *Lotus* commands, but you don't know how to use the commands of the database program. This is also valuable when the *Lotus* commands are more powerful than the commands of the database program. Often, though, if you learn how to use the database program, you'll realize that it's more efficient to use that program for summarizing and analyzing the data in the database than it is to use the *Lotus* commands.

Discussion

When compared with the features of a database program like *Q&A* or *Paradox*, the *Lotus* database features are both limited and difficult to use. Maintaining the data in a *Lotus* database is a relatively inefficient and error prone process. The query features are clumsy and hard to use. And *Lotus* has limited printing capabilities for the records in a database. As a result, it's extremely difficult to do a simple job like printing a mailing label for each record in a database. Because of these limitations, you probably shouldn't use the database feature of *Lotus* for an internal database if you have serious database requirements.

On the other hand, the *Lotus* database features may be satisfactory for small databases with limited processing requirements. The database features may be useful when you want to summarize or analyze the data in an external database. And some of the database features can be useful when you're working on spreadsheets that you don't think of as databases. For instance, you can use the /Data Distribution command to prepare a frequency distribution that becomes part of a report or the basis for a graph. Now that you know what the database features are, you can decide for yourself whether they are practical for your *Lotus* applications.

Terms

field name row
record
database
field
query ranges
input range
criteria range
output range
relational operator
logical operator
argument
bin range
external database
datalens driver
database table

Objectives

1. In general terms, describe the capabilities and limitations of the *Lotus* database feature for working with both internal and external databases.
2. Whenever practical, use one or more of the database features for your spreadsheet or database applications.

Chapter 21

Mouse support and *SmartIcons*

The use of a mouse is supported by *Lotus* releases 2.3 and 2.4. It is also supported when you use *WYSIWYG* with any of the 2.X or 3.X releases. If you enjoy using a mouse with your PC, you may appreciate the mouse support that's offered with *Lotus* and *WYSIWYG*.

SmartIcons became available with *Lotus* releases 2.4 and 3.4. The *SmartIcons* are icons that are arranged in bars to the right of the spreadsheet on the *Lotus* screen. Each one of the icons represents a function that you can start by moving the mouse pointer to it and pressing the left mouse button. This feature lets you access and perform some functions more quickly than you can by using the keyboard.

In this chapter, you'll first learn how to use a mouse with *Lotus*. Then, you'll learn how to use the *SmartIcons*. When you complete this chapter, you'll be able to decide whether or not you can benefit from using a mouse and the *SmartIcons* program.

To use the *SmartIcons* with release 3.4, though, you have to use the *WYSIWYG add-in program*. When you use release 2.4, you have to use the *SmartIcons* add-in program, and most people use *WYSIWYG* with it. So before you start learning how to use the *SmartIcons*, you need to know how to start an add-in program as described in chapter 14. Also, you should realize that the *WYSIWYG* add-in program requires a large amount of internal memory (approximately 105,000 bytes for release 2.4 and 165,000 bytes for release 3.4), and the *SmartIcons* program for release 2.4 requires another 25,000 bytes of memory. As a result, you may not be able to use these add-in programs for large spreadsheets if your PC has a limited amount of memory.

How to use a mouse with *Lotus* releases 2.3, 2.4, and *WYSIWYG*

Figure 21-1 summarizes the basic mouse actions that you need for *Lotus*. If you use a mouse with other programs, you should already know what these are. To *point* to an object on the screen, you move the mouse on the mousepad so the *mouse pointer* (or *mouse cursor*) moves across the screen. When you stop

Mouse term	Mouse action
Point	Move the mouse pointer to an object on the screen.
Click	Without moving the mouse pointer off the object you're pointing to, press and release the left mouse button.
Click-and-drag	Point to an object like a cell or menu highlight; press and hold down the left mouse button while you move the pointer to another object like a cell or menu option; then, release the left mouse button.

Figure 21-1 The basic mouse terms and actions

the movement of the mouse, the mouse pointer points to an object on the screen. This can be a cell, a menu item, or a *SmartIcon*.

To *click* the mouse, you press and release one of the mouse buttons. Unless a specific mouse button is mentioned, "click the mouse" means that you should click the left mouse button. However, some operations require that you click the right mouse button.

To *click-and-drag* the mouse, you point to an object like a cell or the menu highlight. Then, you press and hold the left mouse button, drag the mouse pointer to another object, and release the mouse button. You can use this technique to highlight a range of cells with the mouse. You can also use it to move the menu pointer from one option in a menu to another.

Figure 21-2 summarizes the functions you can do with a mouse when you use *Lotus*. Note, however, that the mouse actions are substitutes for keyboard actions. You can't do anything with a mouse that you can't do by using the keyboard.

How to use the mouse to start and execute commands If you study the summary in figure 21-2, you can see that you can use the mouse to perform *Lotus* commands. To activate the *Lotus* menu, you just move the mouse pointer to the control panel of the spreadsheet screen. Then, to select an option in a menu, you point to it and click. If you want to move the menu pointer to an option without starting it, you click-and-drag the menu pointer from one option to another. If you release the mouse button, you'll start the option. To release the menu pointer without starting an option, you move the pointer off the menu before you release the mouse button.

If you're using *WYSIWYG*, you click the right mouse button to switch from the *Lotus* main menu to the *WYSIWYG* main menu, and you click it again to switch back to the *Lotus* main menu. You also click the right mouse button when you want to back out of a command one level at a time (the equivalent of pressing the Esc key). If you want to exit from the menus altogether, move the mouse pointer out of the control panel.

***Lotus* function**	**Mouse action**
Activate the *Lotus* menu	Move the mouse pointer to the control panel.
Deactivate the *Lotus* menu	Move the mouse pointer out of the control panel.
Switch between the *Lotus* and the *WYSIWYG* main menus	Click the right mouse button.
Select a command or an option from a menu or panel	Point to the command or option that you want and click on it.
Move the menu pointer to an option without starting it	Click-and-drag the menu pointer to the option without releasing the mouse button.
Back up one menu level	Click the right mouse button (same as pressing the Esc key).
Select a name from a list	Point to the name and click on it.
Display a complete list of names when a command prompt asks for one	Point to the word *List* in the first line of the control panel and click on it.
Highlight a range	Point to the first cell in the range; drag the cell pointer to the last cell in the range; and release the left mouse button.
Remove the highlight from a range	Click anywhere outside of the highlighted range.
Move the cell pointer	Point to the cell you want and click on it.
Move the cell pointer to cell A1	Point to the upper left corner of the spreadsheet frame and click on it (same as pressing the Home key).
Accept the range or ranges displayed in the control panel	Click the left mouse button.
Start the Help facility (2.3)	Click on the ? when it's displayed in the control panel or on the right side of the spreadsheet.
Move the cell pointer one cell up, down, left, or right (2.3)	Click on the appropriate arrow symbol when the symbols are displayed in the control panel or on the right side of the spreadsheet.

Figure 21-2 The primary mouse functions that are supported by *Lotus* releases 2.3, 2.4, and *WYSIWYG*

When you start a command that uses names, like the /File Retrieve command, you select one of the names in the control panel by pointing to it and clicking. To display a complete list of names, you point to the word *List* in the first line of the control panel and click. To change the drive, you click on one of the drive letters in the first line of the control panel. To change to the parent directory of the directory that's displayed, you click on the two dots (..) in the first line of the control panel. (The *parent directory* is the one that the current directory is subordinate to.)

When you use a command that requires a range address, you highlight the range by clicking on the first cell in the range and dragging the mouse to the last cell in the range. Often, you highlight the range before you start the command. Otherwise, you highlight the range when the command asks for it. After you highlight a range, you may have to click the left mouse button to tell *Lotus* to continue a command.

Figure 21-3 gives three examples of how you use the mouse to perform commands. In all three, you use the mouse from start to finish; you don't need the keyboard at all. In the second example, the first range that's used by the /Copy command is highlighted after the command is started, but you can also highlight the range before you start this command. In the third example, the range is highlighted before the command is started.

When you enter labels, values, and formulas into a spreadsheet, you can probably work most efficiently by using the keyboard to access a command whenever you need one. Otherwise, you have to switch one hand from the keyboard to the mouse and back again whenever you need a command. And that usually reduces your efficiency.

Perhaps the best time to use a mouse is after you've done most or all of the keyboard entry for a spreadsheet. Then, you can use the mouse to copy formulas from one range to another, to improve the format of the spreadsheet, to print the spreadsheet, and so on. This lets you change your body to a more relaxed position without having much effect on your efficiency.

How to use the mouse to move the cell pointer To move the cell pointer in a spreadsheet, point to the cell that you want to move it to and click. Then, the cell pointer jumps to the location of the mouse pointer. If you want to return the cell pointer to cell A1 (the Home position), you point to the upper left box in the spreadsheet frame and click. This is useful when cell A1 isn't visible in the spreadsheet screen.

If you're using release 2.3 or 2.4, you can move the cell pointer one position up, down, left, or right by clicking on the appropriate arrow symbol when it's displayed to the right of the spreadsheet or in the control panel. But this is an inefficient way to move the cell pointer, so you're better off using the Arrow keys on the keyboard. Also, the arrow symbols don't show on the right side of the spreadsheet when you're using *SmartIcons*.

How to use the mouse to retrieve a file

1. Start the /File Retrieve command by moving the mouse pointer to the control panel, clicking on File, and clicking on Retrieve.
2. In the control panel that's displayed, click on List to display all of the file names in the directory. Click on the two dots (..) to change to the parent directory. Click on one of the drive letters to change drives. Click on a directory name to change the directory. Eventually, click on the file name that you want to retrieve.

How to use a mouse to copy a range of cells

1. Start the /Copy command by moving the mouse pointer to the control panel and clicking on Copy.
2. Highlight the range of cells to be copied by dragging the mouse from the first cell in the range to the last. Then, click the left mouse button to tell *Lotus* that you accept the Copy-from range that's shown in the control panel.
3. Highlight the first cell in the range that the cells should be copied to by pointing to the cell and clicking on it. Then, click the left mouse button to tell *Lotus* that you accept the Copy-to range that's shown in the control panel.

How to use a mouse to erase a range of cells

1. Highlight the range of cells to be erased by dragging the mouse from the first cell in the range to the last.
2. Start the /Range Erase command by moving the mouse pointer to the control panel, clicking on Range, and clicking on Erase.

Figure 21-3 Three examples of how to use the mouse to perform commands

How to use the mouse to access the Help facility If you're using release 2.3 or 2.4, you can access the Help facility with the mouse by clicking on the question mark (?) to the right of the spreadsheet or in the control panel. Then, you can move from topic to topic within the Help facility by clicking on the selected topic or option. You may prefer to work this way when you're looking up several topics in a row, but you can look the topics up just as fast using the keyboard.

How to use *SmartIcons* with *Lotus* releases 2.4 and 3.4

To use the *SmartIcons* feature of *Lotus* release 3.4, you have to attach and invoke the *WYSIWYG* add-in program. To use this feature with release 2.4, you have to attach and invoke the *SmartIcons* add-in program. Then, to make the icons easier to use, you should also attach and invoke *WYSIWYG*. When you install *Lotus*, the default is set so these add-in programs are attached and invoked when you start *Lotus*. But if your PC isn't set up so these programs are started automatically, you can read chapter 14 to learn how to attach and invoke these programs.

When *WYSIWYG* is attached and invoked with *Lotus* release 3.4, the spreadsheet screen looks like the one in figure 21-4. Here, you can see that an *icon bar* is displayed to the right of the spreadsheet, and this bar contains 16 *icons*. Each of these icons represents a function that can be performed by clicking on the icon. The first icon, for example, represents the /File Save function, and the second one represents the /File Retrieve function.

When both *WYSIWYG* and *SmartIcons* are attached and invoked with *Lotus* release 2.4, the spreadsheet screen looks like the one in figure 21-4 with one exception: the small box below the icon bar isn't displayed. When *SmartIcons* is used without *WYSIWYG*, the spreadsheet screen icons look quite different from those in figure 21-4. Although the same icons are there, they're in a form that isn't as easy to interpret. That's why it's best to use *SmartIcons* in combination with *WYSIWYG*. Remember, though, that *WYSIWYG* takes about 105,000 bytes of internal memory with release 2.4, so you may not be able to use both of these add-in programs at the same time. In that case, you can use *SmartIcons* without *WYSIWYG*. Although the icons will look different than those illustrated in this chapter, the techniques for using them are the same.

At the bottom of each icon bar, you can see a number that identifies the bar. In figure 21-4, the first icon bar is displayed. If you study the mouse actions that are summarized in this figure, you can see that you can move from one icon bar to another by clicking on the arrow to the right or left of the bar number at the bottom of the bar. With *Lotus* release 2.4, there are seven icon bars; with release 3.4, there are eight.

When you're using *Lotus* release 3.4, you can remove the icon bar by clicking on the small box below the icon bar. You can also remove it by pressing the Ctrl+F9 key combination. Normally, though, you want the icon bar displayed so you don't need this capability.

Figure 21-5 summarizes some of the most useful *SmartIcons*. As you can see, some of them start *Lotus* commands like the Save, Retrieve, Copy, and Move commands. Some start *WYSIWYG* functions like adding a graph to a spreadsheet or boldfacing the font in the highlighted range of cells. In addition to the *SmartIcons* for release 2.4, the *SmartIcons* for release 3.4 include icons for some of its special features. For instance, release 3.4 has an icon for displaying a 3D spreadsheet in perspective mode. Keep in mind, however, that none of the icons provide for functions that you can't perform using the regular *Lotus* and *WYSIWYG* commands.

A spreadsheet screen with *WYSIWYG* and *SmartIcons* (release 3.4)

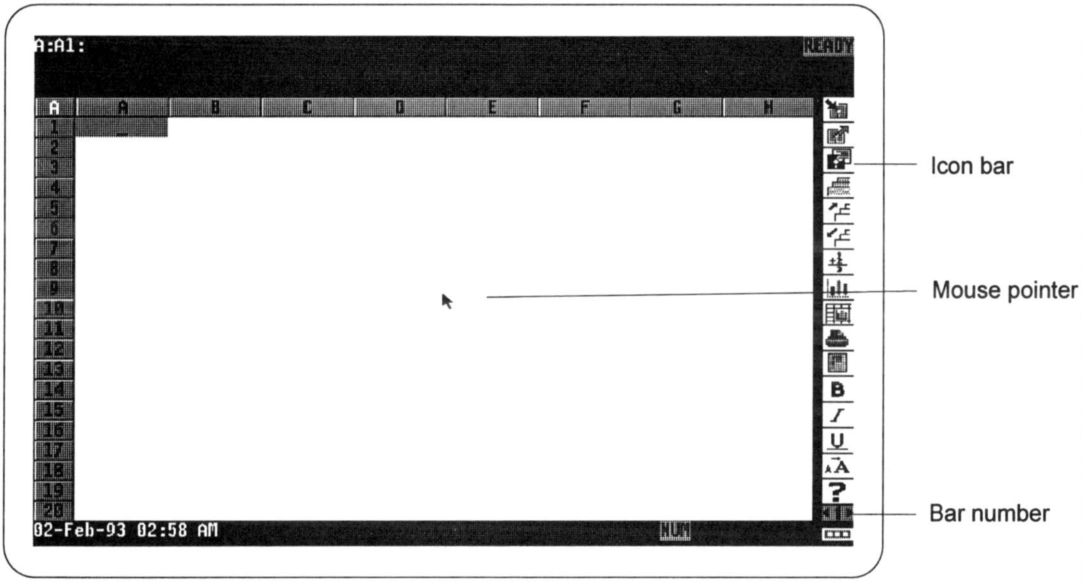

Mouse functions for use with *SmartIcons*

Mouse function	**Mouse action**
Display the description for a *SmartIcon* function	Point to the icon and hold down the right mouse button.
Start a *SmartIcon* function	Point to the icon and click on it.
Move to the next or previous icon bar	Click on the right or left arrow at the bottom of the current icon bar.
Display or remove the icon bar (3.4)	Click on the symbol below the icon bar.

Figure 21-4 How to use the *SmartIcons* (part 1 of 2)

How to review the functions of the icons To find out what the function of an icon is, you simply point to it and hold down the right mouse button. This displays a description of the function in the control panel. However, this is an awkward technique for reviewing the functions of all the icons.

Keystroke combinations for use with *SmartIcons*

Function	Release	Keystrokes
Activate the icon bar for keystroke selection of an icon or to review the icon descriptions	2.4	Alt+F7 or use Alt+F10 to activate the add-in menu and invoke *Icons*; then, use the Left and Right arrow keys to move from icon bar to icon bar and the Up and Down arrow keys to move from icon to icon.
Activate the icon bar for keystroke selection of an icon or to review the icon descriptions	3.4	Ctrl+F10; then, use the Left and Right arrow keys to move from icon bar to icon bar and the Up and Down arrow keys to move from icon to icon.
Display or remove the icon bar	3.4	Ctrl+F9

Figure 21-4 How to use the *SmartIcons* (part 2 of 2)

So if you want to review the descriptions for all of the icon functions, you may want to use the keystroke combinations that are summarized in figure 21-4. To start, you need to activate the icon bar. With release 2.4, you can do this by pressing the Alt+F7 key combination to invoke the *Icons* add-in program if it has been set up that way. Otherwise, you can press the Alt+F10 keystroke combination to display the Add-in menu and invoke the *Icons* add-in program from that menu. With release 3.4, all you have to do is press the Ctrl+F10 key combination to activate the icon bar.

When the icon bar is activated, one of the icons is highlighted and its description is displayed in the control panel. Then, you use the Up and Down arrow keys to move from one icon to another. And you use the Left and Right arrow keys to move from one icon bar to another. This makes it easy for you to review the functions of all the icons. You can also select the highlighted icon by pressing the Enter key, although it's easier to select an icon with the mouse by clicking on it. As a result, I recommend that you use the keyboard with *SmartIcons* only when you want to review the icon functions.

How to use a *SmartIcon* to perform a function Before you click on a *SmartIcon* to start a function, you often use the mouse to highlight the range that you want to perform the function on. To print a range of cells, for example, you use the mouse to highlight the range and then click on the Print icon. And to boldface a range of cells, you highlight the range of cells and then click on the Boldface icon.

Icon	Type	Function
	*Lotus*	Save the current spreadsheet to a disk file.
	*Lotus*	Retrieve a spreadsheet file from disk.
	*Lotus*	Copy a range.
	*Lotus*	Move a range.
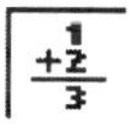	*Lotus*	Create an @SUM function in the empty cell to the right or below the highlighted range. Or, if no range is highlighted, create an @SUM function in the current cell that sums the cells in the column above or in the row to the left of the current cell.
	*Lotus*	Format the highlighted range with the Comma format and zero decimal positions.
	*Lotus*	Format the highlighted range with the Percent format and two decimal positions.
	*Lotus*	Insert the current date with the default date format into the current cell.
	*Lotus*	Erase the highlighted range.
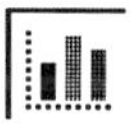	*Lotus*	Graph the highlighted range. Or, if no range is highlighted, graph the data near the cell pointer. This function displays the QuickGraph dialog box.
	*Lotus* or *WYSIWYG*	Print the current or highlighted range.
	*WYSIWYG*	Add the current graph to the highlighted range.
	*WYSIWYG*	Boldface the highlighted range or remove the boldfacing from the range.
	Macro	Assign a macro to a *SmartIcon* from U1 through U12.
	Macro	Run a macro that has been assigned to U1 through U12.

Figure 21-5 Some of the most useful *SmartIcons* for *Lotus* and *WYSIWYG* functions

The QuickGraph dialog box

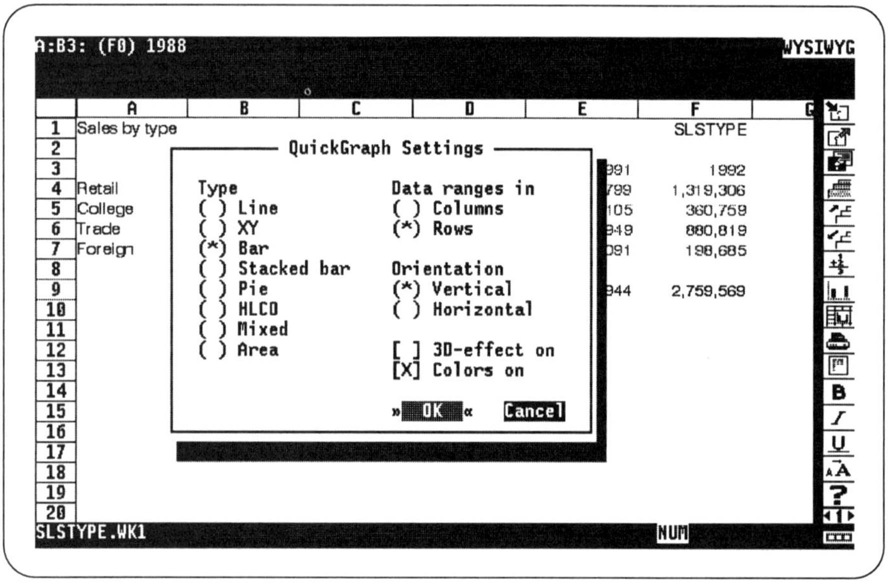

How to create a graph

1. Highlight the range of cells that you want graphed. Then, click on the Graph icon.
2. *Lotus* displays the QuickGraph dialog box shown above. Here, you can specify the graph type, whether the data ranges should be taken from columns or rows in the highlighted range, whether the orientation of the graph should be horizontal or vertical, and whether the 3D effect should be on.
3. Click on the OK box to complete the command and display the graph.

Figure 21-6 How to use the Graph icon to create a graph

In figure 21-6, you can see how the Graph icon is used for graphing the data in a range. In step 1, you highlight the range to be graphed. Then, you click on the Graph icon. This displays the QuickGraph *dialog box* shown in this figure. In step 2, you set the graphing options that are offered by the dialog box. In step 3, you click on OK in the dialog box to complete the command and display the graph.

These icons are called *SmartIcons* because some of them make "smart" assumptions about what the function is supposed to do. This is best illustrated by the Sum icon that is summarized in figure 21-5. If you move the cell pointer to an empty cell below a column of numbers before you click on the Sum icon, this function inserts a complete @SUM function into the current cell with the entire column of numbers as the range. If the assumption that *Lotus* makes is correct, this means that you can enter a correct @SUM function into a cell just by clicking on the Sum icon. Sometimes, though, the assumption isn't correct. So use this *SmartIcon* with caution. When in doubt, highlight the range of cells that you want to sum before you click on the icon.

If you experiment with the *SmartIcons*, you can quickly decide whether or not you want to use this feature. There's no question that using some of the icons, like the Sum icon, can improve your efficiency. There's also no question that using some of the icons can slow you down because they are harder to use than the keystrokes for performing the same functions. Here again, it's probably sensible to use the keyboard for accessing commands while you're entering labels, values, and formulas into a spreadsheet (with the exception of the @SUM function). Later, you can use the mouse with the *SmartIcons* to copy, move, format, graph, and print various ranges within the spreadsheet.

How to set up the custom palette for *SmartIcons* The first icon bar is the *custom palette* of *SmartIcons*. The other icon bars are called *fixed palettes*. The fixed palettes include all of the icons available to your release of *Lotus*. The custom palette can be set up so it includes any of the icons on the fixed palettes.

If you like the idea of using the *SmartIcons* feature of *Lotus*, you should take the time to set up the custom palette so it contains the icons that you will use the most. That way, you usually don't have to switch from one icon bar to another to find the icon that you want to use. When you have to search through the icon bars to find the function that you want, you lose whatever benefits you gain from the *SmartIcons*, and your productivity goes down instead of up.

In figure 21-5, you can see 15 of the most useful icons. But you can add icons to this list or delete icons from it based on your own requirements. Because it's easy to customize a palette, you should be able to develop your own custom palette in less than an hour.

Figure 21-7 presents the procedures you need for setting up the custom palette. To do this, you use functions that are provided by icons themselves. These icons can be found on bar 6 for release 2.4 and bar 7 for release 3.4.

When you add an icon to the custom palette, you use the first procedure in figure 21-7. Then, the new icon is added to the bottom of the custom palette. If another icon was there, it is replaced by the new icon. But remember that all of the icons are included in the fixed palettes so the replaced icon isn't lost. Similarly, when you use the second and third procedures in figure 21-7 to remove or move an icon on the custom palette, no icons are lost.

How to add an icon to the custom palette

1. Click on the icon for adding an icon to the custom palette.
2. Click on the icon you want to add to the custom palette. *Lotus* adds the icon to the bottom of the custom palette. If there is no opening at the bottom of the custom palette, *Lotus* replaces the bottom icon with the icon you've selected.

How to remove an icon from the custom palette

1. Click on the icon for removing an icon from the custom palette.
2. Click on the icon you want to remove from the custom palette.

How to reposition an icon on the custom palette

1. Click on the icon for rearranging the icons on the custom palette.
2. Click on the icon you want to move.
3. Click on the new position for the icon you selected in step 2. *Lotus* then rearranges the custom palette.

Figure 21-7 How to set up the custom icon palette

How to assign macros to the User icons If you've read chapter 19 and like the idea of using macros with your spreadsheets, the *SmartIcons* feature makes it easy for you to set up 12 macros that you can use with all your spreadsheets. You can run these macros by pressing a User-Defined icon from U1 through U12. You'll find the User-Defined icons on the last icon bar.

When you install *Lotus,* these icons have no macros assigned to them. To assign a macro to an icon, you use the Assign-macro icon. This icon is found at the bottom of the second last icon bar. If you're using release 2.4, you use the procedure shown in figure 21-8 to assign a macro to an icon. If you're using release 3.4, you use the procedure in figure 21-9. Both procedures are easy to use, and you shouldn't have any trouble with them.

Usually, it's best to define and test the macro in the spreadsheet before you assign it to an icon. Then, you use the Get-macro-from-sheet function to retrieve the macro from the highlighted range when you're ready to assign it to an icon. That way you know that the macro will work the way you want it to when you select the related icon.

If you want to change a macro after you've assigned it to an icon, you can assign a new set of macro instructions to the icon by using the procedure in figure 21-8 or 21-9. Or, you can use one of the methods in figure 21-10 to edit the macro instructions that you've already assigned to an icon. In the first method, you use the Copy-macro-to-sheet function to copy the assigned

The User-icon-descriptions dialog box

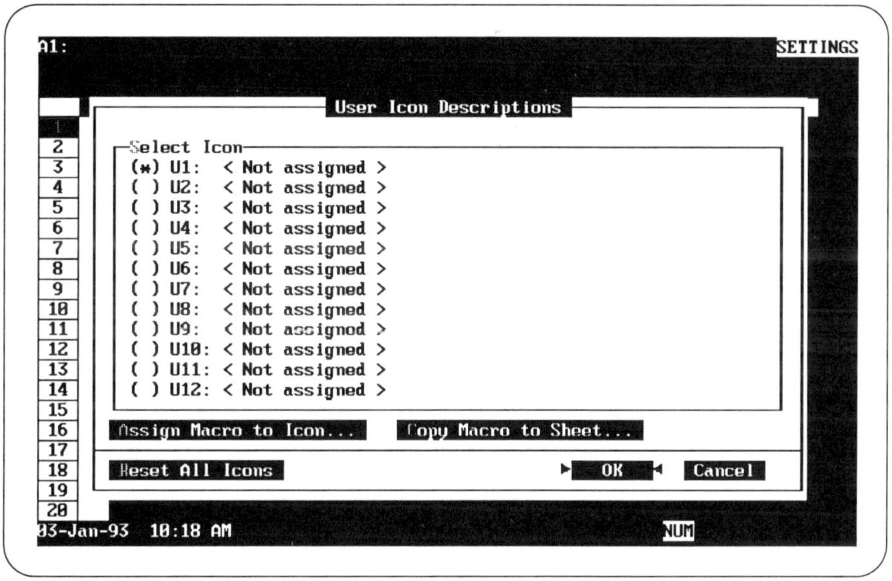

How to assign a macro to a User icon

1. Highlight the range of cells the contains the macro.
2. Click on the Assign-macro icon. This displays a User-icon-descriptions dialog box shown above.
3. Click on the User-icon number that you want to assign a macro to. Then, click on the Assign-macro-to-icon box. This displays the User-defined-icon box (not shown).
4. Enter a description of the macro function in the Icon-description box. This is the description that will get displayed later on when you click on the User icon with the right mouse button.
5. Click on the Get-macro-from-sheet box to get the macro from the range of cells that you highlighted in step 1. This puts the macro instructions in the Macro-text box. As an alternative, you can enter the macro instructions directly into the Macro-text box.
6. Click on the OK box. This displays the User-icon-description dialog box again. Then, you can assign another macro or click on the OK box to end the assignment procedure.

Figure 21-8 How to assign a macro to a User icon (release 2.4)

The Assign-macro dialog box

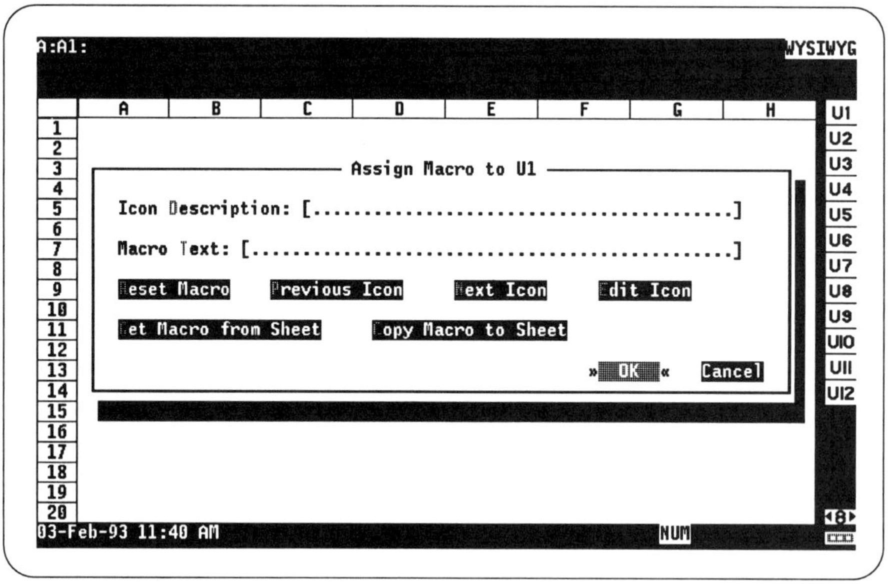

How to assign a macro to a User icon

1. Click on the Assign-macro icon. This displays the Assign-macro dialog box shown above.
2. Click on the User icon that you want to assign a macro to. This displays the User-icon number in the title of the dialog box. Another way to do this is to click on the Previous-icon or Next-icon box until the title shows the number of the icon that you want to assign a macro to.
3. Enter a description of the macro function in the Icon-description box. This is the description that will get displayed later on when you click on the User icon with the right mouse button.
4. Click on the Get-macro-from-sheet box to get the macro. Then, highlight the cells that contain the macro instructions, and click the left mouse button to return to the dialog box. This puts the macro instructions in the Macro-text box. As an alternative, you can enter the macro instructions directly into the Macro-text box.
5. Click on the OK box to complete the assignment.

Figure 21-9 How to assign a macro to a User icon (release 3.4)

Method 1: Edit the macro instructions in the spreadsheet

1. Click on the Assign-macro icon.
2. Select the User-icon number for the macro that you want to edit just as you do if you're assigning a macro to the User icon for the first time.
3. Click on the Copy-macro-to-sheet command to copy the highlighted range in the spreadsheet.
4. Edit and test the macro instructions in the spreadsheet.
5. Use the procedure in figure 21-8 or 21-9 to assign the edited macro instructions to the User icon.

Method 2: Edit the macro instructions in the Macro-text box

1. Click on the Assign-macro icon.
2. Select the User-icon number for the macro that you want to edit just as you do if you're assigning a macro to the User icon for the first time.
3. Edit the macro instructions in the Macro-text box.
4. Click on the OK box to complete the editing.

Figure 21-10 How to edit a macro that has been assigned to a User icon (release 2.4 or 3.4)

macro instructions to the current spreadsheet. Then, you can modify and test the macro before you reassign the macro to the icon. In the second method, you can edit the macro instructions in the Macro-text box without ever putting the macro in the current spreadsheet.

When you assign a macro to an icon, it stays in effect until you change it. That means it stays in effect from one spreadsheet to the next and from one *Lotus* session to the next. So for people who need to use a small number of macros in their spreadsheets, this can be a valuable feature.

Discussion

If you're a fast typist and you remember the keystrokes for most of the commands that you use, using a mouse and *SmartIcons* isn't going to help you get more done. On the contrary, if you use them, they're likely to slow you down.

However, that doesn't mean that you should avoid using the mouse and *SmartIcons* entirely. When you use a mouse, you can change your position to a more comfortable one. This can help you avoid both fatigue and stress. And you can perform a few functions more efficiently by using the *SmartIcons* than you can by using the keyboard. So if you use a mouse and the *SmartIcons* thoughtfully, you can probably work more productively.

In most cases, then, slow typists and occasional *Lotus* users have the most to gain from using the mouse and *SmartIcons*. Often, they can work faster with a mouse than they can with a keyboard. And sometimes, they can find functions more easily on the icon bars than they can in the menus.

In the end, it gets down to individual preferences. If you like using a mouse, you'll probably like using one with *Lotus* and its *SmartIcons*. If you don't like using a mouse, you'll probably prefer using the keyboard.

Terms

SmartIcons
add-in program
point
mouse pointer
mouse cursor
click
click-and-drag
parent directory
icon bar
icon
dialog box
custom palette
fixed palette

Objectives

1. Decide whether using the mouse and *SmartIcons* can help you work more productively.
2. Use the capabilities presented in this chapter that are appropriate for your working style.

Section 5

Practical advice for *Lotus 1-2-3* users

If you're not satisfied with the features that are offered by your release of *Lotus*, you should read the one chapter in this section. It presents practical advice for upgrading to a later release. Similarly, if you aren't satisfied with the performance that you're getting from your PC, you should read the one chapter in this section to get practical advice for improving its performance.

Chapter 22

When to upgrade your *Lotus* release or your PC

If you read the trade magazines for the PC industry, you know that software improvements are offered for all the major programs on a regular basis. And hardware improvements are offered even more frequently. Periodically, then, you need to decide whether you should take advantage of some of these improvements by upgrading your release of *Lotus* or by upgrading the hardware of your PC. In this chapter, I will try to give you some practical advice for making those decisions.

When to upgrade to one of the current releases of *Lotus*

Figure 22-1 summarizes the enhancements that have been made to *Lotus* since 1986. If you read the other chapters in this book, you can learn exactly how most of these enhancements work and what they do. In chapter 14, for example, you can learn how add-in programs work. In chapter 11, you can learn how cell linking works. In chapter 21, you can learn how *Lotus* provides mouse support. And so on.

In figure 22-1, the releases are divided into two parts. First, this figure summarizes the releases from 2.01 through 2.4. Then, it summarizes the releases from 3.0 through 3.4. That's because Lotus Development Corporation is currently maintaining two distinct versions of *Lotus*. These can be referred to as the 2.X and the 3.X releases.

If you study the summary of the 2.X releases, you can see that most of the enhancements since release 2.01 in 1986 have come through add-in programs. Otherwise, the primary enhancements have been cell linking, mouse support, and enhanced graphing. Of these, the most significant enhancement was cell linking, but not everyone needed that feature. Furthermore, this feature had some serious limitations.

If you study the summary of the 3.X releases, you can see that release 3.0 provided three primary improvements over release 2.01, which was the current 2.X release at the time. Most important, release 3.0 let you work on more than one spreadsheet at the same time. This is sometimes referred to as working on a *three-dimensional spreadsheet*, and this makes cell linking much easier. For those *Lotus* users who needed a cell linking capability, this feature was a primary motivation for upgrading to the new release. Beyond that, release 3.0 offered improved graphics and printing capabilities. And it offered background printing and background recalculating.

Today, the current releases of *Lotus* are 2.4 and 3.4. Both are full-featured spreadsheet programs supported by several add-in programs. And the most significant differences between them are the three-dimensional spreadsheet capability, the enhanced graphics capability, and the enhanced printing capability offered by release 3.4. Because most *Lotus* users don't need those capabilities, the 2.X releases are still used by more people than the 3.X releases by a factor of 2 or 3 to 1.

With that as background, you should be able to decide whether you need to upgrade to a new release of *Lotus*. If you have any doubts about a new feature, be sure to read the related chapter to see exactly how it works. Only you can decide whether the benefits that you get from a new feature will justify the time and expense of upgrading to a new *Lotus* release.

If you decide that you should upgrade to a new release of *Lotus*, figure 22-2 summarizes the hardware requirements for the new releases. If you upgrade from a 2.X release to release 3.4, you may need to upgrade your PC to support it. In particular, release 3.4 requires 1MB of internal memory and at least a 286 processor. But if you're used to running *Lotus* 2.X on a 286 processor, release 3.4 is going to seem slow if you run it on a 286. That's why I recommend a faster processor. Beyond these requirements, both release 2.4 and 3.4 require a considerable amount of disk storage. If you store all of the add-in programs that come with release 2.4 on your hard disk, the total requirement is around 5MB. And if you do the same for release 3.4, the total requirement is around 6MB. Now, do you still think it's worth upgrading to a new release of *Lotus*?

When and how to upgrade your PC hardware

If you're not happy with the way *Lotus* runs on your PC, you may be able to improve its performance by upgrading your PC. And if you upgrade your release of *Lotus* from 2.X to 3.X, you may have to upgrade your PC to meet the requirements presented in figure 22-2. Figure 22-3 presents some practical upgrade recommendations for making three types of improvements.

To provide for larger spreadsheets As you use *Lotus*, several software components are stored in internal memory: (1) the resident portion of DOS, (2) the *Lotus* program, (3) any add-in programs that you've attached to *Lotus*, and (4) the spreadsheet that you're working on. If you run out of internal memory as you're working on a large spreadsheet, you can sometimes make

Year	Release number	Primary enhancements	Related chapters	Add-ins	Related chapters
The 2.X releases					
1986	2.01	Add-in program support	14		
1989	2.2	Cell linking	11	*Allways*	
1990	2.3	Mouse support Enhanced graphing	21 17	*WYSIWYG*	18
1991	2.4			*WYSIWYG* *SmartIcons* *Auditor* *Viewer* *Macro Library Manager* *Backsolver*	18 21 2 11, 13 19 14
The 3.X releases					
1989	3.0	3D spreadsheets Enhanced graphing Enhanced printing Background printing Background recalculating	11 17 4, 17 15 7		
1990	3.1			*WYSIWYG*	18
1991	3.1+			*WYSIWYG* *Viewer* *Auditor*	18 11, 13 2
1992	3.4	Enhanced graphing Landscape mode for dot matrix printers Screens for print and graph settings	17 4 3	WYSIWYG (*SmartIcons*) Auditor Viewer Macro Library Manager *Backsolver* *Solver*	18 21 2 2 19 14 14

Figure 22-1 The evolution of *Lotus 1-2-3* for DOS-based PCs

Lotus release	Internal memory	Disk storage	Minimum processor	Recommended processor
2.4	384KB 512KB with *WYSIWYG*	3MB 5MB with add-ins	8088	286 or faster
3.4	1MB	3MB 6MB with add-ins	286	486

Figure 22-2 The hardware requirements for the current releases of *Lotus 1-2-3* for DOS-based PCs

room for it by detaching any add-in programs that are in internal memory. If that isn't possible, you have to divide the large spreadsheet into two or more smaller ones, and that means more work. Normally, though, you can solve this problem by adding more internal memory to your PC.

If your PC doesn't have the maximum amount of *conventional memory* (640KB), you start by adding memory to reach this maximum. If that still isn't enough memory, you can add either *expanded memory* (sometimes called *EMS memory*) or *extended memory* to your PC. Expanded memory can be used by all releases of *Lotus* starting with release 2.01, and extended memory can be used by all 3.X releases. However, only PCs with 286 processors or later ones can use extended memory.

Often, you can find out the types and amounts of internal memory your PC has by just watching the information that's displayed as your PC goes through its start-up routine. But that doesn't tell you how *Lotus* is using the internal memory. To find that out, you can use the /Worksheet Status command that's explained in chapter 7. With releases 2.1 through 2.4, this command displays a screen that shows how much conventional memory is available after *Lotus* has been loaded and how much conventional memory is available for use with the current spreadsheet. This screen provides the same type of information for expanded memory. If you're using release 3.0 or later, the available memory is presented as one block. In other words, the command doesn't provide separate information for conventional, expanded, and extended memory.

If you decide that you want to add memory to your PC, be sure to get the right memory for your PC. In general, the memory must be the right kind (expanded or extended), the right speed, the right memory set size, and the right memory set type. If you're overwhelmed by these factors, it's best to have a PC technician take care of the job for you.

To increase processing speed As a spreadsheet gets larger, it takes more time for your PC's *processor* to recalculate all of the formulas in the

Goal	Upgrade recommendation	Remarks
Provide for larger spreadsheets	Install more memory.	Be sure to get the right kind of memory for your PC.
Increase recalculation speed	Install a math co-processor if your PC doesn't already have one.	Be sure the co-processor matches your processor.
Provide for upgrade from *Lotus* 2.X to 3.X	Replace your old PC with a new one.	This is often both the least expensive and the best solution.

Figure 22-3 Practical recommendations for upgrading your PC

Processor	Abbreviated name	Compatible co-processor
8088	None	8087
80286	286	80287
80386SX	386SX	80387SX
80386DX	386	80387
80486SX	486SX	80487
80486DX	486	Included in the 486 chip

Figure 22-4 A summary of PC processors and co-processors

spreadsheet. At some point, the delay that's required for recalculation may become bothersome or even intolerable. Of course, you'll reach this point sooner if you have an older PC than if you have a newer PC because the newer PCs use faster, more powerful processors.

Figure 22-4 summarizes the processors that are used in PCs today. To illustrate the difference in processor speeds, figure 22-5 shows the amount of time that three different processors required to recalculate the values in the same spreadsheet. Here, you can see that the 8088 PC took 25 seconds to recalculate the spreadsheet. The 286 PC took 9 seconds to perform the same operation. The 386 PC took only 3 seconds. And the 486 PC took less than 1 second. In fact, the 486 was too fast to accurately time.

When the recalculation speed becomes bothersome, one solution is to turn off the recalculation feature as described in chapter 7. Then, *Lotus* only recalculates the formulas in the spreadsheet when you press the F9 (Calc) key. If that solution isn't satisfactory to you, the other alternative is to upgrade the processing speed of your PC.

Unfortunately, it's often difficult to upgrade your processor. Some of the newer PCs provide for processor upgrades. But if you have one of these PCs, you probably have at least a 386 so you don't need to upgrade it for *Lotus*. If you have an older PC, you can add an *accelerator board* that has a faster processor on it. But these boards are often costly ($400 or more), and they don't replace all of the other old and slow components of your PC. That's why it's often better to buy a new PC than to upgrade an older one.

With that as background, the most practical way to increase the processing speed of your PC is to install a *co-processor* chip, if your PC doesn't already have one. This type of chip is specifically designed for mathematical calculations. That's why this chip is also called a *math co-processor*. Working in cooperation with your existing processor chip, the co-processor can substantially reduce the amount of time that's required to recalculate a spreadsheet. In some cases, a PC can perform the calculations in a spreadsheet up to ten times faster with a math co-processor than without one.

If you look back to figure 22-4, you can see that co-processor chips are matched with the processors they are designed to work with; they just end with a 7 instead of a 6. What this figure doesn't show is that co-processors are also matched to the speed of your processor. If, for example, you have a 80386 processor that operates at 25Mhz, make sure you buy a 80387 co-processor that also operates at 25Mhz. Because the 486DX processor has the co-processor built into it, there isn't a co-processor chip available for it. Instead, the 486SX processor is just a 486DX with the co-processor functions disabled.

On most PCs, a co-processor chip is relatively easy to install. Also, co-processor chips are relatively inexpensive. For instance, a co-processor for an 8088 costs around $100, and a co-processor for a 386 costs around $200. That's why a co-processor chip is often the most cost-effective PC upgrade that a *Lotus* user can make.

To provide for a *Lotus* upgrade from release 2.X to 3.X If you look back to figure 22-2, you can see that *Lotus* release 3.4 requires at least 1MB of internal memory and at least a 286 processor. To take full advantage of *Lotus* release 3.4 and its add-ins, though, you are likely to need more than 1MB of memory. And if you're working on a PC with a 286 processor, this release of *Lotus* is going to seem painstakingly slow to you, even though it performs recalculation operations in the background.

With that in mind, the best way to upgrade your PC for release 3.4 if you're using a 286 is to replace the entire PC with a new one. That should provide a faster processor, more internal memory, more disk storage, and a modern monitor. That will save you the time it takes to install hardware upgrades like more memory or a co-processor chip. And that will prepare you for future software upgrades for *Lotus* as well as for other programs.

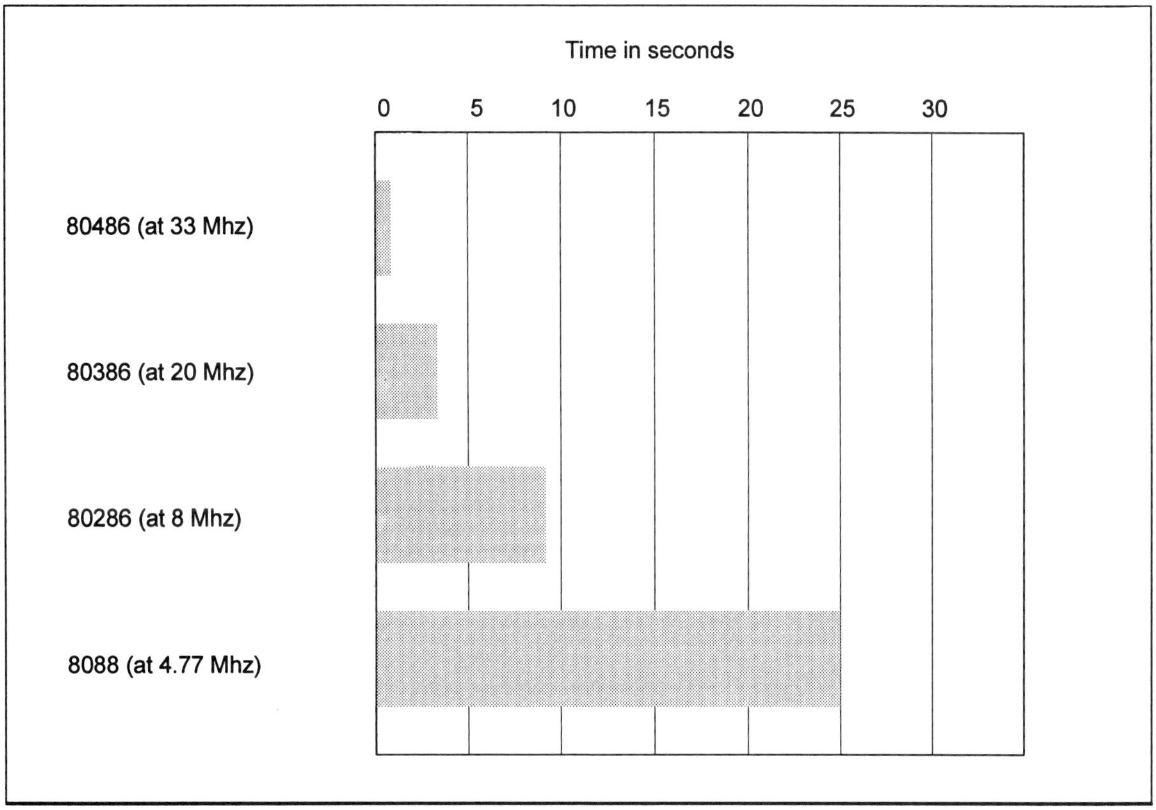

Figure 22-5 The time required to recalculate a spreadsheet using four different processors

When to upgrade to *Lotus for Windows*

With all the talk about *Windows* and *Windows* application programs these days, you may be wondering whether you should upgrade to *Lotus 1-2-3 for Windows*. In general, this program provides all of the features of *Lotus* release 3.4 for DOS with *WYSIWYG*, and its presentation graphics features are better than those provided by release 3.4. That's because *Lotus 1-2-3 for Windows*, like all *Windows* programs, was designed as a graphics-based program in the first place.

Normally, though, you don't just decide whether you should upgrade from one of the *Lotus* for DOS releases to *Lotus for Windows*. The decision is broader than that. Instead, you decide whether you should convert all of your application programs from DOS-based programs to *Windows* programs. If, for example, you're using DOS, *WordPerfect*, and *Lotus* now, you have to decide whether it's worth the effort to convert to *Windows*, *WordPerfect for Windows*, and *Lotus for Windows* (or maybe to *Windows*, *Word*, and *Excel*). Since a change like this can mean a considerable investment in hardware, software, and training, this decision shouldn't be taken lightly.

If you do decide to switch to *Windows*, you're going to need a PC with at least a 386 processor (preferably, a 486), 4MB of internal memory, an 80MB hard drive, a VGA color monitor, and a mouse. You should be ready to spend from 20 to 40 hours learning how to use the *Windows* programs. And you should accept the fact that your productivity is going to go down for the first few months after you convert to *Windows*. After that, you'll probably be delighted that you made the conversion, but don't underestimate the costs of getting to that point. Unless you clearly need the capabilities that are offered by the *Windows* environment, you're better off delaying this move as long as possible. And you certainly don't need to make this move just for the improved *Lotus* capabilities.

Terms

three-dimensional spreadsheet
conventional memory
expanded memory
extended memory
processor
accelerator board
co-processor
math co-processor

Objectives

1. Decide whether you should upgrade to one of the current releases of *Lotus* for DOS.
2. Decide whether you should upgrade your current PC by installing more memory, by installing a math co-processor, or by replacing your old PC with a new one.

Appendix

A quick summary of the *Lotus* keystrokes and commands presented in this book

This appendix summarizes the keystroke meanings and *Lotus* commands presented in this book. In the portion of the appendix that summarizes the commands, the commands are in these groups:

- Worksheet commands (those that apply to the entire spreadsheet)
- Column commands (those that apply to one or more columns)
- Row commands (those that apply to one or more rows)
- Range commands (those that apply to one or more of the cells in a range)
- File commands (those that apply to managing your *Lotus* files)
- Print commands (those that apply to printing a spreadsheet or a 3.X graph)
- Graph commands (those that apply to graphing a spreadsheet)
- *PrintGraph* commands (those that apply to printing a 2.X graph)
- Add-in commands (those that apply to activating and using add-in programs)
- Data commands (those that apply to using the database feature)

If a command can logically be placed in two or more of these groups, it is placed in all of them. For each command, you are referred to the primary figures in the text that present the command.

The primary control keys for *Lotus* operations

Keys	Function
Arrow key	Move the cell pointer one cell in the direction of the arrow.
Page-up	Move the cell pointer up one screen.
Page-down	Move the cell pointer down one screen.
Tab	Move the cell pointer one screen to the right.
Shift+Tab	Move the cell pointer one screen to the left.
Ctrl+Right arrow	Move the cell pointer one screen to the right.
Ctrl+Left arrow	Move the cell pointer one screen to the left.
Home	Move the cell pointer to the home position (A1).
End Home	Move the cell pointer to the cell that is at the intersection of the bottom row and the right-most column that are used in the spreadsheet.
End Right arrow End Left arrow End Up arrow End Down arrow	Move the cell pointer in the direction of the arrow. If the cell pointer starts on an empty cell, move it to the first non-empty cell. If the cell pointer starts on a cell that contains data, move it to the last cell in succession that contains data.
Num-lock (Numeric Lock)	Turn Num-lock on if it's off; turn it off if it's on.
Scroll-lock	Turn Scroll-lock on if it's off; turn it off if it's on. When Scroll-lock is off, the cell pointer moves when you press the Arrow keys. When Scroll-lock is on, the cell pointer stays where it is and the entire window moves. Usually, you'll want to leave it off.
F1	Access the *Lotus* Help feature.
F2	Edit a label, value, or formula.
/	Access the *Lotus* menu system.
Esc (Escape)	Cancel an operation or go back one step within a command or menu.
Ctrl+Page-up (3.X)	Move back one worksheet in a 3D spreadsheet file.
Ctrl+Page-down (3.X)	Move forward one worksheet in a 3D spreadsheet file.

The keys for editing the contents of a cell

Keys	Function
F2	Start the editing operation.
Left arrow	Move the cursor left one character.
Right arrow	Move the cursor right one character.
Backspace	Erase the character to the left of the cursor.
Delete	Erase the character at the cursor position.
Insert	Toggle between the *insert* and *typeover* modes. When the insert mode is activated, the characters you enter are inserted at the cursor position. When the typeover mode is activated, *Lotus* displays a OVR indicator at the bottom of the screen and the characters you enter overwrite the existing characters.
Home	Move the cursor to the first character.
End	Move the cursor to the last character.
Ctrl+Left arrow	Move the cursor to the left by five characters.
Ctrl+Right arrow	Move the cursor to the right by five characters.
Enter	End the editing operation.

The operations of the Function keys

Key	Name	Function
F1	Help	Start the Help facility.
F2	Edit	Enter editing mode.
F3	Name	Display a list of names for any command that uses names.
F4	Absolute	Convert an address from relative to absolute to mixed.
F5	Goto	Jump the cell pointer to a cell or the first cell in a named range that you specify.
F6	Window	Display the current settings for any command that uses a group of settings. With the Window feature, switch between two windows. With 3D spreadsheets, switch between the worksheets.
F9	Calc	Recalculate a spreadsheet when the calculation mode is set to Manual.
F10	Graph	Display the current graph.
Alt+F4 (2.2 and later)	Undo	Reverse the last command, entry, or editing action when the Undo feature is on.
Alt+F5 (2.2 and later)	Learn	Record keystrokes to create a keystroke macro.
Alt+F6 (3.X)	Display	Switch between normal full-screen display to perspective display.

The four label prefixes for entering and aligning labels

Prefix	Meaning
'	Align left
"	Align right
^	Center
\	Repeat the next characters until the current cell is filled

Worksheet commands

Command	Refer to figures	Function
/Worksheet Delete Column	3-9	Delete one or more columns from a spreadsheet.
/Worksheet Delete Row	3-9	Delete one or more rows from a spreadsheet.
/Worksheet Delete Sheet (3.X)	11-6	Delete one or more worksheets from a 3D spreadsheet.
/Worksheet Erase	3-18	Erase a spreadsheet from internal memory without saving it to hard disk or diskette.
/Worksheet Global Column-Width	3-8	Set the widths for all of the columns in the spreadsheet.
/Worksheet Global Default Autoexec	15-2	Automatically execute a macro named \0 (zero) when a spreadsheet containing that macro is loaded.
/Worksheet Global Default Directory	3-3, 3-16	Set the default directory for retrieving and saving files.
/Worksheet Global Default Other	3-3, 14-1, 15-2	Set the defaults for other options such as the status indicator line, the Undo feature, the beeper, and add-ins.
/Worksheet Global Default Printer	3-15, 4-1, 15-11, 5-2, 15-3	Set the global defaults for the printer options, and set the default printer.
/Worksheet Global Default Status	3-3	Display the default setting screen.
/Worksheet Global Default Update	3-3	Update the default settings so they become permanent defaults.
/Worksheet Global Format	3-6, 3-7	Set the formats for all the cells in the spreadsheet.
/Worksheet Global Label-Prefix	3-5	Set the default label prefix for all the labels that are entered into the spreadsheet.

Worksheet commands (continued)

Command	Refer to figures	Function
/Worksheet Global Protection	9-1, 9-2	Activate or deactivate the protection feature for the current spreadsheet. This protects all cells that haven't been unprotected by the /Range Unprotect command.
/Worksheet Global Recalc	7-2	Set the recalculation mode to Automatic or Manual.
/Worksheet Insert Column	3-9	Insert one or more columns into a spreadsheet.
/Worksheet Insert Row	3-9	Insert one or more rows into a spreadsheet.
/Worksheet Insert Sheet (3.X)	11-6, 11-7, 19-4	Insert one or more worksheets into a 3D spreadsheet.
/Worksheet Learn	19-4	Create a "learn range" in which to record the macro.
/Worksheet Page	4-12, 4-13	Insert a page break into a spreadsheet.
/Worksheet Status	2-14, 7-3	Display information about a spreadsheet that includes memory usage or the location of a circular reference.
/Worksheet Titles	3-12	Freeze or unfreeze one or more rows or columns at the top or side of a spreadsheet.
/Worksheet Window	7-4, 7-5	Create two windows so you can view two portions of a spreadsheet simultaneously.
/Worksheet Window Perspective (3.X)	11-6, 11-9	Activate the perspective display for a 3D spreadsheet.
/Quit		Exit from *Lotus*.

Column commands

Command	Refer to figures	Function
/Worksheet Column Column-Range	3-8	Set the column widths for a range of columns.
/Worksheet Column Display	3-10	Display one or more hidden columns.
/Worksheet Column Hide	3-10, 3-11	Hide one or more columns.
/Worksheet Column Reset-Width	3-8	Reset the column widths to the global default.
/Worksheet Column Set-Width	3-8	Increase or decrease the width of one column.
/Worksheet Delete Column	3-9	Delete one or more columns from a spreadsheet.
/Worksheet Global Column-Width	3-8	Set the widths for all of the columns in a spreadsheet.
/Worksheet Insert Column	3-9	Insert one or more columns into a spreadsheet.
/Worksheet Titles	3-12, 3-13	Freeze or unfreeze one or more columns at the left side of a spreadsheet.

Row commands

Command	Refer to figures	Function
/Worksheet Delete Row	3-9	Delete one or more rows from a spreadsheet.
/Worksheet Insert Row	3-9	Insert one or more rows into a spreadsheet.
/Worksheet Titles Horizontal	3-12, 3-13	Freeze or unfreeze one or more rows at the top of a spreadsheet.

Range commands

Command	Refer to figures	Function
/Copy	3-14	Copy the contents of one range of cells to another range of cells.
/Data Fill	1-6, 1-7	Enter a sequence of values into the specified range of cells.
/Data Sort	10-2, 10-3, 10-4	Sort the rows in a specified range.
/Move	3-14	Move the contents of one range of cells to another range of cells.
/Range Erase	3-14	Erase the data from the specified range of cells.
/Range Format	1-2, 3-6, 3-7	Set the format for the specified range of cells.
/Range Input	9-2, 9-3	Restrict the movement of the cell cursor to unprotected cells.
/Range Justify	15-9	Divide a long label in one row into two or more rows.
/Range Label	1-5, 3-5	Change the alignment of the labels in the specified range of cells.
/Range Name	8-2 through 8-6	Assign a name to the specified range; then, the name can be used with commands and formulas.
/Range Protect	9-1, 9-2	Assign the protection attribute to a range in a spreadsheet.
/Range Search	15-11	Search for a character string or search for then replace a character string.
/Range Transpose	15-10	Convert columns to rows or vice versa.
/Range Unprotect	9-1, 9-2	Remove the protection attribute from a range in a spreadsheet.
/Range Value	1-8, 1-9, 1-10	Convert the formulas in the specified range to their current values.
/Worksheet Column Column-Range	3-8	Set the column width for a range of columns.

File commands

Command	Refer to figures	Function
/File Admin Table	13-1, 13-4	Create a table in the spreadsheet of the files in the current directory.
/File Combine	11-1, 11-3	Combine all or part of another spreadsheet into the current spreadsheet.
/File Directory	3-16	Identify the directory that you want to use for your spreadsheet files during the current *Lotus* session.
/File Erase	13-1, 13-2	Erase a *Lotus* file.
/File Import	12-3, 12-4, 12-5	Import an ASCII file into the current spreadsheet.
/File List	13-1, 13-3	List the files in the specified directory.
/File New (3.X)	11-13	Create a new spreadsheet and insert it before or after an open spreadsheet.
/File Open (3.X)	11-12	Load more than one spreadsheet into internal memory.
/File Retrieve	3-16	Retrieve a spreadsheet file.
/File Save	3-16	Save a spreadsheet file to hard disk or diskette.
/File Xtract	11-1, 11-2	Extract the specified range from a spreadsheet and save it to a new file.
/Worksheet Global Default Directory	3-3, 3-16	Set the default directory for retrieving and saving files.

Print commands

Command	Refer to figures	Function
/Print Cancel (3.X)	15-5	Cancel all print jobs.
/Print File	12-5	Transfer the contents of a print range to a nondelimited text file.
/Print Printer Align	3-15	Tell *Lotus* that the paper is aligned properly in the printer.
/Print Printer Clear	4-1, 4-24	Clear some or all of the current print settings.
/Print Printer Go	3-15	Print all of the cells in the print range.
/Print Printer Image (3.X)	15-18, 15-19	Select the current graph or a named graph to be printed.

Print commands (continued)

Command	Refer to figures	Function
/Print Printer Page	3-15	Advance the paper in the printer to the top of the next page.
/Print Printer Range (2.X)	3-15	Set the range of cells that are to be printed.
/Print Printer Range (3.X)	15-6	Set the range or ranges of cells that are to be printed.
/Print Printer Options Advanced Device	15-3	Switch between printers.
/Print Printer Options Advanced Fonts (3.X)	17-16	Specify the font to be used used for a portion of a spreadsheet.
/Print Printer Options Advanced Layout (3.X)	4-1, 4-9, 4-17, 4-22, 4-23	Set the pitch, line spacing and orientation (portrait or landscape) for the printed spreadsheet.
/Print Printer Options Advanced Image (3.X)	17-1, 17-16	Rotate, size, and set the density for the printed graph.
/Print Printer Options Advanced Priority (3.X)	15-5	Set the priority level of a print job.
/Print Printer Options Borders Columns	4-17, 4-20	Identify the columns to be printed on the left side of each page of the spreadsheet.
/Print Printer Options Borders Frame (3.X)	15-6, 15-7	Print a frame around the spreadsheet that consists of column and row identifiers.
/Print Printer Options Borders Rows	4-12, 4-14	Identify the rows to be printed after the header on each page of the spreadsheet.
/Print Printer Options Footer	4-1, 4-4, 4-5	Create a footer that will be printed at the bottom on each page of the spreadsheet.
/Print Printer Options Header	4-1, 4-4, 4-5	Create a header that will be printed on top of each page of the spreadsheet.
/Print Printer Options Margins	3-15, 4-1, 4-3	Set the top, bottom, right, and left print margins for a spreadsheet.
/Print Printer Options Name (3.X)	4-1, 4-25	Create a group of named print settings for a spreadsheet.
/Print Printer Options Other	15-6, 15-7	Print a spreadsheet with its formulas instead of the values the formulas return.
/Print Printer Options Page-Length	3-15, 4-1	Set the number of lines to be printed on each page of a spreadsheet.

Print commands (continued)

Command	Refer to figures	Function
/Print Printer Options Setup	4-1, 4-6, 4-7, 4-8	Set the pitch to be used when the spreadsheet is printed.
/Print Resume (3.X)	15-5	Restart the print jobs that were paused.
/Print Suspend (3.X)	15-5	Pause all current print jobs.
/Worksheet Global Default Printer	3-15, 4-1, 15-1, 15-3	Set the global defaults for the printer options, and set the default printer.
/Worksheet Page	4-12, 4-13	Insert a page break into a spreadsheet.

Graph commands

Command	Refer to figures	Function
/Graph A-F	16-2	Specify the data ranges for a graph.
/Graph Group	16-2	Specify all the data ranges for a graph at one time.
/Graph Name	16-2, 16-13	Save the current graph settings to a named graph.
/Graph Options	16-2, 16-3, 17-1, 17-11	Set graph options that include titles, legends, data labels, and so on.
/Graph Options Advanced Hatches (3.X)	17-1	Set the hatch patterns for a graph.
/Graph Options Advanced Text (3.X)	17-4	Set the style and size of the text used in the graph.
/Graph Reset	16-2, 16-12	Reset some or all of the graph settings.
/Graph Save (2.X)	16-2, 16-14	Save the current graph to a PIC file.
/Graph Save (3.X)	16-14	Save the current graph to a PIC or a CGM file.
/Graph Type	16-2, 16-3	Specify the type of graph to define.
/Graph Type Features	17-4	Enhance a graph by changing the orientation of its axes; putting a frame around it; adding a shadow or 3D effect; adding a table of the graphed data; and so on.
/Graph View	16-2	Display the current graph.

Graph commands (continued)

Command	Refer to figures	Function
/Graph X	16-2	Set the X-axis.
/Print Printer Image (3.X)	16-19	Select the current graph or a named graph to be printed.
/Print Printer Options Advanced Image (3.X)	17-1, 17-16	Rotate, size, and set the density for the printed graph.
/Print Printer Options Advanced Font (3.X)	7-16	Specify the font to be used for a portion of the spreadsheet.
/Worksheet Window Graph (3.X)	17-1, 17-18	Display a spreadsheet and a graph at the same time.

PrintGraph commands (2.X)

Command	Refer to figures	Function
Align	16-17, 16-18	Tells *PrintGraph* that the paper is properly aligned in the printer.
Exit	16-17, 16-18	Exit from the *PrintGraph* program and return to the *Lotus* Access System menu.
Go	16-17, 16-18	Print the specified PIC (graph) files.
Image-Select	16-17, 16-18	Specify the PIC (graph) files you want printed.
Page	16-17, 16-18	Advance the paper to the top of the next page.
Settings	16-17, 16-18	Set the font and image size for the printed graph.

Add-in commands

Command	Refer to figures	Function
/Add-in Attach (2.X)	14-1, 14-2	Load an add-in program into internal memory.
/Add-in Clear (2.X)	14-1	Deactivate all add-in programs by removing them from internal memory.
/Add-in Detach (2.X)	14-1	Deactivate an add-in program by removing it from internal memory.
/Add-in Invoke Alt+F10 Invoke	14-1, 14-3	Activate an add-in program that's in internal memory.

Add-in commands (continued)

Command	Refer to figures	Function
Alt+F10 Load (3.X)	14-1	Load an add-in program into internal memory.
Alt+F10 Remove (3.X)	14-1	Deactivate an add-in program by removing it from internal memory.
Alt+F10 Setting File (3.X)	14-1	Auto-attach an add-in for a specific spreadsheet file only or cancel that setting.
Alt+F10 Setting Systems (3.X)	14-1	Auto-attach an add-in when *Lotus* is started, cancel that setting, or save that setting as the default.
/Worksheet Global Default Other Add-In (2.X)	14-1	Auto-attach an add-in program when *Lotus* is started or cancel that setting.
/Worksheet Global Default Update (2.X)	14-1	Save the auto-attached setting as the default setting.

Data commands

Command	Refer to figures	Function
/Data Distribution	20-8, 20-9	Derive a frequency distribution for a range of cells.
/Data External	20-10 through 20-13	Access an external database so you can use the *Lotus* /Data Query commands on it.
/Data Fill	1-6, 1-7, 20-8	Enter a sequence of values into the specified range.
/Data Matrix	20-8	Invert a matrix, or multiply the columns in one matrix by the rows in another matrix to derive a third matrix.
/Data Parse	12-6, 12-7	Divide up (parse) the data stored in one cell and copy it to separate cells.
/Data Query Criteria	20-3	Identify the range that contains the criteria you'll use to select records in a spreadsheet.
/Data Query Delete	20-3	Delete the records in the input range that meet the criteria.
/Data Query Extract	20-3, 20-4, 20-6	Copy the records from the Input range to the Output range based on the criteria you specified.

Data commands (continued)

Command	Refer to figures	Function
/Data Query Find	20-3	Find the records based on the criteria you specified.
/Data Query Input	20-3	Identify the range that contains the data you want to use.
/Data Query Output	20-3, 20-4, 20-5	Specify the range to copy the records to.
/Data Query Quit	20-3	Exit from the /Data Query command.
/Data Query Reset	20-3	Clear all query settings.
/Data Query Unique	20-3	Copy all records in the input range that meet the criteria, but don't include duplicate records.
/Data Regression	20-8	Perform a regression analysis.
/Data Sort	10-2, 10-3, 10-4	Sort the specified rows in ascending or descending order.
/Data Table	20-8	Calculate a table of values based on the variation of one or two values.

Index

G

H

I

L

M

N

O

P

Q

R

S

T

U

V

W

X-Y

@Function

Comment Form

Your opinions count

If you have any comments, criticisms, or suggestions for us, I'm eager to get them. Your opinions today will affect our products of tomorrow. And if you find any errors in this book, typographical or otherwise, please point them out so we can correct them in the next printing.

Thanks for your help.

Book title: The Practical Guide to *Lotus 1-2-3*

Dear Mike: ______________________________

Name ______________________________

Company (if company address) ______________________________

Address ______________________________

City, State, Zip ______________________________

Fold where indicated and tape closed.

No postage necessary if mailed in the U.S.

fold

fold

NO POSTAGE
NECESSARY
IF MAILED
IN THE
UNITED STATES

BUSINESS REPLY MAIL

FIRST-CLASS MAIL PERMIT NO. 3063 FRESNO, CA

POSTAGE WILL BE PAID BY ADDRESSEE

Mike Murach & Associates, Inc.

4697 W JACQUELYN AVE
FRESNO CA 93722-9888

fold

fold

Order Form

Our Ironclad Guarantee

To our customers who order directly from us: You must be satisfied. Our books must work for you, or you can send them back for a full refund...no questions asked.

Name (& Title, if any) ____________________

Company (if company address) ____________________

Street address ____________________

City, State, Zip ____________________

Phone number (including area code) ____________________

Fax number (if you fax your order to us) ____________________

Qty	Product code and title		*Price
	Lotus 1-2-3		
____	GLOT	The Practical Guide to *Lotus 1-2-3*	$25.00
____	LLOT	The Least You Need to Know about *Lotus 1-2-3*	20.00
	WordPerfect		
____	LWP	The Least You Need to Know about *WordPerfect*	$20.00
	Multiple Programs		
____	DWPL	DOS, *WordPerfect*, and *Lotus* Essentials	$25.00

Qty	Product code and title		*Price
	DOS		
____	LDSR	The Least You Need to Know about DOS (2nd. Ed.)	$20.00
____	DOSR	The Only DOS Book You'll Ever Need (2nd Ed.)	27.50
____	BACK	How to Back Up Your PC	15.00
	Windows		
____	LWIN**	The Least You Need to Know about *Windows*	$20.00
____	LOTW**	The Least You Need to Know about *Lotus 1-2-3* for *Windows*	20.00
	Business Writing		
____	WBPC	Write Better with a PC	$19.95

☐ Bill the appropriate book prices plus UPS shipping and handling (and sales tax in California) to my ____VISA ____MasterCard:

Card number ____________________

Valid thru (month/year) ____________________

Cardowner's signature ____________________

☐ Bill me.

☐ Bill my company. P.O.# ____________________

☐ I want to **save** UPS shipping and handling charges. Here's my check or money order for $_______. California residents, please add sales tax to your total. (Offer valid in the U.S.)

*** Prices are subject to change. Please call for current prices.**

**** Available July 1993**

To order more quickly,

Call **toll-free** 1-800-221-5528

(Weekdays, 8 to 5 Pacific Standard Time)

Fax: 1-209-275-9035

Mike Murach & Associates, Inc.

4697 West Jacquelyn Avenue
Fresno, California 93722-6427
(209) 275-3335